Type

A Visual History
of Typefaces
and Graphic Styles

F d C S M G h P T E R Y j z B i L W v K O A X E N O

Type

A Visual History of Typefaces and Graphic Styles 1628–1900

Edited by Cees W. de Jong
With texts by **Jan Tholenaar** *and* **Cees W. de Jong**

TASCHEN

CONTENTS

A SPECIMEN

By WILLIAM CASLON, Letter-Founder, in Chiſwell-Street, LONDON.

ABCD
ABCDE
ABCDEFG
ABCDEFGHI
ABCDEFGHIJK
ABCDEFGHIJKL
ABCDEFGHIKLMN

French Cannon.

Quouſque tan-
dem abutere,
Catilina, pati-
*Quouſque tandem
abutere, Catilina,
patientia noſtra?*

Two Lines Great Primer.

Quouſque tandem
abutere, Catilina,
patientia noſtra?
quamdiu nos etiam
*Quouſque tandem a-
butere, Catilina, pa-
tientia noſtra? quam-
diu nos etiam furor*

Two Lines Engliſh.

Quouſque tandem abu-
tere, Catilina, patientia
noſtra? quamdiu nos e-
tiam furor iſte tuus elu-
*Quouſque tandem abutere,
Catilina, patientia noſtra?
quamdiu nos etiam furor*

DOUBLE PICA ROMAN.

Quouſque tandem abutere, Catilina, patientia noſtra? quamdiu
nos etiam furor iſte tuus eludet?
quem ad finem ſeſe effrenata jac-
ABCDEFGHIJKLMNOP

GREAT PRIMER ROMAN.

Quouſque tandem abutêre, Catilina, patientia noſtra? quamdiu nos etiam furor iſte tuus eludet? quem ad finem ſeſe effrenata jactabit audacia? nihilne te
nocturnum præſidium palatii, nihil urbis vigiliæ, nihil timor populi, nihil con-
ABCDEFGHIJKLMNOPQRS

ENGLISH ROMAN.

Quouſque tandem abutêre, Catilina, patientia
noſtra? quamdiu nos etiam furor iſte tuus eludet?
quem ad finem ſeſe effrenata jactabit audacia?
nihilne te nocturnum præſidium palatii, nihil
urbis vigiliæ, nihil timor populi, nihil conſenſus bonorum omnium, nihil hic munitiſſimus
ABCDEFGHIJKLMNOPQRSTVUW

PICA ROMAN.

Melium, novis rebus ſtudentem, manu ſua occîdit.
Fuit, fuit iſta quondam in hac repub. virtus, ut viri
fortes acrioribus ſuppliciis civem pernicioſum, quam
acerbiſſimum hoſtem coërcerent. Habemus enim ſenatuſconſultum in te, Catilina, vehemens, & grave:
non deeſt reip. conſilium, neque autoritas hujus ordinis: nos, nos, dico aperte, conſules defumus. DE-
ABCDEFGHIJKLMNOPQRSTVUWX

SMALL PICA ROMAN. No 1.

At nos vigeſimum jam diem patimur hebeſcere aciem horum
autoritatis. habemus enim hujuſmodi ſenatuſconſultum, ve-
rumtamen incluſum in tabulis, tanquam gladium in vagina
recondutum: quo ex ſenatuſconſulto confeſtim interfectum te
eſſe, Catilina, convenit. Vivis: & vivis non ad deponendam,
ſed ad confirmandam audaciam. Cupio, P. C., me
eſſe clementem: cupio in tantis reipub. periculis non diſ-
ABCDEFGHIJKLMNOPQRSTVUWXYZ

SMALL PICA ROMAN. No 2.

At nos vigeſimum jam diem patimur hebeſcere aciem horum
autoritatis. habemus enim hujuſmodi ſenatuſconſultum, ve-
rumtamen incluſum in tabulis, tanquam gladium in vagina
recondutum: quo ex ſenatuſconſulto confeſtim interfectum te
eſſe, Catilina, convenit. Vivis: & vivis non ad deponendam,
ſed ad confirmandam audaciam. Cupio, P. C., me eſſe
clementem: cupio in tantis reipub. periculis non diſſolutum
ABCDEFGHIJKLMNOPQRSTVUWXYZ

LONG PRIMER ROMAN No 1.

Verum ego hoc, quod jampridem factum eſſe oportuit, certa de
cauſſa nondum adducor ut faciam. tum denique interficiam te, cum
jam nemo tam improbus, tam perditus, tam tui ſimilis inveniri po-
terit, qui id non jure factum eſſe fateatur. Quamdiu quiſquam erit
qui te defendere audeat, vives: & vives, ita ut nunc vivis, multis
meis & firmis præſidiis obſeſſus, ne commovere te contra rempub.
poſſis. multorum te etiam oculi & aures non ſentientem, ſicut adhuc
fecerunt, ſpeculabuntur, atque cuſtodient. Etenim quid eſt, Cati-
ABCDEFGHIJKLMNOPQRSTVUWXYZæ

LONG PRIMER ROMAN. No 2.

Verum ego hoc, quod jampridem factum eſſe oportuit, certa de
cauſſa nondum adducor ut faciam. tum denique interficiam te, cum
jam nemo tam improbus, tam perditus, tam tui ſimilis inveniri pote-
rit, qui id non jure factum eſſe fateatur. Quamdiu quiſquam erit
qui te defendere audeat, vives: & vives, ita ut nunc vivis, multis
meis & firmis præſidiis obſeſſus, ne commovere te contra rempub.
poſſis. multorum te etiam oculi & aures non ſentientem, ſicut adhuc
fecerunt, ſpeculabuntur, atque cuſtodient. Etenim quid eſt, Catili-
ABCDEFGHIJKLMNOPQRSTVUWXYZÆ

BREVIER ROMAN.

Novem. C. Manlium audacie ſatellitem atque adminiſtrum tuæ? num me fefellit,
Catilina, non modo res tanta, tam atrox, tam incredibilis, verum, id quod multo
magis eſt admirandum, dies? Dixi ego idem in ſenatu, cædem te optimatum con-
tuliſſe in ante diem v Kalend. Novemb. tum cum multi principes civitatis Rom.
non tam ſui conſervandi, quam tuorum conſiliorum reprimendorum cauſſa profu-
gerunt. num inficiari potes, te illo ipſo die meis præſidiis, mea diligentia circum-
cluſion, commovere te contra rempub. non potuiſſe; cum tu diſceſſu ceterorum,
noſtra tamen, qui remanſiſſemus, cæde contentum te eſſe dicebas? Quid? cum te
ABCDEFGHIJKLMNOPQRSTVUWXYZÆ

NONPAREIL ROMAN.

O dii immortales! ubi-nam gentium ſumus? quam rempub. habemus? in qua urbe vivimus?
hic, hic ſunt in noſtro numero, P. C., in hoc orbis terræ ſanctiſſimo graviſſimoque conſilio, qui
de noſtro, nochumque omnium interitu, qui de hujus urbis, atque adeo orbis terrarum exitio cogitent. hoſce ego video conſul, & de republica ſententiam rogo: & quos ferro trucidari oportebat,
eos nondum voce vulnero. Fuiſti igitur apud Leccam ea nocte, Catilina: diſtribuiſti partes Italiæ: Statuiſti quo quemque proficiſci placeret: delegiſti quos Romæ relinqueres, quos tecum
educeres: deſcripſiſti urbis partes ad incendia: confirmaſti, te ipſum jam eſſe exiturum: dixiſti
paululum tibi eſſe etiam tum moræ, quod ego viverem. Reperti ſunt duo equites Romani, qui te
iſta cura liberarent, & ſe illa ipſa nocte paulo ante lucem me in meo lectulo interfecturos eſſe
pollicerentur. Hæc ego omnia, vix dum etiam cœtu veſtro dimiſſo, comperi: domum meam
ABCDEFGHIKLMNOPQRSTVUWXYZÆ

Double Pica Italick.

*Quouſque tandem abutere, Catili-
na, patientia noſtra? quamdiu
nos etiam furor iſte tuus eludet?
quem ad finem ſeſe effrenata jac-
ABCDEFGHIJIKLMNO*

Great Primer Italick.

*Quouſque tandem abutêre, Catilina, pa-
tientia noſtra? quamdiu nos etiam furor iſte tuus eludet? quem ad finem ſeſe
effrenata jactabit audacia? nihilne te
nocturnum præſidium palatii, nihil urbis vigiliæ, nihil timor populi, nihil con-
ABCDEFGHIJKLMNOPQR*

Engliſh Italick.

*Quouſque tandem abutêre, Catilina, patientia noſ-
tra? quamdiu nos etiam furor iſte tuus eludet?
quem ad finem ſeſe effrenata jactabit audacia?
nihilne te nocturnum præſidium palatii, nihil urbis vigiliæ, nihil timor populi, nihil conſenſus bonorum omnium, nihil hic munitiſſimus habendi ſe-
ABCDEFGHIJKLMNOPQRSTVU*

Pica Italick.

*Melium, novis rebus ſtudentem, manu ſua occîdit.
Fuit, fuit iſta quondam in hac repub. virtus, ut viri
fortes acrioribus ſuppliciis civem pernicioſum, quam a-
cerbiſſimum hoſtem coërcerent. Habemus enim ſenatuſconſultum in te, Catilina, vehemens, & grave: non
deeſt reip. conſilium, neque autoritas hujus ordinis: nos, nos,
dico aperte, conſules defumus. Decrevit quondam ſenatus
ABCDEFGHIJKLMNOPQRSTVUWXYZ*

Small Pica Italick. No 1.

*At nos vigeſimum jam diem patimur hebeſcere aciem horum
autoritatis. habemus enim hujuſmodi ſenatuſconſultum, verum-
tamen incluſum in tabulis, tanquam gladium in vagina recon-
ditum: quo ex ſenatuſconſulto confeſtim interfectum te eſſe, Catilina, convenit. Vivis: & vivis non ad deponendam, ſed ad
confirmandam audaciam. Cupio, P. C., me eſſe clementem:
cupio in tantis reipub. periculis non diſſolutum videri: ſed jam
ABCDEFGHIJKLMNOPQRSTVUWXYZ*

Small Pica Italick. No 2.

*At nos vigeſimum jam diem patimur hebeſcere aciem horum au-
toritatis. habemus enim hujuſmodi ſenatuſconſultum, verum-
tamen incluſum in tabulis, tanquam gladium in vagina recondi-
tum: quo ex ſenatuſconſulto confeſtim interfectum te eſſe, Catilina, convenit. Vivis: & vivis non ad deponendam, ſed ad confirmandam audaciam. Cupio, P. C., me eſſe clementem: cupio in tantis
reipub. periculis non diſſolutum videri: ſed jam meipſum inertiæ
ABCDEFGHIJKLMNOPQRSTVUWXYZ*

Long Primer Italick. No 1.

*Verum ego hoc, quod jampridem factum eſſe oportuit, certa de cauſſa
nondum adducor ut faciam. tum denique interficiam te, cum jam nemo
non jure factum eſſe fateatur. Quamdiu quiſquam erit qui te defendere audeat, vives: & vives, ita ut nunc vivis, multis meis &
firmis præſidiis obſeſſus, ne commovere te contra rempub. poſſis. multorum te etiam oculi & aures non ſentientem, ſicut adhuc fecerunt, ſpeculabuntur, atque cuſtodient. Etenim quid eſt, Catilina, quod jam
ABCDEFGHIJKLMNOPQRSTVUWXYZ*

Long Primer Italick. No 2.

*Verum ego hoc, quod jampridem factum eſſe oportuit, certa de cauſſa
nondum adducor ut faciam. tum denique interficiam te, cum jam nemo
tam improbus, tam perditus, tam tui ſimilis inveniri poteris, qui id non
jure factum eſſe fateatur. Quamdiu quiſquam erit qui te defendere
audeat, vives: & vives, ita ut nunc vivis, multis meis & firmis
præſidiis obſeſſus, ne commovere te contra rempub. poſſis. multorum te
etiam oculi & aures non ſentientem, ſicut adhuc fecerunt, ſpeculabuntur,
atque cuſtodient. Etenim quid eſt, Catilina, quod jam amplius expectes?
ABCDEFGHIJKLMNOPQRSTVUWXYZÆ*

Nonpareil Italick.

*O dii immortales! ubi-nam gentium ſumus? quam rempub. habemus? in qua urbe vivimus? hic, hic
ſunt in noſtro numero, P. C., in hoc orbis terræ ſanctiſſimo graviſſimoque conſilio, qui de noſtro, nochumque
omnium interitu, qui de hujus urbis, atque adeo orbis terrarum exitio cogitent. hoſce ego video conſul, & de
republica ſententiam rogo: & quos ferro trucidari oportebat, eos nondum voce vulnero. Fuiſti igitur apud
Leccam ea nocte, Catilina: diſtribuiſti partes Italiæ: Statuiſti quo quemque proficiſci placeret: delegiſti quos
Romæ relinqueres, quos tecum educeres: deſcripſiſti urbis partes ad incendia: confirmaſti, te ipſum jam eſſe
exiturum: dixiſti paululum tibi eſſe etiam tum moræ, quod ego viverem. Reperti ſunt duo equites Romani, qui te iſta cura liberarent, & ſe illa ipſa nocte paulo ante lucem me in meo lectulo interfecturos
eſſe pollicerentur. Hæc ego omnia, vix dum etiam cœtu veſtro dimiſſo, comperi: domum meam
ABCDEFGHIJKLMNOPQRSTVUWXYZ*

Long Primer Saxon.

Ða he ba uub ʒrummum ꝼ une
neꝡum pæcen pær ꝼ he ealle ba
prꝼu ʃe human byƿe ʒelyboelice
ꝼ ʒepeonbe ꝼon þirlune abæp an

Pica Black.

And be it further enacted by the Authority
aforeſaid, That all and every of the ſaid Exchequer Bills to be made forth by virtue of
this Act, or ſo many of them as ſhall from
ABCDEFGHIJKLMNOPQRST

Brevier Black.

And be it further enacted by the Authority aforeſaid, That all and every
of the ſaid Exchequer Bills to be made forth by virtue of this Act, or ſo
many of them as ſhall from time to time remain undiſcharged and uncan-
celled, until the diſcharging and cancelling the ſame purſuant to this Act,

Pica Gothick.

ATTA ᚢNSAR ΦN IN HIMINAM VEIHNAI
NAMҀ ΦEIN ЧIMAI ΦINDINASSNS ΦEINS
VAIҀΦAI VIAGA ΦEINS SVE IN HIMINA

Pica Coptick.

ϩⲉⲛ ⲟⲩⲁⲣⲭⲏ ⲁϥⲧ ⲟⲙⲓⲟ ⲛ̄ⲧⲫⲉ ⲛⲉⲙ ⲡⲕ-
ⲁϩⲓ· ⲡⲕⲁϩⲓ ⲇⲉ ⲛⲉ ⲟⲩⲟⲛⲁⲧ ⲉϥⲟϥ ⲡⲉ ⲟⲩⲟϩ
ⲏⲧⲟϣⲧ ⲟⲩⲭⲁⲕⲓ ⲛⲁϥⲭⲏ ⲉϫⲉⲛ ⲫⲛⲟⲩⲛ ⲟⲩⲟϩ

Pica Armenian.

Engliſh Syriack.

Pica Samaritan.

Engliſh Arabick.

Hebrew with Points.

בְּרֵאשִׁית בָּרָא אֱלֹהִים אֵת הַשָּׁמַיִם וְאֵת הָאָרֶץ׃ וְהָאָרֶץ
הָיְתָה תֹהוּ וָבֹהוּ וְחֹשֶׁךְ עַל־פְּנֵי תְהוֹם וְרוּחַ אֱלֹהִים
מְרַחֶפֶת עַל־פְּנֵי הַמָּיִם׃ וַיֹּאמֶר אֱלֹהִים יְהִי אוֹר וַיְהִי־אוֹר׃
וַיַּרְא אֱלֹהִים אֶת־הָאוֹר כִּי־טוֹב וַיַּבְדֵּל אֱלֹהִים בֵּין הָאוֹר
וּבֵין הַחֹשֶׁךְ׃ וַיִּקְרָא אֱלֹהִים לָאוֹר יוֹם וְלַחֹשֶׁךְ קָרָא לַיְלָה

Hebrew without Points.

בראשית ברא אלהים את השמים ואת הארץ׃ והארץ
היתה תהו ובהו וחשך על־פני תהום ורוח אלהים
מרחפת על־פני המים׃ ויאמר אלהים יהי אור ויהי־אור׃
וירא אלהים את־האור כי־טוב ויבדל אלהים בין האור
ובין החשך׃ ויקרא אלהים לאור יום ולחשך קרא לילה

Brevier Hebrew.

בראשית ברא אלהים את השמים ואת הארץ׃ והארץ היתה תהו
ובהו וחשך על־פני תהום ורוח אלהים מרחפת על־פני המים׃
ויאמר אלהים יהי אור ויהי־אור׃ וירא אלהים את־האור כי־טוב
ויבדל אלהים בין האור ובין החשך׃ ויקרא אלהים לאור יום ולחשך

Engliſh Greek.

Πρόδικος ὁ σοφὸς ἐν τῷ συγγράμματι τῷ περὶ τῆς Ἡρακλέυς (ὅπερ δὴ καὶ πλείστοις ἐπιδείκνυται) ὥτως περὶ τῆς
ἀρετῆς ἀποφαίνεται, ὧδέ πως λέγων, ὅσα ἐγὼ μέμνημαι.
Φησὶ μὲν Ἡρακλέα, ἐπεὶ ἐκ παίδων εἰς ἥβην ὡρμᾶτο,
ἐν ᾗ οἱ νέοι ἤδη αὐτοκράτορες γιγνόμενοι δηλῦσιν, εἴτε τὴν

Pica Greek.

Πρόδικος ὁ σοφὸς ἐν τῷ συγγράμματι τῷ περὶ τῆς Ἡρακλέυς
(ὅπερ δὴ καὶ πλείστοις ἐπιδείκνυται) ὥτως περὶ τῆς ἀρετῆς ἀποφαίνεται, ὧδέ πως λέγων, ὅσα ἐγὼ μέμνημαι. Φησὶ μὲν
Ἡρακλέα, ἐπεὶ ἐκ παίδων εἰς ἥβην ὡρμᾶτο, ἐν ᾗ οἱ νέοι ἤδη
αὐτοκράτορες γιγνόμενοι δηλῦσιν, εἴτε τὴν δι' ἀρετῆς ὁδὸν τρέψεται

Long Primer Greek.

Πρόδικος ὁ σοφὸς ἐν τῷ συγγράμματι τῷ περὶ τῆς Ἡρακλέυς (ὅπερ δὴ καὶ
πλείστοις ἐπιδείκνυται) ὥτως περὶ τῆς ἀρετῆς ἀποφαίνεται, ὧδέ πως λέγων,
ὅσα ἐγὼ μέμνημαι. Φησὶ μὲν Ἡρακλέα, ἐπεὶ ἐκ παίδων εἰς ἥβην ὡρμᾶτο,

Brevier Greek.

Pica Saxon.

Ða he ba mib ʒrummum
neꝡum pær ꝼ he ealle þa pitu

1734.

Type Specimens

A Book about Diverse Letters and Ornaments, with Examples of Artistic Printing

by Cees W. de Jong

1923, William Caslon's Type Specimen Sheet (Facsimile), *Mergenthaler Linotype Company,* New York

William Caslon was most successful in England. In 1720, his first year of business, he produced a new typeface for the Society for the Propagation of Christian Knowledge to be used for a Bible in Arabic.

He printed sample pages so that he could sell the new typeface to other printers. On these sheets was his name, William Caslon, in roman letters designed specially for the purpose. This new typeface design was the beginning of the popular style we now know as Caslon Old Style. Following this style, Caslon cut a number of non-roman and exotic styles, including Coptic, Armenian, Etruscan, and Hebrew. Caslon Gothic is his version of Old English, or black letter. He published the first and extensive catalog for his type foundry in 1734, presenting a total of 38 typefaces. William Caslon died in 1766, aged 74.

Collector Jan Tholenaar has assembled one of the greatest private collections of type specimens in the world. With his individual preferences setting the tone, the collection focuses on specimens produced between 1830 and 1930.

Extremely diverse fantasy letters and ornaments, with examples of artistic printing. The two volumes of this publication display some wonderful examples, with dazzling construction and color combinations.

Type specimen in letterpress, not in lithography. Here we see magnificent examples of setting, all made up of letters, lines, or intricate ornaments. Applications were devised for all of this material being offered for sale, set, and printed by hand. This chapter in the history of type specimens is endearing, and the infinite variety is glorious.

Until the beginning of the 20th Century, the names of only a handful of famous type designers, such as Garamond, Bodoni, and Fournier, were known. The thousands of typefaces introduced by foundries in the 19th Century were designed and engraved by anonymous workers. In type catalogs, these are referred to as "im Hause" or "Hausschnitt."

It was Klingspor, in particular, who attracted and credited famous designers in the early 20th Century: Otto Eckmann, Rudolf Koch, Walter Tiemann, Imre Reiner. Bauer engaged the services of Heinrich Wieynk, F. H. Ehmcke, Lucian Bernhard, E. R. Weiss, Paul Renner, and F. H. Ernst Schneidler.

Berthold employed designers such as Louis Oppenheim, Georg Trump, and Herbert Bayer. Important designers also worked for the Ludwig und Mayer type foundry, including Heinrich Jost, J. Erbar, and J. V. Cissarz. Georg Belwe and Jan Tschichold designed for Schelter & Giesecke, and

F. W. Kleukens and Hermann Zapf for Stempel. Some designed type for more than one firm.

The Germans were trendsetters in this area. But in other countries, too, there were excellent designers working for type foundries. Georges Auriol and E. Grasset worked for Peignot, for example; A. M. Cassandre and Adrian Frutiger for Deberny & Peignot; Roger Excoffon for Olive; Aldo Novarese for Nebiolo; Warren Chappell and Morris F. Benton for American Type Founders; Rudolph Ruzicka, W. A. Dwiggins, and Walter Tracy for Linotype; and F. W. Goudy, Bruce Rogers, Berthold Wolpe, and Eric Gill for Monotype. S. H. de Roos and Dick Dooijes were employed by Lettergieterij Amsterdam, and J. van Krimpen and S. L. Hartz worked for Enschedé.

German foundries often had a branch either in Moscow or St. Petersburg to serve the Russian market. Also from Berthold is a Hebrew specimen from 1924 with various faces and wonderful color illustrations. In 1925, a similar specimen was published in Eastern languages, including Arabic, Turkish, and Hindi.

For 500 years, the same methods were used for printing—and, suddenly, it was over, owing to new developments. Type foundries that made only lead type have disappeared. Some changed with the times and are still part of the creative process of artistic presentation of messages in the global digital world.

This book would not have been possible without Jan Tholenaar and his international private collection of type specimens, his admiration and love for diverse letters and ornaments, and his examples of artistic printing.

I also wish to thank Alston W. Purvis, professor at the Boston University College of Fine Arts. He has written on a variety of topics relating to graphic design, and now, once again, we have worked together on this book.

The medium is the message; the typeface is the message.

Schriftmuster

Ein Buch über Vielfalt der Schriften und Ornamente in Zeugnissen großer Druckkunst

von Cees W. de Jong

Im Jahr 1720 fertigte der in England überaus erfolgreiche William Caslon für die *Society for the Propagation of Christian Knowledge* eine neue Schrift an, die in einer arabischen Bibelausgabe Verwendung finden sollte.

Um seine Schrift anderen Druckern zum Kauf anzubieten, stellte Caslon Musterblätter her. Auf diesen Bögen war auch sein Name, William Caslon, abgedruckt, und zwar in speziell dafür entworfenen Antiqua-Lettern. Diese neu gestaltete Schrift war der Grundstein für jenen Schriftstil, der heute als Caslon Old Style geläufig ist. In der Folge schnitt Caslon eine Reihe nichtlateinischer, exotischer Stile, darunter koptische, armenische, etruskische und hebräische Schriften. Die Caslon Gothic ist seine Version solcher Schriftarten, die man als Old English oder *black letters* (Frakturschrift) bezeichnet. 1734 veröffentlichte Caslon erstmals einen umfangreichen Katalog seiner Schriftgießerei mit 38 Schriftentwürfen. William Caslon starb 1766 im Alter von 74 Jahren.

Jan Tholenaar hat über viele Jahre eine der eindrucksvollsten privaten Schriftmustersammlungen der Welt aufgebaut. Das Hauptgewicht dieser Sammlung liegt, Tholenaars persönlichen Vorlieben entsprechend, auf der Zeit zwischen 1830 und 1930.

Eine endlose Fülle an fantasievollen Schriften und Ornamenten in Zeugnissen großer Druckkunst – die schönsten Exemplare, Schriftmuster von bestechender typografischer Gestaltung und Farbvielfalt, werden in den beiden Bänden dieser Publikation präsentiert.

Keine Lithografien, sondern Muster im Hochdruckverfahren – die vorgestellten Exemplare zeichnen sich durch ihren hervorragenden Satz aus, sei es der Lettern, der Linien oder der komplexen Ornamente. Für das gesamte seinerzeit feilgebotene Material wurden handgesetzte und -gedruckte Beispiele angefertigt. So eindrucksvoll die unendliche Vielfalt der Schriftmuster aus jener Epoche, so reizvoll ist jedes einzelne Stück für sich.

Bis zu Beginn des 20. Jahrhunderts war nur eine Handvoll berühmter Schriftentwerfer wie Garamond, Bodoni oder Fournier bekannt. Tausende von Schriftentwürfen und -schnitten, die im 19. Jahrhundert von den Schriftgießereien auf den Markt gebracht wurden, stammten von nicht namentlich genannten Mitarbeitern. In Schriftkatalogen sind derartige Entwürfe mit dem Zusatz „im Hause" oder „Hausschnitt" versehen.

Die Gießerei Klingspor wählte im frühen 20. Jahrhundert einen anderen Weg und zog berühmte Gestalter an, die sie später auch als Urheber erwähnte, darunter Otto Eckmann, Rudolf Koch, Walter Tiemann und Imre Reiner. In Bauers Diensten standen Heinrich Wieynk, F. H. Ehmcke, Lucian Bern-

hard, E. R. Weiss, Paul Renner und F. H. Ernst Schneidler. Berthold beschäftige Gestalter wie Louis Oppenheim, Georg Trump oder Herbert Bayer. Auch für die Schriftgießerei Ludwig und Mayer waren bedeutende Gestalter tätig, darunter Heinrich Jost, J. Erbar und J. V. Cissarz. Georg Belwe und Jan Tschichold entwarfen für Schelter & Giesecke, F. W. Kleukens und Hermann Zapf für Stempel. Einige dieser Schriftentwerfer arbeiten für mehrere Unternehmen.

Deutschland hatte eine wegweisende Rolle auf diesem Gebiet inne. Aber auch in anderen Ländern kooperierten die Schriftgießereien mit exzellenten Gestaltern: Georges Auriol und E. Grasset arbeiteten für Peignot, A. M. Cassandre und Adrian Frutiger für Deberny & Peignot, Roger Excoffon für Olive, Aldo Novarese für Nebiolo, Warren Chappell und Morris F. Benton für American Type Founders, Rudolph Ruzicka, W. A. Dwiggins und Walter Tracy für Linotype, F. W. Goudy, Bruce Rogers, Berthold Wolpe und Eric Gill für Monotype; S. H. de Roos und Dick Dooijes waren bei der Lettergieterij Amsterdam angestellt, J. van Krimpen und S. L. Hartz für Enschedé tätig.

Um den russischen Markt zu bedienen, hatten deutsche Gießereien häufig eine Dependance in Moskau oder Sankt Petersburg. Berthold brachte 1924 auch ein hebräisches Schriftmuster mit herrlichen farbigen Illustrationen heraus. Ein ähnliches Muster erschien 1925 für die Sprachen des Nahen und Mittleren Ostens, darunter Arabisch, Türkisch und Hindi.

500 Jahre lang haben sich die Druckverfahren im Wesentlichen nicht verändert – bis aufgrund neuer Technologien plötzlich alles vorbei war. Ausschließlich auf Bleisatzschriften beschränkte Schriftgießereien sind Geschichte. Andere haben sich dem Zeitenwandel angepasst und sind heute Teil jenes kreativen Prozesses, der die künstlerische Gestaltung von Botschaften in einer globalisierten digitalen Welt bestimmt.

Besonders danken möchte ich Jan Tholenaar: Ohne seine Privatsammlung mit ihren Schriftmustern aus aller Welt, ohne seine Leidenschaft und Begeisterung für all die verschiedenen Schriften und Ornamente und nicht zuletzt ohne seine kunstvollen Drucke hätte dieses Buch nicht entstehen können.

Mein weiterer Dank gilt Alston W. Purvis, der als Professor am Boston University College of Fine Arts lehrt und zahlreiche Publikationen zum Thema Grafikdesign verfasst hat. Es war mir eine Freude, bei dem vorliegenden Titel erneut mit ihm zusammenzuarbeiten.

Das Medium ist die Botschaft – die Schrift ist die Botschaft.

Spécimens de caractères

Un ouvrage présentant diverses polices de caractères et ornements, avec des exemples d'impression d'art

par Cees W. de Jong

William Caslon était très célèbre en Angleterre. En 1720, l'année de création de sa fonderie, il conçut une nouvelle police de caractères pour la SPCK (Société pour la promotion du savoir chrétien) pour l'impression d'une bible en arabe.

Il imprima des pages d'échantillon pour pouvoir vendre cette police arabe à d'autres imprimeurs. Sur ces pages, son nom, William Caslon, s'étalait en caractères romains dessinés spécialement pour l'occasion. Cette nouvelle police est à l'origine de la célèbre police que nous connaissons aujourd'hui sous le nom de Caslon Old Style. À la suite de cette police, Caslon grava un certain nombre de caractères non romains et exotiques comme les Coptic, Armenian, Etruscan et Hebrew. Caslon Gothic était sa version de Old English.

Il publia, en 1734, un premier et volumineux catalogue de la fonderie qui présentait un total de 38 caractères. William Caslon mourut en 1766, à l'âge de 74 ans.

Le collectionneur Jan Tholenaar a rassemblé l'une des plus grandes collections privées de spécimens de caractères. Ses préférences individuelles donnant le ton, la collection se concentre sur des pièces réalisées entre 1830 et 1930.

Une variété considérable de caractères fantaisie et d'ornements, ainsi que des exemples d'impression d'art.

Cet ouvrage présente quelques pièces magnifiques, de constructions éblouissantes et de coloris très variés.

Des spécimens de caractères qui sont de la typographie, non de la lithographie.

Nous avons ici de magnifiques exemples de composition, tous faits de lettres, de lignes ou d'ornements complexes. Pour tout ce matériel proposé à la vente, on concevait des démonstrations appliquées, qui étaient composées et imprimées manuellement.

Cette partie de l'histoire des spécimens de caractères est fascinante, et leur infinie variété splendide.

Jusqu'au début du XXᵉ siècle, seul était connu le nom d'une poignée de graphistes typographes comme Garamond, Bodoni ou Fournier. Les milliers de caractères produits par les fonderies au XIXᵉ siècle étaient dessinés et gravés par des ouvriers maison anonymes. Dans les catalogues de caractères, il y est fait référence comme «im Hause» ou «Hausschnitt».

C'est surtout Klingspor qui a su attirer et créditer des graphistes de renom au début du XXᵉ siècle: Otto Eckmann, Rudolf Koch, Walter Tiemann ou Imre Reiner.

Bauer eut, lui, recours aux services d'Heinrich Wieynk, F. H. Ehmcke, Lucian Bernhard, E. R. Weiss, Paul Renner et F. H. Ernst Schneidler.

Berthold employa des graphistes comme Louis Oppenheim, Georg Trump ou Herbert Bayer.

D'importants graphistes ont également travaillé pour la fonderie Ludwig und Mayer, comme Heinrich Jost, J. Erbar ou J. V. Cissarz. Georg Belwe et Jan Tschichold ont travaillé pour Schelter & Giesecke, et F. W. Kleukens et Hermann Zapf pour Stempel. Certains graphistes dessinaient des polices pour plusieurs firmes.

Les Allemands ont été novateurs dans ce domaine. Mais il existait dans d'autres pays aussi d'excellents graphistes travaillant pour les fonderies. Georges Auriol et E. Grasset ont travaillé pour Peignot, par exemple; A. M. Cassandre et Adrian Frutiger pour Deberny & Peignot; Roger Excoffon pour Olive; Aldo Novarese pour Nebiolo; Warren Chappell et Morris F. Benton pour American Type Founders; Rudolph Ruzicka, W. A. Dwiggins et Walter Tracy pour Linotype; et F. W. Goudy, Bruce Rogers, Berthold Wolpe et Eric Gill pour Monotype. S. H. de Roos et Dick Dooijes ont été employés par Lettergieterij Amsterdam, et J. van Krimpen et S. L. Hartz ont travaillé pour Enschedé.

Les fonderies allemandes avaient souvent une filiale à Moscou ou à Saint-Pétersbourg pour desservir le marché russe. Il existe également de chez Berthold un spécimen en hébreu daté de 1924 avec plusieurs styles de caractères et de merveilleuses illustrations en couleur. En 1925, un spécimen similaire fut publié dans des langues orientales, comme l'arabe, le turc ou l'hindi.

On a employé la même méthode d'impression pendant 500 ans – puis soudain, grâce aux nouvelles technologies, tout a changé. Les fonderies de caractères qui ne faisaient que du plomb ont disparu. Quelques-unes se sont adaptées et font toujours partie du processus de création de la présentation artistique des messages dans le monde numérique.

Ce livre n'aurait pu exister sans Jan Tholenaar et son immense collection privée de spécimens de caractères, son amour et son admiration pour les caractères et les ornements, et ses exemples d'impression d'art.

Je voudrais également remercier Alston W. Purvis, professeur au Boston University College of Fine Arts. Il a écrit sur de nombreux sujets relatifs au graphisme, et aujourd'hui, de nouveau, nous nous retrouvons à travailler ensemble sur cet ouvrage.

Le moyen d'expression est le message; la police de caractère est le message.

1923, *The Linotype Bulletin,* **XVII,**
No. 12, *Mergenthaler Linotype Company,*
New York

An initial *T*, a clear accent on the page—
the perfect beginning to any page. This
one is based on the work of William
Caslon.

Initialen setzen klare Akzente – ein per-
fekter Auftakt für eine Seite oder einen
Absatz. Diese *T*-Initiale entstammt dem
Werk William Caslons.

Une lettrine *T*, un accent net sur la
page—rien de tel pour un début. Celle-ci
est basée sur le travail de **William Caslon.**

The Ideal Typeface

by Cees W. de Jong

*What kind of character should letters have, and which aspects
of that character should their content convey? Is the customer a newspaper,
are you designing a letter on your own initiative, just "for fun," or does
a company need a new house style for its communications strategy?*

New innovations have introduced radical changes in typography and
printing, which had seen only slight modifications since the 15th Century.
Craftsmanship was steadily supplanted by machinery, and the increasing
demand for printing required more and improved equipment. Work-
manship became less important, as supervisors and assistants could now
perform tasks that in the past had required hundreds of skilled workers.

Our script has evolved from the flow of writing. Naturally, this eventually
prompted the development of the serif in printed letters. The amazing
thing is that typography developed for hundreds of years internationally,
but only with serif typefaces. The first examples of the new sans serif style
did not appear until 1816 in England.

In the 19th Century, there was a general degeneration of appreciation
for typography, design, or quality in printing material. Printers produced
pages with numerous type sizes and combinations of any typefaces available
in the shop. Except for an occasional superficial imitation of traditional
typography, there was little indication of any concern for page organization
or well-designed typefaces.

In 1951, M. R. Radermacher Schorer, in his *Bijdrage tot de Geschiedenis
van de Renaissance der Nederlandse Boekdrukkunst (Contribution to the History
of the Dutch Printing Arts)*, gave a dismal summary of the period: "When
we compare the 19th-Century book to the incunabula, the type is pallid
and without character, often damaged and badly printed; the arrangement
is confusing; the color is faded; the paper is of bad quality; the spine is
covered with gold stamping without beautiful ornaments … and thicker
paper is used to make the book look larger than it actually is."

Drastic changes in typography and technology occurred in the 19th
Century. For 400 years, the lead setting system had limited the options;
the arrival of new technology changed typography, design, and printing.
New styles and traditions emerged.

After the Arts and Crafts Movement of William Morris and, later, Peter
Behrens, developments were divided into the subjective-expressive and
functional, or elementary, schools of thought.

The expressive position is reflected in the work of Rudolf Koch,
who sought the path of innovation in returning to individualism and
preindustrialization.

In January 1898, two companies, Berthold and Bauer & Co. of Stuttgart,
presented the Akzidenz Grotesk font in advertisements in the *Deutscher
Buch und Steindrucker*. The font was therefore already more than 20 years

old in the heyday of Constructivism, when movements such as De Stijl,
Bauhaus, and Dada adopted the face to great effect. It was present at the
birth of "Swiss typography" as its major typeface. Akzidenz Grotesk still
has a highly visual quality, reminding us that type does not have to be
uniform to be readable and attractive; on the contrary, it is the differences
between characters that make them legible.

Functional typography was developed primarily by designers in the
Soviet Union, Germany, Hungary, and the Netherlands. There was a desire
for a better social, cultural, future-oriented design that reduced ornamentation and the choice of typographical elements. Sans serif typefaces, lowercase letters, and asymmetrical spacing were major characteristics of this
"new typography."

Eric Gill was commissioned by Bristol bookdealer Douglas Cleverdon
to paint a sign with sans serif lettering. Stanley Morison, artistic adviser to
the Monotype Corporation, who was visiting Cleverdon, noticed the sign,
and became convinced that Gill could design a similar sans serif face for
Monotype. Until then, Gill had used only capitals. As usual, the first drawings of the lowercase letters were quite different from the face that was
finally cast. However, when Gill Sans first appeared, toward the end of the
1920s, it was not exactly what the British print establishment had been
waiting for. Its muted reception in the year 1928 was similar to that of Futura in Germany the year before; Paul Renner's design had been called a fashion that would soon be forgotten.

Futura is a timeless, elementary typeface. In 1925, Jan Tschichold published a special edition of *Typographische Mitteilungen* entitled "Elementary
Typography." It was here that he first formulated his attempts to create a
new typography. "Of the typefaces available, the grotesque or block faces
fulfilled the needs of the new typography best, as they were simple
in design and easy to read."

At the same time, Paul Renner's design for a new grotesque style based
on Constructivist principles was in progress. Renner based Futura on
simple, basic forms: the circle, the triangle, and the square. However, his
affinity with books and typography prevented him from casting aside
tradition in favor of a new dogma. The first samples of the new style made
their appearance in 1925.

In 1926, Bauhaus leader László Moholy-Nagy wrote in *Bauhausheft* 7:
"Since all existing grotesque book styles lack basic style, grotesque still
has to be created." Herbert Bayer's essay "Attempt at a New Typeface" and

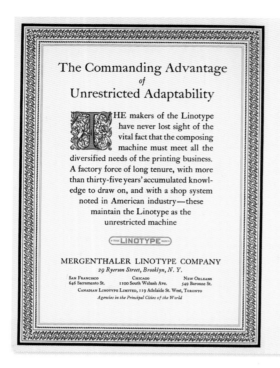

WILLIAM CASLON I

The Editors wish to express their indebtedness
to
LINOTYPE & MACHINERY LIMITED of London
Mr. GEORGE W. JONES of London
and particularly to
"Two Centuries of Typefounding"
A History of the Caslon Foundry
Printed by George W. Jones at The Sign of the Dolphin
London, 1920
from which has been obtained much of the material
used in the following pages

Josef Albers's "Stencil Type as Hoarding Type" were published in the same volume.

Before the start of World War II, the progressive forces in typography were resisted, overcome, and suppressed—just like what was happening in the political arena. Many typographers had to change their style or emigrate. In Germany, archaic design rules were reintroduced and enforced.

In Switzerland, the work of Anton Stankowski earned a great deal of respect for the "new typography." His work developed further and gained fame in the 1950s under the name "Swiss typography." The first generation of this kind of Swiss typographer included Max Bill, Richard P. Lohse, Max Huber, and Emil Ruder.

In addition to the Swiss designers, the former head of the Bauhaus typographical studio, Herbert Bayer, worked in the United States with great success. The link between the strict dogmatism of the sans serif face and aspects of American design led to an interesting form.

The loss of strict grotesque typography and the innovative work from the United States, with a highly pictorial development in the use of letters and text combined with photographs, led to more successful graphic design. It increasingly became a matter of designing total concepts and identity programs.

In 1949, Eduard Hoffmann, head of the Haas Type Foundry in Münchenstein, near Basel, was planning a new grotesque typeface. His model was Schelter Grotesk, the official Bauhaus typeface. Swiss designers at that time were making increasing use of Berthold's Akzidenz Grotesk, and Swiss typography was becoming known throughout the world. Eduard Hoffmann knew exactly how the new typeface should look and entrusted the design to Max Miedinger in Zurich, who was an expert on grotesque typefaces. His sketches were passed to the Haas Type Foundry's in-house punch-cutting works for casting in lead. In 1957, the name of this project was New Haas Grotesque, but Stempel published the new typeface in 1960 under the name Helvetica.

With the arrival of photosetting, typography and design gained unrestricted freedom of movement. For the first time there was access to the most diverse typefaces. This change enabled even better visualization of the content, and words and text images could be set closer together.

In 1973, Günter Gerhard Lange, type director of Berthold and redesigner of Akzidenz Grotesk, described the introduction of this redesigned font: "In this work, the basic proportions of the well-loved Akzidenz Grotesk

semi-bold have been used to determine the average length and individual shapes. Naturally, the family similarities between the individual styles had to be taken into account, as did the mood and fashion of the times." The fashion of that time included the then brand-new Helvetica by Max Miedinger, as well as competing new faces like Adrian Frutiger's Univers and Konrad F. Bauer's Folio.

Helvetica was never intended to be a full range of mechanical and handsetting faces. When Univers, the highly extended typeface family by Adrian Frutiger, was successfully launched, Stempel was forced to redesign the whole range according to the method Frutiger initiated, using numbers for the different members of the Helvetica family. Helvetica was just what designers in the early 1970s were looking for. In 1982, Stempel introduced New Helvetica.

There is a broad interest in the history of typography today, which I hope will extend to the future. We are still looking for new opportunities and "the mood and fashion of the times." The question is, has the ideal typeface been invented yet? That is for you to decide.

Most striking, I find, is that type designers, with their wonderful eye for detail, can determine such a great difference in character. There is a world of difference, for instance, between Caslon (1725) by William Caslon and Baskerville (1754) by John Baskerville. Or compare Berthold's Akzidenz Grotesk (1899) with Paul Renner's Futura (1925). The page looks completely different, and, as a reader, you perceive the message differently, too. The choice of typography and the application of the graphic designer can transport you to another world.

A Small Selection of Type Designers with an Eye for Detail

Claude Garamond: *Garamond*

The French Renaissance Antiqua sees the light of day. Claude Garamond was born in 1480. He learned his craft very early from his father and others in the family circle. Garamond claimed he could cut printed stamps in Cicero size (12 point) at the age of 15. In the first quarter of the 16th Century, French type cutters and printers were the counterparts of Italian creators of the Renaissance Antiqua. Aldus Manutius and Francesco Griffo's Antiqua typefaces came to France, along with those of Pietro Bembo.

Claude Garamond is one of the founding type cutters and casters of the French Renaissance Antiqua and Italica. It was during his era that

Roman capitals and Carolingian lowercase letters were brought together. In centralized France, conditions were more favorable for making progress in typography and letterpress than in Italy or Germany. Claude Garamond gained real fame and his position as royal type caster after the 1543 Greek publication *Grecs du Roy*, which King Francis I, a supporter of letterpress, engaged him to cut. The first Antiqua that can be confidently dated and attributed to Garamond was a large typeface, Gros-Roman, which appeared in an edition of the works of Eusebius and other publications by Robert Estienne in 1544.

After 1545, title pages show, Garamond was also a publisher, both in his own right and together with Pierre Gaultier and Jean Barbé. Examples of a modern Garamond in use today are Jan Tschichold's Sabon and, even better, Sabon Next by Jean François Porchez.

William Caslon: *Caslon*

Caslon, a man with a versatile mind. William Caslon was born in Cradley, Worcestershire, in 1692. At the age of 13, he was apprenticed to an engraver in London. In 1717, he became a citizen of London, where, the year before, he had set himself up as an independent engraver. Two years later, he opened his own type foundry.

It was the bookbinder John Watts who engaged Caslon to design and cast typefaces for his book covers. One of these books then caught the eye of William Bowyer, a well-known London printer. The two became friends, and Bowyer introduced Caslon to other London printers. This was the start of one of the most successful type foundries in England. Initially, Caslon was supported financially by Watts, Bowyer, and his son-in-law James Bettenham, also a printer.

In 1720, his first year of business in the type foundry, he produced a new typeface for the Society for the Propagation of Christian Knowledge to be used for a Bible in Arabic. Having finished the Arabic script, he printed a sample page so that he could sell the new typeface to other printers. On this sheet was his name, William Caslon, in roman letters designed specially for the purpose. This new typeface design was the beginning of the popular style we now know as Caslon Old Style. Following this style, Caslon cut a number of non-roman and exotic styles, including Coptic, Armenian, Etruscan, and Hebrew. Caslon Gothic is his version of Old English, or black letters.

All these typefaces had appeared before Caslon published the first and extensive catalog for his type foundry in 1734, presenting a total of 38 type-faces. Caslon's type foundry moved to the famous Chiswell Street, where Caslon's son and several generations of the family after him ran the business for more than 120 years. In 1749, King George II made Caslon a justice of the peace for the county of Middlesex. He retired and died at his country house in Bethnal Green in 1766, aged 74. His was a success story of an extraordinary engraver.

John Baskerville: *Baskerville*

A quest for the best result. John Baskerville (1706–1775) started cutting and casting his own typefaces around 1754. He was influenced by the lettering of stonemasons, as were other English type designers who developed faces we regard today as typically English: grotesques and Egyptians, which appeared elsewhere in the Industrial Revolution. Baskerville had to imagine what was of great importance for him: how his typefaces would be printed and what they would look like. Paper, ink, typefaces, and printing machines therefore all played equally important roles for him.

In 1750, John Baskerville established a paper mill, type foundry, and printing business. He then came up with the idea of coated paper. After a great deal of painstaking work, in 1754 he presented his first typeface. In 1758, his famous edition of Milton's *Paradise Lost* was produced, a one-man work of art, or *Gesamtkunstwerk*, before the term existed. Baskerville also worked as a printer for the University of Cambridge, where he was promoted director in 1758. One of his most famous publications is *Juvenalis* (1757).

The spacious typefaces Baskerville designed; the open way of typesetting, increasing the spacing between words and lines; the width on the page; and the use of coated paper and very black ink gained him renown throughout Europe. After his death, a large part of Baskerville's typeface material, the secret ink formula, and the manner of producing coated paper were sold to the Frenchman Caron de Beaumarchais. Between 1785 and 1789, he printed 70 volumes of Voltaire using the Baskerville letters. Baskerville would have been very happy with the result.

Giambattista Bodoni: *Bodoni*

"Plenty of white space and generous line spacing, and don't make the type size too miserly. Then you will be assured of a product fit for a king."—Giambattista Bodoni

He has been called the king of printers and the printer of kings. Bodoni's reputation is based on the *Manuale tipografico*, a compilation

TYPOGRAPHY

THE CASLON OLD FACE SERIES

6 Point — THE CASLON OLD FACE SERIES IS THE FRUIT OF MANY YEARS' STUDY of the Caslon types and of their use by those great printers who did their most distinguished and useful work with them in their purity. It was created from the original patterns of William Caslon I, and in all respects a true Caslon, until 1234 *THE CASLON OLD FACE SERIES IS THE FRUIT OF MANY YEARS' STUDY of the Caslon types and of their use by those great printers who did their* VBCD

9 Point — THE CASLON OLD FACE SERIES IS THE FRUIT OF MA ny years' study of the Caslon types and of their use by those gr eat printers who did their most distinguished and useful w 1234 *THE CASLON OLD FACE SERIES IS THE FRUIT OF MA ny years' study of the Caslon types and of their use by tho* VBCD

11 Point — THE CASLON OLD FACE SERIES IS THE fruit of many years' study of the Caslon types and of their use by those great printers who 1234 *THE CASLON OLD FACE SERIES IS THE fruit of many years' study of the Caslon t* VBCD

14 Point — THE CASLON OLD FACE SERIES IS THE FRUIT OF MANY YEARS' STUDY of the Caslon types and of their use by those great printers who did their most disting uished and useful work with them in their purity. It was created from the original 1234 *THE CASLON OLD FACE SERIES IS THE FRUIT OF MANY YEARS' STUDY of the Caslon types and of their use by those great printers who did their most dis* VBCD

18 Point — THE CASLON OLD FACE SERIES IS THE FRUIT OF MANY YEARS' study of the Caslon types and of their use by those great printers who did their most distinguished and useful work with them in their purity. It was c 1234

THE CASLON OLD FACE SERIES IS THE FRUIT OF MANY YE ars' study of the Caslon types and of their use by those great printers who did 1234

24 Point — THE CASLON OLD FACE SERIES IS THE FRUIT OF many years' study of the Caslon types and of their use by those great printers who did their most distinguished and usef 1234

8 Point — THE CASLON OLD FACE SERIES IS THE FRUIT OF MANY years' study of the Caslon types and of their use by those great printers who did their most distinguished and useful work with them in their 1234 *THE CASLON OLD FACE SERIES IS THE FRUIT OF MANY years' study of the Caslon types and of their use by those great pri* VBCD

10 Point — THE CASLON OLD FACE SERIES IS THE FRUIT OF many years' study of the Caslon types and of their use by those great printers who did their most distinguished work wi 1234 *THE CASLON OLD FACE SERIES IS THE FRUIT OF many years' study of the Caslon types and of their use by* VBCD

11 Point — THE CASLON OLD FACE SERIES IS THE FR uit of many years' study of the Caslon types and of their use by those great printers who did their most dist 1234 *THE CASLON OLD FACE SERIES IS THE FR uit of many years' study of the Caslon types and of* VBCD

11 Point — *THE CASLON OLD FACE SERIES IS THE FRUIT of many years' study of the Caslon types and of their use by* 1234

14 Point — THE CASLON OLD FACE SERIES IS THE FR uit of many years' study of the Caslon types and of their use by those great printers who did their most dis 1234

14 Point — *THE CASLON OLD FACE SERIES IS THE FR uit of many years' study of the Caslon types and of the* 1234

30 Point — THE CASLON OLD FACE SERIES IS T he fruit of many years' study of the Cas 1234

36 Point — THE CASLON OLD FACE SER ies is the fruit of many years' 1234

SHORT DESCENDERS

Made for the 18, 21 and 24 point sizes only and will be substituted for the characters regularly furnished, if so ordered, or they may be ordered as an extra. These characters permit the 18 point size to cast on a 16 point body, the 21 on an 18 point body, and the 24 on a 22 point body.

MODERNIZED FIGURES

These figures are made for all sizes and will be regularly furnished with all fonts unless old style figures are specified.

1234567890

SWASH CHARACTERS

A B C D E G M N P T Y

(Included with all fonts)

William Caslon's Foundry

From "Two Centuries of Typefounding", reproduced from a print engraved for the "Universal Magazine," 1750, for F. Hinton, at the King's Corners in St. Paul's Churchyard, London.

THE four men at the left are type casters. At the extreme right (4) is a rubber, and beyond him, seated, is a dresser. The boys (2) at the center table are breaking off the jets of type metal. The devices on either side of the table are almost literal reproductions of two illustrations of a mold in Moxon's "Mechanick Exercises," published in 1683, and for many years thereafter a standard manual on typefounding. As introduced into this print, they are probably ten times larger than their normal size. On the left (5) is the lower half of a mold, which almost duplicates the upper half (6). The reference letters identify the parts, which are listed by Moxon as:

a	The Carriage	g	The Female-Gage	dd	The Throat
b	The Body	h	The Hag	edd	The Pallat
c	The Male-Gage	aaa	The Bottom Plate	f	The Nick
de	The Mouthpiece	bb	The Wood the Bottom Plate	gg	The Stool
fi	The Register		Lies on	hh	The Spring or Bow
		cc	The Mouth		

The LINOTYPE BULLETIN

Devoted to the Linotype and its use

VOLUME XVII   NUMBER 12

Presenting

Linotype Typography Caslon Old Face

CASLON'S English types—so called to distinguish them from the "learned" Gothic or black letter—constitute what is probably the most famous type family in the history of letter founding. The first font, the pica, was cut a little more than two centuries ago, in 1722, and the remaining fonts were completed between that time and 1734, the year in which Caslon issued his famous broadside specimen sheet, reproduced in facsimile in our supplement. The types won an immediate success, and although at one time threatened with extinction, due to the changes in taste which followed the introduction of the "modern" letter, they were revived in 1844 and are today in universal use throughout the English-speaking world. The name Caslon Old Face was given them at the time of their revival to distinguish them from later types cut by the Caslon foundry, and is the name used in England today to designate the original Caslon type.

In America, "Primers and books, newspapers and broadsides, were mostly printed in Caslon old style types in the mid-Eighteenth Century and up to the Revolution. Indeed, the Declaration of Independence itself was printed in

[187]

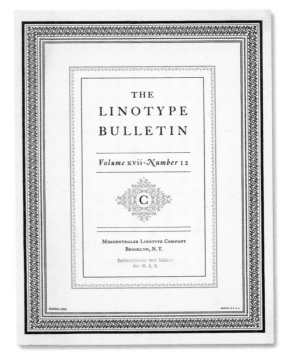

1923, *The Linotype Bulletin*, XVII, **No. 12,** *Mergenthaler Linotype Company,* New York

of his life's work, published posthumously in 1818 in Parma by his widow, Margherita Bodoni. The first copy was dedicated to Her Royal Highness Marie-Louise, Princess of Parma. This handbook on the art of book printing consisted of 546 printed pages with a total of 665 different alphabets, including 100 exotic typefaces and 1,300 vignettes. It contained 170 Latin scripts; some used up to 380 matrices. The edition comprised no more than 150 copies, although the figure of 290 has been quoted.

According to his widow, in 50 years Bodoni made, corrected, and cast over 55,000 matrices. Bodoni was devoted to design, to page harmony in terms of choice and size of typeface, leading, interplay of line length, spacing, and column width. The interaction of black and white and the generous use of space played a major role. The history of Bodoni's emulators is long. Morris Fuller Benton designed a Bodoni face for ATF in 1911. Monotype followed suit, then the Haas Type Foundry in Switzerland in 1924. The Haas Bodoni was copied by the Amsterdam Type Foundry, Berthold, and Stempel. Linotype and Ludlow also followed Haas, while Johannes Wagner introduced a new Bodoni in 1961. There are more than 500 Bodonis in the world. A beautiful example is Zuzana Licko's Filosofia (1996).

Stanley Morison: *Times New Roman*

The search for the best newspaper typeface. In 1923, Stanley Ignatius Arthur Morison (1889–1967) became typographical adviser to Monotype. He was in charge of designing a number of typeface families based on historical fonts, such as those by Eric Gill. The manager of the London *Times,* William Lints-Smith, had heard that Morison had made scathing remarks about the paper's outdated typography. They met and, after a long discussion, Morison's advice was to redesign the *Times* and he became a typographical adviser for the newspaper. He made test pages in different typefaces, including Baskerville, Plantin, Imprint, Ionic, and a version of Perpetua. At the same time, in the United States, Linotype was producing typefaces for setting long texts. The first was Ionic, followed in 1931 by Excelsior, which is still one of the most popular newspaper typefaces today.

After several other presentations, Morison decided that what the *Times* needed was a completely new typeface. In 1931, he presented two designs, an overhauled Perpetua and a modernized Plantin. The committee of the *Times* decided on the second of these. The original face being named Times Old Roman, this new typeface was christened Times New Roman. The face made its first appearance in the edition of the *Times* published

on October 3, 1932. Still a standard typeface today, thanks to wide distribution and marketing, Times New Roman will survive.

Berthold, Günter Gerhard Lange: *Akzidenz Grotesk*

Very simple and highly typical. AG, as connoisseurs like to call this typeface, was already more than 20 years old at the heyday of Constructivism. De Stijl, Bauhaus, Dada, and others used AG to great effect. It was in fashion at the birth of Swiss typography, as its major typeface. AG still has a high visual quality, reminding us that type does not have to be uniform to be legible and attractive; on the contrary, it is the difference between characters that makes them readable. Two companies presented Akzidenz Grotesk in January 1899 in advertisements in the *Deutscher Buch- und Steindrucker*. One was Berthold, the other Bauer & Co. of Stuttgart.

In 1973, Günter Gerhard Lange, redesigner of Akzidenz Grotesk and type director at Berthold, described his new version of the typeface at its introduction as follows: "In this work, the basic proportions of the well-loved Akzidenz-Grotesk semi-bold were used to determine the average length and individual shapes. Naturally, the family similarities between the individual styles had to be taken into account, as did the mood and fashion of the times." The fashion was then Max Miedinger's brand-new Helvetica and other competing new faces, such as Adrian Frutiger's Univers and Konrad F. Bauer's Folio. Nevertheless, good old AG still plays a major role in the ever-changing world of printing and design.

Paul Renner: *Futura*

Though being a typeface of its time, Futura is an ageless, elementary typeface. In 1925, Jan (Ivan) Tschichold published a special edition of *Typographische Mitteilungen* entitled "Elementary Typography," in which he wrote, "Of the typefaces available, the grotesque or block faces fulfilled the needs of the new typography best, as they were simple in design and easy to read. There was no reason, however, why other easy-to-read typefaces should not be used. The right typeface did not yet exist."

Bauhaus leader László Moholy-Nagy wrote in *Bauhausheft* 7 in 1926, "Since all existing grotesque book styles lack basic style, grotesque still has to be created." Herbert Bayer's "Attempt at a New Typeface" and Josef Albers's "Stencil Type as Hoarding Type" were published in the same issue.

At the same time, Paul Renner's design for a new grotesque style based on Constructivist principles was coming along. Designed in 1924, Renner

Technology has made things easier. The process, however, still always begins with an idea, sometimes a hasty sketch to jot down the idea, and then, if it proves to be a good concept, more extensive work on the details. The next morning, the sketch of the day before often turns out to be not quite as innovative as the designer initially imagined.

based his Futura on simple, basic forms—the circle, the triangle, and the square—but Renner's experience with books and typography meant that he did not cast aside tradition in favor of new dogma. The first samples of the new style made their appearance in 1925. A quote from Willy Haas: "With the new Futura, Paul Renner shows a nonhistorical, constructive solution that looks uncommonly noble and pure, is equally at home in classical and modern uses, and, despite its strict design, does not bombard us with doctrine but is easy on the eye. So much personal style with so much abstract strength of form, such a fine, human, noble mixture is not something we are used to seeing very often." In 1933, after the National Socialist Party seized power in Germany, Renner was forced to retire. In 1947, he published the book *Order and Harmony in Color*. At the same time, a reprint was published of his 1939 book, *The Art of Typography*.

Eric Gill: *Gill Sans*

From sculptor to typographer. Arthur Eric Rowton Gill (1882–1940) was trained as an architect around 1900. After he was married, he joined an arts and crafts group in Ditchling, Sussex, where he worked as a graphic designer and illustrator. Later, he worked as a sculptor. His first typeface design, Perpetua, was published in 1925. In 1928, he worked in High Wycombe as a sculptor and mason. In the meantime, he had set up his own hand press, together with his son-in-law René Hague. He published a number of books on industrial design and crafts. Another type design by Eric Gill to become established was Joanna, named after Gill's daughter, which was initially cast solely in 12 point specially for his "Essay on Typography," which appeared in 1931.

Gill Sans, pure and simple.

In 1916, Gill was working on sculptures for the stations of Westminster Cathedral. He was asked to design a simple, geometric typeface to be used for all signage and directions on the London Underground. For this design, he retained the classical proportions (see, for instance, the *g*). But for the *R*, he used his preferred character with its elegant down-sweeping tail.

Monotype's staff created many of the improvements.

In 1928, Gill himself became an adviser for Monotype. When Gill Sans first appeared toward the end of the 1920s, it was not exactly what the British print establishment had been looking for. Its reception was similar to that of Futura in Germany the year before. The comments in the yearbooks on Paul Renner's design spoke of a fashion that would be soon forgotten. The first version of Gill Sans was finished for the annual con-

gress of the British Printing Industries Federation in May 1928, where Stanley Morison gave an address and sent invitations set in the new face. From then on, Gill Sans was a winner.

Max Miedinger: *Helvetica*

Faceless and timeless. In 1949, Eduard Hoffmann, head of the Haas Type Foundry in Münchenstein, near Basel, was planning a new grotesque. His model was Schelter Grotesk, the official Bauhaus typeface. Swiss designers at that time had started to make increasing use of Berthold's Akzidenz Grotesk, which then reentered the world as "Swiss typography." Eduard Hoffmann knew exactly how the new typeface should look and entrusted the design to Max Miedinger in Zurich in 1956. Miedinger was an expert in grotesque typefaces. His sketches were discussed, assessed, and corrected with Hoffmann and passed on to the Haas Type Foundry's in-house punch-cutting works for casting in lead. The working name for this project in 1957 was New Haas Grotesque. In 1960, the new typeface was published by Stempel as Helvetica. When Linotype decided to adopt the new face, initially for mechanical typesetting in lead and later for photosetting, they had to rework the whole design. Helvetica was never planned as a full range of mechanical and hand-setting faces.

Then followed the success of Univers, the highly extended typeface family by Adrian Frutiger. Stempel was forced to redesign the whole range in the method initiated by Frutiger, using numbers for the different members of the Helvetica family. Helvetica Light was designed by Erich Schultz-Anker, artistic director at Stempel, together with Arthur Ritzel. In 1982, Stempel launched New Helvetica. Helvetica was just what designers in the early 1970s were looking for: a faceless, timeless typeface.

Type foundries kept in contact and conducted business with each other at first regionally, and then, quite soon, on an international scale. Letters were sold, copied, adapted, and released under various names, accommodating the trends of the time. If one firm had success, another wanted a piece of the pie.

And to present and sell all these letters, type foundries published and produced the most splendid, magnificent type-specimen proofs.

1894, 75 Jahre, *J.G. Schelter & Giesecke,* Leipzig

Remarkably little changed in the first 75 years of typography, printing, and communication in Leipzig. For nearly a century, artisans labored there with pleasure. The foundry was established in 1819 by Johann Gottfried Schelter and Christian Friedrich Giesecke, who had previously worked for Karl Tauchnitz (see pp. 104–107). The foundation was laid in the 1790s with the construction of letterpress printing machines.

Auffallend wenig haben Typografie, Druck und Kommunikation sich in den 75 Geschäftsjahren in Leipzig verändert. Ein knappes Jahrhundert lang gingen die Arbeiter fröhlich ihrem Tagwerk nach. Die Gießerei öffnete ihre Pforten im Jahr 1819 unter der Ägide von Gott-

fried Schelter und Christian Friedrich Giesecke, der zuvor für Karl Tauchnitz (s. S. 104–107) gearbeitet hatte; vorausgegangen war seit den 1790er-Jahren die Produktion von Druckmaschinen.

Bien peu de choses ont changé, à Leipzig, au cours des 75 premières années de la typographie, de l'imprimerie et de la communication. Pendant près d'un siècle, les artisans ont travaillé là avec plaisir. La fonderie a été fondée en 1819 par Johann Gottfried Schelter et Christian Friedrich Giesecke qui avaient auparavant travaillé pour Karl Tauchnitz (voir pp. 104–107). La première pierre fut posée dans les années 1790 avec la fabrication de machines d'imprimerie typographique.

Giesserei, südlicher Teil.

Aetzung nach photographischer Aufnahme.

Abteilung für Herstellung der Holzgerätschaften.

Ätzung nach photographischer Aufnahme.

One
Hundred
Years

1796
1896

Mackellar, Smiths & Jordan Company

Die ideale Schrift

von Cees W. de Jong

Was für einen Charakter sollte eine Schrift haben, und welche inhaltlichen Aspekte sollten von ihr transportiert werden? Handelt es sich bei dem Kunden um eine Zeitung? Oder entwirft man eine Schrift aus eigenem Antrieb, „nur so zum Spaß"? Oder verlangt eine Firma einen neuen Hausstil für ihre Kommunikationsstrategie?

Nach dem 15. Jahrhundert hatten Typografie und Bruchdruck sich lange Zeit kaum verändert, bis neue Innovationen einen gewaltigen Wandel einleiteten. Der Einsatz von Maschinen sorgte für eine unaufhaltsame Verdrängung des Handwerks, zugleich erforderte die steigende Nachfrage nach Druckerzeugnissen ständig neue und bessere technische Ausrüstungen. Handwerkliche Qualitätsarbeit verlor zunehmend an Bedeutung, da nun wenige Aufseher und Hilfskräfte Arbeiten ausführen konnten, für die früher Hunderte von ausgebildeten Fachkräften benötigt wurden.

Die Form unserer Schrift hat sich aus der fließenden Bewegung beim Schreiben mit der Hand entwickelt. Serifen bei Druckschriften waren eine logische Folge. Erstaunlicherweise hat sich die Typografie jahrhundertelang nur in Form von Serifenschriften entwickelt. Erst 1819 tauchten in England erste Beispiele eines neuen, serifenlosen Stils auf.

Im 19. Jahrhundert wurde Typografie, Gestaltung und Qualität von Druckerzeugnissen meist wenig Wert beigemessen. Drucker stellten Blätter her, die die von ihnen angebotenen Schriftarten in zahlreichen Schriftgrößen und Kombinationen vorführten. Abgesehen von einigen oberflächlichen Nachbildungen traditioneller Typografie gab es kaum etwas, das auf ein Interesse an schön gestalteten Seiten oder Schriften hindeutete. Matthieu René Radermacher Schorer brachte 1951 in seinem *Bijdrage tot de Geschiedenis van de Renaissance der Nederlandse Boekdrukkunst* (Beitrag zur Geschichte der Niederländischen Buchdruckkunst seit der Renaissance) die zu jener Zeit herrschende Trostlosigkeit wie folgt auf den Punkt: „Verglichen mit Inkunabeln ist bei Büchern aus dem 19. Jahrhundert die Schrift glanzlos und ohne Charakter, nicht selten beschädigt und schlecht gedruckt; die Anordnung ist verwirrend, die Farbe verblasst, das Papier von schlechter Qualität, der Rücken mit Goldprägung ohne ansprechende Ornamente versehen … und es wurde dickeres Papier benutzt, damit die Bücher umfangreicher aussahen, als sie in Wirklichkeit waren."

Im 19. Jahrhundert kam es auf dem Gebiet der Typografie und der Drucktechnik zu einschneidenden Veränderungen. 400 Jahre lang hatte der Bleisatz die Möglichkeiten des Machbaren begrenzt. Mit dem Aufkommen neuer Technologien änderten sich Typografie, Gestaltung und Druck, und es entstanden neue, vom bisherigen abweichende Stile und Traditionen.

In der Folge der Reformbewegung William Morris' und der späteren Leistungen Peter Behrens' spaltete sich die Entwicklung in eine subjektiv-expressive Richtung auf der einen und eine funktionale oder elementare Richtung auf der anderen Seite.

Die expressive Position verkörpert sich in den Arbeiten Rudolf Kochs, dessen Neuerungsbemühungen sich als eine Rückkehr zum Individualismus vorindustrieller Zeit darstellten.

Im Januar 1898 erschienen in der Fachpublikation *Deutscher Buch- und Steindrucker* Inserate der beiden in Stuttgart ansässigen Firmen Berthold und Bauer & Co., in denen sie die Schriftart Akzidenz-Grotesk präsentierten. Insofern war die betreffende Schrift zur Blütezeit des Konstruktivismus, als Bewegungen wie De Stijl, Bauhaus und Dada ihr Erscheinungsbild mit großem Erfolg aufgriffen, bereits über 20 Jahre alt. Als einer ihrer Haupteinflüsse stand die Akzidenz-Grotesk Pate bei der Geburt der „Schweizer Typografie". Wie ehedem zeichnet sie sich durch eine hohe visuelle Qualität aus und erinnert daran, dass Schrift nicht gleichförmig sein muss, um gut leserlich und ansprechend zu sein. Im Gegenteil: Gerade die Unterschiede zwischen den einzelnen Typen sorgen für ihre Leserlichkeit.

Die funktionale Typografie wurde vor allem in Deutschland, Ungarn, der Sowjetunion und den Niederlanden entwickelt. Die Reduzierung von Ornamenten und die Verwendung typografischer Grundelemente sollte dem Wunsch nach einem in gesellschaftlicher und kultureller Hinsicht besseren, zukunftsorientierten Design entgegenkommen. Hauptmerkmale dieser „neuen Typografie" waren serifenlose Schriften, Kleinbuchstaben und eine asymmetrische Spationierung.

Eric Gill erhielt von dem Buchhändler Douglas Cleverdon den Auftrag, ein Schild mit einer serifenlosen Beschriftung zu malen. Während eines Besuchs bei Cleverdon wurde Stanley Morison, der künstlerische Berater der Monotype Corporation, auf das Schild aufmerksam und kam zu der Ansicht, dass Gill eine ähnliche serifenlose Schrift für Monotype entwerfen sollte. Bis zu diesem Zeitpunkt hatte Gill ausschließlich Versalien verwendet. Wie so häufig unterschieden sich die ersten Zeichnungen seiner Kleinbuchstaben recht deutlich von den später gegossenen Lettern. Als die Gill Sans Ende der 1920er-Jahre auf den Markt kam, war sie allerdings nicht ganz das, worauf die britische Druckbranche gewartet hatte. Ihre verhaltene Aufnahme bei der Kundschaft im Jahr 1928 ähnelte der der Futura im Jahr zuvor. In Kommentaren zu Paul Renners Entwurf war die Rede von einer Mode, die bald vergessen sein würde.

Die Futura ist eine zeitlose, elementare Schriftart. 1925 gab Jan Tschichold ein Sonderheft der *Typographischen Mitteilungen* mit dem Titel „Elementare Typografie" heraus, in der er erstmals seine Überlegungen zur Schaffung einer neuen Typografie formulierte. Aus den Reihen der bestehenden

The Philadelphia firm MacKellar, Smiths and Jordan began as the first successful American type foundry, Binny and Ronaldson, and helped set a pattern for type design and manufacturing. After the firm changed hands a number of times, in 1860 Thomas MacKellar (1812–1899), the brothers John F. Smith (1815–1899), Richard Smith (1821–1894), and Peter A. Jordan acquired the firm when a previous partner Lawrence Johnson (1801–1860) died at the age of 59. In 1867, the name of the company was officially changed to MacKellar, Smiths & Jordan. Together with other foundries in the United States, MacKellar, Smiths & Jordan implemented in 1886 the American Point system to designate type sizes. In 1892, they joined 22 other foundries to form the American Type Founders Company. By the turn of the century, MacKellar, Smiths and Jordan, then known as the Philadelphia branch of the American Type Founders Company, entered a decline, and in 1893, after producing over 250 original decorative fonts and sets of ornaments, their last typeface was cast.

Die in Philadelphia ansässige Firma MacKellar, Smiths & Jordan ist aus der ersten erfolgreichen Schriftgießerei der Vereinigten Staaten, Binny and Ronaldson, hervorgegangen und war eine richtungweisende Kraft auf dem Gebiet der Schriftgestaltung und -herstellung. Nachdem die Vorgängerfirma durch die Hände verschiedener Besitzer gegangen war, wurde sie im Jahr 1860 von Thomas MacKellar (1812–1899), den Brüdern John F. Smith (1815–1899) und Richard Smith (1821–1894) sowie Peter A. Jordan übernommen; ein weiterer vorgesehener Teilhaber, Lawrence Johnson (geb. 1801), verstarb in selbigem Jahr. 1867 erfolgte die offizielle Änderung des Firmennamens in MacKellar, Smiths & Jordan. Im Verbund mit anderen US-amerikanischen Schriftgießereien führte die Firma 1886 das amerikanische Punktsystem zur Festlegung von Schriftgraden ein. 1892 tat sich MacKellar, Smiths &

Schriftarten kämen Grotesk- oder Blockschriften den Zielen der neuen Typografie am nächsten, da sie schlicht gestaltet und leicht zu lesen seien.

Zur selben Zeit entwickelte Paul Renner einen neuen Groteskstil, der auf konstruktivistischen Prinzipien beruhte. Bei seinem Entwurf für die Futura stützte Renner sich auf die drei einfachen Grundformen Kreis, Dreieck und Quadrat. Dabei hütete er sich vor dem Hintergrund seiner buchgestalterischen und typografischen Erfahrung, die Tradition zugunsten eines neuen Dogmas zu verwerfen. Erste Muster des neuen Stils waren im Jahr 1925 zu sehen. 1926 schrieb der Bauhaus-Meister László Moholy-Nagy im *Bauhausheft* 7 sinngemäß, dass die Grotesk eigentlich erst noch geschaffen werden müsse, da es allen existierenden Grotesk-Buchschriften an Stil mangele. Ebenfalls in dieser Ausgabe erschienen die Aufsätze „Versuch einer neuen Schrift" von Herbert Bayer und „Zur Ökonomie der Schriftform" von Josef Albers.

Im Vorfeld des Zweiten Weltkriegs wurden die progressiven Vertreter der Typografie angefeindet, ausgegrenzt und unterdrückt – nicht anders, als es in der politischen Arena der Fall war. Zahlreiche Typografen mussten ihren Stil ändern oder emigrieren. In Deutschland wurden überholte Gestaltungsrichtlinien wiedereingeführt und als verbindlich durchgesetzt.

In der Schweiz stieß Anton Stankowski mit seinen Arbeiten zur „Neuen Typografie" auf äußerst positive Resonanz. Die Weiterentwicklung seiner Ansätze wurde in den 1950er-Jahren unter der Bezeichnung „Schweizer Typografie" berühmt. Zur ersten Generation dieser Richtung gehörten Typografen wie Max Bill, Richard P. Lohse, Max Huber und Emil Ruder.

Neben den Schweizer Designern verzeichnete der in den Vereinigten Staaten tätige Herbert Bayer, der frühere Leiter der Druck- und Reklamewerkstatt des Bauhauses, großen Erfolg. Die Verknüpfung des strengen Dogmatismus der Groteskschrifen mit den Eigenarten des amerikanischen Designs brachte interessante neue Formen hervor.

Parallel zum Rückgang strenger Groteskschriftarten entstanden in den Vereinigten Staaten innovative Neuansätze, die sich durch eine ausgesprochen bildhafte Entwicklung – die Kombiniation von Buchstaben, Text und Fotografien – auszeichneten und die dem Grafikdesign zu einer wachsenden Bedeutung verhalfen. Dabei ging es immer stärker darum, Gesamtkonzepte und ein geschlossenes Erscheinungsbild zu entwerfen.

1949 plante Eduard Hoffmann, der Leiter der Haas'schen Schriftgießerei in Münchenstein bei Basel, die Entwicklung einer neuen Groteskschrift. Sein Vorbild war die Schelter-Grotesk, die offizielle Bauhaus-Schrift. Damals

griffen Schweizer Designer immer häufiger auf Bertholds Akzidenz-Grotesk zurück, die dann als „Schweizer Typografie" auf die Weltbühne zurückkehrte. Eduard Hoffmann hatte eine genaue Vorstellung davon, wie die neue Schriftart aussehen sollte, und betraute 1956 Max Miedinger in Zürich, der als Experte für Groteskschriften galt, mit dem Entwurf. Die Skizzen dienten als Vorlage für die Stempelschneidemaschine der Haas'schen Schriftgießerei, um anschließend in Blei gegossen zu werden. 1957 trug das Projekt zunächst die Bezeichnung Neue Haas-Grotesk, Stempel brachte die neue Schrift 1960 dann jedoch unter dem Namen Helvetica heraus.

Mit dem Aufkommen des Fotosatzes gewannen Typografie und Grafikdesign eine neue, unbegrenzte Gestaltungsfreiheit. Erstmals standen die unterschiedlichsten Schriftarten nebeneinander zur Verfügung. Die Veränderungen ermöglichten eine noch bessere Visualisierung des Inhalts, und Texte und Illustrationen konnten in enger Kombination gesetzt werden.

1973 erläuterte Günter Gerhard Lange, der für die Überarbeitung der Akzidenz-Grotesk verantwortliche künstlerische Leiter von Berthold, anlässlich ihrer Markteinführung: „Hierbei haben wir auf die Grundproportionen der beliebten Akzidenz-Grotesk zurückgegriffen, um die durchschnittliche Länge und die individuellen Formen festzulegen. Natürlich mussten die Familienähnlichkeiten zwischen den einzelnen Stilen berücksichtigt werden, ebenso wie die Stimmung und Mode der Zeit." Zur Mode der Zeit gehörten die damals brandneue Helvetica von Max Miedinger und konkurrierende Schriften wie Adrian Frutigers Univers und Konrad F. Bauers Folio.

Die Helvetica war ursprünglich gar nicht als komplette Schriftfamilie für den Maschinen- und den Handsatz vorgesehen. Nach dem Erfolg der von Adrian Frutiger gestalteten Schriftfamilie Univers sah Stempel sich jedoch gezwungen, einen kompletten Zeichenbestand nach dem Vorbild von Frutigers Methode neu zu gestalten und ebenfalls Nummern für die verschiedenen Schnitte der Helvetica-Familie zu verwenden. Die Helvetica war genau das, was Gestalter in den frühen 1970er-Jahren suchten. 1982 stellte Stempel die Neue Helvetica vor.

Die Geschichte der Typografie stößt heute auf großes Interesse, und ich hoffe, dass dies auch in Zukunft so sein wird. Die Frage wird immer sein, ob man die ideale Schrift schon gefunden hat. Die Antwort bleibt jedem selbst überlassen. Am meisten beeindruckt mich, wie Schriftentwerfer mit ihrem wunderbaren Blick fürs Detail Schriften von völlig unterschiedlichem Charakter kreieren. Vergleicht man etwa die Caslon (1725) von William Caslon mit der Baskerville (1754) von John Baskerville oder Bertholds

Jordan mit 22 weiteren Gießereien zur American Type Founders Company (ATF) zusammen. Doch auch in seiner Rolle als Ableger der ATF in Philadelphia konnte das Unternehmen seinen noch vor der Jahrhundertwende einsetzenden wirtschaftlichen Niedergang nicht abwenden. Nach einer Gesamtproduktion von 250 Zierschriften und Ornamentpaletten goss MacKellar, Smiths & Jordan im Jahr 1893 seine letzte Schrift.

La firme de Philadelphie, MacKellar, Smiths & Jordan, débute tout d'abord sous le nom de Binny & Ronaldson, première fonderie de caractères américaine prospère, et aide à établir un modèle pour la création et la fabrication de caractères. Après avoir changé de mains un certain nombre de fois, la firme est rachetée, en 1860, par Thomas MacKellar (1812–1899), les frères John F. Smith (1815–1899) et Richard Smith (1821–1894), et Peter A. Jordan, lorsque meurt à l'âge de 59 ans un précédent associé, Lawrence Johnson

(1801–1860). En 1867, le nom de la compagnie fut officiellement changé en MacKellar, Smiths & Jordan. Avec d'autres fonderies des États-Unis, Smiths & Jordan mirent en place, en 1886, le système de points américain pour désigner les tailles de caractères. En 1892, elle se joignit à 22 autres fonderies pour former l'American Type Founders Company. Avant même le début du XXᵉ siècle, MacKellar, Smiths & Jordan, connue comme la branche de Philadelphie de l'American Type Founders Company, connaissait un certain déclin. Après avoir produit 250 caractères originaux fantaisie et des séries d'ornements, elle coula son dernier caractère en 1893.

1796–1896, One Hundred Years,
MacKellar, Smiths and Jordan Foundry,
Philadelphia

SPECIMEN PRINTING DEPARTMENT—COMPOSING ROOM

HAND TYPE-CASTING DEPARTMENT

ELECTROTYPE MOULDING DEPARTMENT

Akzidenz-Grotesk (1899) mit Paul Renners Futura (1925), trifft auf eine ganze Fülle von Unterschieden. Die Druckseiten sehen völlig verschieden aus, und auch als Leser nimmt man die Botschaft anders auf. Die Wahl der Typografie und die Umsetzung durch den Grafikdesigner können den Leser in ganz verschiedene Welten führen.

Hier eine Auswahl von Schriftentwerfern mit einem Blick fürs Detail:

Claude Garamond: *Garamond*

Die Französische Renaissance-Antiqua erblickt das Licht der Welt. Claude Garamond wurde im Jahr 1480 geboren, und schon in jungen Jahren erlernte er sein Handwerk bei seinem Vater und anderen Mitgliedern der Familie. Nach eigener Behauptung konnte Garamond bereits im Alter von 15 Jahren Patrizen in einer Größe von einem Cicero (12 Punkt) schneiden. In den ersten Jahrzehnten des 16. Jahrhunderts standen französische Stempelschneider und Drucker in Konkurrenz zu den italienischen Schöpfern der Renaissance-Antiqua, deren Entwürfe, die Antiqua-Schriften Aldus Manutius' und Francesco Griffos wie auch die Schriften Pietro Bembos, ihren Weg nach Frankreich gefunden hatten.

Claude Garamond ist einer der ersten und wegweisenden Schriftschneider und -gießer der Französischen Renaissance-Antiqua und -Kursive. In seiner Zeit wurden die Römische Capitalis und die Karolingische Minuskel zusammengeführt. Im zentralistischen Frankreich waren die Voraussetzungen für fortschrittliche Entwicklungen auf dem Gebiet der Typografie günstiger als in Italien oder Deutschland. Mit dem Erscheinen seiner griechischem Schrift Grecs du Roy 1543, die König Franz I., ein Verfechter des Buchdrucks, bei ihm in Auftrag gegeben hatte, erwarb sich Garamond einen ausgezeichneten Ruf und den Posten des königlichen Schriftgießers. Die erste Antiqua, die zuverlässig datiert und Garamond zugeschrieben werden kann, ist eine großzügige Schrift namens Gros-Roman, die erstmals in einer Ausgabe der Werke Eusebius' und weiteren im Jahr 1544 von Robert Estienne gedruckten Werken auftaucht.

Wie anhand der Titelblätter zu erkennen, betätigte Garamond sich nach 1545 auch als Verleger, sowohl unter eigener Ägide als auch in Zusammenarbeit mit Pierre Gaultier und Jean Barbé. Als Beispiele für heute verwendete moderne Garamond-Versionen sind Jan Tschicholds Sabon und – hier wird es noch deutlicher – die Sabon Next von Jean François Porchez zu nennen.

William Caslon: *Caslon*

Ein Mann von vielseitiger Begabung. William Caslon wurde 1692 in Cradley in der Grafschaft Worcestershire geboren. Im Alter von 13 Jahren trat er bei einem Londoner Graveur in die Lehre. 1717 wurde er Bürger der Stadt London, in der er sich im vorangegangenen Jahr als Graveur selbstständig gemacht hatte. Zwei Jahre später eröffnete er eine Schriftgießerei.

Von dem Buchbinder John Watts erhielt Caslon den Auftrag, Schriften für dessen Einbände zu entwerfen und zu gießen. Einer dieser Titel fiel William Bowyer, einem bekannten Londoner Drucker, ins Auge. Caslon freundete sich mit Bowyer an, der ihn mit anderen Londoner Druckern bekannt machte. Damit begann die Geschichte einer der erfolgreichsten Schriftgießereien Englands. Finanziell unterstützt wurde Caslon anfänglich von Watts und Bowyer sowie dessen Schwiegersohn, James Bettenham.

1720 – in seinem ersten Geschäftsjahr als Schriftgießer – fertigte Caslon für die *Society for the Propagation of Christian Knowledge* eine neue Schrift für den Druck einer arabischen Bibelausgabe an. Nach Fertigstellung dieser neuen arabischen Schrift druckte er ein Musterblatt, um sie anderen Druckern zum Kauf anzubieten. Auf diesem Bogen war auch sein Name, William Caslon, abgedruckt, und zwar in speziell zu diesem Zweck entworfenen Antiqua-Lettern. Dieser Neuentwurf war der Grundstein für den heute als Caslon Old Style bekannten Schriftstil. Im Anschluss an diesen Stil schnitt Caslon eine Reihe nichtlateinischer, exotischer Stile, darunter koptische, armenische, etruskische und hebräische Schriften. Die Caslon Gothic ist seine Version jener Schriftarten, die als Old English oder „black letters" (Frakturschrift) bezeichnet werden.

Sämtliche dieser Schriften waren bereits auf dem Markt, als Caslon 1734 erstmals einen umfangreichen Katalog für seine eigene Schriftgießerei veröffentlichte, der insgesamt 38 Schriftarten vorstellte. 1737 zog Caslons Gießerei in die berühmte Chiswell Street um, wo seine Geschäfte nach seinem Tod mehr als 120 Jahre lang fortgeführt wurden. 1749 ernannte König Georg II. Caslon zum Schiedsmann für die Grafschaft Middlesex. Nach seinem Rückzug aus dem Geschäft starb Caslon 1766 im Alter von 74 Jahren. Sein Name steht für die Erfolgsgeschichte eines außergewöhnlichen Graveurs.

John Baskerville: *Baskerville*

Auf der Suche nach dem besten Ergebnis. John Baskerville (1706–1775) begann um das Jahr 1754 mit dem Schneiden und Gießen eigener Schriften. Von besonderem Einfluss waren für ihn die Beschriftungen von Stein-

Cees W. de Jong

1796–1896, One Hundred Years,
MacKellar, Smiths and Jordan Foundry,
Philadelphia

On the cover of this publication is a
romantic image of the typesetter at
work. Other images show hand setters
in Philadelphia, working in a highly
concentrated manner.

Ein romantisiert dargestellter Schriftsetzer bei der Arbeit ziert den Umschlag dieser Publikation. Auf den weiteren Bildern
sind Handsetzer in Philadelphia bei ihrer
hochkonzentrierten Tätigkeit zu sehen.

Sur la couverture de cette publication,
l'image romanesque d'un compositeur à
l'ouvrage. D'autres images montrent des
compositeurs manuels, à Philadelphie,
travaillant avec une belle concentration.

metzen, an denen sich auch andere englische Schöpfer von Schriften orientierten, welche man noch heute als typisch englisch ansieht: Grotesk- und
Egyptienne-Schriften, die an anderer Stelle im Zuge der industriellen Revolution auftauchten. Mit großer Aufmerksamkeit widmete Baskerville sich
der Frage, wie sich Schriften am besten drucken ließen und wie das Ergebnis aussehen würde. Folglich maß er Papier, Tinte, Drucklettern und
-maschinen eine gleich große Bedeutung bei. 1750 gründete John Baskerville ein Untenehmen, zu dem eine Papiermühle, eine Schriftgießerei und
eine Druckerei gehörte. Zu dieser Zeit entwickelte er auch die Idee, gestri-
chenes Papier zu verwenden.

Nach langer anstrengender Arbeit präsentierte er im Jahr 1754 seinen
ersten Schriftentwurf. 1758 erschien seine Prunkedition von Miltons *Paradise Lost*, ein Ein-Mann- und zugleich Gesamtkunstwerk, lange bevor dieser
Begriff geprägt wurde. Als Drucker arbeitete Baskerville auch für die Universität Cambridge, zu deren Direktor er 1758 ernannt wurde. Eine seiner
berühmtesten Veröffentlichungen ist sein *Juvenalis* von 1757.

Baskervilles großzügige Letterngestalt, der luftige Textsatz mit erweiter-
ten Abständen zwischen Wörtern und Zeilen, die Breite des Satzspiegels
und die Verwendung von gestrichenem Papier und tiefschwarzer Tinte
machten seinen Namen in ganz Europa bekannt. Nach seinem Tod wurde
ein Großteil von Baskervilles Typenmaterial, seine Geheimformel zur Tin-
tenherstellung und die Anleitung zur Fertigung des gestrichenen Papiers
an den Franzosen Caron de Beaumarchais verkauft. Dieser druckte zwischen 1785 und 1789 mit Baskervilles Typen eine 70-bändige Voltaire-Aus-
gabe. Mit dem Ergebnis wäre Baskerville sehr zufrieden gewesen.

Giambattista Bodoni: *Bodoni*

„Reichlicher Leerraum und großzügiger Durchschuss, und ja die Größe
der Schrift nicht zu bescheiden wählen. Dann darf man sich einer Schöp-
fung sicher sein, die eines Königs würdig ist." – Giambattista Bodoni

Bodoni wurde der König der Drucker und der Drucker der Könige
genannt. Sein Ruf gründete sich auf seinem *Manuale tipografico*, einer
Gesamtschau seines Lebenswerkes, die einige Jahre nach seinem Tod von
seiner Witwe, Margherita Bodoni, veröffentlicht wurde. Das erste Exemplar
war Ihrer Königlichen Hoheit Marie-Louise, Prinzessin von Parma, gewid-
met. Als Handbuch zur Buchdruckkunst präsentierte es auf 546 Druckse-
ten insgesamt 665 verschiedene Alphabete, einschließlich 100 exotischer
Schriften, und 1300 Vignetten. Ferner enthielt es 170 lateinische Schriften,

von denen einige mit bis zu 380 Matrizen hergestellt worden waren. Die
Auflage umfasste wohl weniger als 150 Exemplare, obwohl bisweilen auch
von 290 Exemplaren die Rede ist.

Seiner Witwe zufolge konzipierte, korrigierte und goss Bodoni im Laufe
von 50 Jahren mehr als 55 000 Matrizen. Nichts ging ihm über das Entwerfen und die harmonische Gestaltung von Seiten nach Art und Größe der
Schrift, Durchschuss, dem Zusammenspiel von Zeilenlängen, Abständen
und Spaltenbreiten. Dem Zusammenwirken von Schwarz und Weiß und
der großzügen Verwendung von Leerraum kam eine Hauptrolle zu. Die
Liste von Bodonis Nacheiferern ist lang. 1911 entwarf Morris Fuller Benton
eine Bodonischrift für ATF. Monotype folgte nach und ebenso, im Jahr
1924, die Haas'sche Schriftgießerei in der Schweiz, deren Bodonischrift
wiederum von der Lettergieterij Amsterdam, Berthold und Stempel kopiert
wurde. Linotype und Ludlow orientierten sich ebenfalls an Haas, während
Johannes Wagner im Jahr 1961 eine neue Bodoni herausbrachte. Weltweit
existieren mehr als 500 veschiedene Bodonivarianten. Eine sehr schöne
Version ist Zuzana Lickos Filosofia (1996).

Stanley Morison: *Times New Roman*

Wie sieht die geeignetste Schrift für eine Zeitung aus? Stanley Ignatius
Arthur Morison (1889–1967) wurde im Jahr 1923 typografischer Berater der
Monotype Corporation. Unter seiner Leitung entstand eine Anzahl von
Schriftfamilien, die sich an historischen Schriften orientierten, so etwa die
Entwürfe Eric Gills. Nachdem dem Geschäftsführer der Londoner *Times*,
William Lints-Smith, Morisons vernichtende Kritik an der überholten
Typografie der Zeitung zu Ohren gekommen war, setzte er sich mit dem
Kritiker an einen Tisch, und nach einer langen Diskussion riet Morison
dazu, die *Times* von Grund auf neu zu gestalten. Morison wurde typogra-
fischer Berater der Zeitung und ließ mehrere Probeseiten in verschiedenen
Schriftarten anfertigen, darunter Baskerville, Imprint, Ionic und eine Version der Perpetua. Zur selben Zeit brachte Lynotype in den Vereinigten
Staaten eine Reihe von Schriften für den Mengensatz heraus. Die erste war
die Ionic, gefolgt im Jahr 1931 von der Excelsior, die heute noch immer zu
den populärsten Zeitungsschriften gehört.

Nach einer Reihe weiterer Tests entschied Morison, dass die *Times* eine
komplett neue Schrift bekommen sollte. 1931 präsentierte er zwei Entwürfe,
eine überarbeitete Version der Perpetua und eine modernisierte Plantin.
Das Entscheidungskommitee der *Times* wählte die Letztere der beiden.

 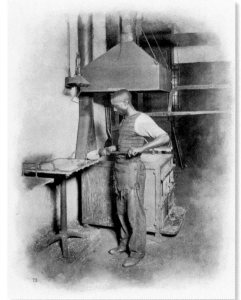

1796–1896, One Hundred Years,
MacKellar, Smiths and Jordan Foundry,
Philadelphia

Angelehnt an den Namen der Vorgängerschrift, Times Old Roman, wurde die neue Schrift Times New Roman getauft. Ihren ersten Auftritt hatte sie in der Ausgabe der *Times* vom 3. Oktober 1932. Dank ihrer Vermarktung und der weltweiten Verbreitung ist sie heute eine Standardschrift.

Berthold, Günter Gerhard Lange: *Akzidenz-Grotesk*

Äußerst schlicht und ausgesprochen charakteristisch. Die AG, wie Liebhaber die Schrift gerne nennen, existierte sie in der Hochzeit des Konstruktivismus bereits seit mehr als 20 Jahren. Höchst wirkungsvoll von De Stijl, Bauhaus, Dada und anderen eingesetzt, war sie später eine der wichtigsten Schriften bei der Entstehung der Schweizer Typografie. Wie ehedem steht die AG für eine hohe visuelle Qualität und erinnert daran, dass Schrift nicht gleichförmig aussehen muss, um gut leserlich und ansprechend zu sein. Im Gegenteil: Gerade die Unterschiede zwischen den einzelnen Typen gewährleisten ihre Leserlichkeit. Erstmals präsentiert wurde die Akzidenz-Grotesk im Januar 1898 in Inseraten in der Zeitschrift *Deutscher Buch- und Steindrucker* von gleich zwei Firmen, der Gießerei Berthold und dem Stuttgarter Unternehmen Bauer & Co.

1973 schrieb Günter Gerhard Lange, als künstlerischer Leiter der Firma Berthold für das Redesign der Akzidenz-Grotesk verantwortlich, zur Einführung der neuen Version: „Hierbei haben wir auf die Grundproportionen der beliebten Akzidenz-Grotesk zurückgegriffen, um die durchschnittliche Länge und die individuellen Formen festzulegen. Natürlich mussten die Familienähnlichkeiten zwischen den einzelnen Stilen berücksichtigt werden, ebenso wie die Stimmung und Mode der Zeit." In Mode waren zur damaligen Zeit Max Miedingers eben erschienene Helvetica und andere neue Schriften wie Adrian Frutigers Univers und Konrad F. Bauers Folio. Dennoch war und blieb die gute alte AG ein Hauptakteur in der sich beständig wandelnden Welt des Drucks und Designs.

Paul Renner: *Futura*

Obwohl ein Kind ihrer Zeit, ist die Futura zugleich eine zeitlose, elementare Schrift. 1925 gab Jan (Iwan) Tschichold ein Sonderheft der *Typographischen Mitteilungen* mit dem Titel „Elementare Typografie" heraus, in der er erstmals seine Überlegungen zur Schaffung einer neuen Typografie formulierte. Von den bestehenden Schriftarten genügten am ehesten Grotesk- oder Blockschriften den Zielen der neuen Typografie, denn sie beruhten auf einem einfachen Entwurf und seien leicht lesbar. Es gebe jedoch keinen Grund, warum nicht auch andere leicht zu lesende Schriftarten benutzt werden sollten; die „richtige" Schriftart würde jedenfalls noch nicht existieren.

Bauhaus-Meister László Moholy-Nagy schrieb im *Bauhausheft* 7 von 1926 sinngemäß, dass die Grotesk eigentlich erst noch geschaffen werden müsse, da es allen existierenden Groteskbuchschriften an Stil mangele. Ebenfalls in dieser Ausgabe erschienen die Aufsätze „Versuch einer neuen Schrift" von Herbert Bayer und „Zur Ökonomie der Schriftform" von Josef Albers.

Zur selben Zeit trat Paul Renner mit seinem Entwurf zu einem neuen, auf konstruktivistischen Prinzipien aufbauenden Groteskstil in Erscheinung. Seine 1924 entstandene Futura beruhte auf einfachen Grundformen – Kreis, Dreieck und Quadrat. Die ersten Proben des neuen Stils erschienen im Jahr 1925. Willy Haas schrieb dazu: „Mit der Futura legt Paul Renner eine vorgängerlose, konstruktive Lösung vor, die sich gleichermaßen klassisch wie modern verwenden lässt und die sich trotz ihrer strengen Gestalt keineswegs schulmeisterlich, sondern wohlgefällig ausnimmt." 1933 musste Renner nach der Machtübernahme der Nationalsozialisten in Deutschland seine Lehrtätigkeit aufgeben und setzte sich am Genfer See zur Ruhe. 1947 veröffentliche er sein Werk *Ordnung und Harmonie der Farben*, sein Buch *Die Kunst der Typographie* von 1939 wurde nachgedruckt.

Eric Gill: *Gill Sans*

Vom Bildhauer zum Schriftentwerfer. Arthur Eric Rowton Gill (1882–1940) studierte zunächst Architektur. Nach seiner Heirat arbeitete er als Grafiker und Illustrator und schloss sich einer Gruppe von Arts-and-Crafts-Künstlern an. Später betätigte Gill sich auch als Bildhauer. Sein erster Schriftentwurf, die Perpetua, erschien im Jahr 1925. 1928 arbeitete er in High Wycombe als Bildhauer und Steinmetz; zwischenzeitlich hatte er sich mit seinem Schwiegersohn René Hague als Kompagnon mit einem Handpressenbetrieb selbstständig gemacht. Daneben verfasste Gill mehrere Bücher zum Thema Industriehandwerk und -design. Eine weitere von Gill entworfene Schrift war die nach seiner Tochter benannte Joanna, die ausschließlich in 12 Punkt und ursprünglich nur für seinen 1931 erschienenen „Essay on Typography" gegossen worden war.

1916 wurde Gill – der damals an den Reliefs der Kreuzwegstationen in der Kathedrale von Westminster arbeitete – um einen Entwurf für eine einfache geometrische Schrift gebeten, die auf sämtlichen Beschilderungen und Linienplänen der London Underground zum Einsatz kommen sollte. Bei seinem Entwurf behielt er die klassischen Proportionen bei, zu erken-

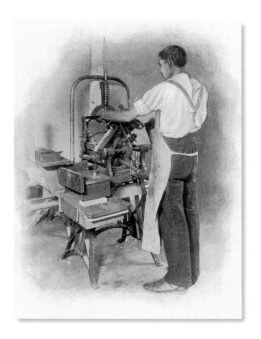

Neue Technologien haben vieles vereinfacht. Doch nach wie vor steht am Anfang des Entwicklungsprozesses immer eine Skizze, der später, wenn sich das Konzept als tragfähig herausstellt, eine genaue Ausarbeitung der Details folgt. Häufig erweist sich die Skizze des Vortags am nächsten Morgen als doch nicht ganz so innovativ, wie man es sich ursprünglich gedacht hatte.

nen etwa beim g, während er das R in seiner dafür bevorzugten Form mit einem elegant gebogenen und weit abgespreizten Fuß gestaltete.

Zahlreiche weitere Überarbeitungen der Schrift stammen von Monotypemitarbeitern. 1928 begann Gill als Berater für die Monotype Corporation zu arbeiten. Als Ende der 1920er-Jahre die Gill Sans erschien, war

sie nicht gerade das, worauf die britische Druckbranche gewartet hatte. Renners Entwurf wurde dahingehend kommentiert, dass es sich um eine bald in Vergessenheit geratene Mode handele. Die erste Version der Gill Sans war im Vorfeld des Jahreskongresses der Britischen Druckindustrie im Mai 1928 fertiggestellt worden. Die Einladungen zu der Veranstaltung hatte Stanley Morison, der dort eine Ansprache hielt, in der neuen Schrift setzen lassen. Damit begann der Siegeszug der Gill Sans.

Max Miedinger: *Helvetica*

Schnörkellos und zeitlos. 1949 plante Eduard Hoffmann, der Leiter der Haas'schen Schriftgießerei in Münchenstein bei Basel, die Entwicklung einer neuen Groteskschrift. Sein Vorbild war die Schelter-Grotesk, die offizielle Bauhaus-Schrift. Damals griffen Schweizer Designer immer häufiger auf Bertholds Akzidenz-Grotesk zurück, die schießlich als „Schweizer Typografie" auf die Weltbühne zurückkehrte. Eduard Hoffmann betraute 1956 Max Miedinger in Zürich, der als Experte für Groteskschriften galt, mit dem Entwurf. Nachdem die Skizzen gemeinsam mit Hoffmann besprochen und korrigiert worden waren, dienten sie als Vorlage für die Stempelschneidemaschine der Haas'schen Schriftgießerei, um anschließend in Blei gegossen zu werden. 1957 trug das Projekt zunächst den Arbeitstitel Neue Haas-Grotesk, 1960 brachte die D. Stempel AG die Schrift indes unter dem Namen Helvetica auf den Markt. Das gesamte Design musste noch einmal überarbeitet werden, als Linotype sich für die Übernahme der Schrift entschied, die anfangs im Maschinensatz und später auch im Fotosatz genutzt wurde.

Als sich jedoch kurz darauf die Univers-Schriftfamilie Adrian Frutigers als großer Erfolg erwies, sah Stempel sich gezwungen, nach dessen Methode einen kompletten Zeichenbestand neu zu gestalten. Der Entwurf zur Helvetica Light stammt von Erich Schultz-Anker, dem künstlerischen Leiter bei Stempel, und Arthur Ritzel. 1982 brachte Stempel die Neue Helvetica auf den Markt.

Schriftgießereien standen untereinander in engem Kontakt und koordinierten ihre Geschäfte in Absprache zunächst regional und bald auch international. Abgestimmt auf jeweils herrschende Trends, wurden Schriften unter verschiedenen Namen herausgebracht, verkauft, kopiert und adaptiert. Erzielte die eine Firma einen Erfolg, wollte auch die andere ein Stück vom Kuchen abbekommen. Und um all diese Schriften den Kunden zu verkaufen, produzierten die Gießereien die prachtvollsten Schriftmuster.

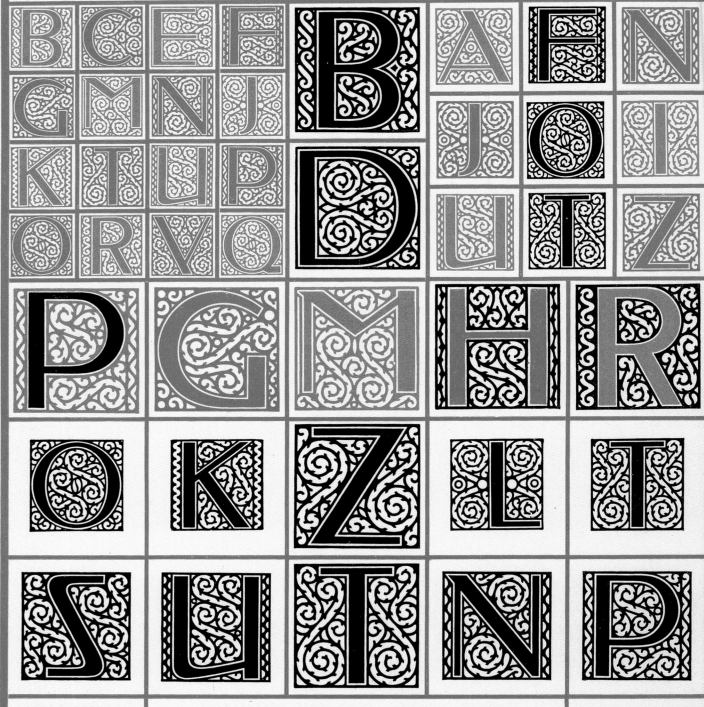

INITIALEN ZUR FEDER-GROTESK
NACH ZEICHNUNGEN VON J. ERBAR · CÖLN

Alle 26 Buchstaben des Alphabets sind in den gezeigten fünf Größen vorrätig (4,5,6,7,8 Cic.) und zwar 1 und 2farbig.

LUDWIG & MAYER
SCHRIFTGIESSEREI · FRANKFURT AM MAIN

Die Initialen werden in starken galvan. Niederschlägen auf Bleifuß geliefert. Auch fertigen wir jede andere Größe.

Le caractère idéal

par Cees W. de Jong

Certaines innovations ont introduit des changements radicaux dans les domaines de la typographie et de l'impression qui n'avaient connu que de légères transformations depuis le XVe siècle. La demande croissante pour des travaux d'impression réclamait un équipement toujours plus important et performant, et la mécanisation supplanta peu à peu la production artisanale. Des surveillants et des assistants pouvaient accomplir des tâches qui nécessitaient par le passé des centaines d'ouvriers qualifiés.

Nos scriptes découlent de l'écriture manuelle, ce qui a naturellement incité à utiliser des empattements dans les caractères typographiques. Il est étonnant que la typographie se soit développée pendant des siècles dans le monde entier, uniquement avec des polices avec empattements. Les premiers exemples des nouveaux styles sans empattements ne sont apparus qu'en 1816 en Angleterre.

Au XIXe siècle, la typographie, le graphisme et la qualité du matériel d'impression ont subi une dégradation généralisée. Les imprimeurs produisaient des pages composées dans tous les corps et tous les styles de caractères disponibles en magasin. À l'exception de quelques imitations superficielles de la typographie traditionnelle, personne ne semblait se soucier ni de la mise en page ni du dessin des caractères.

En 1951, le Dr M. R. Radermacher Schorer, dans sa *Bijdrage tot de Geschiedenis van de Renaissance der Nederlandse Boekdrukkunst (Contribution à l'histoire des arts de l'impression en Hollande)*, faisait un résumé bien sombre de l'époque : « Quand on compare le livre du XIXe siècle aux incunables, le caractère y est terne et sans tempérament, souvent abîmé et mal imprimé, la mise en page déroutante, les couleurs passées, le papier de mauvaise qualité, le dos couvert de simples dorures à la plaque sans ornements… et du papier épais est utilisé pour faire croire que l'ouvrage est plus gros qu'il ne l'est en réalité. »

Des changements radicaux sont survenus dans les domaines de la typographie et de la technologie au cours du XIXe siècle. Pendant 400 ans, le système de la composition au plomb avait limité les choix ; l'arrivée de nouvelles technologies modifia la typographie, le graphisme et l'impression. Des styles nouveaux et différents, de nouvelles traditions virent le jour.

Après le mouvement de réforme de William Morris puis, plus tard, de Peter Behrens, les courants se séparèrent entre écoles subjective-expressive, et fonctionnelle ou élémentaire.

On retrouve la position expressive dans l'œuvre de Rudolf Koch, qui chercha le chemin de l'innovation en renouant avec l'individualisme et la pré-industrialisation.

En janvier 1898, deux entreprises de Stuttgart, Berthold et Bauer & Co, présentaient l'Akzidenz Grotesk dans des publicités insérées dans le *Deutscher Buch und Steindrücker*. Cette police avait donc déjà plus de 20 ans, à l'apogée du constructivisme, quand elle fut adoptée par des mouvements comme de Stijl, le Bauhaus et Dada. Elle fut le symbole de la naissance de la « typographie suisse ». L'Akzidenz Grotesk a toujours une haute qualité visuelle qui nous rappelle qu'une police de caractères n'a pas besoin d'être uniforme pour être lisible et attrayante ; ce sont, au contraire, les différences entre les caractères qui les rendent lisibles.

La typographie fonctionnelle fut d'abord mise au point par des créateurs de l'Union soviétique, d'Allemagne, de Hongrie et des Pays-Bas. Le désir se faisait sentir d'un graphisme plus social, plus culturel et orienté vers l'avenir, à travers une utilisation réduite des ornements et le choix des éléments typographiques. Des caractères sans empattements, des lettres bas de casse et un espacement asymétrique étaient les traits essentiels de cette « nouvelle typographie ».

Un libraire de Bristol, Douglas Cleverdon, demanda un jour à Eric Gill de peindre une enseigne avec des caractères sans empattements. Remarquant l'enseigne à l'occasion d'une visite à Cleverdon, Stanley Morison, conseiller typographique de la Monotype Corporation, fut convaincu que Gill pouvait dessiner une police sans empattements similaire pour Monotype. Jusqu'alors, Gill ne s'était servi que de capitales. Comme à l'accoutumée, les premiers dessins des lettres bas de casse étaient très différents de la police qui fut finalement fondue. Mais, quand Gill Sans fit sa première apparition, vers la fin des années 20, ce n'était pas exactement ce que l'establishment de l'imprimerie britannique attendait. Son accueil mitigé en 1928 ressemblait à celui qui avait été réservé au Futura, l'année précédente, en Allemagne. Les commentaires décrivaient la création de Paul Renner comme une mode qui serait vite oubliée.

Futura est un caractère élémentaire et intemporel. En 1925, Jan Tschichold publia une édition spéciale de *Typographische Mitteilungen* intitulée « Typographie élémentaire ». C'est dans cette publication qu'il formula pour la première fois ses tentatives pour créer une nouvelle typographie. Parmi les caractères disponibles, les Grotesques ou Block,

The foundry Ludwig & Mayer was founded in Frankfurt am Main in 1875 and remained in operation until 1985. The publication *Drucken Sie Kataloge?* (Do you print catalogues?) was meant to inform clients about new fonts and ornaments.

Die Schriftgießerei Ludwig & Mayer wurde 1875 in Frankfurt am Main gegründet und stellte ihren Betrieb erst 1985 ein. Anhand der Broschüre *Drucken Sie Kataloge?* konnten Kunden sich über neue Schriften und Ornamente informieren.

La fonderie Ludwig & Mayer, fondée à Francfort-sur-le-Main en 1875, est restée en activité jusqu'en 1985. La publication *Drucken Sie Kataloge?* (Imprimez-vous des catalogues?) était destinée à informer les clients des nouveaux caractères et ornements disponibles.

Quel genre de caractère faut-il donner aux lettres, et quels aspects de ce caractère veut-on qu'elles transmettent? S'agit-il d'une commande pour un journal, d'une création personnelle pour le plaisir, ou d'une commande pour une entreprise ayant besoin d'une nouvelle identité visuelle pour sa stratégie de communication?

parce qu'ils étaient d'un graphisme simple et faciles à lire, étaient ce qui répondait le mieux aux besoins de la nouvelle typographie.

À la même époque, Paul Renner développait son projet de nouvelle Grotesque fondé sur des principes constructivistes. Renner basait son Futura sur des formes simples : le cercle, le triangle et le carré. Mais ses affinités avec les livres et la typographie l'empêchaient d'abandonner la

tradition au profit d'un nouveau dogme. Les premiers exemples de ce nouveau style firent leur apparition en 1925.

En 1926, László Moholy-Nagy, un des chefs de file du Bauhaus, écrivait dans *Bauhausheft 7* : « Puisque tous les styles de Grotesques existants manquent d'un style fondamental, la Grotesque reste à inventer. » Dans le même numéro figuraient aussi les articles « Essai pour un nouveau caractère » de Herbert Bayer et « Le caractère Stencil comme caractère de titre » de Josef Albers.

Avant le début de la Seconde Guerre mondiale, les forces progressistes furent anéanties dans le domaine de la typographie, tout comme elles le furent dans l'arène politique. De nombreux typographes eurent à choisir entre changer de style ou émigrer. En Allemagne, on réintroduisit en les imposant d'anciennes règles graphiques.

En Suisse, le travail d'Anton Stankowski faisait montre d'un grand respect pour la « nouvelle typographie ». Son travail évolua encore et gagna en renommée dans les années 50 sous le nom de « typographie suisse ». La première génération de typographes suisses se composait de Max Bill, Richard P. Lohse, Max Huber et Emil Ruder.

Hormis les graphistes suisses, le chef d'imprimerie de l'atelier typographique du Bauhaus, Herbert Bayer, trouva la reconnaissance en travaillant aux États-Unis. Le lien qu'il opéra entre le dogmatisme strict de la police sans empattements et les formes du graphisme américain déboucha sur une configuration intéressante.

L'abandon d'une typographie recourant strictement aux Grotesques et un travail novateur en provenance des États-Unis, fondé sur une utilisation hautement picturale de la lettre et du texte, associés à des photos, engendrèrent un graphisme couronné de succès. Il s'agissait de plus en plus de créer des programmes d'identités et des concepts globaux.

En 1949, Eduard Hoffmann, directeur de la fonderie typographique Haas, de Münchenstein, près de Bâle, projetait la création d'une nouvelle Grotesque. Son modèle était le Schelter Grotesk, le caractère officiel du Bauhaus. Les graphistes suisses de l'époque faisaient un usage croissant de l'Akzidenz Grotesk de Berthold, et la typographie suisse devenait connue dans le monde entier. Eduard Hoffmann savait exactement à quoi devait ressembler le nouveau caractère et en confia le dessin à un spécialiste de la famille Grotesque, Max Miedinger, de Zurich. Ses dessins étaient transmis aux ateliers de taille des poinçons de la fonderie Haas pour y être ensuite fondus. En 1957, le nom de ce projet était New Haas

Grotesque, mais, en 1960, Stempel publia le nouveau caractère sous le nom d'Helvetica.

Avec l'arrivée de la photocomposition, la typographie et le graphisme gagnèrent une fabuleuse liberté de mouvement. On avait pour la première fois accès aux caractères les plus divers. Elle permettait des modifications qui amélioraient encore la visualisation du contenu, ainsi qu'un montage plus rapproché des textes et des images.

En 1973, Günter Gerhard Lange, directeur de la typographie chez Berthold présentait sa nouvelle version d'Akzidenz Grotesk en ces termes : « Dans ce travail, on a utilisé les proportions de base du vénérable Akzidenz Grotesk demi-gras pour déterminer la taille moyenne et la forme individuelle des caractères. Il a fallu, bien sûr, tenir compte des ressemblances de famille entre les styles individuels, mais aussi de l'air du temps et de la mode. » La mode était alors au tout nouveau caractère de Max Miedinger, l'Helvetica, ou à des caractères rivaux comme l'Univers d'Adrian Frutiger ou le Folio de Konrad F. Bauer.

L'Helvetica n'avait jamais été conçu comme un jeu complet de caractères pour la composition mécanique et manuelle. Quand l'Univers, la très large famille de caractères d'Adrian Frutiger, fut lancée avec succès, Stempel fut forcé de redessiner toute la gamme selon la méthode mise en place par Frutiger, en attribuant un numéro à chaque membre de la famille Helvetica. L'Helvetica était exactement ce que recherchaient les graphistes du début des années 70. En 1982, Stempel lança son New Helvetica.

Il existe un intérêt marqué pour l'histoire de la typographie à l'heure actuelle, intérêt qui, je l'espère, se prolongera dans l'avenir. Nous sommes toujours à l'affût de nouvelles opportunités, de « l'air du temps » et de « la mode ». Le caractère idéal a-t-il déjà été inventé ? La question reste posée et c'est à vous d'y répondre.

Je trouve très frappant que les créateurs de caractères, avec leur merveilleux sens du détail, puissent autant différencier les choses. Il y a tout un monde, par exemple, entre le Caslon (1725) de William Caslon et le Baskerville (1754) de John Baskerville. Ou comparez l'Akzidenz Grotesk (1899) de Berthold au Futura (1925) de Paul Renner. La page apparaît complètement différente, et, en tant que lecteur, vous percevez aussi le message différemment. Le choix de la typographie et l'implication du graphiste peuvent vous transporter dans un autre monde.

Une petite sélection de quelques créateurs de caractères ayant le sens du détail

Claude Garamond : *Garamond*

Le Romain de la Renaissance française voit le jour. Claude Garamond naquit en 1480. Il apprit très tôt son art auprès de son père et d'autres membres de la famille. Garamond affirmait pouvoir graver des poinçons en Cicero (12 points) à l'âge de 15 ans. Dans le premier quart du XVIe siècle, les graveurs de poinçons et les imprimeurs français étaient les homologues des créateurs italiens du Romain de la Renaissance. Les caractères Antique d'Alde Manuce et de Francesco Griffo arrivèrent en France en même temps que les caractères de Pietro Bembo.

Claude Garamond fait partie des premiers graveurs de poinçons et fondeurs des caractères romains et italiques de la Renaissance française. C'est à son époque que furent rassemblées capitales romaines et bas de casse carolingiennes. Dans une France centralisée, les conditions étaient plus favorables qu'en Italie ou en Allemagne pour faire évoluer la typographie. Claude Garamond gagna la célébrité et le titre de fondeur de caractères du Roi après la publication, en 1543, de ses *Grecs du Roy*, que François Ier, protecteur de la typographie, l'avait poussé à graver. La première Antique que l'on puisse dater et attribuer à Garamond en toute confiance était un Gros-Romain, qui apparaît dans une édition des œuvres d'Eusèbe de Césarée et d'autres publications de Robert Estienne en 1544.

Après 1545, comme le montrent les pages de titre, Garamond devint également éditeur, à la fois en son nom propre et en association avec Pierre Gaultier et Jean Barbe. Le Sabon de Jan Tschichold ou, encore mieux, le Sabon Next de Jean-François Porchez sont des versions modernes des caractères de Garamond.

William Caslon : *Caslon*

Caslon, un homme à l'esprit plein de ressources. William Caslon naquit à Cradley, dans le Worcestershire, en Angleterre, en 1692. À 13 ans, il devint apprenti chez un graveur de Londres. En 1717, il devint citoyen de Londres où il s'installa comme graveur indépendant en 1718. Deux ans plus tard, il ouvrit sa propre fonderie de caractères.

C'est le relieur John Watts qui demanda à Caslon de dessiner et de fondre des caractères pour ses couvertures de livres. Un de ses livres fut remarqué par William Bowyer, célèbre imprimeur londonien. Ils devinrent

1915, *Drucken Sie Kataloge?*,
Schriftgiesserei Ludwig & Mayer, Frankfurt
am Main

amis, et Bowyer présenta Caslon à d'autres imprimeurs londoniens. Ce fut le démarrage de l'une des plus florissantes fonderies de caractères d'Angleterre. À ses débuts, Caslon reçut le support financier de Watts, Bowyer, et de son gendre James Bettenham, qui était aussi imprimeur.

En 1720, la première année de la fonderie, il créa une nouvelle police de caractères pour la SPCK (Société pour la promotion du savoir chrétien) pour l'impression d'une Bible en arabe. Il imprima une page d'échantillon afin de pouvoir vendre cette police arabe à d'autres imprimeurs. Sur cette page, son nom, William Caslon, s'étalait en caractères romains dessinés spécialement pour l'occasion. Cette nouvelle police est à l'origine de la célèbre police que nous connaissons aujourd'hui sous le nom de Caslon Old Style. À la suite de cette police, Caslon grava un certain nombre de caractères non romains et exotiques comme les Coptic, Armenian, Etruscan et Hebrew. Caslon Gothic était sa version de Old English.

Tous ces caractères avaient été créés avant la publication, en 1734, du premier et volumineux catalogue de la fonderie de Caslon, qui présentait un total de 38 caractères. Caslon déménagea sa fonderie à la célèbre adresse de Chiswell Street, d'où son fils et plusieurs générations après lui dirigèrent l'affaire familiale pendant plus de 120 ans. En 1749, le roi George II nomma Caslon juge de paix du comté de Middlesex. Il se retira dans sa maison de campagne de Bethnal Green, où il mourut en 1766, à l'âge de 74 ans. L'histoire de ce graveur extraordinaire fut celle d'une réussite.

John Baskerville : *Baskerville*

La quête de l'excellence. John Baskerville (1706–1775) commença à graver et à fondre ses propres caractères vers 1754. Il fut influencé par l'écriture lapidaire des tailleurs de pierre, à l'instar d'autres créateurs anglais dont les styles de caractères nous paraissent aujourd'hui typiquement anglais : le Clarendon, les Grotesques et les Égyptiennes, qui se propagèrent à la faveur de la révolution industrielle. Baskerville attachait une grande importance à la façon dont ses caractères seraient imprimés et à l'aspect qu'ils auraient une fois sur le papier. Le papier, l'encre, les caractères et les presses à imprimer jouaient donc pour lui des rôles d'une égale importance.

En 1750, John Baskerville fonda un moulin à papier, une fonderie de caractères et une imprimerie. C'est alors qu'il eut l'idée du papier Vélin.

En 1754, après un travail long et minutieux, son premier caractère vit le jour. En 1758, il réalisa son premier livre : la fameuse édition de Milton, un *Gesamtkunstwerk* (une œuvre d'art totale) avant la lettre. Baskerville

fut aussi imprimeur pour l'Université de Cambridge. *Juvenalis*, publié en 1757, est sa production la plus célèbre.

Les caractères spacieux créés par Baskerville, une composition aérée avec un espacement plus grand entre les mots et les lignes, la largeur sur la page et l'utilisation de papier Vélin et d'une encre très noire lui valurent la renommée à travers toute l'Europe. Après sa mort, une grande partie de son matériel, la formule secrète de son encre et sa méthode de fabrication du papier couché furent vendues au Français Caron de Beaumarchais. Entre 1785 et 1789, celui-ci imprima 70 volumes de l'œuvre de Voltaire en utilisant les caractères de Baskerville. Ce dernier eût été ravi du résultat.

Giambattista Bodoni : *Bodoni*

«Beaucoup de blancs et un espacement généreux, et ne faites pas des caractères de taille dérisoire. Vous serez alors assuré d'un résultat digne d'un roi.» – Giambattista Bodoni.

On l'a surnommé le roi des imprimeurs et l'imprimeur des rois. Bodoni doit sa réputation à son *Manuale tipografico*, une compilation posthume de l'œuvre de sa vie, publiée en 1818 à Parme par sa veuve, Margherita Bodoni. L'exemplaire de tête était dédié à son Altesse Royale Marie-Louise, princesse de Parme. Ce manuel sur l'art d'imprimer les livres était constitué de 546 pages imprimées contenant un total de 665 alphabets différents, dont 100 caractères exotiques, et 1300 vignettes. Il contenait 170 écritures latines, certaines nécessitant jusqu'à 380 matrices. L'édition fut limitée à 150 copies, quoique le chiffre de 290 ait été cité.

D'après sa veuve, en 50 ans, Bodoni produisit, corrigea et fondit plus de 55 000 matrices. Bodoni s'était consacré à la création, à l'harmonie de la page en fonction du choix et de la taille de la police de caractères, de la composition et du rapport entre longueur de ligne, espacement et largeur de colonne. L'interaction du blanc et du noir et un usage généreux de l'espace jouaient un rôle prépondérant. L'histoire des émules de Bodoni est longue. Morris Fuller Benton créa un caractère Bodoni pour ATF en 1911. Monotype fit de même, puis la fonderie suisse Haas, en 1924. Le Bodoni Haas fut copié par la fonderie Amsterdam, par Berthold puis Stempel. Linotype et Ludlow suivirent également Haas, et Johannes Wagner sortit un nouveau Bodoni en 1961. Il existe plus de 500 variantes de Bodoni dans le monde. Un beau spécimen en est le Filosofia de Zuzana Licko (1996).

The term *Gesamtkunst* (total art) was known to Jakob Erbar when he made the drawings for Feder-Grotesk. Each one in this type-specimen proof is a fantastic "total picture." Erbar was born in 1878 in Düsseldorf. He was trained as a compositor and took courses in typography with Fritz H. Ehmcke and Anna Simons.

Als Jakob Erbar seine Zeichnungen für die Feder-Grotesk anfertigte, war ihm der Begriff „Gesamtkunst" zweifelsohne geläufig. Jedes Seite seines Schriftmusters ist ein fantastisches, in sich geschlossenes Werk. Der 1878 in Düsseldorf geborene Erbar war gelernter Schriftsetzer und hatte Typografiekurse bei Fritz Helmut Ehmcke und Anna Simons besucht.

Le terme *Gesamtkunst* (art total) était connu de Jakob Erbar quand il réalisa les dessins des Feder-Grotesk. Dans cette épreuve de spécimen de caractères, chacun d'entre eux est un fabuleux dessin à part entière. Erbar est né en 1878 à Düsseldorf. Il a reçu une formation de compositeur et a suivi des cours de typographie avec Fritz H. Ehmcke et Anna Simons.

Stanley Morison : *Times New Roman*

La quête du caractère de journal idéal. En 1923, Stanley Ignatius Arthur Morison (1889–1967) devint conseiller typographique de Monotype. Il était chargé de dessiner plusieurs familles de caractères basés sur des caractères historiques, tels ceux d'Eric Gill. William Lints-Smith, qui dirigeait le journal londonien *Times*, avait ouï dire que Morison s'était montré très méprisant à l'égard de la typographie désuète de son journal. Ils se rencontrèrent et, après une longue discussion, Stanley Morison conseilla une refonte complète du *Times*. Morison devint le conseiller typographique du journal. Il réalisa plusieurs pages de test dans différents caractères, dont Baskerville, Plantin, Imprint, Ionic et une version de Perpetua. Au même moment, aux États-Unis, Linotype développait une série de caractères de labeur. Le premier, Ionic, fut suivi en 1931 par l'Excelsior, qui est, encore aujourd'hui, l'un des caractères de journaux les plus prisés.

Après plusieurs autres essais, Morison décida que ce dont le *Times* avait besoin, c'était d'un caractère entièrement nouveau. En 1931, il proposa deux créations, un Perpetua remanié et un Plantin modernisé. La commission du *Times* se décida pour ce dernier. Le caractère original ayant pour nom Times Old Roman, on baptisa ce nouveau caractère Times New Roman. Il fit sa première apparition dans l'édition du *Times* du 3 octobre 1932. Toujours couramment utilisé aujourd'hui, grâce à une distribution et une commercialisation étendues, le Times New Roman est appelé à survivre.

Berthold, Günter Gerhard Lange : *Akzidenz Grotesk*

Très simple et très caractéristique. L'Akzidenz Grotesk (AG, pour les connaisseurs), avait déjà plus de 20 ans à l'apogée du Constructivisme. De Stijl, le Bauhaus, Dada et d'autres mouvements surent tirer avantage d'AG. Il était à la mode à la naissance de la typographie suisse, dont il fut le caractère de prédilection. AG a toujours une haute qualité visuelle qui nous rappelle qu'un caractère n'a pas besoin d'être uniforme pour être lisible et attrayant ; ce sont, au contraire, les différences entre les caractères qui les rendent lisibles. En janvier 1899, deux entreprises présentaient l'Akzidenz Grotesk dans des publicités insérées dans le *Deutscher Buch und Steindrucker*. L'une était Berthold et l'autre Bauer & Co, de Stuttgart.

En 1973, Günter Gerhard Lange, directeur de la typographie chez Berthold, présentait sa nouvelle version d'Akzidenz Grotesk en ces termes : «Dans ce travail, on a utilisé les proportions de base du vénérable Akzidenz Grotesk semi-gras pour déterminer la taille moyenne et la forme indivi-

duelle des caractères. Il a fallu bien sûr tenir compte des ressemblances de famille à l'intérieur de chaque style individuel, mais aussi de l'air du temps et de la mode. » La mode était alors au tout nouveau caractère de Max Miedinger, l'Helvetica, ou à des caractères rivaux comme l'Univers d'Adrian Frutiger ou le Folio de Konrad F. Bauer. Cependant le bon vieil AG joue toujours un rôle de premier plan dans le monde toujours en mouvement de l'imprimerie et de la création graphique.

Paul Renner : *Futura*

Bien de son époque, Futura est un caractère élémentaire et intemporel. En 1925, Jan (Ivan) Tschichold publia une édition spéciale de *Typographische Mitteilungen* intitulée «Typographie élémentaire», dans laquelle il décrivait ses efforts pour créer une nouvelle typographie. «Parmi les caractères disponibles», écrivait-il, «les caractères Grotesque ou Block répondaient le mieux aux besoins de la nouvelle typographie, parce qu'ils étaient d'un dessin simple et faciles à lire. Rien n'interdisait cependant d'utiliser d'autres caractères faciles à lire. Le caractère idéal n'était pas encore né.»

En 1926, l'un des chefs de file du Bauhaus, László Moholy-Nagy, écrivait dans *Bauhausheft 7* : «Puisque tous les styles de Grotesques existants manquent d'un style fondamental, la Grotesque reste à inventer.» Dans le même numéro figuraient aussi les articles «Essai pour un nouveau caractère» de Herbert Bayer et «Le caractère Stencil comme caractère de titre» de Josef Albers.

Au même moment, Paul Renner développait son projet de nouvelle Grotesque fondé sur des principes constructivistes. En 1924, Renner créait le Futura, basé sur des formes simples – cercle, triangle et carré – mais, avec son expérience du livre et de la typographie, il n'était pas question de se débarrasser de la tradition au profit d'un nouveau dogme. Les premiers exemples de ce nouveau style firent leur apparition en 1925. Comme l'expliquait Willy Haas : «Avec le nouveau Futura, Paul Renner nous propose une solution constructive intemporelle qui paraît exceptionnellement noble et pure, qui convient aussi bien à un usage classique que moderne et qui, en dépit de son dessin strict, ne nous bombarde pas de doctrine mais se lit facilement. On a rarement l'occasion de voir un style aussi personnel associé à une telle force d'abstraction de la forme, un tel mélange de raffinement, d'humanité et de noblesse.» En 1933, après que le parti nazi eut pris le pouvoir en Allemagne, Renner démissionna de son école et se retira au lac de Genève. En 1947, il publia l'ou-

Monotype Corporation publications are immediately recognizable due to their highly specific design. In the early years of the 20th Century, Monotype produced original typefaces for their mechanical production process, proving that they could achieve the quality of traditional type foundries.

Publikationen der Firma Monotype lassen sich dank ihrer ganz speziellen Gestaltung auf den ersten Blick erkennen. Um zu beweisen, dass man mit dem maschinellen Herstellungsverfahren die gleiche Qualität wie traditionelle Schriftgießereien erzielen konnte, produzierte Monotype in den ersten Jahren des 20. Jahrhunderts auch eigene Schriften.

Les publications de Monotype sont immédiatement reconnaissables à leur graphisme très spécifique. Au début du XXᵉ siècle, Monotype a réalisé des caractères originaux pour son procédé de production mécanique, prouvant qu'elle pouvait obtenir la même qualité que des fonderies de caractères traditionnelles.

*La technologie a rendu les choses plus faciles.
Mais le processus débute toujours par une idée,
parfois rapidement notée à l'aide d'un croquis,
et se poursuit, si le concept s'avère bon,
par un travail plus approfondi sur les détails.
Au matin, le croquis de la veille s'avère souvent
moins novateur que ce que le graphiste avait
d'abord imaginé.*

vrage *Ordre et harmonie des couleurs*. À la même époque, on rééditait son *Art de la typographie* de 1939.

Eric Gill : *Gill Sans*

De la sculpture à la typographie. Arthur Eric Rowton Gill (1882–1940) reçut une formation d'architecte aux alentours de 1900. Après son mariage, il rejoignit un groupe d'artisans de Ditchling, dans le Sussex, où il travailla comme graphiste et illustrateur. Plus tard, il travailla comme sculpteur. Sa première création de caractère, Perpetua, fut publiée en 1925. En 1928, il travailla à High Wycombe comme sculpteur et maçon. Entre-temps, il avait fabriqué une presse manuelle avec l'aide de son gendre, René Hague. Il publia plusieurs ouvrages sur la création industrielle et l'artisanat. Un autre de ses caractères sut s'imposer. Il s'agit du Joanna, ainsi nommé en l'honneur de sa fille, et initialement fondu exclusivement en corps 12, pour l'impression de son *Essay on Typography* publié en 1931.

Gill Sans, pur et simple.

En 1916, Gill travaillait à des sculptures pour les stations de métro de Westminster Cathedral. On lui demanda de concevoir un caractère géométrique simple pour toute la signalétique du métro londonien. Pour cette création, il garda les proportions classiques (cf. le *g*, par exemple). Pour le *R*, il utilisa son caractère de prédilection, avec son élégante boucle descendante. L'équipe de Monotype y apporta de nombreuses améliorations.

En 1928, Gill devint lui-même conseiller pour Monotype. Quand Gill Sans fit sa première apparition, à la fin des années 20, il ne correspondait pas vraiment à ce que recherchait l'establishment de l'imprimerie britannique. Son accueil fut similaire à celui réservé au Futura l'année précédente, en Allemagne. Les annuaires décrivaient la création de Paul Renner comme une mode qui serait vite oubliée. La première version de Gill Sans fut achevée pour le congrès annuel de la British Printing Industries Federation. Stanley Morison devait y prononcer une allocution pour laquelle il envoya ses invitations composées dans ce nouveau caractère. Dès lors, Gill Sans avait gagné.

Max Miedinger : *Helvetica*

Impersonnel et intemporel. En 1949, Eduard Hoffmann, directeur de la fonderie Haas de Münchenstein, près de Bâle, projetait la création d'une nouvelle Grotesque. Son modèle était le Shelter Grotesk, le caractère officiel du Bauhaus. Les graphistes suisses de l'époque faisaient un usage croissant de l'Akzidenz Grotesk de Berthold qui connut alors une renaissance sous l'appellation «typographie suisse». Eduard Hoffman savait exactement à quoi devait ressembler son caractère et en confia le dessin à Max Midinger, de Zurich, en 1956. Midinger était un spécialiste de la famille Grotesque. Ses dessins étaient discutés, évalués et corrigés avec Hoffman, avant de passer à l'étape de la gravure des poinçons, puis à celle de la fonte, dans les ateliers de la fonderie Haas. En 1957, le nom de ce projet était New Haas Grotesque. En 1960, le nouveau caractère fut publié par Stempel sous le nom d'Helvetica. Quand Linotype décida d'adopter le nouveau caractère, d'abord pour la composition mécanique au plomb puis, plus tard, pour la photocomposition, il fallut retravailler complètement le dessin. L'Helvetica n'avait jamais été conçu comme un jeu complet de caractères pour la composition mécanique et manuelle.

Puis vint le succès de l'Univers, la famille très étendue créée par Adrian Frutiger. Stempel fut forcé de redessiner toute la gamme Helvetica selon la méthode inaugurée par Adrian Frutiger, en attribuant un numéro à chaque membre de la famille. L'Helvetica light fut dessiné par Erich Shulz-Anker, directeur artistique chez Stempel, en collaboration avec Arthur Ritzel. En 1982, Stempel lança son New Helvetica. L'Helvetica était exactement ce que recherchaient les graphistes du début des années 70 : un caractère impersonnel et intemporel.

Les fonderies de caractères restaient en contact et entretenaient des relations commerciales d'abord au plan régional, puis assez rapidement, à l'échelle internationale. Les lettres étaient vendues, copiées, adaptées et distribuées sous des noms divers, s'adaptant aux tendances du moment. Dès qu'une firme connaissait un succès, une autre voulait sa part du gâteau.

Et pour présenter et vendre ces lettres, les fonderies publièrent et produisirent de somptueuses épreuves de spécimens de caractères.

'MONOTYPE'

GILL SANS

A

Specimen of Printing Types,

BY WILLIAM CASLON,

𝕷𝖊𝖙𝖙𝖊𝖗-𝕱𝖔𝖚𝖓𝖉𝖊𝖗 𝖙𝖔 𝖍𝖎𝖘 𝕸𝖆𝖏𝖊𝖘𝖙𝖞.

Five-Line Pica.

ABCD
abcdeg

Four-Line Pica.

ABCDE
abcdefgh

Two-Line Double Pica.

ABCDEF
ΓΔΘΞΩ

Two-Line Great Primer.

ABCDEFG
ΓΔΘΞΠΩ

Two-Line English.

ABCDE FGJ
ΓΔΠΣΥΦΨΩ

Two-Line Pica.

ABCDEFGHIM
ΓΔΘΞΠΣΥΦΩ

Two-Line Small Pica

ABCDEFGHIKL
ΓΔΘΞΠΣΥΦΨΩ

Two-Line Long Primer.

ABCDEFGHIJKM
ΓΔΘΞΠΣΥΦΧΨΩ

Two-Line Brevier.

ABCDEFGHIKLMN
ΓΔΕΘΚΛΞΟΠΣΥΨΩ

French Cannon.

Quousque tan-
dem abutere,
Quousque tandem

Two-Line Double Pica.

Quousque tand-
em abutere, Ca-
Quousque tandem

　　　　　　　　　　　　　　　　　　　　　　　Jan Tholenaar

Collecting Type Specimens

by Jan Tholenaar
With an introduction by Casper Gijzen

The type specimens from the end
of the 19th Century are really endearing;
their infinite variety is glorious.

Collector Jan Tholenaar has assembled one of the greatest private collections of type specimens in the world. With his individual preferences setting the tone, the collection focuses on specimens produced between 1830 and 1930. The many highlights of that century include extremely diverse fantasy letters and ornaments, with examples of artistic printing. The tension mounts as Tholenaar displays some of the wonderful examples and enthuses: "Such a wealth, such dazzling color combinations. Such complex constructions; these took weeks of work. All those letters and all those ornaments in all those different colors. That pale green and brown and that light grey next to each other, there's no clash there. And look at the way that fits, unbelievable! All of it letterpress, no lithography. It does sometimes lead to abnormalities; just look at this piece of work, all set entirely in copper lines! They were secured in plaster; nobody knows how to do that these days. Sometimes there's a lovely signature, too, also constructed the same way."

Tholenaar does, indeed, show magnificent examples of setting, all made up of letters, lines, or intricate ornaments. Applications were devised for all of this material being offered for sale, set, and printed by hand. Tholenaar leafs further through the book: "The type specimens from the end of the 19th Century are really endearing; their infinite variety is glorious."

Tholenaar continually expresses his admiration for the love with which type specimens were evidently composed during that era. He points out a specimen in which a single letter is presented as an artful example of the designer's typography, and another that features various printing procedures: letterpress, engraving, and offset.

The only restriction Tholenaar imposes on his collecting is that the specimens must be set in lead. He has examples from foundries and printers, but an advertisement in a magazine, for instance, can also be a specimen. He buys them from antiquarian booksellers all around the world. Having long worked in the book business, he is used to dragging around a heavy case of books. Naturally, he also gets to see a lot of catalogs. He cites the example of the famous Jammes type catalog: "No point in even thinking about it. … Just look at the prices. And they're all like that. It was terrible, real torture, nothing but type specimens."

Some specimens he finds "amusing," others simply "nice." He doesn't have much enthusiasm for all the sans serifs designed in the last century, with the exception of Paul Renner's Futura. "But if you compare all those Victorian fantasy letters with the postwar, perfect, but stiff Swiss typography, for example, then the former have far more appeal."

It's not so easy to collect type specimens these days; they've become scarce and expensive. You have to buy virtually everything from an antiquarian bookseller or at an auction. That burns a big hole in your pocket. It would be impossible to start my collection of several thousand examples all over again. If I go into a bookseller's (something I find hard to resist, wherever I am in the world) and ask if they have any type specimens, often the reply is, "No, and whenever I do get one, it goes quickly; they seem to be real collectors' items nowadays."

I remember one of my first purchases, a Schelter & Giesecke *Mustersammlung* from 1886. I bought it at Kok in Oude Hoogstraat, Amsterdam.

My love for type was aroused while I was training at the Amsterdam Graphic School in Dintelstraat from 1945 to 1947. I was taught typesetting by J. Aarden, known for his Linotype, or "new trend," courses (1920–28) and "illustrative typography" (1928–34). In Möllenkamp's drawing class, we sat endlessly fiddling with Hollandse Medieval; I will never forget, as long as I live, that the capital *A* has a little flag on it. We had letters such as Nobel, Romulus, Bodoni, Studio, Libra, and Iris. My favorites were Trajanus and Gravure, with its long ascenders and descenders.

I really got a kick when I visited the library of the Amsterdam Type Foundry (formerly the Nicolaas Tetterode Foundry in Rotterdam, then located in Bilderdijkstraat, Amsterdam). It was there that I saw, for the first time, a Derriey specimen from 1862, probably the most beautiful ever made. It was years before I managed to get one of those.

On a visit to the St. Bride Printing Library in London, I made the acquaintance of the Printers' International Specimen Exchange publications. From 1880 onwards, 16 yearbooks were published in editions of 200 to 450 copies. English printers, in particular, submitted their most magnificent work for these books, thus preserving it for posterity. The books featured complex setting work (artistic printing), with many colors and a vast array of both beautiful and ugly letters. It is Victorian printing, in particular, of which I'm extremely fond; sometimes it is truly lovely, and sometimes only beautiful in its ugliness. The Germans picked up the idea of these yearbooks, and I feel privileged to have a number of both the English and the German series in my library. A similar product of Dutch manufacture is the *Uitwisseling van kunstdrukwerk in Nederland*, of which I possess the first—and immediately last?—volume, from 1893. It contains little more than 20 pages.

I used to have to travel a lot for my work (book co-productions). It was

Casper Gijzen

1785, Specimen of Printing Types,
William Caslon, London

Shown here is a complete, eight-page proof of a type specimen by His Majesty's letter-founder, including Greek, Latin, Hebrew, music, and floral decorations.

Dieser Druckbogen des königlichen Schriftgießers William Caslon präsentiert auf seinen acht – hier vollständig abgebildeten – Seiten griechische, lateinische und hebräische Schriftbeispiele sowie Noten und florale Ziermuster.

L'épreuve complète de huit pages d'un spécimen de caractères du fondeur de lettres de sa Majesté, comprenant du grec, du latin, de l'hébreu, de la musique et des décorations florales.

in 1963, during the first children's book fair in Bologna, that I found a broadsheet type specimen from a Bolognese printer, folded in four, in an antique shop. I think I paid the equivalent of about 20 euros (30 U. S. dollars) for it, calculating backwards—a lot of money for me at that time. The specimen had lain in a drawer for years until collecting became all the rage. I sent a photocopy of it to the University of Bologna, asking for information. The specimen proved to be from the Benacci printing family, which was active in Bologna in the 16th and early 17th Centuries. The Bolognese university library informed me that they had many specimens from these printers, but not this one. I now flatter myself with the thought that it is a unique copy and one of the very oldest type specimens. The antiquarian bookseller Herzberger offered me a good price for it, but I'm glad I resisted the temptation. A couple of years ago, I was able to purchase an extremely rare duodecimo publication of madrigals printed and published by Alessandro and Vittorio Benacci between 1588 and 1590, with lavish, whimsical use of their vignettes. That's what really brings a type specimen to life.

In principle, I collect anything in the way of specimens, from any country and from any period, the only restriction being the lead era. There are various producers: type foundries, printers, and bookbinders—although the last group is small. The specimens demonstrate type cast in lead or made from materials such as wood, brass, and iron (for impressions). There are also vignettes and ornaments, stereotypes of woodcuts, and all kinds of copper lines. I do have a number of photosetting specimens, but I pay little or nothing for them. In most cases, they excel in their dullness, if not ugliness. But there are, naturally, exceptions. One lovely example is the three-part Compugraphic specimen, printed in two colors and designed by Jost Hochuli, with a playful, humorous application of the type on each right-hand page.

Type specimens come in all shapes and sizes. Those with a complete range are often bound in a hard cover. One extremely large specimen is Stempel's 1925 *Hauptprobe*. It is around 1,200 pages long and more than 10 centimeters thick; it weighs 7 kilos and is bound in half parchment. There are also slim volumes eulogizing the qualities of a single typeface each. Often, they are stapled, but some are sewn with cahier stitch, in a soft binding. Years ago, I bought two boxes of this kind of specimen from the bookseller Horodisch, who had evidently just acquired them at an auction. He remarked at the time that those thin booklets with a specimen of a single type each were far more beautiful and interesting

than the thick volumes. He was quite right. They show various applications of the type and are often extremely stylishly designed, sometimes by the type designer himself. The use of color was not shunned.

Type specimens are, naturally, not only found in special publications; they were also incorporated into the foundries' in-house magazines, such as the Amsterdam Type Foundry's *Typografische Mededeelingen*; Johannes Enschedé & Zonen's *Letterproef*; Nebiolo's *Archivio tipografico*; Schelter & Giesecke's *Typographische Mitteilungen*; and *La crónica* by Richard Gans in Madrid. There are also the world-famous publications: the *Monotype Recorder* and the *Linotype Bulletin*. Type specimens can also be found as advertisements in trade journals such as *Graphicus*, *The British Printer*, *Typographische Jahrbücher*, *Deutscher Buch- und Steindrucker*, and the Swiss *Les archives de l'imprimerie*. The French type foundries had a joint magazine in the early 1900s called *La fonderie typographique*. They displayed magnificent examples of all the new types, ornaments, and so forth, often pure Art Nouveau. In Germany, there was the *Journal für Buchdruckerkunst, Schriftgießerei und die verwandten Fächer* in the mid-19th Century, and, later in the century, *Archiv für Buchdruckerkunst und verwandte Geschäftszweige*. Innumerable appendices were bound into them, sometimes folding out to big broadsheets, with the most complicated setting and printed in several colors—beautiful enough to frame. Today, the appendices are often missing, but the volumes in my collection are complete.

Type specimens were also printed in manuals and encyclopedias. One 36-page Caslon specimen from 1763 was included in P. Luckombe's *The History and Art of Printing* (1770). Eight pages from 1785 were featured in Chambers's *Cyclopaedia*, which also includes a Fry broadsheet. In 1767, 10 pages by Fournier were incorporated into the *Encyclopédie élémentaire* ("*Tableau des vingt corps de caractères, d'usage ordinaire dans l'imprimerie*") and, naturally, into the second part of his *Manuel typographique*, printed in 1766. *Die so nöthig als nützliche Buchdruckerkunst und Schriftgießerey* presented the "*Schrift-Probe, oder kurzes Verzeichniss derjenigen Hebräisch-, Griechisch-, Lateinisch-, und Teutschen Schriften, welche in Herrn Bernhard Christoph Breitkopfs Schriftgießerey allhier befindlich sind. Dabey man mehrentheils bemerket hat, von wem eine jede Schrift in Messing oder Stahl ist geschnidten worden.*" A treatise by Ernesti on typecasting and printing from 1721 (*Die wol-eingerichtete Buchdruckerey*) features type specimens probably by Endters, who printed and published the book.

Following the chronology of my collection for a moment: I bought an

English Syriac.

ـحـٮـمـ ,حـمـمـٮـٮـا ٮـمـمـٮ مـمـحـٮ ٮٲٮٮا مـحـٮ
صـٮـٲلٮ ٮـٮـٮٮ٦ٮ ٮحـٮمٮ ٮٮٮـٮ ,حـمـمـٮا
ٮٮ مٲٮٮـٮا ٮٮ٦ حـٮ حـمـمـٮ ,مـٮٮمـٮ ٮٮ
مـحـٮ مـمـحـمـم حـٮ مـمـمٮ ٮٮٮـٮ ٮٲ
مـ ٮـٮٮ مـحـمٮ حـٮٮٮمـٮ ٮٮ ٮلحٮٮ
ٮ حـٮٮمـمـمـٮ ٮلٮ ٮٮ حـٮ مـٮ حـمـٮا

Long-Primer Syriac.

أ ٮٮٮ: ٮٮٮٮ٦ٮ, حـٮمـمٮٮ ٮحـٮٮ . مـحـٮٮ مـحـٮٮ
ٮٮٮٮ ٮٲمٮ حـٮ . مـٮ حـمٮ ٮٮ ٮٮٮٲ ٮٮٮٮ. ٮٮ
ٮٮ ٮٮٮ ٮٮٮٮ . حـٮمٮٮ ٮٮٮ ٮٮٮٮٮ ٮٮٮٮٮٮ٦ٮ
ٮٮٮٮ . ٮٲ ٮٮحـٮٮ ٮٮٮٲ, حـمـٮٮ حـٮٮٮٮ حـحـمـمٮ. حـٮٮـٮٲ
٦ٮ ٮٲٮٮ . مـمـٮ حـٲحـٮ حـٮٲ, حـٲٮ٦حـٮٮ مـمٲحٮٮ حـٮٲ . مـٮٮٲ
ٮ-: ٲٲ؛ ٮمٮٲ ٮحـٲ مـٮ حـٮٲ ٮحـٲ . مـحـٮٲٮمٲٮ
مـٮٮٮمٲٮ مـمٲمٮ ٮٮٮٲ ٮحـٲٮ حـٲٲ . مـٮٮٮٲ

English Arabic.

لعلم ايها الاخ الحبيب القاري اللبيب ٭ ان الاب الفاضل
الكلي احترامه والذايع في كافة العلوم نامه ٭ كبر كبر
اثاناسيوس البطريرك الانطاكي علي الملة الرومية في الامصار
الشامية ٭ قد اصرف اتعابا جسيمة ومجاهدات عظيمة في
نظام الكتب الالهية والاسفار البيعية ٭ لفايدة الشعوب المس
ـيحية ٭ المؤتمن علي سياستهم بغبطتة الابوية ٭ فابرز مندذ

Pica Armenian.

Քանբայա խանագման Ես ատտունծայնցն
՛ի քեզ Սնրգագհ, ե գանէնւ Հգւնոյն ՛ի վէ-
րայ քոյ խանգֆիւածոցդ գ շարֆնիւն ձանեայ
՛ի ձեռն գէրեցիկ խանրոյս, առապ քան ղէ-
ապինոյս, ՝գՏօգւոյցնկայնայ գանԽնգէ-
ոըեսերերեքէ խֆնկան ապոռ՚ժ ապագէ, առաւ
ել ես սմֆօրուԽֆգայ Ա՛ս ողոյ, Աոյ մֆայն գ-

Pica Samaritan.

ᛮᛗᚹᛚᛉ ᛉᚢᛉ᛬ᛘᚹᛘᛈ ᛘᛉᛚ ᛉᛘᚹᚹᛘᛈ᛬ᛘᚢᚢᛘᛘᛗ ᛚᛘᛗᛉᛈ
ᛘᛉᚹ ᛈᛉᛘᛚ᛬ᚹᛗᚹᛉᛘ ᛉᚢᛈ ᛈᛘᚹ᛬ᛉᛘᚹ ᛉᛉᚹᛉ᛬ᛘᛗᛘᛉᛚᛉ
ᛈᛈᚹ ᛉᛘᛗ ᛈᛚᛈᛚᛈᛚ ᛉᛗ ᛉᛉᛘᛉ ᛉᛉᛈᛉᛘᛘ᛬ᛉᛘ ᛉᛗ
ᛉᛘᛉ᛬ᛉᛗᛉ ᛉᛘᛈᛉᛚ ᛉᛈᛉᛘ ᛈᛉᛗᛈᛉᛘ᛬ᛈᛈᛉ᛬ᛉᛘᛉ
ᛈᛉ ᛉᛘ ᛈᛘᛘᛈ᛬ᛉᛉᛘᛘᛉᛉ ᛉᛈᛉ᛬ᛉᛈᛈ ᛉᛉᛘᛘ᛬ᛉᛘ
᛬ᛉᛘᛉᚹᛉ ᛉᛗᛘᚹᛘᛉᚹ ᛘᛘᚹᛈᛉ ᛘᚹᛘᛚᛘ ᚹᛘᛘᛈᛘᛈ
᛬ᛉᛗᛉᛈᛚ ᚹᛈᛘᛚ᛬ᛉᛘᛚ ᚹᛈᛘᛉ ᛘᛈᚹᛚᚹᛘ ᛈᚹᛉ᛬ᛘᚹᛘᛈᛈᛗ

Pica Gothic.

ΛΤΤΛ ꞐꞐSΛꞰ ΦꞐ ĨꞐ ꞪΙΜΙꞐΛΜ: ᚹΕΙꞪ-
ꞐΛΙ ꞐΛΜꞀ ΦΕΙꞐ: ᚹΙΜΛΙ ΦΙꞐⰄΙꞐΛSSꞐS
ΦΕΙꞐS: ᚹΛΙꞰΦΛΙ ᚹΙΛꞀΛ ΦΕΙꞐS SᚹΕ ĨꞐ
ꞪΙΜΙꞐΛ ᚵΛꞪ ΛꞐΛ ΛΙꞰΦΛΙ: ꞪΛΛΙΕ ꞐꞐS-
SΛꞰΛꞐΛ ΦΛꞐΛ SΙꞐΤΕΙꞐΛꞐ ΓΙΕ ꞐꞐS
ꞪΙΜΜΛⰄΛΓΛ: ᚵΛꞪ ΛΕΛΕΤ ꞐꞐS ΦΛΤΕΙ
SꞰꞐΛΛꞐS SΙᚵΛΙΜΛ. SᚹΛ SᚹΕᚵΛꞪ ᚹΕ-
ΙS ΛΕΛΕΤΛΜ ΦΛΙΜ SꞰꞐΛΛΜ ꞐꞐSΛꞰΛ-

Pica Coptic.

Ⲡⲉⲛⲓⲱⲧ ⲉⲧⲃⲉⲛ ⲛⲓ ⲫⲏⲟⲩⲓ ⲁⲣⲉϥ ⲧⲟⲩⲃ-
ⲟⲛϫⲉ ⲡⲉⲕⲣⲁⲛ ⲁⲣⲉⲥⲛ ⲓⲭⲉ ⲧⲉⲕ ⲙⲉ ⲧⲟⲩⲣⲟ
ⲡⲉⲧⲉϩ ⲛⲁⲕ ⲁⲣⲉϥ ϣⲱⲡⲓ ⲁⲫⲣⲏ ϯ ϧⲉⲛ ⲧ ⲫⲉ
ⲛⲉⲙ ϩⲓϫⲉ ⲛⲡⲓⲕⲁϩⲓ ⲡⲉⲛ ⲱⲓⲕ ⲛ ⲧⲉⲣⲁⲥ ⲧ ⲁⲁ
ⲛⲓϧ ⲛⲁⲛ ⲁⲓ ϥⲟⲟⲩ ⲟⲩⲟϩ ⲭⲁⲛ ⲛⲉⲧⲉⲣⲟⲛ ⲛⲁⲛ ⲉⲃ
ⲟⲗ ⲁⲫⲣⲏ ϯ ⲛ ⲱ ⲛ ⲧ ⲉⲛ ⲭ ⲱ ⲉⲃ ⲟⲗ ⲛ ⲛⲏ ⲉⲧⲉ-
ⲟⲩⲟⲛ ⲛ ⲉⲣ ⲧ ⲉⲛ ⲁⲟⲩ ⲉⲛ ⲓⲡⲣⲁⲥ ⲙⲟⲥ ⲁⲗⲗⲁ
ⲛⲁ ⲅ ⲙ ⲉⲛ ⲉⲃ ⲟⲗ ϧⲉⲛ ⲡⲓⲡⲉⲧ ϩ ⲱ ⲟⲩ ⲡⲉⲛⲓ-

Pica Æthiopic.

 አቡኅ፡ ዘበሰማያት፡ ይትቀደስ፡ ስምከ፡፡ ተመጻእ፡ መንግ
ሥትከ፡፡ ይኩኅ፡ ፈቃድከ፡ በከመ፡ በሰማይ፡ ወበምድርኒ፡፡
ሲሳየ፡ ዘለለ፡ ዕለተ፡ ሀበነ፡ ዮም፡ ኅድግ፡ ለነ፡ አበሳነ፡
ከመ፡ ንሕነኒ፡ ንኅድግ፡ ለአ፡ አበሰ፡ ለነ፡ ወኢታብአነ፡
ዎስተ፡ መንሱተ፡ አላ፡ አድኅነነ፡ ወባልሕነ፡ አምኲሉ፡
እኩይ፡፡ እስመ፡ ዚአከ፡ ይእቲ፡ መንግሥት፡ ኃይል፡ ወስብ
ሐት፡ ለዓለም፡ ዓለም፡ አሜን፡፡ አቡኅ፡ ዘበሰማያት፡
ተቀደስ፡ ስምከ፡፡ ተመጻእ፡ መንግሥትከ፡ ይኩኅ፡ ፈቃድ

Etruscan.

ᛖᛋ ᛏᛈ ᛏᛈ ᛗᛖᛏᛗᛖᛁᛋ ᛏᛈᛏᛘᛏᛖᛉ ᛋᛈᛈᛉᛏᛏᛉᛈ
ᛈᛘᛑᛑ ᛖᛏ ᛈᛏᛘᛏᛚ ᛏᛈᛗ ᛏᛈᛉᛉᛉᛑ ᛈᛈᛉᛏ
ᛁᛉᛑ ᛉᛈᛗᛈᛑ ᛏᛖᛖ ᛗᛏᛈᛑᛖ ᛉᛈᛉ ᛑᛉ ᛏᛑᛘᛖ
ᛏᛗᛖ ᛈᛖᛉᛉᛏ ᛉᛘ ᛗᛈᛈᛑ ᛑᛈ ᛖᛑᛑᛈ ᛖᛈᛑᛈᛉ
ᛈᛈ ᛗᛑᛖᛏ ᛈᛑ ᛈᛖᛈᛈᛘ ᛉᛈᛘ ᚹᛏ ᛗᛑᛈᛑᛉ

English Saxon.

Fæðeр uрe þu þe eaрt on heoꝝenum. Sı þın
nama ᵹehalᵹoꝺ. To-becume þın рıce. Leрuꝝðe þın
pılla on eoꝛþan. ꞃpa ꞃpa on heo-
ꝛenum. Uꞃne ꝺæᵹhꝝamlıcan hlaꝝ ꞃẏle uꞃ
to ꝺæᵹ. Anꝺ ꝼoꞃᵹyꝝ uꞃ uꞃe ᵹẏltaꞃ. ꞃpa ꞃ-
pa þe ꝼoꞃᵹıꝝað uꞃum ᵹẏltenꝺum. Anꝺ ne
ᵹelæꝺꝺe þu uꞃ on coꞃtnunᵹe. ac alẏꞃ uꞃ oꝝ

Pica Saxon.

Fæðeр uрe þu þe eaрt on heoꝝenum. Sı þın nama ᵹehalᵹoꝺ. To-becume þın рıce. Leрuꝝðe þın
pılla on eoꝛþan. ꞃpa ꞃpa on heoꝛenum. Uꞃne ꝺæᵹhꝝamlıcan hlaꝝ ꞃẏle uꞃ to ꝺæᵹ. Anꝺ ꝼoꞃᵹyꝝ uꞃ
uꞃe ᵹẏltaꞃ. ꞃpa ꞃpa þe ꝼoꞃᵹıꝝað uꞃum ᵹẏltenꝺ-
ꝺum. Anꝺ ne ᵹelæꝺꝺe þu uꞃ on coꞃtnunᵹe. ac

Long Primer Saxon.

Fæðeр uрe þu þe eaрt on heoꝝenum. Sı þın nama ᵹehalᵹoꝺ.
To-becume þın рıce. Leрuꝝðe þın pılla on eoꝛþan. ꞃpa ꞃpa
on heoꝛenum. Uꞃne ꝺæᵹhꝝamlıcan hlaꝝ ꞃẏle uꞃ to ꝺæᵹ.
Anꝺ ꝼoꞃᵹyꝝ uꞃ uꞃe ᵹẏltaꞃ. ꞃpa ꞃpa þe ꝼoꞃᵹıꝝað uꞃum ᵹẏltenꝺum. Anꝺ ne ᵹelæꝺꝺe þu uꞃ on coꞃtnunᵹe. ac alẏꞃ uꞃ

Brevier Saxon.

Fæðeр uрe þu þe eaрt on heoꝝenum. Sı þın nama ᵹehalᵹoꝺ. To-becume
þın рıce. Leрuꝝðe þın pılla on eoꝛþan. ꞃpa ꞃpa on heoꝛenum. Uꞃne
ꝺæᵹhꝝamlıcan hlaꝝ ꞃẏle uꞃ to ꝺæᵹ. Anꝺ ꝼoꞃᵹyꝝ uꞃ uꞃe ᵹẏltaꞃ. ꞃpa ꞃpa
þe ꝼoꞃᵹıꝝað uꞃum ᵹẏltenꝺum. Anꝺ ne ᵹelæꝺꝺe þu uꞃ on coꞃtnunᵹe. ac
alẏꞃ uꞃ oꝝ ẏꝝele. So ꝺlıce. Fæðeр uрe þu þe eaрt on heoꝝenum. Sı þ-

Two-Line Great-Primer Black.

And be it further he

Double Pica Black.

And be it further hereby ena-cted, That the Mayors, Bai-

Great Primer Black.

And be it further hereby enacted, That the Mayors, Bailiffs, or o-

English Black.

And be it further hereby enacted, That the Mayors, Bailiffs, or other head Officers of every
Town and place corporate, and City within

English Black. No 2.

And be it further hereby enacted, That the
Mayors, Bailiffs, or other head Officers of
every Town and place corporate, and City

Pica Black.

And be it further hereby enacted, That the Mayors, Bailiffs, or other head Officers of every
Town and place corporate, and City within

Pica Black. No 2.

And be it further hereby enacted, That the Mayors,
Bailiffs, or other head Officers of every Town and
place corporate, and City within this Realm, being

Small Pica Black.

And be it further hereby enacted, That the Mayors,
Bailiffs, or other head Officers of every Town and
place corporate, and City within this Realm, being

Long Primer Black.

And be it further hereby enacted, That the Mayors, Bailiffs, or o-
ther head Officers of every Town and place corporate, and City within this Realm, being Justice or Justices of Peace, shall have the same
authority by vertue of this Act, within the limits and precincts of their

Brevier Black.

And be it further hereby enacted, That the Mayors, Bailiffs, or other head
Officers of every Town and place corporate, and City within this Realm,
being Justice or Justices of Peace, shall have the same authority by vertue
of this Act, within the limits and precincts of their Jurisdictions, as well our
of Sessions, as at their Sessions, if they hold any, as is herein limited, pre-
scribed and appointed to Justices of the Peace of the County, or any two

1785, Specimen of Printing Types,
William Caslon, London

At the age of 13, William Caslon (1692–1766) was apprenticed to a London engraver and in 1718 established his own engraving business. After beginning a type foundry two years later, the bookbinder John Watts engaged him to design and cast typefaces for his bindings. William Bowyer, an eminent London printer, noticed one of these books, and this was the beginning of the most successful English type foundries at that time. Initially, Watts, Bowyer, and his son-in-law James Bettenham, also a printer, backed Caslon financially. In 1720, his first year as a type founder, Caslon produced a new typeface for the Society for the Propagation of Christian Knowledge to be used for a Bible in Arabic. He printed a sample page to market the Arabic type and on the flyer printed his name in a typeface design that would become the

extremely old specimen, after hemming and hawing for more than a year, in the hope that no other interested party would appear who was prepared to buy it without negotiating the price. I went to fetch the specimen myself, in this case from London. You don't entrust something like that to the post. It was the 1628 Brogiotti, the Stampa Vaticana. The significance of this old specimen is demonstrated by the fact that a facsimile edition was produced. I can summarize a few of the specimens in my possession of which facsimiles exist: the 1742 Claude Lamesle, the 1773 Du Sieur Delacologne, and the Enschedé specimens from 1768 and 1773. Further 18th-Century specimens in my collection include the 1748 Enschedé, the 1764 Fournier, the 1740 Louis Luce, the 1778 Gillé, the specimen by J. de Groot of The Hague from 1781, the 1783 and 1789 Wilsons, the 1785 Caslon—with 21 pages of wonderful, ingenious applications of flowers—the 1787 Fry, and the 1799 specimen from Imprenta Real in Madrid. I also have a number of lovely 19th-Century specimens by, for example, Bodoni (1818), Didot (1819), and Fry (1824). It is a fair number for a private individual, but only a fraction of what they have in public collections. There are major collections of this sort in, for example, the Bibliothèque nationale in Paris, Amsterdam's university library (including the Tetterode collection and the Royal Society of the Dutch Book Trade library), the St. Bride Printing Library, and the Newberry Library in Chicago. I, myself, have quite a few old Caslon and Figgins specimens, but if I consult the St. Bride Foundation catalog from 1919 (then already almost 1,000 pages), I count 70 Caslon specimens, primarily from the 19th Century, and 31 Figgins specimens.

One special example in my collection is a Bodoni Greek specimen, which is unusual in that the first name, Giambatista, is spelled with two *t*'s rather than three (the typical spelling is Giambattista). Each of the 28 pages, the letters ascending in size, has its own unique typeface. The specimen was published in 1788, the year in which his most important specimen, *Serie di majuscole*, from which Greek is derived, appeared. In Birrell & Garnett's exemplary sales catalog of famous typefounders' specimens (1928), the slim volume is referred to as "extremely rare," with a price of 15 guineas (the aforementioned Vaticana, Lamesle, and Enschedé are offered for sale at 15 to 18 guineas). I bought Bodoni's specimen at a Beijers auction for considerably more. The Parisian publisher and bibliophile Renouard once said of Bodoni, "In the evenings, conversing with his friends and in distinguished company, during meals, he was always busy with his typefaces, justifying a matrix, filing a die, designing a capital."

I find the 19th-Century book letters rather dull; this is primarily the realm of Didot and Bodoni. A Turlot specimen from around 1885, published in Paris, for example, has 27 pages of 8-point typefaces and they all look practically the same, each just a tiny bit smaller or larger or fractionally different in thickness from the next. I can't see the point. But the display letter, on the other hand. … I already sang the praises of those thousands of Victorian typefaces and their infinite variety above: classic, decadent, chic, touching, hideous, course or refined, straight or italic, *egyptiennes, américaines, italiennes, syriennes, elzéviriennes, babyloniennes, pompéiennes, japonaises, milanaises, orientales, latines*, letters in two colors, innumerable *fantaisies, Zierschriften, Grotesken und Antiquas, Fraktur-Schriften, Rustic* (treebranch letters) … the list is endless. And then there are the *filets, vignettes, lettrines, coins, ornements, Zierleisten, Polytypen, Untergrunde, Einfassungen*, and books full of *Messinglinien*.

Around 1820, heavy competition arrived in the form of lithography. While the book printers, with their rigid, rectangular blocks of lead, were limited in their possibilities, lithographic draftsmen could put any design onto a plate, as they did for stocks and bonds, calligraphic visiting and business cards, calendars, and other commercial printing work. I have a number of examples of these in my collection. In their fight to compete with lithographers, typefounders devised ways of setting lead lines diagonally or in a circle and engraved more and prettier ornaments. I already mentioned the 1862 Charles Derriey, which measures more than 40 x 30 centimeters. The first part, "Spécimen," shows the vignettes. These are wonderful designs, sometimes for two- or three-color printing. Then come the *"Caractères ornés,"* the *"Trais de plumes,"* the sophisticated *"Coins composés, filets, passe-partouts,"* and so forth. The second part, "Album," demonstrates applications. This is so magnificent, so stylish, and in such delicate colors that I can only describe it in superlatives. And to think that it was all printed on a hand press: a tremendous feat, considering the wide spectrum of colors. I have one other comparable specimen: The one from the Imprimerie Royale from 1845 also contains such an album. If you have ever used a setting stick, you will realize how terribly complicated it must have been to produce those pieces of printing. The competition with lithography also led to ridiculous abnormalities and unnatural typography.

So where did I find all those extraordinary type specimens? Well, I was always a good customer of the antiquarian bookseller Frits Knuf (Vendôme, France), one of the few specializing in bibliography in the broadest sense.

popular style now known as Caslon Old Style. Caslon then cast a number of nonroman and exotic styles, including Coptic, Armenian, Etruscan, Hebrew, and Caslon Gothic, the latter being his version of Old English or black letters. In 1734, Caslon published the first catalog for his type foundry, presenting a total of 38 typefaces. He then moved to the Chriswell Street Foundry, where his son and generations after him would continue the business for over 120 years.

William Caslon (1692–1766) trat im Alter von 13 Jahren bei einem Londoner Graveur in die Lehre, 1718 machte er sich mit einem eigenen Graveurbetrieb selbstständig. Nach der Eröffnung einer Schriftgießerei zwei Jahre darauf erhielt er von dem Buchbinder John Watts den Auftrag, Schriften für dessen Bucheinbände zu entwerfen und zu gießen. Auf eines dieser Bücher wurde der bedeutende Londoner Drucker William Bowyer aufmerk-

sam, womit die Geschichte einer der erfolgreichsten englischen Schriftgießereien der damaligen Zeit begann. Bowyer und Watts sowie Bowyers ebenfalls im Druckgewerbe tätiger Schwiegersohn, James Bettenham, boten Caslon in der Frühphase seines Gewerbes finanzielle Unterstützung. Im Jahr 1720, seinem ersten Geschäftsjahr als Schriftgießer, fertigte Caslon für die *Society for the Propagation of Christian Knowledge* eine neue Schrift für eine arabische Ausgabe der Bibel an. Zur Vermarktung dieser arabischen Schrift stellte er ein Musterblatt her, auf dem sich sein eigener Name in einem Stil abgedruckt findet, der heute als Caslon Old Style geläufig ist. In der Folgezeit goss Caslon eine Reihe exotischer, nichtlateinischer Entwürfe, darunter koptische, armenische, etruskische und hebräische Schriften, sowie die Caslon Gothic, Letztere eine Variante jener Schriftarten, die man als Old English oder „black letters" (Frakturschrift) bezeich-

net. Am neuen Standort des Unternehmens in der Chiswell Street führten nach Caslons Tod sein Sohn und dessen Nachfolgegenerationen das Geschäft noch mehr als 120 Jahre lang fort.

À 13 ans, William Caslon (1692–1766) devient apprenti chez un graveur de Londres. Il s'installe comme graveur indépendant en 1718, et, deux ans plus tard, ouvre sa propre fonderie de caractères. C'est le relieur John Watts qui lui demande de dessiner et de fondre des caractères pour ses couvertures de livres. William Bowyer, célèbre imprimeur londonien, remarque un de ses livres et c'est le démarrage de l'une des plus florissantes fonderies de caractères d'Angleterre. À ses débuts, Caslon reçoit le soutien financier de Watts, Bowyer, et de son gendre James Bettenham, également imprimeur. En 1720, la première année de la fonderie, il crée une nouvelle police de caractères pour la SPCK (Société pour

la promotion du savoir chrétien) pour l'impression d'une Bible en arabe. Pour pouvoir vendre cette police arabe à d'autres imprimeurs, il imprime une page d'échantillon sur laquelle son nom s'étale en caractères qui sont à l'origine de la célèbre police connue aujourd'hui sous le nom de Caslon Old Style. Caslon grave ensuite un certain nombre de caractères non romains et exotiques comme les Coptic, Armenian, Etruscan, Hebrew et Caslon Gothic, ce dernier étant sa version de Old English. En 1734, Caslon publie le premier catalogue de la fonderie qui présente un total de 38 caractères. Il déménage ensuite sa fonderie sur Chiswell Street, d'où son fils et plusieurs générations après lui dirigèrent l'affaire familiale pendant plus de 120 ans.

Through Knuf's bookshop, I acquired specimens from the G. W. Ovink library, for example. In England, I bought the Lamesle from Tony Appleton. Other suppliers were Keith Hogg, Questor Rare Books, S. P. Tuohy, Barry McKay, and the London antiquarian booksellers Marlborough, Maggs, and Quaritch. There are a couple of booksellers in Germany who sometimes have a reasonable *Buchwesen* range. In America, I have a good relationship with Bob Fleck of Oak Knoll, and the Delacologne specimen came from Kraus in New York. With a lot of rummaging and a bit of luck, I sometimes find something at an antiquarian book fair, a book market, or a collectors' fair. And then there are the Dutch auctions, such as Bubb Kuyper's. Sometimes I buy a whole stack for a single book I'm missing. Once or twice on a viewing day, I've left a note in such a pile, after which the buyer has contacted me and I've been able to purchase the desired item.

Naturally, with the advent of the Internet, I've also started looking for type specimens online. I've bought them from booksellers in places from Switzerland to Sweden, via their online catalogs.

In the early 1980s, the famous Parisian antiquarian bookseller Jammes published a typography catalog. This included the library of the ancient, bankrupt type foundry Deberny & Peignot, with more than 400 chiefly unusual and rare specimens. The prices were high and, at that moment, there was no way I could even think of buying anything. With a lump in my throat, I laid the catalog aside. It was not until several years later that I was able to purchase a few specimens from this wonderful Jammes catalog. It was of some consolation to me that, before the catalog was released, various pieces had already been offered to the Bibliothèque nationale, the St. Bride Printing Library (which had to draw on special funds from the British Library), and the Newberry Library. The Taylor Institution in Oxford had also bought a number of important items. It was rather a disappointment for me, but a large proportion of the type specimens described had already found a good home even before the catalog came out.

Incidentally, the Jammes catalog reminds me of one kind of type specimen that doesn't interest me: the smoke impression. If a letter engraver wanted to make an impression of a die, he did it not with ink, but with soot from a smoking candle, which gives an especially sharp impression.

In his bibliography *Die deutsche Schriftgießerei* (1923), Oscar Jolles mentions specimens from some 120 19th-Century type foundries. There were far more, though, such as small in-house foundries affiliated with a printer.

I imagine they must all have produced type specimens at some time, but what has happened to them? Some are in libraries and archives, perhaps, but an awful lot must have been lost in World War II alone. And we all know the stories of printers and other firms moving and clearing out their attics and archives. It wasn't any different in the 19th Century. Personally, I have specimens from some 60 German foundries, but that's counting the single sheets. I've never found anything from the others in any antiquarian booksellers' catalogs. *Buchdruckschriften im 20. Jahrhundert* (1995) says there were 73 type foundries in Germany in 1889; this number diminished drastically in the 20th Century due to mergers and takeovers. More recently, between the wars, there was a vast range of new typefaces created, and printing runs of 10,000 were not unusual for advertising work. Nevertheless, most specimens from that time are now rare, having been lost during World War II. Hans Adolf Halbey writes in his book, *Karl Klingspor, Leben und Werk* (1991), that the Klingspor foundry was almost entirely obliterated by bombing in March 1944. Some 200 tons of type, the print shop, tens of thousands of type specimens and other publications, designs, and 120 files of correspondence with artists were lost.

In general, it's not at all easy to date specimens. Some dutifully state the year in the preliminary pages, such as one specimen from Wimble & Co., New Zealand, dated July 1, 1928, which happens to be my date of birth. To date most specimens, however, you have to wade through typographical literature, searching for references. Sometimes you can find a clue in the specimen itself: a dated medal or—for script letters—a sample letter with a date, a dated invitation for a party, or a wine list.

I can estimate the period from which a specimen stems fairly well on the basis of the type and style. But one can be gravely mistaken if, for example, a printer in the 1930s was still using all the Art Nouveau ornaments and Victorian letters. Berthold made it easy and numbered his specimens. The Journal-Antiqua specimen, for example, Heft 198, was produced around 1920. And the Boulevard Probe 448 originates from around 1960. Schelter & Giesecke did the same. Woellmer numbered his pages consecutively. In his *Brokat-Einfassung* specimen from around 1902, for example, the pages are numbered 1324–1331, and, in the *Deutsche Reichsschrift* specimen from around 1920, 6974–6996.

Incidentally, in German type specimens from the years preceding World War II, one comes across the odd National Socialist (Nazi) text and—here and there—a swastika. One of Trennert's specimens, for the

Jan Tholenaar

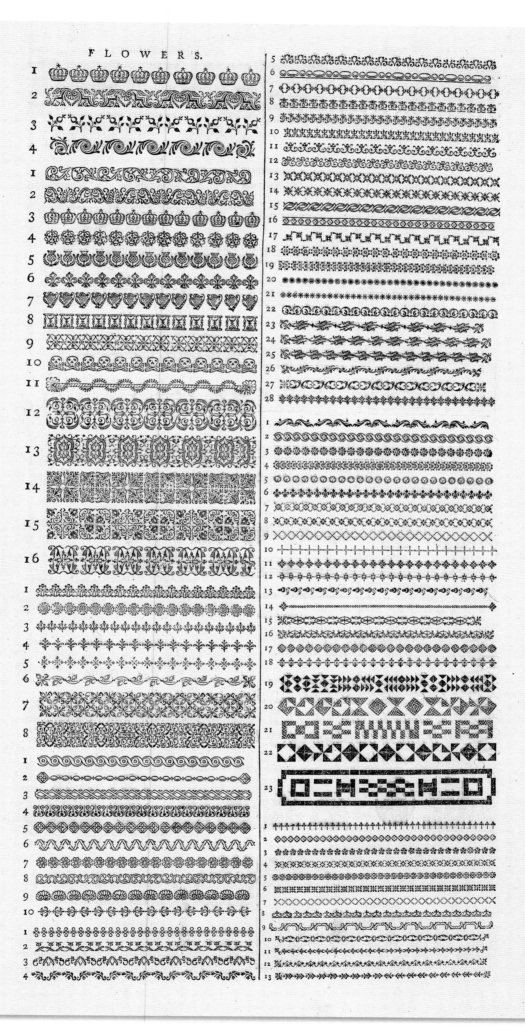

FLOWERS.

typeface Blizzard, from around 1938, expressly uses *Heil Hitler* to demonstrate the type.

Until the beginning of the 20th Century, the names of only a handful of famous type designers, such as Garamond, Bodoni, and Fournier, were known. The thousands of typefaces introduced by foundries in the 19th Century were designed and engraved by anonymous workers. In type catalogs, these are referred to as "*im Hause*" or "*Hausschnitt.*" It was Klingspor, in particular, who attracted and credited famous designers in the early 20th Century: Otto Eckmann, Rudolf Koch, Walter Tiemann, Imre Reiner, and so forth. Bauer engaged the services of Heinrich Wieynk, F. H. Ehmcke, Lucian Bernhard, E. R. Weiss, Paul Renner (designer of the Futura typeface), and F. H. Ernst Schneidler, for example. Berthold employed designers such as Louis Oppenheim, Georg Trump, and Herbert Bayer (of the Bauhaus). Important designers also worked for the Ludwig und Mayer type foundry, including Heinrich Jost, J. Erbar, and J. V. Cissarz. Georg Belwe and Jan Tschichold designed for Schelter & Giesecke, and F. W. Kleukens and Hermann Zapf for Stempel. Some designed type for more than one firm. The specimens devoted to these designs are generally typographical tours de force and little gems of the printing art.

It is indeed so that, for a large part of the 19th and 20th Centuries, the Germans were trendsetters in this area. But in other countries, too, there were excellent designers working for type foundries. Georges Auriol and E. Grasset worked for Peignot, for example; A. M. Cassandre and Adrian Frutiger for Deberny & Peignot; Roger Excoffon for Olive; Aldo Novarese for Nebiolo; Warren Chappell and Morris F. Benton for American Type Founders; Rudolph Ruzicka, W. A. Dwiggins, and Walter Tracy for Linotype; and F. W. Goudy, Bruce Rogers, Berthold Wolpe, and Eric Gill for Monotype. In the Netherlands, in the 20th Century, S. H. de Roos and Dick Dooijes were employed by Lettergieterij Amsterdam, and J. van Krimpen and S. L. Hartz worked for Enschedé.

I would like to mention a number of type specimens in my collection that I consider unusual for one reason or another. I have a specimen dating from 1832 from the F. Dresler und Rost-Fingerlin foundry in Frankfurt, which was set up five years earlier, the successor to the 18th-Century Schleussnersche Schriftgießerei. Later in the century, they were taken over by Flinsch, which was swallowed up by Bauersche Gießerei.

The publications produced by Typis Sacrae Congregationis de Propaganda Fide in Rome, established in 1626 with the intention of spreading

the Christian faith among the peoples of the East, are an entirely different kettle of fish. These printers operated in the 17th and 18th centuries, and it is with them that Bodoni learned his trade. They cut exotic letters for their

Around 1820, type foundries received fierce competition in the form of lithography. While the book printers, with their rigid, rectangular blocks of lead, were limited in their possibilities, lithographic draftsmen could put any design onto a plate, as they did for stocks and bonds, calligraphic visiting and business cards, calendars, and other commercial printing work.

publications: Coptic, Tibetan, Persian, and so forth. Some of them were foreign-language grammar textbooks with the Lord's Prayer in that language. In 1798, the typefaces were transferred to Paris, where, in 1805, the Lord's Prayer was published in 150 languages as the Pope's homage to Napoleon on the occasion of his coronation. Many faces are still in the Imprimerie Nationale. I have 14 of these publications, dated from 1629 to 1789.

Edmund Fry should also be mentioned in this context. His 1787 specimen includes Hebrew, Greek, Ethiopian, Samaritan, Arabic, Persian, Turkish, Tartar, and Malay. In 1799, he published *Pantographia*, a work of 320 pages containing accurate representations with explanations of all the known alphabets of the world. He cut most of the typefaces for this publication himself.

The first major type specimen from the Schelter & Giesecke type foundry, established in 1819, was published in 1836. In their 1894 commemorative book, I read that, in the early 19th Century, a good type caster could cast 5,000 to 6,000 letters a day by hand! The number Friedrich Bauer mentions in his *Chronik der Schriftgießereien* (1928) is 2,000 to 4,000. After the invention of the casting machine in the mid-19th Century, the speed increased six-fold.

Proben aus der Schriftgiesserey der Andreäischen Buchhandlung, published in 1834 in Frankfurt am Main, is also rare. On the title page, an announcement reads that, as of July 1, 1839, the business has been taken over by Benjamin Krebs's Schriftgießerei, Buch-, Congrève- und Steindruckerei. And so this foundry, started in 1581 by Johann Wechsel, moved forth into the 20th Century.

From the same period is a specimen by Eduard Haenel (1837), from shortly before his foundry in Magdeburg was destroyed by fire; he continued his business in Berlin.

German foundries often had a branch in either Moscow or St. Petersburg to serve the Russian market. I have a large broadsheet Berthold specimen, produced toward the end of the 19th Century, entirely in Russian, with extensive examples in many colors. Also from Berthold is a Hebrew specimen from 1924—reading from back to front, naturally—with various faces and wonderful color illustrations. In 1925, a similar specimen was published in Eastern languages, including Arabic, Turkish, and Hindi.

In 1990, another lead-set type specimen was published: *A Miscellany of Type*. This broadsheet specimen is printed on 148 pages of heavy, mold-made paper and is a bibliophilic publication (540 numbered copies) by the English Whittington Press, printers and publishers of the fabulous *Matrix* yearbook. *A Miscellany of Type* is an exemplary model of printing, with wood engravings and other illustrations in color taken from other publications by this press.

When I bought it, the book *Ornamented Types*, printed and published by Ian Mortimer in London, was not to be found in any public collection in the Netherlands. It contains impressions of decorated wooden pattern letters that came from the London typefounder Pouchée in the early 19th Century. In 1936, the Monotype Corporation bought up this material from the liquidated Caslon foundry. It survived the bombing during the war and is now in the St. Bride Printing Library. It took years to print the 200 copies on an old hand press. The book consists of 24 alphabets—altogether 45 pages—printed on 170-gram Zerkall-Bütten (53 x 38 centimeters). The whole thing comes in a slipcase, with an introduction by James Mosley. This specimen is expensive, which is not surprising considering the immense amount of work involved. It is worth every penny.

A specimen from the Gurajati Type Foundry in Bombay, established in 1900, contains more than 400 pages in many colors and was published in a run of 10,000 copies. An article on this piece of work in *Matrix* 2 says that they started it in 1926, and, as far as production and technical quality were concerned, it was intended to "outdo" the Western foundries. An experienced printer and display setter were taken on and a new German press was acquired; art printing paper was bought in America, and ink was purchased from Manders in England. The job was completed in 1937—a production time of 11 years, which is why I don't want to make too much of an issue of that "outdoing."

There are also small specimens from private presses. I paid a lot of money for one simple sheet: "Specimens of Type Used at The Ashendene Press." What is special about it is that it includes two letters designed and cut for Ashendene's owner, Mr. Hornby: Subiaco and Ptolemy. A specimen by Hans Mardersteig for Monotype (1928) features Pastonchi, specially cut for a new series of Italian classics. This appeared in a bibliophile edition of 200, hand-printed on Fabriano and with pasted-in models.

In this context, the type specimens of Paul Hayden Duensing (who cut punches and founded type himself) are worth a mention, as are the Harrisfeldwegpresse, the Alembic Press, a really sweet little book from the Overbrook Press (1934), the Harbor Press, the Kit-Cat Press, the Sandelswood

Plakathände.

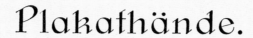

Nr. 1085. Per Stück fl. 1.50.   Nr. 1084. Per Stück fl. 1.—.

Nr. 1083. Per Stück 60 kr.

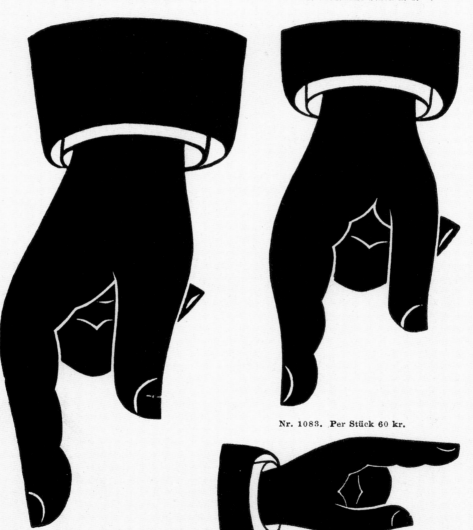

J. H. Rust & Co. in Wien.

1887, Schriftproben, *Schriftgiesserei und mechanische Werkstätte J. H. Rust & Co.,* Vienna

Press, and Philippsberger Werkstatt, not forgetting Charles Whitehouse of Edition Seefeld. This last press issued, for example, a sheet of Jan van Krimpen's Romanée, with a beautiful classic design, hand-printed on a Kniehebelpresse on mold-made paper with a rough surface. The paper was moistened before printing, and the result is fabulous: The small, narrow 10-point italics are incredibly sharp, really black, and yet not too bold. What makes it special is that almost three-dimensional effect, the relief you don't get with offset. It brings it home to me that the disappearance of lead was a heavy, irretrievable loss to the art of printing.

Naturally, the marginal Dutch printers should not be omitted here: De Vergulde Maatlat, Eric van der Wal, Ter Lugt Pers, De Vier Seizoenen, Willem Muilenburg, Triona Pers, Exponent, Elze ter Harkel, Tuinwijkpers (Rosart), Castanha Pers (Garamond), and Drukschuur Blaricum. One highly original example is De Dwarsbomen (Gert van Oortmerssen). The basic item is made from hard material, and the separate spine, which weighs a kilo, is cast in recycled lead type. The Surrealist artist Johannes Moesman also designed a typeface, Petronius. It was first used in 1975 in a type specimen. I don't know whether this typeface has ever been used again.

The Curwen Press, the renowned printers of *The Fleuron,* commissioned Oliver Simon to compile and design a type specimen in 1928. The specimen is expensive, not so much because of the limited edition (135 copies) but because it is so exceptionally beautifully made, with austere, classic design and hand-molded paper with its own watermark. The ornaments and such were specially made for Curwen by artists such as Claud Lovat Fraser, Paul Nash, and Percy Smith. The typefaces were designed by artists such as Rudolf Koch and Jan van Krimpen.

Theodore Low De Vinne (1828–1914) was a well-known New York printer, author of various books on printing, and cofounder and president of the first syndicate of American master printers. I'll mention two specimens of his that I own. He was still associated with the printer Francis Hart when he published a 96-page specimen in 1878, *Specimens of Pointed Texts and Black Letters.* Black letters are what we call gothic letters, and pointed letters are roughly the same thing—they were used for Bibles, but also circulars and such. The specimen contains about 50 typefaces. The second is from the De Vinne Press, from 1891. It contains some 144 pages of book type and would be a boring book, in itself, were it not for the fact that each page features different initials, for which no effort or cost has been spared: varying sizes and designs, most of them in two colors and gold.

Along the same lines is a small-format specimen from 1903, featuring nothing but book typefaces. It was published by the Copenhagen printer Martius Truelsen in an edition of 1,500 *"maskinnummerede"* copies. I was often in Copenhagen and always visited the antiquarian bookseller Busck. I bought the specimen there in 1979 and, a few years later, I bought a second copy. The book has 176 pages, is bound entirely in leather, and is blind-stamped. The quires are not sewn but stapled, and staples can rust. But the inside is beautiful. Each double page is different, with a decorated header to the left and an initial at the beginning of the text, which together form a whole, often pure Art Nouveau. There are wonderful (anonymous) designs in three or four colors and different colors on each page. A total of perhaps 300 colors were used.

My copy of the 1902–03 *Boktryckeri calendar* (with the signature of the printer-publisher, Waldemar Zachrisson, and the dedication "Hommage à Mr. Theo L. De Vinne") features a printed photograph of Martius Truelsen. He tells how he was orphaned at the age of 15 and, from then on, had to fend for himself. At the age of 30, with a few hundred crowns he had earned, he started his own business, and, in 1903, by the age of 50, he was running a printing firm with a workforce of some 50 men. In addition to my two copies of the Truelsen specimen, I have boxes full of fantastic duplicates.

I'd like to mention a few other nice pieces from my collection. Signature, new series, number 5, discussed type specimens. It said of a 1939 specimen from Shenval Press, "printed in superbly black ink, an all too exceptional virtue these days." And I agree wholeheartedly there; black can be beautiful.

A 200-page 1934 specimen from Imprimerie Darantière in Dijon, printed in an edition of 800 copies, features a continuous novel, running through all kinds of fonts, large and small. The pages are beautifully laid out with spacious margins and printed in black and red. What a shame that support colors like that are no longer used these days. One specimen from Buchdruckerei August Hopfer only uses quotes from Goethe. Both specimens are a pleasant change from the stock pattern of endlessly repeated texts.

My 1835 specimen from the Boston Type Foundry is quite old by American standards. It contains more than 200 pages, printed on one side. Half are devoted to ornaments (wood engravings), including household items and cattle, and there are foldouts with steamboats and paddle steamers, sailing ships and horses with coaches.

At the end of the 19th Century, 11 major American foundries decided to

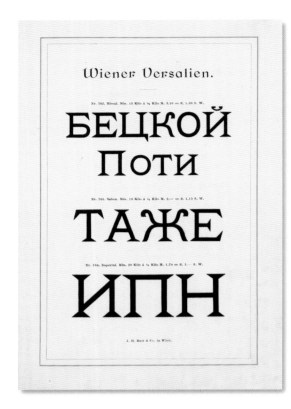

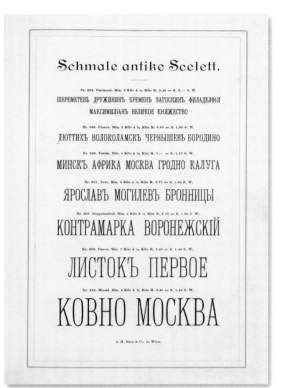

collaborate, resulting in the establishment of the American Type Founders. Their first type specimen, a heavy tome of more than 800 pages, appeared in 1896.

In the *Hauptprobe*, you can see that toward the end of the 19th Century special attention was paid to titles and subheadings, which were presented with colorful settings, in many hues, and with lavish use of ornaments, many of them very lovely. All this must have stemmed from striving to compete with lithography—a successful effort, it seems, as these specimens are sometimes referred to in the catalogs of antiquarian booksellers and auction houses as chromolithos, although the relief on the back clearly indicates letterpress.

In the early 19th Century, at the age of 66, the French letter engraver Henri Didot did the almost impossible by engraving a microscopically tiny 2.5-point type, the smallest ever made. Later, the punches and matrices ended up in the possession of Johannes Enschedé & Zonen, who, in 1861, printed the Dutch constitution, a booklet measuring 4.5 x 6.5 centimeters. I bought one of the last copies at the Haarlem train station. Various firms, including Enschedé, were selling off their remainders on the occasion of an antiquarian book fair. Henri Didot was also the inventor of the polyamatype, a mold with which you could cast up to 120 small letters at a time. His cousin, Pierre Didot, who had inherited a printer's press, also developed into a letter engraver. In 1819, his first specimen, *Spécimen des nouveaux caractères de la fonderie etc.*, was published. The texts are poems from his own hand.

In 19th-Century specimens from countries such as Germany, the Netherlands, and America, the same ornaments, wood engravings, and such are often found. You might wonder whether all of that was actually organized, with contracts and royalties. Stereotypy had been in use for some time already, and, from roughly 1840 onwards, it was easy to copy things galvanically. Copyright was not protected in those days. (Mind you, I read somewhere that, these days, 80 percent of software is used illegally …)

Specimens including first showings of types are especially valuable to collectors. I have one of Centaur, for example, with a preface by the designer, Bruce Rogers; one of van Krimpen's Lutetia; and one featuring Cartier (1966), the first text letter designed in Canada, by Carl Dair.

One also, unfortunately, comes across type specimens on poor-quality paper. Some paper from the second half of the 19th Century has failed to survive the ravages of time and crumbles between your fingers. Sometimes

the quires of books were not sewn but stapled onto a linen strip. This method may have been cheaper, but it was certainly not stronger. After all, the staples rust. Type specimens weighing kilos, even very expensive ones, were sometimes bound in a paper binding. The large Imprimerie Nationale specimen, for example, was bound in fine, delicate *glacé* paper—which is asking for trouble.

But damage can also be the work of vandals. Sometimes pieces have simply been cut out of specimens, despite the request at the front of the book not to do so! A good bookseller will check the volume for such damage and mention it in his catalog. Jammes uses the nice term *fenêtres* (windows) for such holes.

I have an extensive specimen from Gebroeders Hoitsema in Groningen, with the date 1897 on the cover. The unusual thing about this specimen is that the year of purchase, the supplier, and the weight are noted for each type. A clear majority of them are from German foundries, which is perhaps not so astounding, in view of the geographical location. It would be interesting to find out whether the German foundries sent their representatives directly to the Dutch printers. In a few cases, an agent is named: Klinkhardt (Van Meurs), Huck (P. van Dijk), and so forth. It is also interesting to see the mention of smaller Dutch foundries such as G. W. van der Wiel & Onnes and De Boer & Coers. In 1869, the Hoitsema brothers also purchased from Reed and Fox, the late R. Besley & Co, London (two-line English Courthand).

Old specimens from printers are rare. I'll name a few firms from which I have old copies: Bricx in Ostend (around 1787); H. Martin & Comp. (1829), J. Ruys (1908), Pieper & Ipenbuur (1828), and the Stads en Courant drukkerij (1834) in Amsterdam; M. Wijt (1828) and J. W. van Leenhoff (1837) in Rotterdam; B. Henry (1828) in Valenciennes; the university printer Johan Frederik Schultz (1805) in Copenhagen (the second copy, in Copenhagen's Royal Library, was mislaid years ago!); De Bachelier (1842) in Paris; Michael Lindauer (1825) in Munich; Osvalda Lucchini (1853) in Guastalla; Rand and Avery (1867) in Boston—then the second-largest printer in America—and John F. Trow (1856) in New York (from whom I have an example of "rainbow printing," a kind of iris printing).

One showpiece in my collection is a specimen from around 1847 from the Groningen type foundry Van der Veen Oomkens & Van Bakkenes. In the back, printed in color, are "Plates for Congreve printing." This system was intended for printing stocks and bonds in more than one color at a time (in letterpress). This foundry, established in 1843 by Alle van der Veen Oomkens, was taken over in 1857 by Onnes, De Boer & Coers and moved the following year to Arnhem. In 1894, Enschedé took over the matrices. I purchased a compiled Enschedé type specimen from the end of the 19th Century that contains 145 wonderful pages by these type founders from Groningen and Arnhem.

One special specimen from the United States is the 1882 Bruce. It is comparable with the Derriey in its enormous range of borders and decorated letters. There is also a vast array of lovely electrotyped ornaments illustrating professions, shop interiors, trade articles, and so forth. Bound in is a sizable work by De Vinne on the invention of book printing.

Especially unusual are the broadsheet type specimens, all on one sheet. The oldest surviving specimens are largely broadsheets. In the 20th Century, Monotype, for example, produced some creditable work in this format. Highlights include the sheets Stanley Morison made for Monotype, the Pelican Press, and the Cloister Press.

In the 1930s, the firm of Bom was used when the material from a printing firm had to be auctioned, generally due to bankruptcy. I have 75 auction catalogs with the auctioneers' notes. The type up for auction was printed in the catalog—in a single line and without the name, to be sure, but these are nonetheless type specimens.

If you ask anyone which is the oldest surviving printer in the Netherlands, they will probably say Enschedé. But it is, in fact, Van Waesberge. You can read the company history in a type specimen from 1918. Van Waesberge was established more than 400 years ago in Rotterdam.

According to a specimen from 1852, N. Tetterode, later Lettergieterij Amsterdam, also started in Rotterdam. In part two of this specimen, from 1856, Tetterode calls himself an Amsterdam type founder. It was there that he took over the De Passe & Menne foundry (I have their 1843 *Proeve van drukletteren* specimen) in Bloemgracht. In the first supplement, he has pasted his own name over the name of De Passe & Menne. In his early specimens he still used the classic example text, which can also be seen in 18th-Century specimens by Caslon, Fry, Wilson, and Bodoni: "*Quousque tandem abutere, Catilina, patientia nostra?*"

Setting-machine manufacturers also often produced very thick type specimens: Linotype, Intertype, Monotype, and Ludlow. I have a specimen from Typograph. These generally use typefaces licensed from foundries.

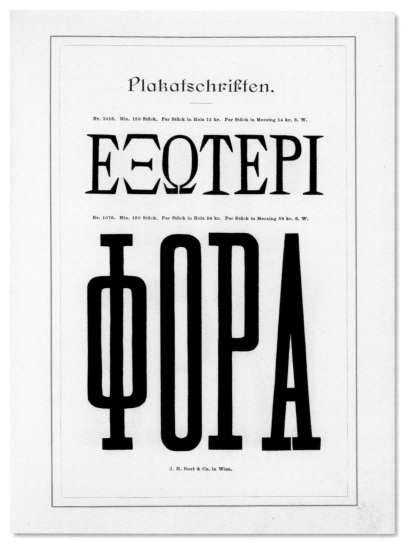

One coincidence: At one point I only had three slim specimens by Heinrich Hoffmeister, who started a type foundry in 1898 in Leipzig. So when a specimen in book form came up for auction in Berlin, I put in a

No.-Zeichen.

Nr. 1 pr. 100 St. M. 1.70 = fl. 1.— ö. W.

№ № № № № № № № № № № № № № №

Nr. 2 pr. 80 St. M. 1.70 = fl. 1.— ö. W.

№ № № № № № № № № № № № № № №

Nr. 3 pr. 60 St. M. 1.70 = fl. 1.— ö. W.

№ № № № № № № № № № №

Nr. 4 pr. 40 St. M. 1.70 = fl. 1.— ö. W.

№ № № № № № № № № №

Nr. 5 pr. 20 St. M. 1.70 = fl. 1.— ö. W.

№ № № № № № № №

Nr. 6 pr. St. 10 Pf. = 06 kr. ö. W.	Nr. 7 pr. St. 15 Pf. = 08 kr. ö. W.
№ № №	№ № №

Nr. 10 pr. St. 10 Pf. = 06 kr. ö. W.	Nr. 11 pr. St. 15 Pf. = 08 kr. ö. W.
№ № №	№ № №

Nr. 8 pr. St.	Nr. 9 pr. St.	Nr. 12 pr. St.	Nr. 13 pr. St.
№	№	№	№
18 Pf. = 10 kr. ö. W.	20 Pf. = 12 kr. ö. W.	18 Pf. = 10 kr. ö. W.	20 Pf. = 12 kr. ö. W

Nr. 14 pr. 60 St. M. 1.70 = fl. 1.— ö. W.	Nr. 15 pr. 40 St. M. 1.70 = fl. 1.— ö. W.
№ № № № № № № № № № №	№ № № № № № № № № №

Nr. 16 pr. 30 St. M. 1.70 = fl. 1.— ö. W.	Nr. 17 pr. 15 St. M. 1.70 = fl. 1.— ö. W.
№ № № №	№ № № №

J. H. Rust & Co. in Wien.

1887, **Schriftproben,** *Schriftgiesserei und mechanische Werkstätte J. H. Rust & Co.,* Vienna

bid and was able to acquire it. The day after I received the specimen by post, I was at the antique fair in Haarlem. And what did I find there? Two bound specimens by Hoffmeister, an earlier one (the first, only containing vignettes) and a later one.

A couple of years ago, I lent some material to the Gutenberg Museum in Mainz for an exhibition of type specimens. On that occasion, I was allowed to browse through the library, and, to my amazement, I found a number of unusual, old, and in some cases rare specimens that the museum staff themselves had hardly been aware of. They also had some unusual things from Dutch foundries from the 19th Century, including specimens from Hendrik Bruyn & Comp., Broese & Comp., Elix & Co., and J. de Groot (1781). Of these I unfortunately have only the de Groot. For the record, all other items mentioned in this book are in my own library.

I'd like to mention one last specimen: that by the typefounder Louis Vernange in Lyon, from 1770, which comprises 64 pages. The three other known copies are all slightly smaller. The bookseller I bought it from told me he had never come across one before in the 35 years of his career.

Well, those are some examples from my own collection. I keep my bound copies in bookshelves, arranged by height, because of the space they take up. The slim specimens are stored in archive boxes, classified by foundry and date. Although everything is recorded in the computer, I sometimes forget and buy one I already have.

The value of type specimens is largely determined by their physical condition. The 1768 Enschedé specimen could fetch tens of thousands of euros; the 1628 Vatican specimen even more. For a good bound specimen over 100 years old, you have to pay hundreds of euros; slim specimens cost around 20 euros, and a nice Rudolf Koch specimen will set you back more than 100 euros. Prices for rare or special things—unusual items such as an 80-page Peter Behrens stitched specimen from 1902 or the 1928 Curwen Press specimen—are slightly higher than average. Also unusual in relation to their peers are the three rare 1833 Andreäische broadsheets I once purchased from Jammes and the double 1926 Ashendene Press sheet I mentioned earlier.

Is there anything else I want? Well, there's quite a list, at the top of which used to be the three Bodoni specimens, *Fregi e majuscole* (1771), *Serie di majuscole* (1788), and *Manuale tipografico* (1818). I now have the last one, and it is the pride of my collection.

Quite a lot has been written about specimens and foundries. The standard works include *Chronik der Schriftgiebereien* by Friedrich Bauer (1928,

first impression 1914), *Les livrets typographiques des fonderies françaises créées avant 1800* by Marius Audin (1964, first impression 1933), *British Type Specimens before 1831* by James Mosley (1984), *Schweizer Stempelschneider und Schriftgiesser* by Albert Bruckner (1943), *Type Foundries of America and Their Catalogs* by Maurice Annenberg (1994, first impression 1975), and, last but not least, *Type Foundries in the Netherlands* by Charles Enschedé, translated and adapted by Harry Carter (1978, first impression 1908).

If you think that lead type is never cut or cast these days, you are mistaken. Not so long ago, the American poet Dan Carr felt he should design his own typeface for his poems and cut the dies himself. An appendix to the aforementioned *Matrix* featured Regulus, which turned out to be a really nice typeface. I immediately wrote to Carr's Golgonooza Letter Foundry & Press to order the bibliophile collection of the first application, asking for a real type specimen.

In the past, setting up a well-stocked hand-setting shop meant a considerable investment. These days, anyone who produces printed matter on the computer can choose from an infinite range of typefaces on the Internet that cost only a couple of euros each. If you buy 10 at the same time, you get a free mountain bike.

The same printing methods were used for 500 years—and, suddenly, it was over, thanks to Mr. Senefelder. Type foundries that made only lead type have disappeared. Some changed with the times and built photosetting machines—sometimes successfully, like Berthold (they had been engraving the matrices for the German Linotype system since 1900), and sometimes with less success, like Deberny & Peignot, who went bankrupt with their Lumitype system. Others already had a sideline; Enschedé, for example, had a print shop, and Lettergieterij Amsterdam dealt in printing machines. The commercial type foundries disappeared, but fortunately there is a foundation in the Netherlands by the name of Stichting Lettergieten that presents the former art of typography. Anyone who loves the old business should support them!

Once, when I was visiting the Amsterdam University library, a librarian casually remarked, "We've got 70 meters of type specimens here." I must have blushed. At home, I took out a tape measure and established that I measured up to perhaps half of that. A lesson in humility.

1922, Arabisch-Türkisch, type specimen
from *D. Stempel*, Frankfurt, Leipzig,
Vienna, Budapest

4,5 Cicero, 54 Punkte ٥٤ پونطو

8 Cicero, 96 Punkte ٩٦ پونطو

6 Cicero, 72 Punkte ٧٢ پونطو

Die Initial-Umrahmungen sind aus Einfassungen zusammengesetzt الدوائر الموجوده حول الحروف مركبة من نقوش مختلفة

Schriffgießerei D. Stempel, Akf.-Gef., Frankfurf am Main, Leipzig, Wien und Budapeff

حروفات دوكمخانه‌سی ، توزیع جدوللر فابریقه‌سی ٭ حکاکلر وحروف‌اتجیار :: د. شته‌مپل آنونیم شرکتی ٭ فرانقفورت ماین ، لایپچیغ ، ویه‌نا و پشته ١٢

Über das Sammeln von Schriftmustern

von Jan Tholenaar
Mit einer Einführung von Caspar Gijzen

*Die Schriftmuster vom Ende
des 19. Jahrhunderts sind wirklich hinreißend;
diese unendliche Vielfalt ist großartig.*

Jan Tholenaars private Schriftmustersammlung ist eine der eindruckvollsten ihrer Art weltweit. Tholenaars persönlichen Vorlieben entsprechend liegt der Schwerpunkt seiner Sammlung auf Mustern aus der Zeit zwischen 1830 und 1930. Einige der vielen Glanzstücke aus diesen 100 Jahren, fantasievolle Schriften und Ornamente unterschiedlichster Form, sind zugleich herausragende druckkünstlerische Werke. Wenn Tholenaar beim Vorführen einiger besonders schöner Stücke ins Schwärmen gerät, kann man kaum anders als mitgerissen sein: „Diese Fülle, diese bezaubernden Farbkombinationen. Und wie komplex das aufgebaut ist – da stecken Wochen an Arbeit drin. Dieses blasse Grün und Braun und das Hellgrau da direkt nebeneinander, ohne dass sich irgendetwas beißt. Schau dir nur an, wie gut das zusammenpasst, unglaublich! Und alles Hochdruck, keine Lithografien. Da kann es schon einmal zu Absonderlichkeiten kommen; zum Beispiel bei diesem Exemplar hier: komplett mit Kupferzeilen gesetzt! Die wurden in Gips befestigt, heutzutage weiß überhaupt niemand mehr, wie so etwas geht. Manchmal stößt man auch auf eine schöne kleine Signatur, die genauso entstanden ist."

Die Beispiele, die Tholenaar vorführt, sind wirklich ausgezeichnet gesetzt, ob es nun die Schrift, Linien oder komplexe Ornamente betrifft. Für das gesamte damals feilgebotene Material wurden handgesetzte und -gedruckte Anwendungsbeispiele erstellt. Tholenaar blättert weiter durch das Buch: „Die Schriftmuster vom Ende des 19. Jahrhunderts sind wirklich hinreißend; diese unendliche Vielfalt ist großartig."

Immer wieder unterstreicht Tholenaar seine Bewunderung für die offenkundige Hingabe, mit der Schriftmuster zu jener Zeit komponiert wurden. Er greift eines heraus, bei dem die Gestaltungskunst des Typografen anhand eines einzelnen Buchstaben vorgeführt wird, und dann ein anderes, das verschiedene Drucktechniken vorführt: Hochdruck, Stich, Offset.

Eine einzige Beschränkung erlegt Tholenaar sich beim Sammeln auf: Die Muster müssen in Blei gesetzt sein. Er besitzt Exemplare von Schriftgießereien und Druckereien, aber auch ein Inserat in einer Zeitschrift etwa kann ein Muster sein. Die Stücke ersteht Tholenaar bei Antiquariaten auf der ganzen Welt. Nach vielen Jahren im Verlagsgeschäft ist er es gewohnt, schwere Bücherkoffer mit sich herumzuschleppen. Natürlich schaut er sich auch eine Vielzahl an Katalogen an; als Beispiel nennt er den berühmten Schriftenkatalog des Antiquariats Jammes: „Man braucht gar nicht erst darüber nachzudenken … Schau dir nur die Preise an. Und die sind alle so. Es war furchtbar, eine richtige Qual, nichts als Schriftmuster."

Manche Muster findet er „amüsant", andere einfach nur „nett". Nicht sonderlich begeistern kann Tholenaar sich indes für die zahllosen im vergangenen Jahrhundert entstandenen Groteskschriften, mit Ausnahme von Paul Renners Futura.

„Aber wenn man einmal all diese viktorianischen Fantasielettern hier etwa mit der perfekten, aber steifen Schweizer Typografie aus der Zeit nach dem Zweiten Weltkrieg vergleicht, sind Erstere doch weitaus attraktiver."

Caspar Gijzen

Schriftmuster zu sammeln ist gar nicht so leicht heutzutage. Sie sind nämlich selten und teuer geworden. Man muss praktisch alles in Antiquariaten oder bei Auktionen erstehen. Das hinterlässt ein ordentliches Loch im Geldbeutel. Ich könnte heute unmöglich mit meiner Sammlung noch einmal ganz bei null anfangen. Wenn ich in eine Buchhandlung gehe (eine Sache, der ich kaum widerstehen kann, egal in welchen Breiten ich mich gerade aufhalte) und mich erkundige, ob sie irgendwelche Schriftmuster dahaben, bekomme ich oft zu hören: „Nein, und wenn ich schon mal eins hereinbekomme, bin ich's auch sofort wieder los. Das scheinen heute alles echte Sammlerstücke zu sein."

Ich erinnere mich noch an eine meiner ersten Erwerbungen, eine Mustersammlung von Schelter & Giesecke aus dem Jahr 1886, die ich bei Kok in der Oude Hoogstraat in Amsterdam gekauft habe.

Meine Liebe zu typografischen Schriften entdeckte ich während meiner Ausbildung an der Amsterdamse Grafische School in der Dintelstraat von 1945 bis 1947. Bei J. Aarden, der für seine Kurse zu den Themen „Neuer Trend" (1920–28, ein Linotypekurs) und „Illustrative Typografie" (1928–34) bekannt war, habe ich Schriftsetzen gelernt. In Möllenkamps Zeichenklasse mühten wir uns endlose Stunden an der Hollandse Mediaeval. Ich werde mein Lebtag nicht vergessen, dass an dem großen A ein kleines Fähnchen hängt. Zum Unterrichtsstoff gehörten Schriften wie Nobel, Romulus, Bodoni, Studio, Libra und Iris. Am liebsten mochte ich die Gravure mit ihren langen Ober- und Unterlängen und die Trajanus.

Ein ganz besonderes Vergnügen war es für mich immer, die Bibliothek der Lettergieterij Amsterdam (die vormalige Schriftgießerei Nicolaas Tetterode in Rotterdam, die später ihren Sitz in die Amsterdamer Bilderdijkstraat verlegte) zu besuchen. Dort bekam ich beispielsweise zum ersten Mal ein Derriey-Muster von 1862 zu Gesicht, wahrscheinlich das schönste, das jemals entstanden ist. Erst Jahre später sollte ich ein solches ergattern.

Bei einem Besuch der St. Bride Printing Library in London lernte ich die *Printers' International Specimen Exchange*-Jahrbücher kennen, von denen ab 1880 16 Ausgaben in Auflagen von 200 bis 450 Exemplaren erschienen.

Vor allem englische Drucker steuerten dazu ihre gelungensten Arbeiten bei, die so der Nachwelt erhalten geblieben sind. Kennzeichnend für die Bücher war ihre aufwendige Satzgestaltung (Kunstdruck), die Verwendung vieler Farben und die Unmenge an Schriften, schöner wie hässlicher. Speziell Drucke aus viktorianischer Zeit reizen mich; manchmal sind sie wirklich hübsch, manchmal sind sie bloß schön ob ihrer Hässlichkeit. Der Jahrbuchidee nahm man sich jedenfalls auch in Deutschland an, und ich darf mich glücklich schätzen, einige Exemplare sowohl aus der englischen als auch aus der deutschen Reihe zu besitzen. Ein ähnliches Produkt holländischer Provenienz ist das *Uitwisseling van kunstdrukwerk in Nederland*, von dem ich den ersten – und zugleich letzten? – Band aus dem Jahr 1893 habe, der nur etwas mehr als 20 Seiten umfasst.

Aufgrund meiner beruflichen Tätigkeit (Buchkoproduktionen) musste ich früher für gewöhnlich viel reisen. Als ich 1963 anlässlich der ersten internationalen Kinderbuchmesse in Bologna war, entdeckte ich in einem Antiquitätengeschäft einen großformatigen Schriftmusterbogen, doppelt gefaltet, von einem Bologneser Drucker. Der Preis, den ich dafür bezahlt habe, mag heute 20 Euro entsprechen – was damals viel Geld für mich war. Das Muster hatte jahrelang in einer Schublade gelegen, bis das Sammeln zu einer großen Mode wurde. Ich schickte eine Fotokopie an die Universität Bologna mit der Bitte um Informationen. Wie sich herausstellte, stammte es von der Druckerfamilie Benacci, die in Bologna im 16. und frühen 17. Jahrhundert aktiv gewesen war. Die Universität teilte mir mit, dass sie zwar viele Musterblätter dieser Dynastie besäße, aber nicht dieses eine. Ich schmeichle mir heute mit dem Gedanken, dass es sich um ein einzigartiges Exemplar und eines der ältesten Schriftmuster überhaupt handelt. Das Antiquariat Herzberger bot mir einen guten Preis für das Stück, aber ich bin froh, dass ich der Versuchung widerstanden habe. Vor ein paar Jahren hatte ich die Gelegenheit, eine extrem seltene Duodezausgabe mit Madrigalen zu erstehen, gedruckt und veröffentlicht zwischen 1588 und 1590 von Alessandro und Vittorio Benacci. Das Werk ist auf skurrile Weise vollgepfropft mit ihren Vignetten. So etwas macht ein Muster erst richtig lebendig.

Im Prinzip sammle ich so ziemlich alles an Schriftmustern, egal aus welchem Land und welcher Zeit. Die einzige Einschränkung besteht darin, dass sie aus der Ära des Bleisatzes stammen müssen. Produziert wurden die Muster von verschiedener Seite: von Schriftgießereien und Druckern sowie von Buchbindern, wobei letztere Gruppe recht klein ist. Die Muster führen Schriften vor, deren Drucklettern aus Blei gegossen oder aus Materialien wie Holz, Messing oder Eisen (für den Hochdruck) gefertigt sind. Ich habe zwar auch ein paar Fotosatzschriftmuster, aber dafür gebe ich nur wenig oder gar nichts aus. In den meisten Fällen sind sie langweilig, wenn nicht sogar hässlich. Aber es gibt natürlich auch Ausnahmen. Ein hübsches Beispiel ist das dreiteilige, von Jost Hochuli entworfene und zweifarbig gedruckte Compugraphic-Muster, das sich durch seine verspielt-humorvolle Verwendung der Schrift auf der rechten Seite auszeichnet.

Schriftmuster gibt es in den verschiedensten Formen und Formaten. Solche, die eine komplette Schriftfamilie vorstellen, haben oft einen festen Einband. Ein extrem umfangreiches Muster ist die 1925 von Stempel herausgebrachte *Hauptprobe*. Mit ihren rund 1200 Seiten ist sie mehr als zehn Zentimeter dick, wiegt sieben Kilo und ist in Halbpergament gebunden. Ebenso gibt es dünnere Ausgaben, die jeweils die besonderen Eigenschaften einer einzelnen Schriftart anpreisen. Häufig sind sie mit Klammern geheftet, manche haben aber auch eine Fadenheftung und einen flexiblen Einband. Vor Jahren habe ich zwei Kisten mit solchen Mustern von dem Buchhändler Horodisch erworben, der sie offensichtlich kurz zuvor bei einer Auktion erstanden hatte. Die Broschüren führen verschiedene Verwendungsarten der jeweiligen Schrift vor und sind oft überaus stilvoll gestaltet, manchmal von den Schriftentwerfern selbst. Auch wurde mit Farbe nicht gespart.

Natürlich trifft man Schriftmuster nicht nur als eigenständige Drucke an, sondern auch als Bestandteil von Unternehmenspublikationen wie den *Typografische Mededeelingen* der Lettergieterij Amsterdam, Johannes Enschedé en Zonens *Letterproef*, Nebiolos *Archivio tipografico*, Schelter & Gieseckes *Typographischen Mitteilungen* oder *La crónica* von Richard Gans in Madrid. Dazu kommen so weltberühmte Publikationen wie *Monotype Recorder* und *Linotype Bulletin*. Außerdem finden sich Schriftmuster in Form von Anzeigen in Branchenzeitschriften wie *Graphicus*, *The British Printer*, *Typographische Jahrbücher*, *Deutscher Buch- und Steindrucker* und den Schweizer *Les archives de l'imprimerie*. In Frankreich existierte in den ersten Jahren des 20. Jahrhunderts eine Gemeinschaftspublikation der französischen Schriftgießereien, die den Titel *La fonderie typographique* trug. Präsentiert wurden prächtige Beispiele sämtlicher neuer Schriften sowie Ornamente und dergleichen, oftmals reinster Art Nouveau. In Deutschland erschien Mitte des 19. Jahrhunderts das *Journal für Buchdruckerkunst, Schriftgießerei und die verwandten Fächer*, und im späteren 19. Jahrhundert das *Archiv für Buchdruckerkunst und verwandte Geschäftszweige*. Darin waren zahllose Einlagen einge-

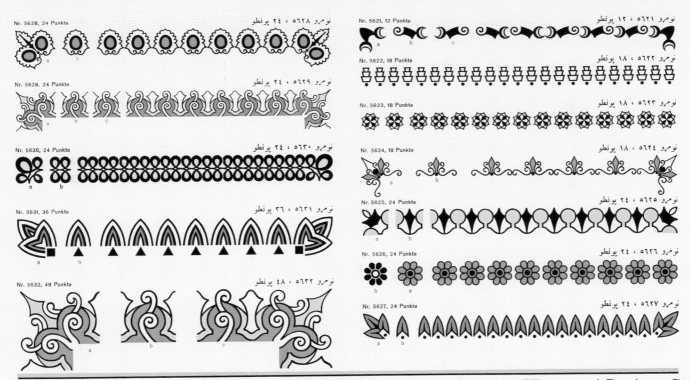

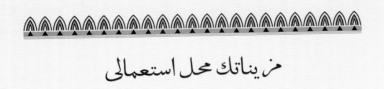

مزيناتك محل استعمالى

Anwendungen

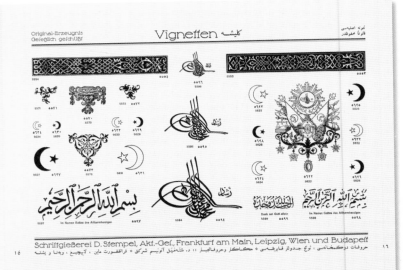

bunden, die sich manchmal zu großen Druckbögen auffalten ließen und die höchst aufwändig gesetzt und in mehreren Farben gedruckt waren – so schön, dass man sie rahmen konnte.

Auch in Handbüchern und Enzyklopädien wurden Schriftmuster abgedruckt. P. Luckombes *The History and Art of Printing* (1770) beinhaltete ein 36-seitiges Caslon-Muster. Acht Seiten aus dem Jahr 1785 waren auch in Chambers *Cyclopaedia* enthalten, die außerdem mit einem Bogen von Edmund Fry aufwartete. 1767 wurden zehn Seiten von Fournier in die *Encyclopédie élémentaire* (*Tableau des vingt corps de caractères, d'usage ordinaire dans l'imprimerie*) aufgenommen, die natürlich auch in seinem 1766 gedruckten *Manuel typographique* enthalten waren. *Die so nöthig als nützliche Buchdruckerkunst und Schriftgießerey* präsentierte eine *Schrift-Probe, oder kurzes Verzeichniss derjenigen Hebräisch-, Griechisch-, Lateinisch-, und Teutschen Schriften, welche in Herrn Bernhard Christoph Breitkopfs Schriftgießerey allhier befindlich sind. Dabey man mehrentheils bemerket hat, von wem eine jede Schrift in Messing oder Stahl ist geschnidten worden.* Eine Abhandlung zu Letternguss und Druckkunst von Ernesti aus dem Jahr 1721 (*Die wol-eingerichtete Buchdruckerey*) stellt Schriftmuster vor, die vermutlich von Endters stammen, der das Buch druckte und verlegte.

Zurück zur Chronologie meiner Sammlung: Ein extrem altes Muster habe ich nach über einem Jahr des Zögerns und Zauderns gekauft, die ganze Zeit hoffend, dass kein anderer Interessent auftauchen und den geforderten Preis anstandslos akzeptieren würde. Ich machte mich persönlich auf den Weg nach London, um das Muster abzuholen. Es handelte sich nämlich um das Brogiotti von 1628 aus der Stampa Vaticana. Die Bedeutung dieses alten Schriftmusters lässt sich daran ermessen, dass eine Faksimile-Edition von ihm erstellt wurde. Weitere Muster aus meinem Besitz, von denen Faksimiles existieren, sind das von Claude Lamesle aus dem Jahr 1742, das von Du Sieur Delacologne von 1773 und zwei von Enschedé aus den Jahren 1768 und 1773. Zu den aus dem 18. Jahrhundert stammenden Mustern meiner Sammlung gehören das Enschedé von 1748, das Fournier von 1764, das Louis Luce von 1740, das Gillé von 1778, das Muster von J. de Groot in Den Haag von 1781, die Wilson-Muster von 1783 und 1789, das Caslon von 1785 – mit 21 Seiten voller wunderbarer kunstvoller Blumenverzierungen –, das Fry von 1787 und das Muster von 1799 aus der Imprenta Real, in Madrid. Daneben besitze ich eine Reihe schöner Muster aus dem 19. Jahrhundert, zum Beispiel von Bodoni (1818), Didot (1819) und Fry (1824). Für einen privaten Sammler ist das eine hübsche Menge, doch nur

ein Bruchteil dessen, was sich in öffentlichen Sammlungen befindet. Bedeutende Sammlungen dieser Art existieren beispielsweise in der Bibliothèque nationale in Paris, der Bibliothek der Universität von Amsterdam (darunter die Sammlung Tetterode und die Bibliothek der Koninklijke Vereeniging ter Bevordering van de Belangen des Boekhandels), der Londoner St. Bride Printing Library und der Newberry Library in Chicago. Ich selbst besitze zwar schon eine ganze Reihe alter Caslon und Figgings-Muster, aber wenn ich den Katalog der St. Bride Foundation von 1919 zur Hand nehme (damals schon an die 1000 Seiten), zähle ich 70 Caslon-Muster, vornehmlich aus dem 19. Jahrhundert, und 31 Figgins-Muster.

Ein besonderes Stück aus meiner Sammlung ist das Muster einer griechischen Bodoni. Jede der 28 Seiten zeigt, mit aufsteigendem Schriftgrad, eine eigene Schriftart. Erschienen ist das Exemplar 1788, in jenem Jahr, in dem Bodonis bedeutendstes Muster, die *Serie di majuscole*, herauskam, von der sich die griechische Variante ableitete. In Birrell & Garnetts vorbildlichem Verkaufskatalog mit Mustern berühmter Schriftgießer (1928) ist die dünne Publikation als „extrem selten" und mit einem Preis von 15 Guinea aufgeführt (die zuvor erwähnten Muster der Vaticana, von Lamesle und Enschedé werden für 15 bis 18 Guinea angeboten). Das Bodoni-Muster habe ich bei einer Beijers-Auktion zu einem weitaus höheren Betrag erstanden. Der Pariser Verleger und Bibliophile Renouard erzählte einmal über Bodoni: „Des Abends im Gespräch mit Freunden oder bei Tisch in erlesener Gesellschaft war er stets mit seinen Schriften beschäftigt, stets richtete er eine Matrize, feilte an einem Stempel, entwarf eine Majuskel."

Die Buchschriften des 19. Jahrhunderts finde ich uninteressant; beherrscht wurde das Gebiet vor allem von Bodoni und Didot. Ein um 1885 in Paris erschienenes Turlot-Muster etwa umfasst 27 Seiten mit 8-Punkt-Schriften, die praktisch alle gleich aussehen, nur dass sie sich ein winziges bisschen in ihrer Größe oder Strichstärke voneinander unterscheiden. Was soll daran so spannend sein? Dagegen die Akzidenz- und Auszeichnungsschriften … Ich habe oben schon das Loblied auf die Tausenden von viktorianischen Schriftarten und ihre unendliche Vielfältigkeit angestimmt: klassische, ausladende, elegante, anmutige, hässliche, schlichte oder aufwendige, normale oder kursive, *Egyptiennes, Américaines, Italiennes, Syriennes, Elzéviriennes, Babyloniennes, Pompéiennes, Japonaises, Milanaises, Orientales, Latines*, zweifarbige Lettern, unzählige *Fantaisies*, Zierschriften, Grotesk- und Antiquaschriften, Frakturschriften, rustikale alte Schriften – die Liste ist endlos. Und dann wären da noch all die *Filets, Vignettes, Lettrines, Coins,*

Jan Tholenaar

1922, Arabisch-Türkisch, type specimen from *D. Stempel*, Frankfurt, Leipzig, Vienna, Budapest

The market was supplied with letters in Arabic and Turkish from various offices in Europe. The D. Stempel AG was founded in 1895 by David Stempel (1869–1927) in Frankfurt am Main, and in 1897 the firm began manufacturing type after purchasing the Offenbach based Juxberg-Rust Foundry. In the same year, Stempel's brother in law, Wilhelm Cunz (1869-1951) joined the company, and Cunz and Peter Scondo (1854-1908) later became partners. Berthold and Bauer had launched Akzidenz Grotesk in 1898 and, inspired by its popularity, Stempel AG produced Reform Grotesk between 1904 and 1910. In 1900 D. Stempel had already began with the production of matrices for Linotype typesetting machines.

Den Markt für arabische und türkische Schriften versorgten verschiedene Firmen mit Sitz in Europa. Die Gießerei D. Stempel AG wurde 1895 von David Stempel (1869–1927) in Frankfurt am Main gegründet. 1897 nimmt die Firma nach der Übernahme der Schriftgießerei Juxberg-Rust in Offenbach die Herstellung von Schriften auf. Im selben Jahr tritt Stempels Stiefbruder Wilhelm Cunz (1869–1951) dem Unternehmen bei, der später neben Peter Scondo (1854–1908) Teilhaber wird. Angeregt durch den großen Erfolg der Akzidenz-Grotesk, die Berthold und Bauer im Jahr 1898 auf den Markt gebracht hatten, produzierte die D. Stempel AG von 1904 bis 1910 die Reform-Grotesk. Bereits vor 1900 hatte Stempel die Matrizenproduktion für Linotype-Setzmaschinen aufgenommen.

Le marché était approvisionné en lettres arabes et turques par différents bureaux en Europe. La fonderie D. Stempel AG a été fondée en 1895 à Francfort par David Stempel (1869–1927). En 1897, la firme se lance dans la fabrication de caractères après avoir racheté la fonderie Juxberg-Rust, à Offenbach. La même année, le beau-frère de Stempel, Wilhelm Cunz (1869–1951) rejoint la compagnie ; Cunz et Peter Scondo (1854–1908) en deviennent plus tard associés. Berthold et Bauer ont lancé Akzidenz Grotesk en 1898 et, devant sa popularité, Stempel AG sort Reform Grotesk entre 1904 et 1910. Dès 1900, D. Stempel avait commencé la production de matrices pour les composeuses Linotype.

Ornements, Zierleisten, Polytypen, Untergrunde, Einfassungen und ganze Bücher voller Messinglinien.

Um 1820 tauchte scharfe Konkurrenz in Form der Lithografie auf. Während die Buchdrucker mit ihren starren rechteckigen Bleiplatten in ihren Möglichkeiten eingeschränkt waren, konnten Lithografen jeden beliebigen Entwurf auf eine Platte übertragen, zum Beispiel für Wertpapiere, kalligrafisch gestaltete Visiten- und Geschäftskarten, Kalender und sonstige kommerzielle Druckerzeugnisse. Auch davon habe ich mehrere Exemplare in meiner Sammlung. Um im Wettbewerb gegen die Lithografen zu bestehen, entwickelten Schriftgießer Verfahren, mit denen sich Bleisatzzeilen diagonal oder bogenförmig anordnen ließen, außerdem fertigten sie eine größere Auswahl an schöneren Ornamenten an. Ich erwähnte bereits Charles Derrieys Muster von 1862, das ein Format von über 40 x 30 Zentimeter hat. Im ersten Teil, *Spécimen*, werden die Vignetten gezeigt, wundervolle Entwürfe, manchmal für den zwei- oder dreifarbigen Druck. Danach folgen die *Caractères ornés*, die *Trais de plumes*, die exquisiten *Coins composés*, *Filets*, *Passe-partouts* und so fort. Der zweite Teil, das *Album*, stellt praktische Anwendungen vor. Das Ganze ist derart prächig und stilvoll und in so exzellenten Farben ausgeführt, dass ich es nur in Superlativen beschreiben kann. Und wenn man bedenkt, dass all das auf einer Handpresse gedruckt wurde – eine unglaubliche Meisterleistung angesichts des breiten Farbspektrums. Ich besitze noch ein anderes Muster, das mit dem Derriey vergleichbar ist: Das der Imprimerie Royal von 1845, das ebenfalls eine Art Album enthält. Wer jemals mit einem Winkelhaken gearbeitet hat, kann sich vorstellen, wie schrecklich kompliziert die Anfertigung solcher Druckwerke gewesen sein muss. Allerdings führte der Wettbewerb mit der Lithografie auch zu albernen Auswüchsen und unnatürlichen Typografien.

Wo habe ich nun all diese außergewöhnlichen Schriftmuster herbekommen? Ich war immer ein guter Kunde des Antiquariats Frits Knuf in Vendôme in Frankreich, eines der wenigen auf buchkundliche Werke im weitesten Sinne spezialisierten Häuser. Über Knuf gelangte ich beispielsweise an ein Muster aus der Bibliothek G. W. Ovink. Mein Lamesle-Muster habe ich in England bei Tony Appleton gekauft. Weitere Quellen waren Keith Hogg, Questor Rare Books, S. P. Tuohy, Barry McKay und das Londoner Antiquariat Marlborough, Maggs, and Quaritch. In Deutschland gibt es eine Reihe von Buchhandlungen, die manchmal eine passable Auswahl zum Thema Buchwesen anbieten. Was Amerika betrifft, stehe ich auf gutem Fuße mit Bob Fleck von Oak Knoll, und das Delacologne-Muster habe ich von Kraus

in New York. Wenn ich ordentlich stöbere, finde ich mit einem Quäntchen Glück manchmal etwas bei einer Messe für antiquarische Bücher, einer Sammlermesse oder einem Büchermarkt. Außerdem gibt es noch die holländischen Auktionshäuser wie Bubb Kuyper. Manchmal kaufe ich einen ganzen Stapel wegen eines einzigen Buches, das mir noch fehlt. Ein- oder zweimal habe ich am Besichtigungstag in einem solchen Stapel eine Notiz hinterlassen, woraufhin der Verkäufer mich kontaktiert hat und ich so das gewünschte Stück erstehen konnte. Natürlich habe ich mit dem Aufkommen des Internets auch angefangen, online nach Schriftmustern zu suchen. Über die entsprechenden Onlinekataloge bin ich bei Buchhändlern von der Schweiz bis nach Schweden fündig geworden.

In den frühen 1980er-Jahren veröffentliche das berühmte Pariser Antiquariat Jammes einen speziellen Typografiekatalog. Darin war die Bibliothek der alten, Konkurs gegangenen Schriftgießerei Deberny & Peignot vertreten, zu der mehr als 400 meist ungewöhnliche und seltene Muster gehörten. Die Preise waren erklecklich, und zu diesem Zeitpunkt war für mich nicht im Geringsten daran zu denken, irgendetwas zu kaufen. Mit einem Kloß im Hals legte ich den Katalog wieder zur Seite. Erst mehrere Jahre später war ich in der Lage, einige der Muster aus dem wunderbaren

Nr. 12009, 6 Punkte نومرو ۱۲۰۰۹ ، ٦ پونطو	Nr. 12001, 3 Punkte نومرو ۱۲۰۰۱ ، ۳ پونطو	Nr. 11601, 2 Punkte نومرو ۱۱٦۰۱ ، ۲ پونطو
Nr. 12010, 6 Punkte نومرو ۱۲۰۱۰ ، ٦ پونطو	Nr. 12002, 3 Punkte نومرو ۱۲۰۰۲ ، ۳ پونطو	Nr. 11602, 3 Punkte نومرو ۱۱٦۰۲ ، ۳ پونطو
Nr. 12012, 8 Punkte نومرو ۱۲۰۱۲ ، ۸ پونطو	Nr. 12003, 4 Punkte نومرو ۱۲۰۰۳ ، ٤ پونطو	Nr. 11603, 4 Punkte نومرو ۱۱٦۰۳ ، ٤ پونطو

Nr. 11517, 1 Punkt نومرو ۱۱٥۱۷ ، ۱ پونطو
Nr. 11533, 1 Punkt نومرو ۱۱٥۳۳ ، ۱ پونطو
Nr. 11556, 1 Punkt نومرو ۱۱٥٥٦ ، ۱ پونطو
Nr. 11552, 2 Punkte نومرو ۱۱٥٥۲ ، ۲ پونطو
Nr. 11519, 2 Punkte نومرو ۱۱٥۱۹ ، ۲ پونطو
Nr. 11525, 2 Punkte نومرو ۱۱٥۲٥ ، ۲ پونطو
Nr. 11502, 2 Punkte نومرو ۱۱٥۰۲ ، ۲ پونطو
Nr. 11512, 2 Punkte نومرو ۱۱٥۱۲ ، ۲ پونطو
Nr. 11550, 2 Punkte نومرو ۱۱٥٥۰ ، ۲ پونطو
Nr. 11558, 2 Punkte نومرو ۱۱٥٥۸ ، ۲ پونطو

Nr. 12014, 8 Punkte نومرو ۱۲۰۱٤ ، ۸ پونطو
Nr. 12016, 8 Punkte نومرو ۱۲۰۱٦ ، ۸ پونطو
Nr. 12017, 8 Punkte نومرو ۱۲۰۱۷ ، ۸ پونطو
Nr. 12015, 8 Punkte نومرو ۱۲۰۱٥ ، ۸ پونطو
Nr. 12018, 12 Punkte نومرو ۱۲۰۱۸ ، ۱۲ پونطو
Nr. 12019, 12 Punkte نومرو ۱۲۰۱۹ ، ۱۲ پونطو
Nr. 12021, 12 Punkte نومرو ۱۲۰۲۱ ، ۱۲ پونطو

Nr. 12004, 4 Punkte نومرو ۱۲۰۰٤ ، ٤ پونطو
Nr. 12005, 4 Punkte نومرو ۱۲۰۰٥ ، ٤ پونطو
Nr. 12006, 6 Punkte نومرو ۱۲۰۰٦ ، ٦ پونطو
Nr. 12011, 6 Punkte نومرو ۱۲۰۱۱ ، ٦ پونطو
Nr. 12013, 6 Punkte نومرو ۱۲۰۱۳ ، ٦ پونطو
Nr. 12007, 6 Punkte نومرو ۱۲۰۰۷ ، ٦ پونطو
Nr. 12008, 6 Punkte نومرو ۱۲۰۰۸ ، ٦ پونطو

Nr. 11604, 6 Punkte نومرو ۱۱٦۰٤ ، ٦ پونطو
Nr. 11559, 3 Punkte نومرو ۱۱٥٥۹ ، ۳ پونطو
Nr. 11560, 4 Punkte نومرو ۱۱٥٦۰ ، ٤ پونطو
Nr. 11561, 6 Punkte نومرو ۱۱٥٦۱ ، ٦ پونطو
Nr. 11562, 8 Punkte نومرو ۱۱٥٦۲ ، ۸ پونطو
Nr. 11563, 10 Punkte نومرو ۱۱٥٦۳ ، ۱۰ پونطو
Nr. 11564, 12 Punkte نومرو ۱۱٥٦٤ ، ۱۲ پونطو

Weitere Linienmuster stehen auf Verlangen zu Diensten ديگر جدول اورنكلرى طلبى اوزرينه خدمتكره افاده بولنور

Schriftgießerei D. Stempel, Akt.-Ges., Frankfurt am Main, Leipzig, Wien und Budapest
حروفات دوكمخانه‌سى ، توغ جدوللر فابريقه‌سى ٭ حكاكر وحروفاتجيار :: د. شته‌مبل آنونيم شركتى ٭ فرانقفورت ماين ، لايپچيغ ، ويه‌نا و پشته

13   ۱۳

Nr. 5612, 12 Punkte نومرو ٥٦۱۲ ، ۱۲ پونطو
Nr. 5613, 12 Punkte نومرو ٥٦۱۳ ، ۱۲ پونطو
Nr. 5614, 12 Punkte نومرو ٥٦۱٤ ، ۱۲ پونطو
Nr. 5615, 12 Punkte نومرو ٥٦۱٥ ، ۱۲ پونطو
Nr. 5616, 12 Punkte نومرو ٥٦۱٦ ، ۱۲ پونطو
Nr. 5617, 12 Punkte نومرو ٥٦۱۷ ، ۱۲ پونطو
Nr. 5618, 12 Punkte نومرو ٥٦۱۸ ، ۱۲ پونطو
Nr. 5619, 12 Punkte نومرو ٥٦۱۹ ، ۱۲ پونطو
Nr. 5620, 12 Punkte نومرو ٥٦۲۰ ، ۱۲ پونطو

Nr. 5601, 6 Punkte نومرو ٥٦۰۱ ، ٦ پونطو
Nr. 5602, 6 Punkte نومرو ٥٦۰۲ ، ٦ پونطو
Nr. 5603, 6 Punkte نومرو ٥٦۰۳ ، ٦ پونطو
Nr. 5604, 6 Punkte نومرو ٥٦۰٤ ، ٦ پونطو
Nr. 5605, 6 Punkte نومرو ٥٦۰٥ ، ٦ پونطو
Nr. 5606, 6 Punkte نومرو ٥٦۰٦ ، ٦ پونطو
Nr. 5607, 6 Punkte نومرو ٥٦۰۷ ، ٦ پونطو
Nr. 5608, 6 Punkte نومرو ٥٦۰۸ ، ٦ پونطو
Nr. 5609, 12 Punkte نومرو ٥٦۰۹ ، ۱۲ پونطو
Nr. 5610, 12 Punkte نومرو ٥٦۱۰ ، ۱۲ پونطو
Nr. 5611, 12 Punkte نومرو ٥٦۱۱ ، ۱۲ پونطو

Schriftgießerei D. Stempel, Ak.-Ges., Frankfurt am Main, Leipzig, Wien und Budapest
حروفات دوكمخانه‌سى ، توغ جدوللر فابريقه‌سى ٭ حكاكر وحروفاتجيار :: د. شته‌مبل آنونيم شركتى ٭ فرانقفورت ماين ، لايپچيغ ، ويه‌نا و پشته

14   ۱٤

Jammes-Katalog zu erwerben. Es war ein gewisser Trost für mich, dass vor der Veröffentlichung des Katalogs verschiedene Stücke bereits der Bibliothèque nationale, der St. Bride Printing Library (die auf Sonderbudgets der British Library zurückgreifen musste) und der Newberry Library angeboten worden waren. Die Taylor Institution in Oxford hatte ebenfalls einige bedeutende Stücke erworben. Wenn es also für mich selbst auch recht enttäuschend war, hatte doch ein großer Anteil der beschriebenen Schriftmuster ein gutes Zuhause gefunden, noch bevor der Katalog herauskam.

Im Zusammenhang mit dem Jammes-Katalog fällt mit eine Art von Muster ein, das mich nicht interessiert, nämlich der Rauchabdruck. Wenn ein Schriftgraveur einen Probedruck von einer Druckplatte machen wollte, tat er dies nicht mit Tinte, sondern mit dem Ruß einer Räucherkerze, da dieser einen besonders scharf gezeichneten Abdruck erzeugt.

In seiner Bibliografie *Die deutsche Schriftgießerei* (1923) erwähnt Oscar Jolles Muster von rund 120 im 19. Jahrhundert betriebenen Schriftgießereien. Es existierten allerdings weit mehr von ihnen, etwa kleine, direkt an bestimmte Druckereien angeschlossene Betriebe. Ich denke mir, dass alle diese Gießereien doch irgendwann einmal Schriftmuster angefertigt haben müssen – nur was ist damit passiert? Manche befinden sich vielleicht in Bibliotheken und Archiven, aber furchtbar viele müssen allein im Zweiten Weltkrieg verlorengegangen sein. Oder Druckereien haben bei Umzügen ihre Lager und Archive entrümpelt. Ich für meinen Teil habe Muster von etwa 60 deutschen Gießereien, wobei sich die Zahl auf die einzeln gezählten Blätter bezieht. Von den übrigen Betrieben habe ich in keinem Antiquariatskatalog etwas ausfindig machen können. In *Buchdruckschriften im 20. Jahrhundert* (1995) heißt es, dass im Jahr 1889 in Deutschland 73 Schriftgießereien existierten; im 20. Jahrhundert ging diese Zahl aufgrund von Zusammenschlüssen und Übernahmen drastisch zurück. Einige Jahre später, zwischen den beiden Weltkriegen, entstand eine ungeheure Vielfalt an neuen Schriften, und Druckdurchläufe mit einem Ausstoß von 10 000 Exemplaren waren bei Werbedrucksachen nichts Ungewöhnliches. Wie Hans Adolf Halbey in seinem Buch *Karl Klingspor, Leben und Werk* (1991) schreibt, wurde die Schriftgießerei Klingspor bei einem Bombenangriff im März 1944 fast vollständig zerstört. Rund 200 Tonnen an Letternmaterial, die Druckmaschinen, Zehntausende Schriftmuster und sonstige Druckerzeugnisse, Entwürfe und 120 Ordner mit Künstlerkorrespondenzen gingen verloren.

Schriftmuster zu datieren, ist meist alles andere als einfach. Bei einigen ist das Jahr pflichtschuldig in der vorgeschalteten Einführung angegeben, so etwa bei einem Muster von Wimble & Co. aus Neuseeland, datiert auf den 1. Juli 1928, was zufälligerweise mein Geburtstag ist. Bei den meisten Mustern muss man sich zur Datierung durch Literatur zur Typografie kämpfen und nach Anhaltspunkten suchen. Manchmal findet man auch einen Hinweis im Muster selbst: eine datierte Medaille oder – bei Schreibschriften – einen Musterbrief mit Datum, eine datierte Einladung zu einer Feier oder eine Weinkarte.

Anhand der Schrift und des Stils kann ich den Entstehungszeitraum eines Musters einigermaßen zuverlässig bestimmen. Man kann sich aber auch sehr irren, wenn etwa ein Drucker in den 1930er-Jahren immer noch seine kompletten Jugendstilornamente und viktorianische Buchstaben verwendet hat. Berthold hat einem die Sache einfacher gemacht, denn die Muster sind nummeriert. Das zur Journal-Antiqua beispielsweise wurde um 1920 als Heft 198 angefertigt. Die Boulevardprobe 448 entstand um 1960. Schelter & Giesecke verfuhren nach demselben Prinzip. Die Gießerei Woellmer wiederum nummerierte die Seiten fortlaufend durch. Zum Beispiel tragen die Seiten in ihrem Muster zur Brokateinfassung von circa 1902 die Zahlen 1324 bis 1331; in dem Muster zur Deutschen Reichsschrift, entstanden um 1920, laufen sie von 6974 bis 6996.

In deutschen Schriftmustern aus den Jahren vor dem Zweiten Weltkrieg stößt man gelegentlich auf Textausschnitte aus nationalsozialistischen Publikationen und da und dort auch auf ein Hakenkreuz. Eines der Muster von Trennert – für die Schriftart Blizzard – von circa 1938 verwendet demonstrativ die Worte *Heil Hitler* zur Präsentation der Schrift.

Bis Anfang des 20. Jahrhunderts war nur eine Handvoll von Namen berühmter Schriftentwerfer wie Garamond, Bodoni oder Fournier bekannt. Die Entwürfe und Schnitte von Tausenden von Schriften, die die Schriftgießereien des 19. Jahrhunderts herausgebracht haben, stammen von anonymen Angestellten. In Schriftkatalogen werden diese als „im Hause" oder „Hausschnitt" aufgeführt. Vor allem die Gießerei Klingspor zog zu Beginn des 20. Jahrhunderts berühmte Gestalter an und erwähnte sie als Urheber, darunter Otto Eckmann, Rudolf Koch, Walter Tiemann und Imre Reiner. Bauer verpflichtete unter anderem Heinrich Weiynk, F. H. Ehmcke, Lucian Bernhard, E. R. Weiss, Paul Renner (den Entwerfer der Futura) und F. H. Ernst Schneidler. Berthold stellte Gestalter wie Louis Oppenheim, Georg Trump oder Herbert Bayer (vom Bauhaus) in seine Dienste. Auch für die Schriftgießerei Ludwig und Mayer arbeiteten bedeutende Gestalter, unter ihnen Heinrich Jost, Jakob Erbar und J. V. Cissarz. Georg Belwe und

1922, Arabisch-Türkisch, type specimen
from *D. Stempel*, Frankfurt, Leipzig,
Vienna, Budapest

Man kann zu Recht sagen, dass die Trendsetter des Metiers über weite Strecken des 19. und 20. Jahrhunderts aus Deutschland kamen. Aber auch in anderen Ländern waren exzellente Designer für Schriftgießereien am Werk. Georges Auriol und E. Grasset arbeiteten für Peignot, A. M. Cassandre und Adrian Frutiger für Deberny & Peignot, Roger Excoffon für Olive, Aldo Novarese für Nebiolo, Warren Chappell und Morris F. Benton für American Type Founders, Rudolph Ruzicka, W. A. Dwiggins und Walter Tracy für Linotype, F. W. Goudy, Bruce Rogers, Berthold Wolpe und Eric Gill für Monotype. In den Niederlanden waren im 20. Jahrhundert S. H. de Roos und Dick Dooijes bei der Lettergieterij Amsterdam angestellt, J. van Krimpen und S. L. Hartz arbeiteten für Enschedé.

Ich möchte noch eine Reihe weiterer Schriftmuster erwähnen, die sich in meiner Sammlung befinden und die ich aus dem einen oder anderen Grunde für ungewöhnlich halte. Dazu gehört eines aus dem Jahr 1832 von der fünf Jahre zuvor gegründeten Frankfurter Gießerei Dresler und Rost-Fingerlin, der Nachfolgerin der im 17. Jahrhundert aktiven Schleussner-schen Schriftgießerei. Später im 19. Jahrhundert wurde sie von Flinsch übernommen und diese wiederum von der Bauerschen Gießerei.

Ein ganz anderes Paar Schuhe sind die Druckwerke der Typis Sacrae Congregationis de Propaganda Fide in Rom, die im Jahr 1626 zur Verbreitung des christlichen Glaubens unter den Völkern des Ostens eingerichtet wurde. In ebendieser Druckerei erlernte Bodoni im 18. Jahrhundert sein Handwerk. Für ihre Publikationen, darunter fremdsprachige Lehrbücher mit dem Vaterunser in der jeweiligen Sprache, wurden eigens exotische Schriften geschnitten – koptische, tibetanische, persische und so weiter. 1785 verbrachte man die Schriften nach Paris, wo 1805, als päpstliche Hommage an die Kaiserkrönung Napoleons, das Vaterunser in 150 Sprachen veröffentlicht wurde. Ein großer Teil der Drucktypen befindet sich noch heute in der Imprimerie Nationale. Von den betreffenden Publikationen besitze ich 14 Stück aus der Zeit von 1629 bis 1789.

In diesem Zusammenhang ist auch Edmund Fry zu erwähnen. Sein Muster aus dem Jahr 1787 enthält hebräische, äthiopische, samaritanische, arabische, persische, türkische, tatarische und malaiische Schriften. 1799 veröffentliche Fry seine *Pantographia*, in der auf 320 Seiten sämtliche bekannten Alphabete der Welt exakt dargestellt und erläutert werden. Die meisten Schriftarten für das Werk schnitt Fry selbst.

Das erste umfassendere Schriftmuster der 1819 gegründeten Schriftgießerei Schelter & Giesecke kam 1836 heraus. Wie ich in einer 1894 erschiene-

Jan Tschichold entwarfen für Schelter & Giesecke, F. W. Kleukens und Hermann Zapf für Stempel. Manche waren auch für mehrere Unternehmen als Schriftentwerfer tätig. Die diesen Entwürfen gewidmeten Muster sind zumeist typografische Glanzleistungen und kleine Perlen der Druckkunst.

Um 1820 tauchte für die Schriftgießereien scharfe Konkurrenz
in Form der Lithografie auf. Während die Buchdrucker mit ihren
starren rechteckigen Bleiplatten in ihren Möglichkeiten eingeschränkt waren, konnten Lithografen jeden beliebigen Entwurf
auf eine Platte übertragen, zum Beispiel für Wertpapiere,
kalligrafisch gestaltete Visiten- und Geschäftskarten, Kalender
und sonstige kommerzielle Druckerzeugnisse.

nen Festschrift der Firma gelesen habe, konnte im 19. Jahrhundert ein guter
Schriftgießer täglich 5000 bis 6000 Drucklettern von Hand gießen! Friedrich Bauer nennt in seiner *Chronik der Schriftgießereien* (1928) eine Anzahl
von 2000 bis 4000 Lettern. Durch die Erfindung der Gießmaschine Mitte
des 19. Jahrhunderts erhöhte sich die Geschwindigkeit um das Sechsfache.

Ein ebenfalls seltenes Muster sind die 1834 in Frankfurt am Main
erschienenen *Proben aus der Schriftgiesserey der Andreäischen Buchhandlung*.
Wie ein auf das Titelblatt aufgeklebter Hinweis besagt, war das Unternehmen mit Wirkung vom 1. Juli 1839 von Benjamin Krebs' Schriftgießerei,
Buch-, Congrève- und Steindruckerei übernommen worden. So bestand
die einst von Johann Wechsel im Jahr 1581 gegründete Gießerei unter
neuem Dach bis ins 20. Jahrhundert fort. Aus derselben Zeit wie das zuvor
genannte stammt ein Muster von Eduard Haenel (1837), dessen Magdebur-
ger Gießerei kurze Zeit später durch einen Brand zerstört wurde, worauf
Haenel sein Gewerbe in Berlin fortsetzte.

Deutsche Gießereien führten häufig eine Dependance in Moskau oder
Sankt Petersburg, um den russischen Markt zu bedienen. Von Berthold
besitze ich einen großen, gegen Ende des 19. Jahrhunderts angefertigten
Musterbogen, komplett auf Russisch und mit ausführlichen, vielfarbig
gestalteten Schriftbeispielen. Ebenfalls von Berthold stammt ein hebräisches Muster von 1924 – angeordnet natürlich in der Leserichtung von
rechts nach links – mit herrlichen farbigen Illustrationen. 1925 kam ein
ähnliches Muster für östliche Sprachen, darunter Arabisch, Türkisch und
Hindi, heraus.

1990 erschien ein Bleisatzmuster mit dem Titel *A Miscellany of Type*. Bei
diesem großformatigen Muster, gedruckt auf 148 Seiten aus schwerem Büttenpapier, handelt es sich um eine bibliophile Ausgabe der englischen
Whittington Press, die das fantastische *Matrix*-Jahrbuch druckt und heraus-
gibt. *A Miscellany of Type* ist ein Beispiel für musterhafte Druckkunst und
umfasst Holzstiche und andere farbige Illustrationen, die früheren Publikationen der Druckerei entnommen sind.

Als ich das von Ian Mortimer in London gedruckte und herausgegebene
Buch *Ornamented Types* erwarb, war es in den Niederlanden in keiner einzigen öffentlichen Sammlung zu finden. Es enthält Drucke von Schmucklettern aus Holz, die von dem Anfang des 19. Jahrhunderts aktiven Londoner
Schriftgießer Pouchée stammen. 1936 hatte die Monotype Corporation das
Material aus der Konkursmasse der Caslon Foundry aufgekauft. Es überleb-
te die Bombenangriffe während des Krieges und befindet sich heute in der

St. Bride Printing Library. Die 200 Exemplare auf einer alten Handpresse zu
drucken, hat mehrere Jahre gedauert. Das Buch besteht aus 24 Alphabeten
auf insgesamt 45 Seiten und wurde auf 170 Gramm schwerem Zerkall-Bütten (53 x 38 Zentimeter) gedruckt. Zu dem Werk gehören ein Schuber und
ein separater Einleitungsband von James Mosley. Dass dieses Muster seinen
Preis hat, kann in Anbetracht der vielen Arbeit, die in ihm steckt, nicht
überraschen. Es ist jeden Cent wert.

Mein Muster der im Jahr 1900 in Bombay gegründeten Schriftgießerei
Gurajati umfasst mehr als 400 vielfarbige Seiten und erschien in einer Auflage von 10 000 Exemplaren. In einem in *Matrix 2* erschienen Artikel zu diesem Exemplar heißt es, dass die Arbeit an dem Muster 1926 begann und es
die westlichen Gießereien in herstellerischer und technischer Hinsicht
„ausstechen" sollte. Dazu wurden ein erfahrener Drucker und ein Akzi-
denzsetzer angeheuert und eine neue Druckerpresse aus Deutschland ange-
schafft; aus Amerika importierte man Kunstdruckpapier, die Tinte stammte
von Manders in England. Abgeschlossen wurde das Werk 1937 – eine Pro-
duktionszeit von elf Jahren also, weshalb ich das „Ausstechen" nicht allzu
hoch hängen möchte.

Daneben gibt es auch kleine Muster von Privatdruckereien. Ein solches
ist *Specimens of Type Used at The Ashendene Press*, ein schlichtes Einzelblatt,
für das ich sehr viel Geld bezahlt habe. Das Besonders an diesem Muster
ist, dass es zwei Schriften enthält, die für den Besitzer von Ashendene,
Mr. Hornby, entworfen und geschnitten wurden: die Subiaco und die Ptolemy. Ein Muster von Hans Mardersteig für Monotype (1928) stellt die Pastonchi vor, die speziell für eine neue Reihe italienischer Klassiker geschnitten
wurde. Es erschien als bibliophile Edition von 200 Exemplaren, handgedruckt auf Fabriano-Papier und mit eingeklebten Einzelmustern.

In diesem Zusammenhang sind auch die Schriftmuster von Paul Hay-
den Duensing (der selbst Stempel schnitt und Typen goss) erwähnenswert,
ferner die Harrisfeldwegpresse, die Alembic Press, ein sehr reizendes kleines
Buch der Overbrook Press (1934), die Harbor Press, die Kit-Cat Press, die
Sandelswood Press, die Philippsberger Werkstatt und nicht zu vergessen
Charles Whitehouse von der Edition Seefeld. Letztere brachte beispielsweise ein Blatt zu van Krimpens Romanée in einem schönen klassischen
Design heraus, handgedruckt auf Büttenpapier mit rauer Oberfläche auf
einer Kniehebelpresse. Vor dem Druck wurde das Papier angefeuchtet – das
Ergebnis ist fantastisch: Die kleine, eng laufende Kursive in 10 Punkt ist
unglaublich scharf, tiefschwarz und dennoch nicht zu fett. Das Besondere

1922, Arabisch-Türkisch, type specimen
from *D. Stempel*, Frankfurt, Leipzig,
Vienna, Budapest

an ihr ist eine beinahe dreidimensionale, reliefartige Wirkung, wie sie sich beim Offsetdruck nicht erzielen lässt. Hieran wird in meinen Augen ersichtlich, dass das Verschwinden des Bleisatzes ein schwerer, unwiederbringlicher Verlust für die Druckkunst war.

Selbstverständlich sollen die etwas weniger bekannten niederländischen Drucker hier nicht unerwähnt bleiben: De Vergulde Maatlat, Eric van der Wal, Ter Lugt Pers, De Vier Seizoenen, Willem Muilenburg, Triona Pers, Exponent, Elze ter Harkel, Tuinwijkpers (Rosart), Castanha Pers (Garamond) und Drukschuur Blaricum. Ein höchst originelles Exemplar ist De Dwarsbomen (Gert van Oortmerssen). Der Buchblock besteht aus festem Material, und der separate, ein Kilo schwere Rücken wurde aus recycelten Bleilettern gegossen. Der Surrealist Johannes Hendrikus Moesman hat ebenfalls eine Schrift entworfen, die Petronius, die erstmals 1975 als Schriftmuster zu sehen war. Ich weiß nicht, ob die Schrift danach überhaupt je in Gebrauch war.

Die Curwen Press, die namhafte Druckerei des Magazins *The Fleuron*, betraute im Jahr 1928 Oliver Simon mit der Zusammenstellung und dem Entwurf eines Schriftmusters. Seinen hohen Preis hat dieses Muster weniger aufgrund der geringen Auflage (135 Exemplare), sondern weil es eine so außergewöhnlich schön gefertigte Arbeit ist, in nüchtern-klassischer Gestaltung auf handgeschöpftem Papier mit eigenem Wasserzeichen. Ornamente und sonstigen Dekor ließ Curwen speziell von Künstlern wie Claud Lovat Fraser, Paul Nash oder Percy Smith anfertigen. Die Schriftentwürfe stammten von Künstlern wie Rudolf Koch oder Jan van Krimpen.

Theodore Low De Vinne (1828–1914) war ein bekannter New Yorker Drucker, Autor von mehreren Büchern zum Thema Druckkunst und Mitbegründer und Präsident der ersten Vereinigung amerikanischer Meisterdrucker. Von ihm möchte ich zwei Muster vorstellen, die ich besitze. Im Jahr 1878, noch während seiner Zusammenarbeit mit dem Drucker Francis Hart, brachte Low De Vinne ein 96-seitiges Muster mit dem Titel *Specimens of Pointed Texts and Black Letters* heraus. „Black letters" entsprechen dem, was wir unter gebrochenen Schriften verstehen, „pointed letters" sind in etwa dasselbe – verwendet wurden sie für Bibeln, aber auch für Rundschreiben und dergleichen. Dieses Muster enthält rund 50 Schriftarten. Das andere, 1891 von der De Vinne Press gedruckte, umfasst 144 Seiten mit Buchschriften und wäre für sich genommen ein langweiliges Buch, wäre da nicht der Umstand, dass jede Seite unterschiedliche Initialen vorführt, für die weder Kosten noch Mühen gescheut wurden: Die

meisten der in Größe und Form variierenden Initialen sind zweifarbig und golden.

In eine ähnliche Richtung geht ein kleinformatiges Muster von 1903, das ausschließlich Buchschriften präsentiert. Herausgebracht hat es der Kopenhagener Drucker Martius Truelsen in einer Auflage von 1500 maschinennummerierten Exemplaren. Bei meinen häufigen Aufenthalten in Kopenhagen habe ich stets das Antiquariat Busck besucht, wo ich 1979 ein erstes und ein paar Jahre später noch ein zweites Exemplar des betreffenden Musters erstanden habe. Das Buch hat 176 Seiten, ist komplett in Leder gebunden und mit Blindprägungen versehen. Die Lagen sind nicht genäht, sondern geheftet – und eine Heftung kann natürlich rosten. Aber das Innere ist sehr schön. Alle Doppelseiten sind unterschiedlich gestaltet, jeweils mit einer verzierten Kopfleiste auf der linken Seite und einer Initiale am Textbeginn, die eine gemeinsame Einheit bilden, das Ganze oft reinster Jugendstil. Man trifft auf wundervolle (anonyme) Entwürfe in drei oder vier Farben, wobei sämtliche Seiten sich in ihrer Farbgestaltung unterscheiden. Insgesamt wurden um die 300 Farben verwendet.

In meinem Exemplar des *Boktryckeri*-Kalenders von 1902/03 (inklusive Signatur des Druckers und Verlegers Waldemar Zachrisson und der Widmung „Hommage à Mr. Theo L. De Vinne") findet sich auch eine Fotografie von Martius Truelsen abgedruckt. Truelsen erzählt, wie er im Alter von 15 Jahren zum Waisen wurde und sich von da an alleine durchs Leben schlagen musste. Als er 30 war, machte er sich mit ein paar Hundert gesparten Kronen selbstständig; 1903 dann leitete er, inzwischen 50 Jahre alt, eine Druckerei mit rund 50 Angestellten. Neben meinen beiden Exemplaren des Truelsen-Musters habe ich noch ganze Kisten voller fantastischer Duplikate.

Noch ein paar weitere schöne Stücke aus meiner Sammlung möchte ich erwähnen. Im Zusammenhang mit der in Ausgabe Nummer 5 der Zeitschrift *Signature* (New Series) behandelten Schriftmuster heißt es über eines der Shenval Press von 1939: „Druck in vorzüglich-schwarzer Tinte, wie man es heutzutage nur noch höchst selten antrifft." Dem kann ich voll und ganz zustimmen – „black can be beautiful".

Ein 200-seitiges Muster von 1934 aus der Imprimerie Darantière in Dijon, gedruckt in einer Auflage von 800 Exemplaren, ist als zusammenhängender Roman angelegt, in dessen Verlauf die verschiedensten Schriftarten – in großen wie kleinen Schriftgraden – vorgestellt werden. Die Seitengestaltung zeichnet sich durch breite Ränder und einen in Rot und Schwarz gedruckten Text aus. Es ist bedauerlich, dass man heute nicht

mehr mit derartigen Zusatzfarben arbeitet. Ein Muster der Buchdruckerei August Hopfer wiederum verwendet ausschließlich Goethe-Zitate. Diese beiden Muster sind eine nette Abwechslung zu dem stereotypen Schema sich endlos wiederholender Texte.

Von der Boston Type Foundry besitze ich ein für amerikanische Verhältnisse recht altes Muster von 1835. Die Hälfte der mehr als 200 einseitig bedruckten Buchseiten versammelt ausschließlich Ornamente (Holzstiche), darunter Abbildungen von Haushaltswaren und Zuchtvieh. Außerdem enthält es Faltblätter mit Dampfschiffen, Raddampfern, Segelschiffen und Pferdekutschen.

Gegen Ende des 19. Jahrhunderts vereinbarten elf führende amerikanische Schriftgießereien eine engere Zusammenarbeit, aus der schließlich die American Type Founders hervorgingen. Ihr erstes Muster, ein schwerer Wälzer von mehr als 800 Seiten, erschien 1896.

Wie man anhand der *Hauptprobe* erkennen kann, wurde gegen Ende des 19. Jahrhunderts den Überschriften und Zwischentiteln besonders viel Aufmerksamkeit geschenkt, sie wurden in verschiedenen Tönen vor farbigen Hintergründen und mit üppigem Einsatz von häufig sehr reizvollen Ornamenten präsentiert. Dieser Aufwand dürfte zurückzuführen sein auf das Bemühen, sich gegen die Lithografie zu behaupten – was offenbar insofern gelang, als die betreffenden Muster in Antiquariatskatalogen bisweilen als Chromolithografien aufgeführt werden, obwohl die Erhebungen auf der Rückseite eindeutig auf Hochdruck als Herstellungsverfahren schließen lassen.

Anfang des 19. Jahrhunderts vollbrachte der französische Schriftschneider Henri Didot das nahezu Unmögliche und schnitt eine mikroskopisch kleine 2,5-Punkt-Schrift, die kleinste jemals angefertigte Schrift. Die Stempel und Matrizen gelangten später in den Besitz der Firma Johannes Enschedé & Zonen, die im Jahr 1861 die niederländische Verfassung druckte, ein Büchlein im Format 4,5 x 6,5 Zentimeter. Eines der letzten Exemplare davon habe ich am Bahnhof von Haarlem erstanden. Verschiedene Firmen, unter ihnen Enschedé, verramschten ihre Restauflagen anlässlich einer Messe für antiquarische Bücher. Henri Didot erfand des Weiteren eine als Polymatype bezeichnete Gussform, mit der man bis zu 120 kleine Lettern gleichzeitig gießen konnte. Sein Cousin, Pierre Didot, der eine Druckerpresse geerbt hatte, betätigte sich ebenfalls als Schriftschneider. 1819 brachte er sein erstes Muster, *Spécimen des nouveaux caractères de la fonderie…*, heraus, mit Gedichten aus seiner eigenen Feder als Textbeispielen.

Häufig finden sich in Schriftmustern des 19. Jahrhunderts aus Ländern wie Deutschland, den Niederlanden und den USA die gleichen Ornamente, Holzstiche etc. Man könnte fragen, ob dem womöglich ein systematisches Vorgehen inklusive Verträgen und Lizenzvergaben zugrunde liegt. Bereits seit geraumer Zeit war die Stereotypie ein gängiges Verfahren; ab etwa 1840 konnte man Vorlagen ohne Schwierigkeiten mithilfe der Galvanoplastik kopieren. Ein Urheberrecht existierte zu dieser Zeit noch nicht. (Wohlgemerkt werden in unseren Tagen, wie ich irgendwo gelesen habe, 80 Prozent der benutzten Software illegal verwendet …)

Muster mit Erstpräsentationen neuer Schriften sind für Sammler besonders wertvoll. Ich besitze beispielsweise eines der Centaur inklusive einer Einleitung ihres Schöpfers, Bruce Rogers, eines von van Krimpens Lutetia und eines der Cartier (1966), der ersten in Kanada entstandenen Schreibschrift, entworfen von Carl Dair. Leider trifft man auch auf Schriftmuster mit schlechter Papierqualität. Manchen Papiersorten aus der zweiten Hälfte des 19. Jahrhunderts ist der Zahn der Zeit deutlich anzumerken – sie zerbröseln einem zwischen den Fingern. Mitunter wurden die Lagen eines Buches nicht auf einen Leinenstreifen aufgenäht, sondern aufgeheftet. Dieses Verfahren war zwar billiger, aber, da Heftungen rosten, mitnichten haltbarer. Kiloschwere Schriftmuster, selbst sehr hochpreisige, erhielten manchmal einen Papiereinband. Das Muster der Imprimerie Nationale zum Beispiel wurde in ein feines dünnes Glacépapier eingeschlagen – womit Unannehmlichkeiten vorprogrammiert sind.

Aber auch Vandalismus kann der Grund für Beschädigungen sein. Manchmal wurden einfach Teile aus den Mustern herausgeschnitten, ungeachtet der im Eingangsteil geäußerten Bitte, davon abzusehen! Ein guter Buchhändler überprüft ein Stück auf solcherlei Beschädigungen und erwähnt sie in seinem Katalog. Jammes verwendet für derartige Löcher den netten Ausdruck *fenêtres* (Fenster).

Von den Gebroeders Hoitsema in Groningen besitze ich ein umfangreiches Schriftmuster, das auf der Titelseite auf das Jahr 1897 datiert ist. Ungewöhnlich an diesem Stück ist, dass für jede Schrift das Jahr des Erwerbs, der Einlieferer und das Letterngewicht vermerkt sind. Die große Mehrheit der aufgeführten Schriften stammt aus deutschen Gießereien, was in Anbetracht der geografischen Nähe vielleicht nicht allzu erstaunlich ist. Es wäre aber interessant herauszufinden, ob diese Gießereien ihre Geschäftsvertreter direkt zu den holländischen Druckern geschickt haben. In einigen Fällen ist der Name des Vertreters angegeben: Klinkhardt (Van Meurs), Huck

1922, Arabisch-Türkisch, type specimen from *D. Stempel*, Frankfurt, Leipzig, Vienna, Budapest

(P. van Dijk) und so weiter. Interessant ist außerdem, dass kleinere holländische Gießereien wie G. W. van der Wiel & Onnes und De Boer & Coers erwähnt werden. 1869 erwarben die Gebrüder Hoitsema die Gießerei Reed and Fox, vormals Besley & Co, London (doppelzeilige English Courthand).

Alte Schriftmuster von Druckereien sind selten – ich führe einige Firmen an, von denen ich alte Exemplare besitze: Bricx in Ostende (um 1787), H. Martin & Comp. (1829), J. Ruys (1908), Pieper & Ipenbuur (1828) und Stads en Courant drukkerij (1834) in Amsterdam, M. Wijt (1828) und J. W. van Leenhoff (1837) in Rotterdam, B. Henry (1828) in Valenciennes, die Universitätsdruckerei Johan Frederik Schultz (1805) in Kopenhagen (das zweite Exemplar in der Kopenhagener Dänischen Königlichen Bibliothek, gilt seit Jahren als vermisst!), De Bachelier (1842) in Paris, Michael Lindauer (1825) in München, Osvalda Lucchini (1853) in Guastalla, Rand and Avery (1867) in Boston – damals die zweitgrößte Druckerei in den USA – und John F. Trow (1856) in New York.

Ein Glanzstück meiner Sammlung ist ein circa 1847 erschienenes Muster der Groninger Schriftgießerei Van der Veen Oomkens & Van Bakkenes. Darin befinden sich im hinteren Teil „Tafeln zum Congrevedruck" als Farbdrucke. Mithilfe dieses Systems ließen sich Wertpapiere in mehreren Farben gleichzeitig drucken (im Hochdruckverfahren). Die 1843 von Alle van der Veen Oomkens gegründete Gießerei wurde 1857 von Onnes, De Boer & Coers übernommen und zog im darauffolgenden Jahr nach Arnheim um. 1894 gingen die Matrizen an die Gießerei Enschedé, von der ich eine Kompilation aus mehreren Ende des 19. Jahrhunderts entstandenen Schriftmustern erworben habe, die 145 herrliche Seiten aus den beiden Gießereien in Groningen und Arnheim umfasst.

Ein besonderes Stück aus den Vereinigten Staaten ist das Bruce-Muster von 1882. Angesichts der enormen Auswahl an Einfassungen und Schmucklettern lässt es sich mit dem Derriey-Muster vergleichen. Außerdem enthält es Unmengen von reizvollen galvanoplastisch hergestellten Ornamenten für Gewerbezwecke, Ladeneinrichtungen, Waren und so weiter. Zusätzlich mit eingebunden ist eine recht große Arbeit von De Vinne zur Erfindung des Buchdrucks.

Besonders ungewöhnlich sind großformatige Musterbögen, wo also sämtliche Schriftmuster auf einem einzelnen Blatt präsentiert werden. Bei einem Großteil der ältesten heute noch existierenden Schriftmuster handelt es sich um eben solche Bögen. Im 20. Jahrhundert fertigte unter anderem Monotype einige beachtliche Stücke in diesem Format. Die Bögen, die

Stanley Morison für Monotype, die Pelican Press und die Cloister Press anfertigte, gehören zu den Highlights ihrer Art.

Wenn in den 1930er-Jahren Materialien aus einer Druckerei, meistens nach einem Konkurs, unter den Hammer kommen sollten, trat das Auktionshaus Bom auf den Plan, von dem ich 75 kommentierte Auktionskataloge besitze. Auch wenn die zu versteigernden Schriften in den Katalogen mit nur einer einzigen Zeile und ohne den dazugehörigen Namen abgedruckt wurden, handelt es sich doch ebenfalls um Schriftmuster.

Fragt man jemanden nach der ältesten Druckerei der Niederlande, wird die Antwort wahrscheinlich Enschedé lauten. Tatsächlich aber ist es Van Waesberge; die Firmengeschichte lässt sich in einem Schriftmuster von 1918 nachlesen. Van Waesberge wurde vor mehr als 400 Jahren in Rotterdam gegründet. Auch N. Tetterode, die spätere Lettergieterij Amsterdam, hatte laut einem Muster von 1852 seinen Sitz anfangs in Rotterdam. In einem zweiten Teil des Musters, von 1856, bezeichnet Tetterode sich als Amsterdamer Schriftgießer. Dort in Amsterdam, an der Bloemgracht, hatte die Schriftgießerei De Passe & Menne (deren Muster *Proeve van drukletters* von 1843 ich besitze) ihren Sitz, die von Tetterode übernommen worden war. In seiner ersten Beilage überklebte er den Namen De Passe & Menne mit seinem eigenen. Die frühen Muster verwendeten noch die klassischen Textbeispiele, wie man sie auch in Mustern des 19. Jahrhunderts, bei Caslon, Fry, Wilson und Bodoni, findet: *„Quousque tandem abutere, Catilina, patientia nostra?"*

Auch die Setzmaschinenhersteller Linotype, Intertype, Monotype und Ludlow fertigten häufig recht umfangreiche Schriftmusterbücher an; auch von Typograph besitze ich ein reizendes kleines Exemplar. Für diese Muster wurden im Allgemeinen von Gießereien lizenzierte Schriften benutzt.

An dieser Stelle möchte ich von einem netten Zufall erzählen: Von Heinrich Hoffmeister, der 1898 eine Schriftgießerei in Leipzig eröffnete, besaß ich zuerst nur drei dünne Schriftmuster. Als bei einer Auktion in Berlin ein Schriftmuster in Buchform von Hoffmeister zu versteigern war, bot ich mit und bekam den Zuschlag. Einen Tag nachdem das Stück mit der Post bei mir angekommen war, besuchte ich die Antiquitätenmesse in Haarlem. Und was fand ich da? Zwei gebundene Muster von Hoffmeister, ein älteres (sein erstes, ausschließlich mit Vignetten) und ein jüngeres.

Vor ein paar Jahren lieh ich dem Gutenberg-Museum in Mainz einige Materialien für eine Ausstellung über Schriftmuster. Bei dieser Gelegenheit ließ man mich in der Bibliothek herumstöbern, wobei ich zu meinem Erstaunen auf eine Reihe von ungewöhnlichen alten und in einigen Fällen

Jan Tholenaar

seltenen Mustern stieß, über die die Museumsangestellten selbst kaum im Bilde waren. Außerdem fand ich außergewöhnliche Stücke aus holländischen Gießereien, die im 19. Jahrhundert aktiv waren, darunter Muster von Hendrik Bruyn & Comp., Broese & Comp., Elix & Co. und J. de Groot (1781). Von all diesen besitze ich leider nur das von de Groot. Um es an dieser Stelle nicht ungesagt zu lassen: Sämtliche anderen in diesem Buch aufgeführten Stücke befinden sich in meiner eigenen Bibliothek.

Ein letztes Muster möchte ich gerne noch erwähnen, und zwar das des Lyoneser Schriftgießers Louis Vernange von 1770, das 64 Seiten umfasst. Die übrigen drei bekannten Ausgaben sind etwas weniger umfangreich. Der Buchhändler, bei dem ich es gekauft habe, erzählte mir, dass ihm in den 35 Jahren seiner Tätigkeit noch nie ein Schriftmuster begegnet sei.

So, das wären also ein paar Beispiele aus meiner Sammlung. Meine gebundenen Exemplare bewahre ich in Bücherregalen auf, der Größe nach geordnet, damit sie nicht ganz so viel Platz benötigen. Die dünnen Muster sind in Archivkästen untergebracht und nach Gießerei und Datum sortiert. Obwohl ich alles auch im Computer festhalte, verliere ich manchmal den Überblick und kaufe ein Exemplar, das ich schon besitze.

Der Wert von Schriftmustern bestimmt sich vor allem anhand ihres Erhaltungszustands. Das Enschedé-Muster von 1768 könnte auf mehrere Zehntausend Euro kommen, das der Stampa Vaticana sogar auf noch mehr. Für ein gut erhaltenes, gebundenes Muster, das mehr als 100 Jahre alt ist, muss man einige Hundert Euro bezahlen; Muster mit wenigen Seiten kosten um die 20 Euro, und ein schönes Exemplar von Rudolf Koch schlägt mit 100 Euro zu Buche. Die Preise für seltene Stücke – ungewöhnliche Exemplare wie ein 80-seitiges fadengeheftetes Muster von Peter Behrens oder das Muster der Curwen Press von 1928 – liegen etwas über dem Durchschnitt. Teurer als ähnliche Stücke sind die drei seltenen Bögen der Andreäischen Gießerei von 1833, sowie das erwähnte Doppelmuster der Ashendene Press von 1926.

Gibt es sonst noch irgendetwas, das ich gerne hätte? Nun, eigentlich eine ganze Liste, auf der eine Zeitlang drei Muster von Bodoni, *Fregi e majuscole* (1771), *Serie di majuscole* (1788) und *Manuale tipografico* (1818), ganz oben standen. Das Letztere besitze ich inzwischen, und es ist der Stolz meiner Sammlung.

Über Schriftmuster und Gießereien ist eine ansehnliche Menge an Literatur erschienen. Zu den Standardwerken gehören die *Chronik der Schriftgießereien* von Friedrich Bauer (1928, erste Auflage 1914), *Les livrets typographiques des fonderies françaises créées avant 1800* von Marius Audin (1964,

erste Auflage 1933), *British Type Specimens before 1831* von James Mosley (1984), *Schweizer Stempelschneider und Schriftgiesser* von Albert Bruckner (1943), *Type Foundries of America and Their Catalogs* von Maurice Annenberg (1994, erste Auflage 1975) und nicht zuletzt *Type Foundries in the Netherlands* von Charles Enschedé, übersetzt und bearbeitet von Harry Carter (1978, erste Auflage 1908).

Wer meint, dass heute keine Schriften mehr geschnitten oder gegossen werden, liegt falsch. Vor nicht allzu langer Zeit hatte der amerikanische Dichter Dan Carr das Gefühl, eine eigene Schrift für seine Gedichte kreieren zu müssen, woraufhin er sich seine eigenen Formen schnitt. In einem Anhang des bereits erwähnten *Matrix*-Jahrbuches wurde Carrs Regulus vorgestellt, die sich als eine wirklich schöne Schrift herausstellte. Ich schrieb sofort an Carrs Golgonooza Letter Foundry & Press, um die bibliophile Kollektion des Erstdrucks zu bestellen und mich nach einem richtigen Schriftmuster erkundigen.

In der Vergangenheit erforderte der Aufbau einer gut ausgestatteten Handsetzerei noch beträchtliche Investitionen. Heute kann jeder, der Drucksachen am Computer erstellt, im Internet aus einer endlosen Bandbreite von Schriften auswählen, die alle nur ein paar Euro kosten. Und wenn man zehn auf einmal kauft, bekommt man noch ein Mountainbike gratis dazu.

500 Jahre lang haben sich die Druckverfahren nicht verändert – und plötzlich war alles vorbei, dank des Herrn Senefelder. Schriftgießereien, in denen ausschließlich Bleisatzschriften hergestellt wurden, sind verschwunden. Manche haben sich dem Wandel der Zeit angepasst und Maschinen für den Fotosatz gebaut – einige mit Erfolg, wie etwa Berthold (die seit 1900 die Matrizen für das deutsche Linotype-System schnitten), andere waren weniger erfolgreich, wie Deberny & Peignot, die mit ihrem Lumitype-System Pleite gingen. Wieder andere verfügten über ein zweites Standbein; Enschedé etwa besaß eine Druckerei, die Lettergieterij Amsterdam stieg in den Handel mit Druckmaschinen ein. Zwar sind die kommerziellen Schriftgießereien verschwunden, doch erfreulicherweise gibt es in den Niederlanden eine Stiftung namens Stichting Lettergieten, die die Kunst der Typografie hochhält. Jeder, der dieses alte Gewerbe liebt, sollte sie unterstützen!

Einmal bei einem meiner Besuche in der Amsterdamer Universitätsbibliothek bemerkte ein Bibliothekar nebenbei zu mir: „Wie haben hier 70 Meter an Schriftmustern." Mir muss das Blut in den Kopf geschossen sein. Zuhause nahm ich ein Maßband und stellte fest, dass ich vielleicht auf die Hälfte kam. Eine Lektion in Sachen Bescheidenheit.

96 פונקט נומער 83841

באַראָק־איניציאלן סעריע

48 פונקט נומער 83842

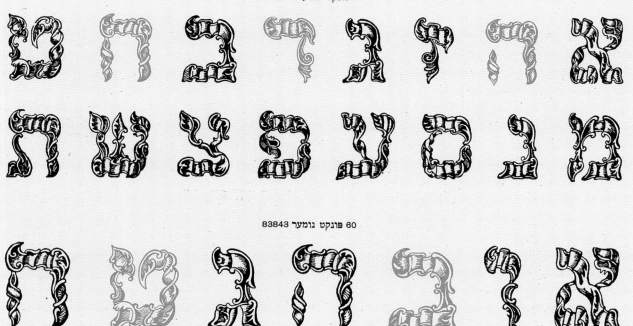

60 פונקט נומער 83843

H. BERTHOLD AG — ה. בערטהאלד אנ

Collectionner les spécimens de caractères

par Jan Tholenaar
Avec une introduction de Casper Gijzen

Les spécimens de caractères de la fin
du XIXe siècle sont vraiment séduisants ;
leur infinie variété est merveilleuse.

Le collectionneur Jan Tholenaar a rassemblé l'une des plus grandes collections privées de spécimens de caractères. Ses préférences individuelles donnant le ton, la collection se concentre sur des pièces réalisées entre 1830 et 1930. Ces 100 années ont vu se créer une variété considérable de caractères fantaisie et d'ornements, ainsi que des exemples d'impression d'art. Plein d'enthousiasme, Tholenaar présente quelques-unes de ces pièces magnifiques et s'exalte : « Toute cette richesse, toutes ces associations de couleurs éclatantes. Ces constructions tellement complexes ; regardez ça, il a fallu des semaines de travail. Et toutes ces lettres et ornements dans des coloris aussi variés. Ce vert et ce brun pâles à côté de ce gris léger, ça ne jure pas du tout. Et regardez la façon dont ça s'accorde, incroyable ! Et tout est de la typographie, pas de lithographie. On trouve parfois des objets singuliers ; regardez donc cette pièce, composée entièrement en lignes de cuivre ! Elles étaient fixées avec du plâtre ; personne ne sait plus faire ça. Il arrive qu'on trouve une très belle signature, faite avec le même procédé. » Et Tholenaar montre, effectivement, de magnifiques exemples de composition, tous faits de lettres, de lignes ou d'ornements complexes. Pour tout ce matériel proposé à la vente, on concevait des démonstrations appliquées, qui étaient composées et imprimées à la main. Tholenaar feuillette l'ouvrage plus avant : « Les spécimens de caractères de la fin du XIXe siècle sont vraiment séduisants ; leur infinie variété est merveilleuse. »

Tholenaar exprime son admiration sans réserve pour l'amour avec lequel les spécimens étaient composés à cette époque. Il montre un spécimen dans lequel un seul caractère est présenté comme exemple ingénieux de la typographie du graphiste, et un autre qui propose différents procédés d'impression : typographie, gravure et offset.

Seule restriction que Tholenaar s'impose pour sa collection, tous les spécimens doivent être composés au plomb. Il possède des échantillons de fonderies ou d'imprimeurs, mais un spécimen peut également exister sous forme de publicité dans un magazine, par exemple. Il les achète à des marchands de livres anciens dans le monde entier. Il a naturellement l'occasion de voir de nombreux catalogues. Il cite en exemple le fameux catalogue de caractères de Jammes : « Ce n'est même pas la peine d'y songer… Regardez les prix. Et ils sont tous comme ça. C'était terrible, une vraie torture, rien que des spécimens de caractères. »

Il trouve certains spécimens « amusants », d'autres simplement « jolis ». Il ne montre pas beaucoup d'enthousiasme pour les caractères sans empattements dessinés au siècle dernier, exception faite du Futura de Paul Renner. « Mais si on compare les lettres fantaisie de l'époque victorienne avec la typographie suisse de l'après-guerre, parfaite mais austère, les premières ont beaucoup plus de charme. »

Casper Gijzen

Il n'est pas si facile de collectionner des spécimens de caractères aujourd'hui ; ils sont devenus rares et coûteux. Tout ou presque doit être acheté chez des marchands de livres anciens ou dans des ventes aux enchères. Un sacré trou dans le porte-monnaie. Il me serait impossible de recommencer à zéro ma collection de plusieurs milliers de pièces. Quand j'entre dans une librairie ancienne (chose à laquelle il m'est difficile de résister où que je sois dans le monde) et que je demande s'ils ont des spécimens de caractères, on me répond souvent : « Non, et quand il m'arrive d'en avoir, ils partent vite ; ce sont de vraies pièces de collection maintenant. »

Je me souviens d'un de mes premiers achats, un *Muster-Sammlung* de Schelter & Giesecke de 1886. Je l'ai trouvé chez Kok sur Oude Hoogstraat, à Amsterdam.

C'est en prenant des cours à l'École de graphisme d'Amsterdam sur Dintelstraat, entre 1945 et 1947, qu'est né mon amour des caractères. Je suivais les classes de composition de J. Aarden, connu pour ses cours de linotypie, ou « nouvelle vague » (1920–1928), et de « typographie illustrative » (1928–1934). Dans la classe de dessin de Möllenkamp, nous restions des heures à traficoter avec le Hollandsche Medieval ; je n'oublierai jamais, aussi longtemps que je vivrai, que le *A* a un petit drapeau. Nous avions des lettres comme Nobel, Romulus, Bodoni, Studio, Libra ou Iris. Mes préférées étaient Trajanus et Gravure, avec ses longues hampes ascendantes et descendantes.

J'ai vraiment adoré visiter la bibliothèque de la fonderie de caractères Amsterdam (anciennement fonderie Nicholas Tetterode, à Rotterdam, située ensuite sur Bilderdijkstraat, à Amsterdam). C'est là que j'ai vu pour la première fois un spécimen de Derriey de 1862, probablement le plus beau jamais produit. Il a fallu des années avant que je réussisse à m'en procurer un.

À l'occasion d'une visite à St. Bride Printing Library à Londres, j'ai appris l'existence des publications de Printers' International Specimen Exchange. Seize annuaires ont été publiés depuis 1880, en éditions de 200 à 450 exemplaires. Les imprimeurs anglais, en particulier, soumettaient leur plus belle œuvre pour qu'elle apparaisse dans ces annuaires, la préservant ainsi pour la postérité. Les annuaires présentaient des travaux de compositions complexes (impression d'art), avec des couleurs en grand nombre et toute une panoplie de lettres, belles ou laides. Je suis particulièrement friand de l'impression de l'époque victorienne ; c'est parfois vraiment charmant, et parfois joliment laid. Les Allemands ont repris l'idée de ces annuaires, et j'ai la chance de posséder un certain nombre de ces ouvrages

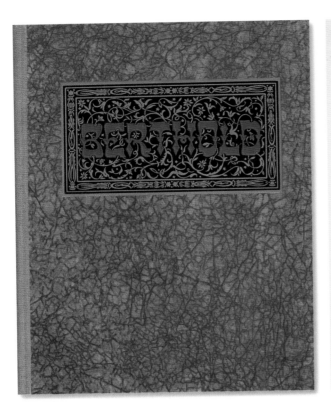

anglais et allemands dans ma bibliothèque. Il existe un produit similaire de fabrication hollandaise, le *Uitwisseling van kunstdrukwerk in Nederland*, dont je possède le premier – et dernier ? – volume, datant de 1893. Il contient à peine plus de 20 pages.

J'avais l'occasion de beaucoup voyager pour mon travail (coproduction de livres). C'est en 1963, pendant la première Foire du livre pour la jeunesse de Bologne, que j'ai trouvé chez un antiquaire un spécimen de caractères grand format d'un imprimeur bolognais, plié en quatre. Je crois que je l'ai payé l'équivalent de 20 euros environ, une grosse somme pour moi à l'époque. Le spécimen est resté dans un tiroir pendant des années, jusqu'à ce que la collection en devienne à la mode. J'en ai envoyé une photocopie à l'université de Bologne, en demandant des informations. Le spécimen s'est révélé provenir de la famille d'imprimeurs Benacci, en activité à Bologne au XVIe siècle et au début du XVIIe siècle. La bibliothèque de l'université de Bologne m'informa qu'ils avaient de nombreux spécimens de ces imprimeurs, mais pas celui-ci. Je peux maintenant me flatter de l'idée qu'il s'agit d'un exemplaire unique et de l'un des plus vieux spécimens de caractères. Le marchand de livres anciens Herzberger m'en a offert un bon prix, mais je ne regrette pas d'avoir résisté à la tentation. Il y a deux ans environ, j'ai pu acheter un très rare volume in-douze de madrigaux, imprimé et publié, entre 1588 et 1590, par Alessandro et Vittorio Benacci qui ont fait un usage original et généreux de leurs vignettes. Voilà qui donne vraiment du relief à un spécimen de caractères.

En principe, je collectionne tout ce qui est spécimen, de tous les pays et de toutes les époques, me donnant comme unique restriction l'époque du plomb. Il existe différentes sources de spécimens : les fonderies de caractères, les imprimeurs et un petit nombre de relieurs. Les spécimens illustrent l'usage des caractères en plomb ou fabriqués dans des matériaux comme le bois, le cuivre ou le fer (pour impressions). Il y a aussi des vignettes et des ornements, des stéréotypes de gravures sur bois, et toutes sortes de lignes de cuivre. J'ai bien un certain nombre de spécimens de photocomposition, mais je les ai eus pratiquement pour rien. Ils brillent souvent par leur aspect terne, si ce n'est par leur laideur. Il y a des exceptions, bien sûr, comme par exemple le joli spécimen Compugraphic en trois parties, imprimé en deux couleurs et composé par Jost Hochuli, avec une application humoristique du caractère sur chaque page de droite.

Il existe une variété infinie de spécimens de caractères, de toutes les formes et de toutes les tailles. Ceux qui présentent une gamme complète ont souvent une reliure cartonnée. Il existe un très gros spécimen, le *Hauptprobe* de 1925, de Stempel, qui fait environ 1200 pages et plus de 10 centimètres d'épaisseur ; relié en demi-parchemin, il pèse 7 kilos. Il y a également de minces volumes vantant les qualités d'un seul caractère. Ils sont souvent agrafés, mais il arrive que certains soient cousus en cahiers, avec une couverture souple. Il y a des années, j'ai acheté deux cartons de spécimens de ce genre au marchand de livres anciens Horodisch, qui venait apparemment de les acquérir dans une vente aux enchères. Il me fit observer à l'époque que ces minces brochures, avec un spécimen d'un seul caractère, étaient bien plus belles et plus intéressantes que les gros volumes. Il avait raison. Elles présentent différentes applications du caractère et sont souvent très élégamment composées, parfois même par le graphiste du caractère. L'usage de la couleur n'y est pas ignoré.

Les spécimens de caractères ne se trouvaient pas uniquement dans les publications spécialisées, bien sûr ; ils étaient aussi intégrés dans les revues internes des fonderies, comme le *Typografische mededelingen* de la fonderie Amsterdam ; celle de Johannes Enschedé & Zonen ; l'*Archivio tipografico* de Nebiolo ; le *Typographische Mitteilungen* de Schelter & Giesecke ; et *La crónica* de Richard Gans à Madrid. Il y a aussi les publications mondialement connues : le *Monotype Recorder* et le *Linotype Bulletin*. On trouve également des spécimens de caractères sous forme de publicité dans des revues professionnelles comme *Graphicus*, *The British Printer*, *Typographische Jahrbücher*, *Deutscher Buch- und Steindrucker*, et la revue suisse *Les archives de l'imprimerie*. Les fonderies de caractères françaises avaient une revue commune au début du XXe siècle appelée *La fonderie typographique*. Elles y présentaient de superbes exemples des nouveaux caractères, ornements etc., souvent du plus pur style Art Nouveau. En Allemagne, il y eut le *Journal für Buchdruckerkunst, Schriftgießerei und die verwandten Fächer* vers le milieu du XIXe siècle, et, plus tard dans le siècle, *Archiv für Buchdruckerkunst, Schriftgießerei…* Une infinité d'appendices étaient reliés à l'intérieur, se dépliant parfois en grands formats, avec une composition des plus complexes et une impression en plusieurs couleurs – dignes d'être encadrés. Aujourd'hui, les appendices ont souvent disparu, mais les volumes de ma collection, eux, sont complets.

Les spécimens de caractères étaient également imprimés dans des manuels ou des encyclopédies. *The History and Art of Printing* (1770) de P. Luckombe contenait un spécimen de Caslon de 36 pages, de 1763. Huit pages de 1785 figuraient dans le *Cyclopaedia* de Chambers, qui comprenait aussi un grand format de Fry. En 1767, 10 pages de Fournier furent incluses dans l'*En-

Jan Tholenaar

1924, Die Hebräische Schrift,
H. Berthold AG, Berlin, Leipzig, Stuttgart,
Vienna, Riga

The Bible, the best-selling book of all
time. In 1924, there was a wonderful collection of typefaces available for producing the Torah and other texts in Hebrew.

Die Bibel, der größte Bestseller aller
Zeiten. 1924 existierte eine wunderbare
Auswahl an Schriften für die Thora und
andere hebräische Texte.

La Bible, éternel best-seller. En 1924,
il existait un magnifique ensemble de
caractères disponibles pour fabriquer en
hébreu la Torah ainsi que d'autres textes.

cyclopédie élémentaire (« *Tableau des vingt corps de caractères, d'usage ordinaire
dans l'imprimerie* ») et, naturellement, dans la seconde partie de son *Manuel
typographique*, imprimé en 1766. *Die so nöthig als nützliche Buchdruckerkunst
und Schriftgießerey* présentait le « *Schrift-Probe, oder kurzes Verzeichniss derjenigen Hebräisch-, Griechisch-, Lateinisch-, und Teutschen Schriften, welche in Herrn
Bernhard Christoph Breitkopfs Schriftgießerey allhier befindlich sind. Dabey man
mehrentheils bemerket hat, von wem eine jede Schrift in Messing oder Stahl ist geschnidten worden* ». Un traité d'Ernesti sur la fonte de caractères et l'imprimerie, de 1721 (*Die wol-eingerichtete Buchdruckerey*), contient des spécimens de
caractères probablement créés par Endters qui a imprimé et publié l'ouvrage.

Faisons un peu la chronologie de ma collection : j'ai acheté un très vieux
spécimen après avoir hésité plus d'une année, dans l'espoir que personne ne
serait prêt à l'acquérir sans en négocier le prix. Je suis allé chercher ce spécimen moi-même, à Londres en l'occurrence. On ne confie pas pareil colis à
la poste. Il s'agissait du Stampa Vaticana de 1628 de Brogiotti. Il en a été
publié un fac-similé, prouvant s'il en est besoin l'importance de ce spécimen ancien. Voici un récapitulatif des quelques spécimens en ma possession dont il existe un fac-similé : le Claude Lamesle de 1742, le Du Sieur
Delacologne de 1773, et les spécimens Enschedé de 1768 et 1773. Les spécimens du XVIIIᵉ siècle de ma collection comprennent l'Enschedé de 1748, le
Fournier de 1764, le Louis Luce de 1740, le Gillé de 1778, le spécimen de J. de
Groot de La Haye de 1781, les Wilsons de 1783 et 1789, le Caslon de 1785 (avec
21 pages de merveilleuses et astucieuses applications de Flowers), le Fry de
1787 et le spécimen d'Imprenta Real de Madrid de 1799. Je possède également quelques très jolis spécimens du XIXᵉ siècle, de Bodoni (1818), Didot
(1819), ou encore Fry (1824). C'est un nombre assez important pour un
collectionneur privé, mais une fraction à peine de ce qu'on trouve dans les
collections publiques. Il existe d'importantes collections de cette sorte par
exemple à la Bibliothèque nationale de Paris, à la bibliothèque universitaire
d'Amsterdam (dont la collection Tetterode et la bibliothèque de la Société
royale du commerce du livre hollandais), la St. Bride Printing Library, et la
Newberry Library à Chicago. Je possède moi-même un certain nombre de
vieux spécimens Caslon et Figgins, mais si je consulte le catalogue de la St.
Bride Foundation de 1919 (qui faisait déjà presque 1000 pages), j'y trouve 70
spécimens Caslon, essentiellement du XIXᵉ siècle, et 31 spécimens Figgins.

J'ai, dans ma collection, un spécimen spécial du Bodoni Grec, qui a ceci
de particulier que le prénom, Giambatista, est écrit avec deux « t » au lieu de
trois (on l'écrit d'habitude Giambattista). Chacune des 28 pages est compo-

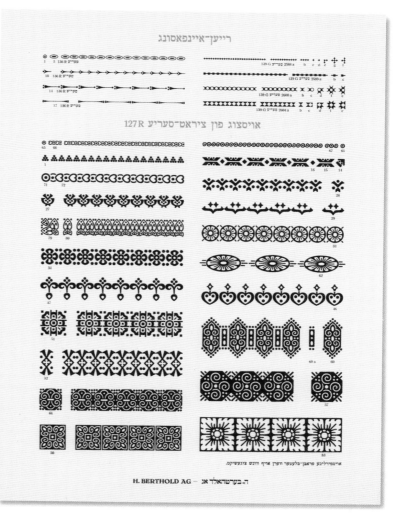

sée dans son propre caractère unique, de taille croissante. Le spécimen a été
publié en 1788, l'année où est paru son plus important spécimen, *Serie di
majuscole*, dont le Grec est dérivé. Dans le catalogue Birrell & Garnett des
exemplaires de vente de spécimens de fonderies célèbres (1928), référence
est faite à la mince brochure comme étant « extrêmement rare », au prix de

1924, Die Hebräische Schrift,
H. Berthold AG, Berlin, Leipzig, Stuttgart,
Vienna, Riga

15 guinées (les Vaticana, Lamesle et Enschedé susmentionnés y sont en vente à un prix variant entre 15 et 18 guinées). J'ai acheté le spécimen de Bodoni dans une vente aux enchères de Beijers pour bien plus que ça. L'éditeur et bibliophile parisien Renouard a dit un jour de Bodoni : « Le soir, tout en conversant avec ses amis ou en bonne compagnie, au cours des repas, il était toujours occupé avec ses caractères, justifiant ou limant une matrice, dessinant une capitale. »

Je trouve les caractères de labeur du XIXe siècle plutôt quelconques : c'est essentiellement le royaume de Didot et Bodoni. Un spécimen Turlot de 1885 environ, publié à Paris, est composé par exemple de 27 pages de caractères en corps 8 qui sont tous pratiquement identiques, si ce n'est qu'ils sont à peine un peu plus larges, un peu plus petits ou épais que le précédent. Je ne vois pas l'intérêt. Quant au caractère de titre, lui… J'ai déjà chanté plus haut les louanges de ces milliers de polices de l'époque victorienne et leur infinie variété : classiques, décadentes, chics, touchantes, hideuses, grossières ou raffinées, droites ou italiques, *égyptiennes, américaines, italiennes, syriennes, elzéviriennes, babyloniennes, pompéiennes, japonaises, milanaises, orientales, latines,* lettres en deux couleurs, innombrables *fantaisies, Zierschriften, Grotesken und Antiquas, Fraktur-Schriften, Rustic* (caractère en branche d'arbre)… la liste est infinie. Et il y a encore les *filets, vignettes, lettrines, coins, ornements, Zierleisten, Polytypen, Untergrunde, Einfassungen,* et des livres remplis de *Messinglinien.*

Vers 1820, la lithographie fit une entrée en force dans la compétition. Alors que les imprimeurs du livre, avec leurs blocs de plomb rectangulaires et rigides, étaient limités dans leurs possibilités, les dessinateurs lithographes pouvaient mettre n'importe quel dessin sur une pierre, comme ils le faisaient pour les bons et titres, les cartes de visite calligraphiées, les calendriers et autres travaux d'impression. J'en ai un certain nombre d'exemples dans ma collection. Dans leur ardeur à combattre les lithographes, les fondeurs de caractères imaginèrent des façons de composer des lignes de plomb en diagonale ou en cercle et gravèrent des ornements toujours plus nombreux et plus jolis. J'ai déjà mentionné le Charles Derriey de 1862, qui mesure plus de 40 x 30 centimètres. La première partie, « Spécimen », y présente les vignettes. Ce sont des graphismes magnifiques, parfois pour des impressions en deux ou trois couleurs. Puis viennent les « *Caractères ornés* », les « *Trais de plumes* », les « *Coins composés, filets, passe-partouts* » sophistiqués, etc. La seconde partie, « Album », montre des applications. Cet ouvrage est tellement superbe, tellement élégant et de couleurs si délicates que je ne

peux le décrire qu'avec des superlatifs. Et quand on pense qu'il a été imprimé sur une presse manuelle : une prouesse extraordinaire, vu l'étendue de la gamme de couleurs. Je possède un autre spécimen comparable : celui de l'Imprimerie Royale de 1845 contient également un tel album. S'il vous est déjà arrivé de vous servir d'un composteur, vous vous rendrez compte à quel point il a dû être compliqué de réaliser ces pièces d'imprimerie. La compétition avec la lithographie a aussi occasionné des bizarreries ridicules et une typographie affectée.

Où ai-je donc trouvé tous ces extraordinaires spécimens de caractères ? Eh bien, j'ai toujours été un bon client du marchand de livres anciens Frits Knuf, un des rares à être spécialisé dans la bibliographie au sens large du terme. Dans la boutique de Knuf, j'ai acquis par exemple des spécimens de la bibliothèque de G. W. Ovink. En Angleterre, j'ai acheté le Lamesle de Tony Appleton. J'ai eu comme autres fournisseurs Keith Hogg, Questor Rare Books, S. P. Tuohy, Barry McKay, et les marchands de livres anciens de Londres, Marlborough, Maggs et Quaritch. Il y a un ou deux marchands de livres en Allemagne qui ont parfois une variété non négligeable de *Buchwesen.* En Amérique, j'ai de bons rapports avec Bob Fleck, d'Oak Knoll, et mon spécimen Delacologne venait de Kraus, à New York. En farfouillant beaucoup et avec un peu de chance, je trouve parfois quelque chose dans une foire aux livres anciens, un marché aux livres ou une foire aux collectionneurs. Et puis il y aussi les ventes aux enchères hollandaises comme chez Bubb Kuyper. Il m'arrive parfois d'acheter toute une pile de livres pour un seul qui me manque. Une fois ou deux, il m'est arrivé de laisser un mot sur une pile de ce genre, lors du jour de visite, après quoi, l'acheteur m'ayant contacté, j'ai pu acquérir l'objet convoité.

Naturellement, avec l'arrivée de l'Internet, je me suis mis à chercher des spécimens en ligne. J'en ai acheté à des marchands de livres, en Suisse comme en Suède, grâce à leur catalogue en ligne.

Au début des années 80, Jammes, célèbre marchand de livres anciens parisien, publiait un catalogue typographique. Il incluait la bibliothèque de l'ancienne fonderie Deberny & Peignot qui avait fait faillite, avec plus de 400 spécimens rares et insolites. Les prix étaient élevés et, à l'époque, il n'était pas question que j'achète quoi que ce soit. Une boule dans la gorge, j'ai reposé le catalogue. Ce n'est que plusieurs années plus tard que j'ai pu acheter quelques spécimens de ce merveilleux catalogue Jammes. Il m'a un peu consolé de savoir qu'avant même la publication du catalogue, certaines pièces avaient déjà été proposées à la Bibliothèque nationale, à la St. Bride

פראנק־ריהל 12 פונקט Nr. 33714

אין הבדל באושר חיי האדם בעולם, בין העשירים או בין העניים. העני
סובל, אך גם העשיר סובל לא פחות ממנו; וההבדל הוא במין וצורת הסבל.
והמאושר הוא איננו מצטער בקושי חייו. הנאהבים והנעימים בחייהם

פראנק־ריהל 16 פונקט Nr. 33716

בראשית ברא אלהים
את השמים ואת הארץ

פראנק־ריהל 14 פונקט Nr. 33715

שם בארץ הצבי במושבות
אחינו חיים חדשים יפרחו

פראנק־ריהל 24 פונקט Nr. 33718

והתורה היא חיים
למחזיקיה. אשה

פראנק־ריהל 20 פונקט Nr. 33717

והארץ היתה תהו
ובהו וחשך על פני

פראנק־ריהל 28 פונקט Nr. 33719

ויפח באפיו נשמת חיים ויהי

פראנק־ריהל 36 פונקט Nr. 33720

מצב היהודים בבוווריה

פראנק־ריהל 48 פונקט Nr. 33721

בספר חיים ברכה

פראנק־ריהל 72 פונקט Nr. 33723

האורכיטוב

H. BERTHOLD AG — ה. בערטהאלד אג

In 1858, Hermann Berthold (1831–1904) began a brass rule factory in Berlin that would eventually become the leading company of its kind in Germany. After Berthold's death, the firm entered the type founding field and acquired a number of established German foundries. Soon, Berthold type measurements would form the basis of the Didot type measurement system still in use today. In 1919, the company bought the original Walbaum foundry. This was originally sold to the publisher and printer F. A. Brockhaus in 1836 and moved to Leipzig from Weimar after the death of Walbaum's son. In the future, Berthold would use the services of many eminent type designers, including Herbert Post, Imre Reiner, and Günter Gerhard Lange. After World War II, Berthold became a leader in phototypesetting. In 1958, at its 100th anniversary, the company produced the first commercial phototypesetting system, Diatype, which was followed by Diatext in 1975, and Berthold ads 3000 in 1977 (the akzidenz-dialog-system). Continuing as a major force in typeface production, Berthold licensed 500 typefaces to ADOBE for use as PostScript fonts.

Hermann Berthold (1831–1904) gründete 1858 in Berlin eine Messinglinienfabrik, die in der Folge zum Marktführer auf ihrem Gebiet wurde. Nach Bertholds Tod wandte sich das Unternehmen dem Gießen von Schriften zu und übernahm eine Reihe namhafter deutscher Gießereien. Auf der Grundlage des von Berthold verwendeten Schriftsatzmaßes erfolgte die Überarbeitung des Didot-Maßsystems, das in dieser Form bis heute gebräuchlich ist. 1919 übernahm die H. Berthold AG die ehemalige Gießerei Walbaum. Diese war 1836 an das Verlagshaus und Druckerei F. A. Brockhaus verkauft und nach dem Tod von Justus Erich Walbaums Sohn von Weimar nach Leipzig verlegt worden. Die H. Berthold AG nahm später zahlreiche bedeutende Schriftentwerfer in ihre Dienste, darunter Herbert Post, Imre Reiner und Günter Gerhard Lange. Nach dem Zweiten Weltkrieg wurde Berthold zum führenden Unternehmen auf dem Gebiet des Fotosatzes. Zum 100. Geburtstag der Firma kam im Jahr 1958 mit dem Diatype-Gerät das erste Fotosatzsystem auf den Markt, dem 1975 das System Diatext und 1977 das ads 3000 (Akzidenz-Dialog-System) folgten. Noch für geraume Zeit einer der wichtigsten Schrifthersteller, überließ Berthold schließlich der Firma Adobe 500 seiner Schriftarten als PostScript-Fonts.

Printing Library (qui a dû faire appel à des fonds spéciaux de la British Library), et à la Newberry Library. La Taylor Institution à Oxford avait également acheté un certain nombre de pièces importantes. C'était une déception pour moi, mais une partie importante des spécimens décrits avaient déjà trouvé un bercail avant même la sortie du catalogue.

Soit dit en passant, le catalogue Jammes me fait penser à un type de spécimen qui ne m'intéresse guère : l'impression à la fumée. Quand un graveur de caractères voulait faire une impression d'une matrice, il ne la faisait pas avec de l'encre mais avec du noir de fumée provenant d'une chandelle fumante, ce qui donne une impression particulièrement précise.

Dans sa bibliographie *Die deutsche Schriftgießerei* (1923), Oscar Jolles fait mention de spécimens de quelque 120 fonderies du XIXe siècle. Mais il y en avait beaucoup plus, comme par exemple de petites fonderies en interne affiliées à un imprimeur. J'imagine qu'ils ont tous dû fabriquer des spécimens de caractère à un moment ou à un autre, mais qu'en est-il advenu ? Il en reste peut-être dans des bibliothèques ou des archives, mais une grande partie doit avoir disparu, ne serait-ce que pendant la Seconde Guerre mondiale. Et nous connaissons tous des histoires d'imprimeurs ou autres maisons faisant le vide dans leur grenier et leurs archives avant de déménager. Il se passait la même chose au XIXe siècle. J'ai personnellement des spécimens de 60 fonderies allemandes, mais c'est en comptant les feuilles simples. Je n'ai jamais rien trouvé en provenance des autres fonderies dans aucun catalogue de marchands de livres anciens. Le *Buchdruckschriften im 20. Jahrhundert* (1995) dit qu'il existait 73 fonderies en Allemagne en 1889 ; en raison de fusions et de rachats, ce nombre a diminué de façon drastique au XXe siècle. Plus récemment, dans l'entre-deux-guerres, il y a eu une création de quantité de nouveaux caractères, et des tirages à 10 000 exemplaires étaient monnaie courante pour du matériel publicitaire. Néanmoins, les spécimens de cette époque sont devenus rares, la plupart ayant disparu pendant la Seconde Guerre mondiale. Hans Adolf Halbey écrit dans son livre, *Karl Klingspor, Leben und Werk* (1991), que la fonderie Klingspor a été presque entièrement détruite par des bombardements en mars 1944. Quelque 200 tonnes de caractères, l'imprimerie, des dizaines de milliers de spécimens de caractères et autres publications, des dessins et 120 dossiers de correspondance avec des artistes ont été perdus.

Il n'est, en général, pas facile de dater les spécimens. Certains affichent l'année dans les pages préliminaires, comme ce spécimen de Wimble & Co., Nouvelle-Zélande, daté du 1er juillet 1928, qui se trouve être ma date de naissance. Mais pour dater la plupart des spécimens, il faut chercher des références dans la littérature typographique, ce qui n'est pas une mince affaire. On trouve parfois un indice dans le spécimen lui-même : une médaille datée ou – pour des caractères en script – une lettre échantillon avec une date, une invitation datée pour une soirée, ou une carte des vins.

Jan Tholenaar

En 1858, Hermann Berthold (1831–1904) fonde, à Berlin, une fabrique de règles en laiton qui va devenir la plus importante d'Allemagne. Après la mort de Berthold, la firme s'intéresse à la fonderie de caractères et rachète un certain nombre de fonderies allemandes. Le système de mesure des caractères de Berthold va vite former la base du système de mesure en points Didot toujours en vigueur aujourd'hui. En 1919, la compagnie achète la fonderie Walbaum qui avait été vendue à l'éditeur-imprimeur F. A. Brockhaus en 1836, et transférée de Weimar à Leipzig après la mort du fils de Walbaum. Berthold fera plus tard appel aux services d'éminent dessinateurs de caractères,

comme Herbert Post, Imre Reiner ou Günter Gerhard Lange. Après la Seconde Guerre mondiale, Berthold devient leader dans la photocomposition. En 1958, centième anniversaire de la compagnie, ils fabriquent le premier système commercial de photocomposition, la Diatype, suivie en 1975 de la Diatext, puis de la Berthold ADS (Akzidenz-Dialog-System) 3000 en 1977. Tenant toujours une place importante dans le domaine de la production de caractères, Berthold vend sous licence 500 polices de caractères à Adobe comme fontes PostScript.

1924, Die Hebräische Schrift,
H. Berthold AG, Berlin, Leipzig, Stuttgart, Vienna, Riga

Je peux estimer avec une relative précision la période de provenance du spécimen à partir de la police et du style. Mais on peut lourdement se tromper quand on a affaire, par exemple, à un imprimeur des années 30 qui utilisait encore tous les ornements Jugendstil ainsi que les caractères victoriens. Berthold a facilité les choses en numérotant ses spécimens. Le spécimen Journal-Antiqua, par exemple, Heft 198, a été produit aux alentours de 1920. Et le Boulevard Probe 448 date d'environ 1960. Schelter & Giesecke ont fait la même chose. Woellmer a numéroté ses pages à la suite. Dans son spécimen *Brokateinfassung,* produit vers 1902, par exemple, les pages sont numérotées de 1324 à 1331, et, dans le spécimen *Deutsche Reichsschrift*, produit vers 1920, de 6974 à 6996.

Soit dit en passant, dans des spécimens de caractères allemands précédant la Seconde Guerre mondiale, il arrive qu'on tombe sur un texte national-socialiste (nazi) et, ici ou là, sur une croix gammée. Un des spécimens de Trennert, pour le caractère Blizzard, aux environs de 1938, utilise explicitement *Heil Hitler* pour en faire la démonstration.

Jusqu'au début du XXe siècle, seul était connu le nom d'une poignée de graphistes typographes comme Garamond, Bodoni ou Fournier. Les milliers de caractères produits par les fonderies au XIXe siècle étaient dessinés et gravés par des ouvriers anonymes. Dans les catalogues de caractères, il y est fait référence comme « *im Hause* » ou « *Hausschnitt* ». C'est surtout Klingspor qui a su attirer et créditer des graphistes de renom au début du XXe siècle : Otto Eckmann, Rudolf Koch, Walter Tiemann, Imre Reiner, etc. Bauer, par exemple, eut recours aux services d'Heinrich Wieynk, F. H. Ehmcke, Lucian Bernhard, E. R. Weiss, Paul Renner (concepteur de la police Futura) et F. H. Ernst Schneidler. Berthold employa des graphistes comme Louis Oppenheim, Georg Trump ou Herbert Bayer (du Bauhaus). D'importants graphistes ont également travaillé pour la fonderie Ludwig und Mayer, comme Heinrich Jost, J. Erbar ou J. V. Cissarz. Georg Belwe et Jan Tschichold ont travaillé pour Schelter & Giesecke, et F. W. Kleukens et Hermann Zapf pour Stempel. Certains graphistes dessinaient des polices pour plusieurs firmes. Les spécimens dédiés à ces créations sont généralement des tours de force typographiques et de petites merveilles d'impression.

Il est certain que, pour une grande partie des XIXe et XXe siècles, les Allemands ont été novateurs dans ce domaine. Mais dans d'autres pays aussi, il existait d'excellents graphistes travaillant pour les fonderies. Georges Auriol et E. Grasset ont travaillé pour Peignot, par exemple ; A. M. Cassandre et Adrian Frutiger pour Deberny & Peignot ; Roger Excoffon

pour Olive ; Aldo Novarese pour Nebiolo ; Warren Chappell et Morris F. Benton pour American Type Founders ; Rudolph Ruzicka, W. A. Dwiggins et Walter Tracy pour Linotype ; et F. W. Goudy, Bruce Rogers, Berthold Wolpe et Eric Gill pour Monotype. Aux Pays-Bas, au XXe siècle, S. H. de Roos et Dick Dooijes ont été employés par Lettergieterij Amsterdam, et J. van Krimpen et S. L. Hartz ont travaillé pour Enschedé.

J'aimerais mentionner plusieurs spécimens de ma collection que je considère insolites pour une raison ou une autre. J'ai un spécimen datant de 1832 provenant de la fonderie F. Dresler und Rost-Fingerlin de Francfort, créée cinq ans auparavant et qui succédait à la Schleussnersche Schriftgießerei, fondée au XVIIIe siècle. Plus tard dans le siècle, elle fut reprise par Flinsh, qui fut à son tour avalée par la Bauersche Gießerei.

Les publications produites à Rome par la Typis Sacrae Congregationis de Propaganda Fide, fondée en 1626 pour propager la foi chrétienne parmi les peuples de l'Orient, sont une tout autre affaire. C'est avec ces imprimeurs, qui opéraient aux XVIIe et XVIIIe siècles, que Bodoni apprit son métier. Ils gravaient les alphabets exotiques destinés à leurs publications : copte, tibétain, persan, etc. Certains de leurs ouvrages étaient des manuels de grammaire de langue étrangère avec le Pater Noster dans cette langue. En 1798, les caractères furent transférés à Paris, où fut publié en 1805 le Pater Noster en 150 langues, en hommage du pape à Napoléon, à l'occasion de son couronnement. De nombreux caractères sont toujours conservés à l'Imprimerie Nationale. Je possède 14 de ces publications, datant de 1629 à 1789.

Edmund Fry doit également être mentionné dans ce contexte. Son spécimen de 1787 inclut l'hébreu, le grec, l'éthiopien, le samaritain, l'arabe, le persan, le turc, le tartare et le malais. En 1799, il publia *Pantographia,* un ouvrage de 320 pages, contenant les représentations exactes de tous les alphabets connus, assorties d'explications. Edmund Fry grava lui-même la plupart des caractères de cette publication.

Le premier spécimen important de la fonderie Schelter & Giesecke, fondée en 1819, fut publié en 1836. Dans leur livre commémoratif de 1894, j'ai lu qu'au début du XIXe siècle, un bon fondeur de caractères pouvait produire de 5 à 6000 lettres par jour, à la main ! Dans son livre *Chronik der Schriftgießereien* (1928), Friedrich Bauer avance le chiffre de 2 à 4000. Après l'avènement de la fonte mécanique, au milieu du XIXe siècle, le chiffre fut multiplié par 6. *Proben aus der Schriftgiesserey der Andreäischen Buchhandlung,* publié en 1834 à Francfort-sur-le-Main, est également rare. Sur la page de titre, une annonce a été collée, précisant que, depuis le 1er juillet 1839, l'affai-

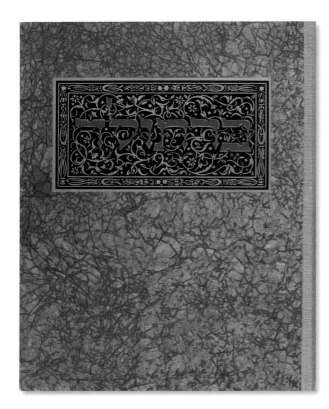

re a été rachetée par la Schriftgießerei, Buch-, Congrève- und Steindruckerei, de Benjamin Krebs. Et c'est ainsi que cette fonderie, fondée en 1581 par Johann Wechsel, œuvra jusqu'au XXe siècle.

De la même époque, j'ai un spécimen produit par Eduard Haenal (1837) peu avant la destruction de sa fonderie de Magdebourg par un incendie; il poursuivit son activité à Berlin.

Les fonderies allemandes avaient souvent une filiale à Moscou ou à Saint-Pétersbourg pour desservir le marché russe. J'ai un spécimen de grand format de chez Berthold, produit à la fin du XIXe siècle, entièrement en russe, avec de multiples exemples en de nombreuses couleurs. Il y a également de chez Berthold un spécimen en hébreu daté de 1924 – qui se lit naturellement à l'envers – avec plusieurs styles de caractères et de merveilleuses illustrations en couleur. En 1925, un spécimen similaire fut publié dans des langues orientales, comme l'arabe, le turc ou l'hindi.

En 1990 parut un autre spécimen de caractères au plomb: *A Miscellany of Type*. Ce spécimen de grand format est imprimé sur 148 pages d'un papier de fort grammage fabriqué à la forme, et publié en édition limitée (540 exemplaires) par English Whittington Press, imprimeur et éditeur du fabuleux annuaire *Matrix. A Miscellany of Type* est un modèle exemplaire d'impression, avec des gravures sur bois et d'autres illustrations en couleur empruntées à d'autres publications de cet imprimeur.

Lorsque j'ai acheté le livre *Ornamented Types*, publié et imprimé à Londres par Ian Mortimer, on ne le trouvait dans aucune collection publique hollandaise. Il contient des impressions de lettres ornées en bois, produites par la fonderie londonienne Pouchée au début du XIXe siècle. En 1936, Monotype Corporation acquit ce matériel lors de la liquidation de la fonderie Caslon. Il a survécu aux bombardements de la guerre et se trouve maintenant à la St. Bride Printing Library. Il a fallu des années pour imprimer les 200 exemplaires sur une vieille presse manuelle. L'ouvrage consiste en 24 alphabets – 45 pages en tout – imprimés sur un papier Zerkall-Bütten (53 x 38 cm) de 170 g. Le tout est présenté dans un coffret, avec une introduction séparée de James Mosley. Ce spécimen est cher, ce qui n'est pas surprenant si l'on considère la somme énorme de travail qu'il a nécessité. Son prix est tout à fait mérité.

Un spécimen de la fonderie Gurajati de Bombay, fondée en 1900, contient plus de 400 pages dans de nombreuses couleurs et fut tiré à 10 000 exemplaires. Un article publié dans *Matrix* 2 à propos de cet ouvrage dit qu'il fut commencé en 1926 et qu'il visait à «surpasser» les fonderies occi-

dentales au niveau de la qualité technique et de la production. Un imprimeur et un compositeur expérimentés furent engagés et une nouvelle presse allemande achetée; le papier pour impression d'art fut acheté en Amérique et l'encre en Angleterre, chez Manders. Le travail fut achevé en 1937 – une production de 11 ans qui explique pourquoi je n'ai pas envie de m'étendre sur cette question du «surpassement».

Il existe aussi des petits spécimens d'imprimeries privées. J'ai payé très cher une simple feuille: «Specimens of Type Used at The Ashendene Press». Ce qu'elle a de spécial, c'est qu'elle inclut deux polices de caractères originales, Subiaco et Ptolemy, créées et gravées pour le propriétaire d'Ashendene, M. Hornby. Un spécimen de Hans Mardersteig pour Monotype (1928) présente Pastonchi, gravé spécialement pour une nouvelle série de classiques italiens. Il parut en édition limitée à 200 exemplaires, imprimés à la main sur papier Fabriano, incluant des exemples collés.

Dans ce contexte, les spécimens de Paul Hayden Duensing (qui gravait ses poinçons et fondait ses caractères lui-même) méritent d'être mentionnés, tout comme Harrisfeldwegpresse, Alembic Press, Overbrook Press, Harbor Press, avec un petit livre vraiment charmant de 1934, Kit-Cat Press, Sandelswood Press et Philippsberger Werkstatt, sans oublier Charles Whitehouse d'Edition Seefeld. Ce dernier éditeur publia par exemple une feuille du Romanée de Van Krimpen, d'une belle composition classique et imprimée à la main avec une presse Kniehebel sur un papier à grain fabriqué à la forme. Le papier était humidifié avant l'impression et le résultat est fabuleux. Les italiques étroits en corps 10 sont incroyablement précis et vraiment noirs, sans être trop gras. Ce qui rend cette feuille spéciale, c'est cet effet presque tridimensionnel, ce relief qu'on n'obtient pas avec la technique de l'offset. Elle me conforte dans l'idée que la disparition du plomb fut une perte irréparable pour l'art d'imprimer.

Naturellement, les imprimeurs hollandais de seconde importance ne doivent pas être omis ici: De Vergulde Maatlat, Eric van der Wal, Ter Lugt Pers, De Vier Seizoenen, Willem Muilenburg, Triona Pers, Exponent, Elze ter Harkel, Tuinwijkpers (Rosart), Castanha Pers (Garamond) et Drukschuur Blaricum. Un exemple de spécimen très original est celui de De Dwarsbomen (Gert van Oortmerssen). L'élément de base est en matériau rigide, et le dos séparé, qui pèse un kilo, est fondu avec des caractères recyclés. L'artiste surréaliste Moesman a aussi créé un caractère, Petronius. Il fut employé pour la première fois en 1975 dans un spécimen de caractères. Je ne sais pas s'il a jamais été utilisé depuis.

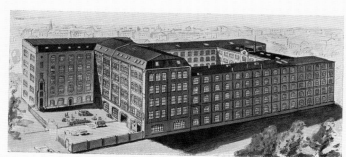

filigrane. Les ornements et autres furent créés spécialement pour Curwen par des artistes comme Claud Lovat Fraser, Paul Nash ou Percy Smith et les caractères par des artistes comme Rudolf Koch ou Jan van Krimpen.

Theodore Low De Vinne (1828–1914) était un imprimeur renommé de New York, auteur de divers ouvrages consacrés à l'imprimerie, et co-fondateur et président du premier syndicat de maîtres imprimeurs américains. Je mentionnerai deux de ses spécimens que je possède. Il était encore associé avec l'imprimeur Francis Hart lorsqu'il publia le premier, un spécimen de 96 pages intitulé *Specimens of Pointed Texts and Black Letters,* en 1878. Les *black letters* sont ce qu'on appelle les lettres gothiques et les *pointed letters* sont à peu près la même chose – ce type de caractères était utilisé pour les bibles, mais aussi pour des prospectus ou autres. Ce spécimen contient environ 50 caractères. Le second fut publié par de De Vinne Press en 1891. Il contient quelque 144 pages en caractères de labeur et serait en soi un livre ennuyeux, n'était-ce que chaque page présente des lettrines différentes, pour lesquelles on n'a lésiné ni sur la peine ni sur la dépense : tailles et dessins variés, et la plupart d'entre elles en deux couleurs et or.

Dans la même veine, il y a un spécimen de petit format de 1903, exclusivement consacré à des caractères de labeur. Il fut imprimé et publié en édition limitée à 1500 «*maskinnummerede*» exemplaires par l'imprimeur Martius Truelsen. J'allais souvent à Copenhague où je rendais chaque fois visite au marchand de livres anciens Busck. C'est là que j'ai acheté le spécimen, en 1979, puis un autre exemplaire, quelques années plus tard. L'ouvrage contient 176 pages, sous une reliure entièrement en cuir estampillé. Les cahiers ne sont pas cousus mais agrafés, et les agrafes peuvent rouiller. Mais l'intérieur est beau. Chaque double page est différente, avec un en-tête décoré à gauche et des lettrines en début de texte qui forment un ensemble souvent du plus pur style Art Nouveau. Il y a de merveilleuses compositions (anonymes) en trois ou quatre couleurs et des couleurs différentes sur chaque page. Il a peut-être nécessité 300 couleurs au total.

Mon exemplaire du *Boktryckeri calendar* de 1902–1903 (avec la signature de l'imprimeur-éditeur Wald. Zachrisson et la dédicace «Hommage à Mr. Theo L. De Vinne») contient une photo imprimée de Martius Truelsen. Il raconte comment, devenu orphelin à l'âge de 15 ans, il dut dès lors se débrouiller seul. À 30 ans, avec les quelque centaines de couronnes qu'il avait gagnées, il démarra sa propre affaire et, en 1903, à 50 ans, il dirigeait une imprimerie de 50 employés. Outre mes deux exemplaires des spécimens de Truelsen, j'ai des boîtes pleines de doubles fantastiques.

Curwen Press, les imprimeurs renommés de *The Fleuron,* demandèrent à Oliver Simon de compiler et de concevoir un spécimen en 1928. Le spécimen est cher, non tant qu'il s'agisse d'une édition limitée (135 exemplaires) que parce qu'il est exceptionnellement bien réalisé, d'une austère composition classique sur un papier fabriqué à la main et comportant son propre

שריפט מיריאם, ראמזעס־וויגנעטן,
אקסידידענץ־שמוק סעריע R 138 .Nr

מיר האבן אין פיל גרעסערע שטעט ווי בערלין,
לייפציג, דרעזדען, האמבורג געעפנט גרויסע
מוסטער־אויסשטעלונגען וועלכע מיר בעטן די
געערטע געזעלשאפט צו באזוכן. דאס הויפט־
געשעפטס־ביורא געפינט זיך אין בערלין מאטץ־
גאס 69, הויפט־קאנטאר פאטסדאמער־גאס 82.

1924, Die Hebräische Schrift,
H. Berthold AG, Berlin, Leipzig, Stuttgart,
Vienna, Riga

J'aimerais mentionner quelques autres jolies pièces de ma collection. Signature, nouvelle série, numéro 5, spécimens commentés. Il est dit d'un spécimen de Shenval Press, datant de 1939 : « imprimé avec une excellente encre noire, une qualité trop rare de nos jours ». Et j'approuve ici de tout cœur ; oui, le noir peut être beau.

Un spécimen de 1934 de 200 pages de l'imprimerie Darantière, de Dijon, édité à 800 exemplaires, se présente comme un vrai roman, où se succèdent toutes sortes de styles et de tailles de caractères. Les pages sont joliment composées et imprimées en rouge et noir avec des marges spacieuses. Quel dommage que ce genre de couleurs de soutien ne soit plus utilisé de nos jours. Un spécimen de chez Buchdruckerei August Hopfer utilise exclusivement des citations de Goethe. Ces deux spécimens nous changent agréablement du motif habituel de textes répétés sans fin.

Mon spécimen de la Boston Type Foundry, daté de 1835, est un modèle assez ancien selon les critères américains. Il contient plus de 200 pages, imprimées sur une seule face. La moitié d'entre elles sont dédiées aux ornements (gravures sur bois), incluant des ustensiles et des animaux domestiques, ainsi que des encarts dépliants avec des bateaux à vapeurs ou à aubes, des voiliers et des voitures attelées.

À la fin du XIXᵉ siècle, 11 des principales fonderies américaines décidèrent de s'associer pour fonder l'American Type Founders. Leur premier spécimen, un lourd volume de plus de 800 pages, parut en 1896.

Dans le *Hauptprobe*, on peut voir que, vers la fin du XIXᵉ siècle, une attention spéciale était portée aux titres et sous-titres qui étaient composés dans une grande variété de teintes et avec une profusion d'ornements, souvent très jolis. Tout ceci est probablement né d'un désir de rivaliser avec la lithographie – un effort payant si l'on en juge par le fait que ces spécimens sont souvent mentionnés comme chromolithographies dans les catalogues de marchands de livres anciens ou de vente aux enchères, bien que le relief au dos de l'impression indique clairement qu'il s'agit de caractères typographiques.

Au début du XIXᵉ siècle, à l'âge de 66 ans, le graveur de caractères Henri Didot accomplit l'exploit presque impossible de graver un caractère microscopique en corps 2,5, le plus petit jamais réalisé. Plus tard, les poinçons et matrices finirent dans les mains de Johannes Enschedé & Zonen, qui imprimèrent en 1861 la constitution hollandaise, un livret de 4,5 x 6,5 cm. J'ai acheté un des derniers exemplaires à la gare de Haarlem. Diverses maisons, dont Enschedé, y soldaient leurs invendus à l'occasion d'une foire

au livre ancien. Henri Didot fut aussi l'inventeur du polyamatype, un moule qui permettait de fondre jusqu'à 120 petits caractères à la fois. Son cousin, Pierre Didot, qui avait hérité d'une presse, devint aussi graveur de caractères. En 1819, il publia son premier spécimen, *Spécimen des nouveaux caractères de la fonderie etc*. Les textes sont des poèmes de sa composition.

Dans les spécimens du XIXᵉ siècle provenant de pays comme l'Allemagne, les Pays-Bas ou l'Amérique, on trouve souvent les mêmes ornements, les mêmes gravures sur bois, etc. On peut se demander si tout cela était vraiment organisé, avec contrats et versements de droits d'auteur. Cela faisait déjà un moment qu'on utilisait la stéréotypie et, à partir des années 1840, la galvanoplastie facilita la copie. Le droit de reproduction n'était pas protégé à l'époque. (Notez que j'ai lu quelque part qu'à notre époque 80 % des logiciels sont piratés…)

Les spécimens contenant la première publication d'un caractère sont particulièrement recherchés par les collectionneurs. J'en ai un, par exemple, qui présente le Centaur, avec une préface de son créateur, Bruce Rogers, un autre qui présente le Lutetia de Van Krimpen et encore un autre qui présente le Cartier, premier caractère de labeur canadien, créé par Carl Dair, en 1966.

On rencontre également, hélas, des spécimens de caractères sur des papiers de mauvaise qualité. Certains papiers de la seconde moitié du XIXᵉ siècle n'ont pas survécu aux ravages du temps et tombent en poussière entre les doigts. Parfois, les cahiers des livres ne sont pas cousus mais agrafés sur une bande de lin. Cette méthode était peut-être meilleur marché, mais en aucun cas plus solide. Les agrafes finissent par rouiller. Des spécimens de plusieurs kilos, même très chers, étaient parfois reliés sous couverture de papier. Le gros spécimen de l'Imprimerie Nationale, par exemple, était relié avec du fin et délicat papier *glacé* – c'était chercher les ennuis.

Mais les dommages peuvent être aussi le fait de vandales. Il arrive que des morceaux aient été tout simplement découpés dans des spécimens, en dépit de la demande figurant expressément sur la couverture de l'ouvrage ! Un bon marchand de livres anciens se doit de vérifier la présence de tels dommages et de les indiquer dans son catalogue. Pour désigner de telles lacunes, Jammes utilise le joli terme de *fenêtres*.

J'ai un gros spécimen de Gebroeders Hoitsema, de Groningue, daté 1897 sur la couverture. Ce que ce spécimen a d'exceptionnel, c'est que l'année d'acquisition, le vendeur et le poids de chaque caractère y sont notés. La grande majorité proviennent de fonderies allemandes, ce qui n'est peut-être pas si surprenant, étant donnée la situation géographique. Il serait intéressant

Vers 1820, la lithographie fit une entrée en force dans la compétition avec les fonderies de caractères. Alors que les imprimeurs du livre, avec leurs blocs de plomb rectangulaires et rigides, étaient limités dans leur possibilités, les dessinateurs lithographes pouvaient mettre n'importe quel dessin sur une pierre, comme ils le faisaient pour les bons et titres, les cartes de visite calligraphiées, les calendriers et autres travaux d'impression.

1924, Die Hebräische Schrift,
H. Berthold AG, Berlin, Leipzig, Stuttgart, Vienna, Riga

de savoir si les fonderies allemandes envoyaient leurs représentants directement chez les imprimeurs hollandais. Dans quelques cas, un agent est mentionné : Klinkhardt (Van Meurs), Huck (P. van Dijk) etc. Il est également intéressant de voir mentionner des petites fonderies hollandaises comme G. W. van der Wiel & Onnes et De Boer & Coers. En 1869, les frères Hoitsema se fournirent chez Reed and Fox, anciennement R. Besley & Co (two-line English Courthand).

Les spécimens anciens d'imprimeurs sont rares. Je citerai quelques-uns d'entre eux, dont je possède des exemplaires anciens : Bricx d'Ostende (vers 1787) ; H. Martin & Comp. (1829), J. Ruys (1908), Pieper & Ipenbuur (1828) et le Stads en Courant drukkerij (1834) d'Amsterdam ; M. Wijt (1828) et J. W. van Leenhoff (1837) de Rotterdam ; B. Henry (1828) de Valenciennes ; l'imprimeur de l'Université de Copenhague, Johan Frederik Schultz (1805) (le second exemplaire conservé à la Bibliothèque Royale de Copenhague a été égaré il y a des années !) ; De Bachelier (1842) de Paris ; Michael Lindauer (1825) de Munich ; Osvalda Lucchini (1853) de Guastalla ; Rand and Avery (1867) de Boston – à l'époque le deuxième plus important imprimeur d'Amérique – et John F. Trow (1856) de New York (dont je possède un exemple de « rainbow printing », un type d'impression irisée).

Une des pièces de choix de ma collection est un spécimen des alentours de 1847 de la fonderie Van der Veen Oomkens & Van Bakkenes, de Groningue. Au dos, figure, imprimée en couleur, la mention « Plaques pour impression Congreve ». Ce système était conçu pour imprimer des actions et obligations en plusieurs couleurs, en une seule passe (en typographie). Cette fonderie, fondée en 1843 par Allen van der Veen Oomskens, fut reprise par Onnes, De Boer & Coers en 1857 et déménagea l'année suivante à Arnhem. En 1894, Enschedé récupéra les matrices. J'ai acheté le spécimen d'une compilation de caractères d'Enschedé de la fin du XIXᵉ siècle, contenant 145 pages magnifiques par ces deux fondeurs de Groningue et d'Arnhem.

Un spécimen spécial, des États-Unis, est le Bruce de 1882. Il est comparable au Berriey pour son extraordinaire gamme de bordures et lettres ornées. Il contient aussi un vaste assortiment de jolis ornements produits par électrotypie, illustrant des métiers, des intérieurs de boutiques, des articles de commerce, etc. Un assez long texte de De Vinne sur l'invention de l'imprimerie y est inséré.

Les spécimens de caractères en une seule feuille de grand format sont particulièrement rares. Les plus anciens spécimens conservés sont en majorité des feuilles de grand format. Au XXᵉ siècle, Monotype, par exemple,

a produit des pièces de grand format honorables. Les feuilles de Stanley Morison pour Monotype, Pelican Press et Cloister Press sont parmi les plus marquantes.

Dans les années 1930, on avait recours à la firme Bom lorsque des imprimeries étaient vendues aux enchères, en général pour cause de faillite. Je possède 75 catalogues de ventes annotés par les commissaires-priseurs. Il est vrai que les caractères mis aux enchères y sont imprimés sur une seule ligne, et bien sûr sans mention de leur nom, mais ils n'en restent pas moins des spécimens de caractères.

Demandez à n'importe quel Hollandais de citer le nom du plus ancien imprimeur de Hollande encore en activité, il y a de fortes chances qu'il réponde Enschedé. Mais il s'agit en fait de Van Waesberge. On retrouve l'histoire de cette compagnie dans un spécimen de 1918. Van Waesberge fut fondée à Rotterdam il y a plus de 400 ans.

Selon un spécimen de 1852, N. Tetterode, devenu plus tard Lettergieterij Amsterdam, débuta aussi son activité à Rotterdam. Dans la seconde partie de ce spécimen, datée de 1856, il se présente comme un fondeur d'Amsterdam. C'est à cette époque qu'il prit le contrôle de la fonderie De Passe & Menne (je possède leur spécimen *Proeve van drukletteren*, de 1843) à Bloemgracht. Dans le premier supplément, il a collé son nom sur celui de De Passe & Menne. Dans ses premiers spécimens, il utilisait encore l'exemple classique de texte qu'on trouve également dans les spécimens du XVIIIᵉ siècle de Caslon, Fry, Wilson et Bodoni : « *Quousque tandem abutere, Catilina, patientia nostra ?* »

Les fabricants de matériel de composition produisaient souvent des spécimens très épais : Linotype, Intertype, Monotype et Ludlow. Je possède également un charmant petit spécimen de chez Typograph. Ceux-ci utilisaient généralement des caractères de fonderie, achetés sous licence.

Une coïncidence. Je ne possédais que trois minces spécimens de la fonderie Heinrich Hoffmeister, créée à Leipzig en 1898, quand un spécimen de format livre fut mis aux enchères à Berlin. Je fis donc une offre et put l'acquérir. Le jour suivant sa réception par la poste, j'allais à la foire aux antiquités de Haarlem. Et qu'est-ce que j'y ai trouvé ? Deux spécimens d'Hoffmeister reliés, l'un plus ancien (leur premier, ne contenant que des vignettes) et un autre plus récent.

Il y a quelques années, je prêtais des pièces au musée Gutenberg de Mayence pour une exposition sur les spécimens de caractères. À cette occasion, je fus autorisé à flâner dans la bibliothèque et, à mon grand étonne-

ment, j'y découvris un certain nombre de spécimens insolites, anciens et même des raretés, dont même l'équipe du musée semblait à peine consciente. Il y avait aussi des pièces insolites de fonderies hollandaises du XIXᵉ siècle, dont des spécimens de Hendrik Bruyn & Comp., Broese & Comp., Elix & Co., et J. de Groot (1781). De cet ensemble, je ne possède, hélas, que le de Groot. Je précise que toutes les autres pièces mentionnées ici sont dans ma bibliothèque.

Je voudrais mentionner un dernier spécimen : celui du fondeur lyonnais Louis Vernange, daté de 1770 et qui s'étend sur 64 pages. Les trois autres exemplaires connus sont tous légèrement plus petits. Le marchand qui me l'a vendu m'a dit que c'était la première fois qu'il en croisait un, en 35 ans de carrière.

Voilà pour ces quelques exemples de ma collection personnelle. Mes exemplaires reliés, qui prennent de la place, sont conservés sur des étagères et rangés par tailles. Les spécimens plus minces sont conservés dans des boîtes d'archivage et classés par fonderie et par date. Bien que tout soit enregistré sur ordinateur, il m'arrive d'oublier et d'acheter une pièce dont je possède déjà un exemplaire.

La valeur des spécimens de caractères est largement déterminée par leur état. Le spécimen d'Enschedé de 1768 vaut sans doute des dizaines de milliers d'euros ; le spécimen du Vatican de 1628 encore plus.

Pour un bon spécimen de plus de 100 ans, il faut compter en centaines d'euros ; les spécimens minces valent une vingtaine d'euros et un joli spécimen de Rudolf Koch vous coûtera plus de 100 euros. Le prix des pièces rares ou spéciales – pièces insolites, comme ce spécimen cousu de 80 pages de 1902 par Peter Behrens ou le spécimen de 1928 de Curwen Press – est légèrement plus élevé que la moyenne. Sont également insolites, comparés aux pièces du même type, les trois rares grands formats de Andreäische, de 1833, que j'ai achetés un jour chez Jammes, et la double feuille d'Ahendene Press, de 1926, que j'ai mentionnée plus haut.

Y a-t-il autre chose dont j'aurais envie ? La liste est ma foi assez longue, et j'avais placé en tête les trois spécimens de Bodoni, *Fregi e majuscole* (1771), *Serie di majuscole* (1788) et *Manuale tipografico* (1818). Je possède à présent ce dernier et c'est le joyau de ma collection.

On a beaucoup écrit sur les spécimens et les fonderies. Les ouvrages de base incluent *Chronik der Schriftgießereien* de Friedrich Bauer (1928, première édition en 1914), *Les livrets typographiques des fonderies françaises créées avant 1800* de Marius Audin (1964, première édition en 1933), *British Type Specimens*

Before 1831 de James Mosley (1984), *Schweizer Stempelschneider und Schriftgießer* d'Albert Bruckner (1943), *Type Foundries of America and Their Catalogs* de Maurice Annenberg (1994, première édition en 1975), enfin et non des moindres, *Type Foundries in the Netherlands* de Charles Enschedé, traduit et adapté en anglais par Harry Carter (1978, première édition en 1908).

Si vous pensez que la gravure et la fonte de caractères au plomb ne se pratiquent plus de nos jours, vous vous trompez. Il n'y a pas si longtemps, le poète américain Dan Carr éprouva le besoin de créer son propre caractère pour ses poèmes et grava lui-même les poinçons. Ce caractère, nommé Regulus, que l'annuaire *Matrix*, mentionné plus haut, publia dans un appendice, s'avère être un très joli caractère. J'ai immédiatement écrit à Golgonooza Letter Foundry & Press, la fonderie de Carr, pour commander l'édition à tirage limité de sa première application, en demandant un vrai spécimen de caractères.

Autrefois, l'installation d'un atelier de composition manuelle bien fourni demandait un investissement considérable. De nos jours, pour préparer sur ordinateur un document à imprimer, on peut choisir sur Internet une infinité de polices de caractères pour quelques euros chacune. Et si vous en prenez 10, on vous offre en prime un vélo tout terrain.

On a employé la même méthode d'impression pendant 500 ans – et soudain, grâce à M. Senefelder, tout a changé. Les fonderies de caractères qui ne faisaient que du plomb ont disparu. Quelques-unes se sont adaptées et ont fabriqué du matériel de photocomposition – parfois avec succès, comme Berthold (qui gravait les matrices du système Linotype allemand depuis 1900) et parfois avec moins de succès, comme Deberny & Peignot, qui fit faillite avec son système Lumitype. D'autres avaient déjà une activité secondaire ; Enschedé, par exemple, avait une imprimerie et Lettergieterij Amsterdam vendait des machines d'imprimerie. Les fonderies commerciales ont disparu, mais il existe heureusement aux Pays-Bas la fondation Stichting Lettergieten qui perpétue l'art typographique du passé. Tous ceux qui aiment l'ancien métier devraient la soutenir !

Un jour, alors que je visitais la bibliothèque de l'Université d'Amsterdam, un bibliothécaire fit incidemment cette remarque : « Ici, nous avons 70 mètres de spécimens de caractères. » Je crois que j'ai rougi. Arrivé chez moi, j'ai sorti un mètre ruban et constaté que je parvenais à peine à la moitié de cette longueur. Une leçon d'humilité.

1628, Indice de Caratteri, *Stampa Vaticana, Andreas Brogiotti,* Rome

Al Lettore (To the Reader), 1628. This extraordinary greeting was offered in Italian, Latin, and Greek. (And the reader was expected to sing, too!) In 1628, the Stampa Vaticana published for the first time a specimen featuring their available types. They also published a specimen of their Arabic types.

Al Lettore (An den Leser) – 1628 veröffentlichte die Stampa Vaticana erstmals ein Muster mit ihren diversen Schriften, in dem der Leser auf Italienisch, Deutsch und Lateinisch willkommen geheißen wurde (zu singen gab es auch etwas!). Später folgte auch ein Muster zu arabischen Schriften.

Al Lettore (Au lecteur), 1628. Cette extraordinaire adresse était proposée en italien, latin et grec. (Et on s'attendait aussi à ce que le lecteur chante!) En 1628, la Stampa Vaticana publia, pour la première fois, un spécimen de leurs caractères disponibles. Elle publia également un spécimen de caractères arabes.

ABCD
EFGH
IKLM
NOPQ
RSTV
XYZ.

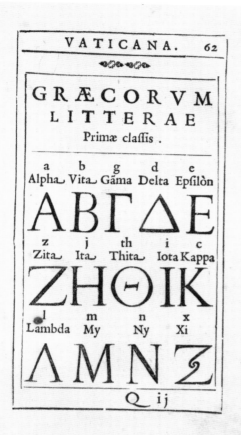

GRÆCORVM
LITTERAE
Primæ classis.

a	b	g	d	e
Alpha	Vita	Gāma	Delta	Epsilòn

A B Γ Δ E

z	j	th	i	c
Zita	Ita	Thita	Iota	Kappa

Z H Θ I K

l	m	n	x
Lambda	My	Ny	Xi

Λ M N Ξ

Q ij

Idem.

o	p	r	s
Omicròn	Pi	Rho	Sigma

O Π P Σ

t	y	ph	ch
Tau	Ypsilòn	Phi	Chi

T Y Φ X

pſ	o
Pſi	Omega

Ψ Ω.

Q iij

Turba multa, quæ conuenerat ad diem fe-

ſtum clamabat Domino, Benedictus qui

ve nit in nomine Do mini.

S iij

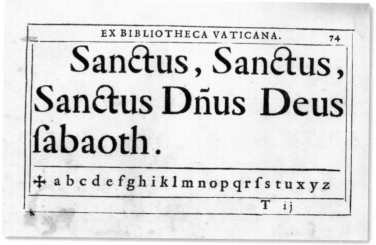

Sanctus, Sanctus,
Sanctus Dñus Deus
ſabaoth.

✠ a b c d e f g h i k l m n o p q r ſ s t u x y z

T ij

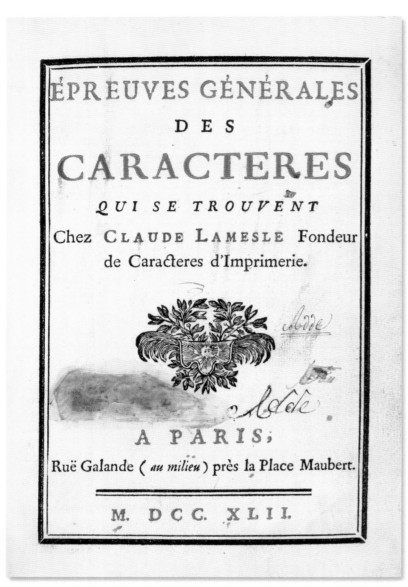

ÉPREUVES GÉNÉRALES
DES
CARACTERES
QUI SE TROUVENT
Chez CLAUDE LAMESLE Fondeur
de Caracteres d'Imprimerie.

A PARIS;
Ruë Galande (au milieu) près la Place Maubert.

M. DCC. XLII.

Civilité au Corps de Gros Romain,
Numero XLIX.

1742, Épreuves Générales des Caractères, *Claude Lamesle,* Paris

It was an honor to have one's name (here, Claude Lamesle) set on such a lovely publication.

Wer für ein so reizvolles Druckwerk verantwortlich war (wie hier Claude Lamesle), konnte mit Stolz seinen Namen auf dem Titel präsentieren.

C'était un honneur d'avoir son nom (en l'occurrence, Claude Lamesle) composé dans une si belle publication.

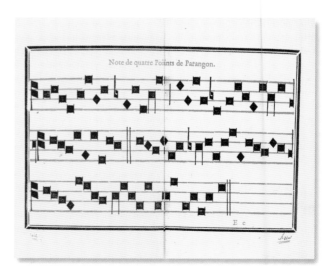

Gros Canon gros œil,
Numero LXII.
donna en l'Isle de Lemnos. Tou-
te-fois les Grecs voyant que sans
les fléches d'Hercule, dont il é-
toit le maître, ils ne pouvoient
réuffir à Troye, ils déléguerent
Ulyffe, qui l'amena au Siege, &
depuis fut guéri par Machaon,
X

Gros Canon Italique maigre,
Numero LIX.
défefpoir, il fe jetta dans un bûcher ardent, & y fut
réduit en cendre: le ferviteur Lycas fe précipita dans
la Mer, où il fut transformé en un Rocher: Déjanire
de déplaifir fe tua d'un coup de la Maffue de fon
Mari.

Hercule pourtant, avant que de mourir obligea
par ferment Philoctete fils de Péan, fon compagnon
S

Gros Canon quatre points de
Cicero, Numero LXIV.
temps d'Hercule, & lui touchoit de
quelque parenté. Auffi fut-il fou-
vent compagnon de fes avantures,
& fe rendit parfait imitateur de fa
générofité, après avoir évité un breu-
vage empoifonné que Medée, fa
z

Gros Canon Italique Ordinaire,
Numero LXI.
de déclarer le lieu où il les avoit cachées ; & pour
ne point fauffer fon ferment, il les montra feulement
du pied: dequoi il fut bien puni. Car étant fur le
chemin pour aller à Troye, l'une de ces fléches-là
lui bleffa le pied qui avoit été l'inftrument de fa per-
fidie ; & la playe rendit tant de puanteur, qu'il en
devint infupportable, ce qui fut caufe qu'on l'aban-
V

Dubbelde Auguſtyn Capitalen.

ABCDEFGH
IJKLMNOP
QRSTVUW
XYZÆ-,;:.

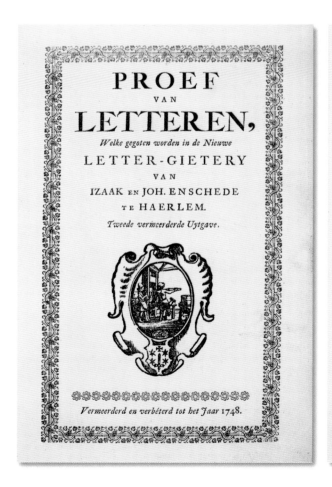

Deum revereri & prae-
cepta ejus obſervare:
hoc eſt totum hominis.
Virtute et Genio. abcd
efghijklmnopqrſstuvw
xyz ABCDEFGHIJK
LMNOPQRSTVUY
WZÆ; ABCDEFGZJ Æ?:!

*Nos ad Patriam feſtinan-
tes mortiferos Sirenum
cantus ſurda aure tranſi-
re debemus. Hieronimus.
Per Anguſta ad Auguſta.
abcdefghijklmnopqrſstuv
wxyz. ,,;:'!??-*

Eer vaed Konſt.
Keyzer Carolus
Magnus zette eens
zyn Kroon op den
Bybel / geevende
daar mede te kennen
deſſelfs groote ach-
ting voor dat Boek.
A D F G H I L
M N O P Q R S T
C U V W X Y Z &c.

Deeze bovenſtaande Canon Duyts is in 't Jaar 1748 op nieuw geſneden/
en overtreft/zo wy meenen/ zeer verre in fraayheyd de Plantynſe/ dewelke tot
hier toe beſtend en in gebruyk is geweeſt. De Kleyne Canon Duyts, die voor
onze Voorzaten nooit is gemaakt en vertoont geworden/ is mede onder han-
den; dezelve zal miſſchien noch voor zen Jaare of in 't begin van 1749 mede het
licht zien/ ten dienſte en gebruyk der reſpective Boekdzukkers en Lief-
hebbers der Edele Boekdzukkonſt.

1748, Proef van Letteren,
Izaak en Joh. Enschedé, Haarlem

Izaak and Johan Enschedé of Haarlem
were a father and son who followed pan-
European typographical developments
from the Netherlands. In 1703, Izaak
Enschedé established a printing press in
Haarlem. His son Johan acquired the
foundry of Rudolph Wetstein in Amsterdam. In 1773, the firms came together
under the name Joh. Enschedé & Zonen.

An den gesamteuropäischen Entwick-
lungen auf dem Gebiet der Typografie
waren die Niederlande mit Izaak
Enschedé aus Haarlem und seinem Sohn
Johan beteiligt. 1703 gründete Izaak
Enschedé in Haarlem ein Druckerei.
Johan erwarb die Amsterdamer Gießerei
Rudolph Wetsteins. 1773 schlossen sich
die beiden Firmen unter dem Namen
Joh. Enschedé & Zonen zusammen.

Izaak (le père) et Johan (le fils) Enschedé
de Harlem, observèrent, des Pays-Bas,
tous les progrès de la typographie pan-
européenne. En 1703, Izaak Enschedé
avait ouvert une imprimerie à Harlem.
Son fils Johan acheta la fonderie de
Rudolph Wetstein à Amsterdam. En
1773, les deux maisons fusionnèrent
pour devenir Joh. Enschedé en Zonen.

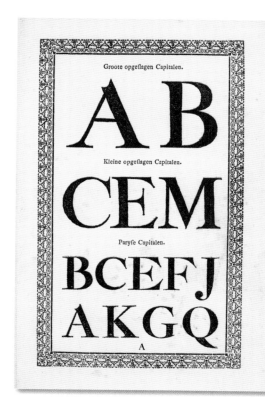

A B

CEM

BCEFJ
AKGQ

Typographia,
Ars Artium om-
nium Conferva-
trix, hic primum
Inventa, circa an-
num 1440. HAR-
LEMI. & ABSEM

*Non inchoantibus
præmium promitti-
tur, ſed perſeveran-
tibus datur.* c-d-

1768, Proef van Letteren,
J. Enschedé, Haarlem

Typefaces in Dutch, Greek, and Hebrew stand next to one another with ease in this exceptional type specimen.

Niederländische, griechische und hebräische Schriften stehen in diesem außergewöhnlichen Schriftmuster einträchtig nebeneinander.

Des caractères en hollandais, en grec et en hébreu se côtoient avec aisance dans ce spécimen de caractères exceptionnel.

Top: Double paragon Greek capitals. *Bottom*: Double text Greek capitals

ΑΒΓΔΕΖΗΘΙΚΛΜ
ΝΞΟΠΡΣΥΦΧΨΩ

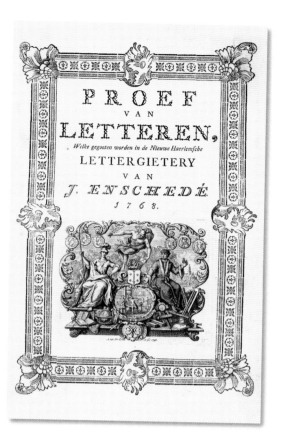

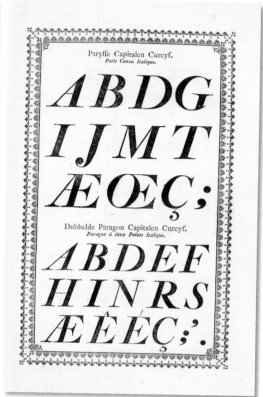

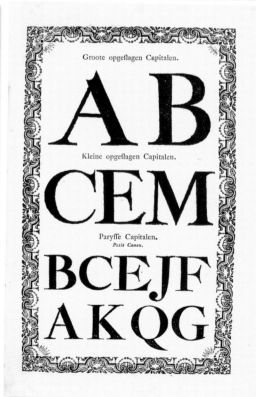

Proef van Letteren, 1768

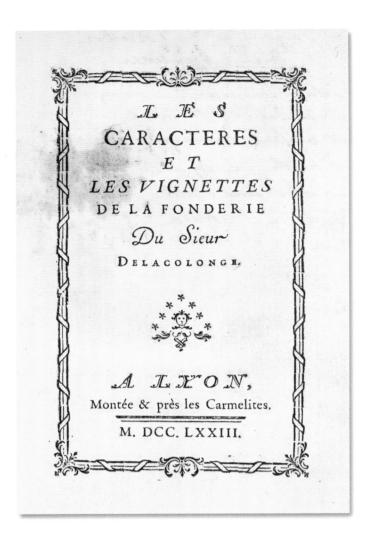

1773, Les Caractères et les Vignettes,
Fonderie du Sieur Delacologne, Lyon

Design like this, featuring an attractive
layout and decorative elements, made
the customer's choice easy.

Ein Entwurf wie der abgebildete, der
mit einem attraktiven Layout und Zier-
elementen aufwartete, machte dem
Kunden die Entscheidung leicht.

Une composition telle que celle-ci, dans
une mise en page séduisante qui poposait
des éléments décoratifs, facilitait le choix
du client.

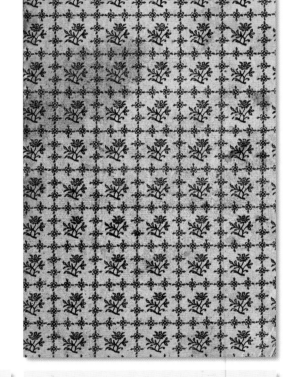

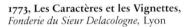

GROS CANON ITALIQUE ŒIL MAIGRE.

*Il faut crain-
dre, dit M. l'ab-
bé de Condillac,
d'étouffer la cu-
riosité des enfans
en n'y répondant
pas.*

AUTRE PARANGON A SON ŒIL ITAL.

L'Invention est l'art de
rapprocher les idées qui pa-
roissoient les plus éloignées,
d'en faire sentir le rapport,
& de présenter les objets sous
un aspect nouveau. L'invention est le fruit du génie & de
la pénétration.

Quiconque n'est pas né
stupide a de l'invention; mais
elle est surtout le caractere du
génie.

(90)

Parangon romain.

ABCDF EGHM

Italique.

ABCDF EHIJM

Palestine.

ABCF

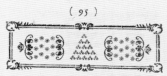

(95)

CIVILITE' DE CICERO.

Soyez propre en votre personne, vos habits, linges, meubles, toutefois sans vanité ni affectation.

Peignez-vous tous les jours proprement, prenant garde de ne pas salir vos habits. Ne vous frisez ni poudrez. Faites-vous couper de temps en temps les cheveux : ne les laissez pas tomber sur vos yeux : ne les retroussez pas sur l'oreille.

Lavez votre visage, vos mains, vos yeux, vos dents, votre bouche quand il sera nécessaire, sans toutefois vous farder : si vous avez besoin de vous moucher, faites-le sans bruit avec le mouchoir, & non avec les doigts ni le bout de votre manche, & sans regarder ensuite dans votre mouchoir : détournez un peu le visage, & couvrez-le de votre chapeau ou du mouchoir.

(105)

GREC DE PARANGON.

ΚΑΡΧΗΔΟΝΙΟΙ δὲ, ξένου ἐν τῇ πόλει συχνῶν παρ αὐτοῖς γινομένων, ὀφείλοντες αὐτοῖς μισθὸν, ἐκ ἠδύναντο διαλῦσαι ἀπέγγελαν ἐν, εἰ τις, ῶν πολιτῶν, οἱ μετων σίλαν ἔχει κατὰ πόλεως, ἢ ἰδιάτε, εἰ βέλεται λαβεῖν ἀπογράψαθαι. ἀπογραψαμένων δὲ συχνῶς, τὰ πλοῖα τὰ πλέοντα εἰς τὸν Πόντον ἐσύλων, μετὰ προφάσεος εὐλόγε.

(107)

HEBREU PONCTUE' DE CICERO. *

בְּאוֹר פְּנֵי מֶלֶךְ חַיִּים וּרְצוֹנוֹ כְּעָב מַלְקוֹשׁ :
חֶסֶד וֶאֱמֶת יִצְּרוּ מֶלֶךְ וְסָעַד בַּחֶסֶד כִּסְאוֹ :
מֶלֶךְ יֹשֵׁב עַל כִּסֵּא דִין מְזָרֶה בְּעֵינָיו כָּל רָע :
פַּלְגֵי מַיִם לֵב מֶלֶךְ בְּיַד יְהוָה עַל כָּל אֲשֶׁר
יַחְפֹּץ יַטֶּנּוּ : יִרְא אֶת יְהוָה בְּנִי וָמֶלֶךְ עִם
שׁוֹנִים אַל תִּתְעָרָב : רְצוֹן מְלָכִים שִׂפְתֵי
צֶדֶק וְדֹבֵר יְשָׁרִים יֶאֱהָב : חֲמַת אִישׁ מְדָנִים
בִּמְלָאכְתּוֹ .

מְכַהֲרִים בְּכֹחַ נָאוֹר פְּנְבוּרָה : מַשְׁבִּיחַ
שְׁאוֹן יַמִּים שְׁאוֹן גַּלֵּיהֶם וַהֲמוֹן לְאֻמִּים :
וַיִּירְאוּ שֹׁבֵי קְצָוֹת מֵאוֹתֹתֶיךָ מוֹצָאֵי בֹקֶר וָעֶרֶב

* J'ai des Hébreux au corps de Petit-Texte,
de Petit-Romain, de Philosophie, de Cicero,
de Saint-Augustin, & de Gros-Romain.
Les points d'hébreu sont toujours au corps de
nompareille pour tous les corps.

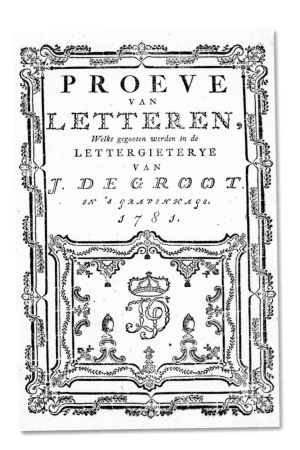

1781, Proeve van Letteren,
J. de Groot, The Hague

This firm from The Hague is one of the oldest type foundries in the Netherlands. Take note of the *0*.

J. de Groot in Den Haag war eine der ältesten Schriftgießereien der Niederlande. Beachtenswert ist die Ziffer *0*.

Cette firme de La Haye est l'une des plus vieilles fonderies de caractères des Pays-Bas. On remarquera le *0*.

AB
CD
EF

1234
567
890

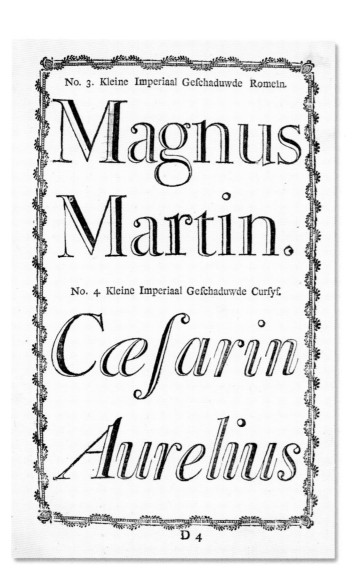

No. 3. Kleine Imperiaal Geschaduwde Romein.

Magnus Martin.

No. 4. Kleine Imperiaal Geschaduwde Curfyf.

Cæfarin Aurelius

D 4

No. 5. Groote Kanon Romein.

Marcus Aurelius zegd, al word den Wyzen gevraagd, zo antwoorden zy nauwlyks, maar de Gekken antwoorden fonder vragen. abcdefghiklmnpqs ABCDEFGHK' IJLMNOPQRS TUVWXYZabc DEFGHIKLMNOPQRS.

D 5

No. 1. Groote Kanon Duits.

Pompejus Magnus zegt / de grootste fortuyne dien ik oont gehadt hebbe / die heeft my noyt trots of opgeblasen gemaakt; en de alder zwaarste tegenspoedt die my oont bejegent is / die heeft my noyt doen brezen. ABCDEF

H 3

Dubbelde Paragon Hoogduitfche Gefchreven Capitalen.

No.	Vervolg van Paragon.
11	
12	
13	
14	
15	
16	
17	
18	
19	
20	AAAAAAAAAAA
21	
22	
23	

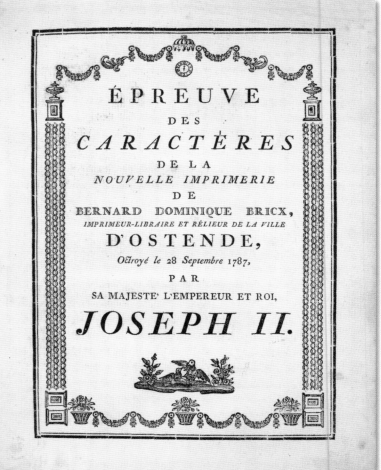

1787, Épreuve des Caractères,
Bernard Dominique Bricx, Ostende

This type specimen is dedicated to
Central European monarch Joseph II,
yet it features the lion and the unicorn,
symbols of the United Kingdom. It was
printed in Ostend, on the Belgian coast
just across from England.

Dieses Schriftmuster ist „Seiner Majestät
dem Kaiser und König Joseph II." gewid-
met. Obgleich es mit dem Löwen und
dem Einhorn die Wappentiere des Vereinigten Königreichs trägt, wurde es nicht
auf der britischen Seite des Ärmelkanals,
sondern in dem belgischen Küstenort
Ostende gedruckt.

Bien que ce spécimen de caractères soit
dédié au monarque d'Europe centrale,
Joseph II, on y retrouve le lion et la
licorne, symboles du Royaume-Uni.
Il a été imprimé à Ostende, sur la côte
belge juste en face de l'Angleterre.

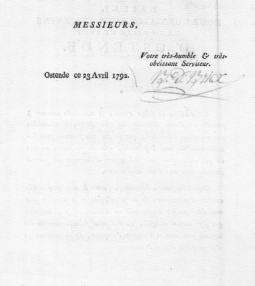

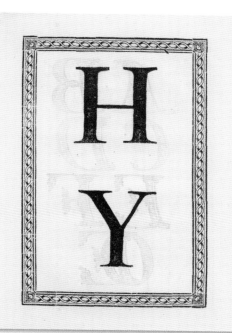

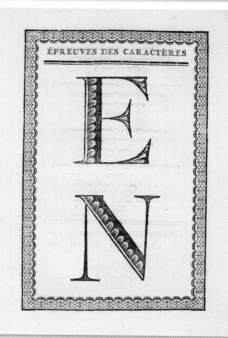

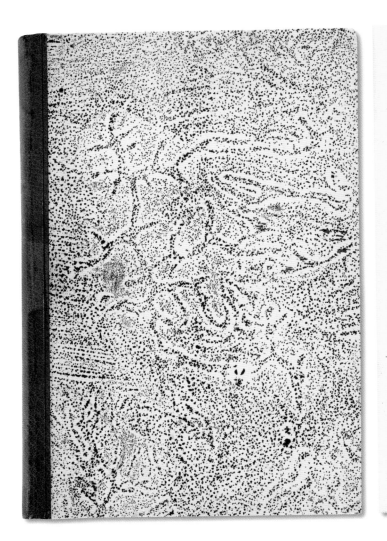

Serie
de' Caratteri Greci
di
Giambatista Bodoni
1788

1788, Serie de Caratteri Greci,
Giambattista Bodoni, Parma

GRECO

Οταν κλαιοντα ιδης τινα εν πενθει η απο-
δημουντος τεκνου η αποθανοντος, η απολω-
λεκοτα τα εαυτου, προσεχε, μη σε η φαντασια συναρπαση, ως εν κακοις ουτος αυτου
τοις εκτος· αλλ' ευθυς διαιρει παρα σεαυτω,
και λεγειν εσΙω προχειρον, οτι, τουτος θλιβει, ου το συμβεβηκος, αλλον γαρ ου θλιβει,
αλλα το δογμα το περι τουτου. μεχρι μεν
τοι λογου, μη οκνει συμπεριφερεσθαι αυτω,
καν ουτω τυχη, συνεπιστεναξαι. προσεχε
μεν τοι, μη και εσωθεν στεναξης. Κοραξ ο-
ταν μη αισιον κεκραγη, μη συναρπαζετω σε
η φαντασια. αλλ' ευθυς διαιρει παρα σεαυτω, και λεγε, οτι, τουτων εμοι ουδεν επιση-
μαινεται, αλλ' η τω σωματιω μου. η τω κτη-
σιδιω μου, η τω δοξαριω, η τοις τεκνοις, η
τη γυναικι· εμοι δε παντα, αισια σημαινε-
ται, εαν εγω θελω. ο, τι γαρ αν τουτων απο-
βαινη, επ'εμοι εστιν ωφεληθηναι απ'αυτου.
Ορκον παραιτεσαι. ει μεν οιοντε, εισαπαν.
ει δε μη, εκ των εχοντων. Επικτετου εγχειρ.

GRECO

Εν ταις ομιλιαις απ-
εσΙω το τινα των εαυ-
του εργων η κινδυνων
επι πελυ και αμετρως
μεμνησθαι· ου γαρ ως
σοι ηδυ εσΙι Ιο Ιων σων
κινδυνων μεμνησθαι,
ουτω και τοις αλλοις
ηδυ εστι το των σοι
συμβεβηκοτων ακου-
ειν. Επικτετος εγχειρ.

The extremely small type sizes in this Greek specimen were cut by hand by Giambattista Bodoni himself. Every size has its own script.

Die Schnitte dieser griechischen Schriftprobe mit ihren ausgesprochen kleinen Schriftgraden stammen von Giambattista Bodonis Hand persönlich. Jede Größe hat ihre eigene Schrift.

Les tailles de caractères extrêmement petites de ce spécimen de grecques ont été coupées à la main par Giambattista Bodoni en personne. Chaque taille a ses propres scriptes.

Και τα μεν εφ'
ημιν, εσ]ι φυσει
ελευθερα ευσθε-
νη, ακωλυτα, α-
παρεμϖοδιστα.
τα δε ουκ εφ'η-
μιν, ασ]ενη, δου-
λα, κωλυτα, αλ-
λοτρια. Επικτη.

Πολις εσ]ι Λεσ-
6ου, Μιτυληνη,
μεγαλη και κα-
λη· διειληϖται
γαρ ευριϖοις,
υϖεισρεουσης
της ϑαλατ]ης,
και κεκοσμηται

An extreme contrast between thick and thin strokes of letters, a generous use of white space in page design, and wide line spacing characterize the work of Giambattista Bodoni (1740–1813). Early in his career, he copied the types of Pierre Simone Fournier, who in turn had been influenced by the Romaine du Roi commissioned by Louis XIV. In 1768, Bodoni was appointed Director of the Stamperia Reale, the private press of the Duke of Parma. Important folio editions included works by Horace (1791), Virgil (1793), and Homer (1808). During his 50-year career, Bodoni made, corrected, and cast over 55,000 matrices, and he was committed to page harmony through choice and size of typeface, leading, line length, spacing, and column width. Officially limited to 150 copies, the two-volume *Manuale tipografico*, a compilation of his life's work which was published posthumously in 1818 by his widow Margherita, consists of 546 pages with 665 alphabets, including 100 exotic typefaces and 1,300 vignettes. In 1911, the American Type Founders issued a revival of Bodoni designed by Morris Fuller Benton, and Monotype and the Haas foundry soon issued one as well. The Haas Bodoni was copied by the Amsterdam Type Foundry, Berthold, Stempel, and Linotype, and Johannes Wagner issued a new Bodoni in 1961. Introduced in 1926, Bauer Bodoni is closest to the original version. A more recent addition is Zuzana Licko's Filosofia released in 1996.

Kennzeichnend für die Arbeiten Giambattista Bodonis (1740–1813) ist der extreme Strichstärkenkontrast zwischen Grund- und Haarstrichen der Lettern sowie der großzügige Umgang mit Leerraum und Durchschuss bei der Seitengestaltung. Zu Beginn seiner Laufbahn orientierte Bodoni sich an den Schriftentwürfen Pierre Simone Fourniers, der sich wiederum durch die von Ludwig XIV. in Auftrag gegebene Romaine du Roi hatte anregen lassen. 1768 wurde Bodoni zum Leiter der Stamperia Reale ernannt, der Privatdruckerei des Herzogs von Parma. Zu seinen bedeutendsten Druckwerken zählen Ausgaben mit ausgewählten Werken des Horaz (1791), Vergils (1793) und Homers (1808). Im Laufe seines 50 Jahre umspannenden Schaffens fertigte, korrigierte und goss Bodoni mehr als 55 000 Matrizen. Größten Wert legte er auf den Aufbau eines harmonischen Seitenspiegels durch die Wahl der Schriftart und -größe und das Zusammenspiel von Durchschuss, Zeilenlängen, Abständen und Spaltenbreiten. Bodonis offiziell auf eine Auflage von 150 Exemplaren limitiertes, zweibändiges *Manuale Tipografico* – eine Gesamtschau seines Lebenswerkes, die nach seinem Tod von seiner Witwe Margherita im Jahr 1818 veröffentlicht wurde – umfasst 546 Druckseiten mit insgesamt 665 verschiedenen Alphabeten, einschließlich 100 exotischen Schriften, und 1300 Vignetten. 1911 läuteten die American Type Founders mit einer von Morris Fuller Benton entworfenen Bodoni ein Revival ein, zu dem bald darauf Monotype und die Haas'sche Schriftgießerei mit eigenen Versionen beitrugen. Als Nächstes folgten die Lettergieterij Amsterdam, Berthold, Stempel und Linotype mit Bodoni-Entwürfen. 1961 brachte Johannes Wagner eine neue Bodoni heraus. Die größte Nähe zum Original weist die 1926 von Bauer veröffentlichte Bodoni auf. Eine Version aus jüngerer Zeit ist Zuzana Lickos 1996 herausgekommene Filosofia.

Le travail de Giambattista Bodoni (1740–1813) se caractérise par des pleins et des déliés finement contrastés et une composition aérée, réservant des marges généreuses. Au début de sa carrière, Bodoni copie les caractères de Pierre-Simon Fournier, lui-même influencé par les «Romains du Roi», que Louis XIV avait commandés. En 1768, Bodoni est nommé maître-imprimeur à la Stamperia Reale, l'imprimerie privée de Ferdinand, duc de Parme. Parmi ses importantes éditions in-folio, on trouve des œuvres d'Horace (1791), Virgile (1793), et Homère (1808). Au cours de ses 50 ans de carrière, Bodoni fabrique, corrige et moule plus de 55 000 matrices, en s'attachant à une mise en page harmonieuse par le choix de la taille des caractères, des blancs, de la longueur des lignes, des espacements et de la largeur des colonnes. Officiellement limité à 150 exemplaires, le *Manuale tipografico* en deux volumes – une compilation du travail de toute une vie publié après sa mort, en 1818, par sa veuve Margherita – consiste en 546 pages comprenant 665 alphabets, 100 caractères exotiques et 1300 vignettes. En 1911, American Type Founders sort une nouvelle interprétation du Bodoni dessinée par Morris Fuller Benton, et Monotype et la fonderie Haas en lancent bientôt chacun un. Haas est suivie dans la création d'un Bodoni par Amsterdam Type Foundry, Berthold, Stempel, et Linotype. Johannes Wagner sort un nouveau Bodoni en 1961. Lancé en 1926, le Bauer Bodoni est le plus proche de la version originale. Sorti en 1996, le Filosofia de Zuzana Licko est le Bodoni le plus récent.

A

SPECIMEN

OF

PRINTING TYPES,

BY

FRY and STEELE,

𝕷𝖊𝖙𝖙𝖊𝖗=𝕱𝖔𝖚𝖓𝖉𝖊𝖗𝖘

TO THE

PRINCE OF WALES.

TYPE-STREET.

London:

PRINTED BY T. RICKABY.

MDCCXCIV.

Advertisement.

WARMED *with sincere Gratitude to their Friends, and the Public, The Proprietors of the* TYPE-STREET LETTER-FOUNDERY *present them with a new Specimen of Printing-Types, which, with indefatigable Assiduity. and at a very great Expence, they have now compleated.*

In appealing to the ingenious Artist, they do not wish to hazard an unqualified Assertion, but rather desire he may be convinced by comparison, that this Specimen is enriched with such Improvements, and Additions of variety of useful Types, including GREEKS, HEBREWS, *and the other* ORIENTALS, *as no Letter-Foundery in Europe besides can produce.*

Desirous that their sense of Obligation may ever be equal to the pleasure arising from successful industry, They thankfully

acknowledge

1794, A Specimen of Printing Types,
Fry and Steele, London

Although the Prince of Wales receives the dedication on the title page, all the attention here goes to the limitless possibilities of the table of "metal space-lines" from which a typesetter could choose.

Die Titelseite mag eine Widmung an den Prinzen von Wales zieren, die Hauptaufmerksamkeit gilt jedoch den unerschöpflichen Kombinationsmöglichkeiten der „Metallenen Abstandlinien", die dem Schriftsetzer in Tabellenform vorgestellt wurden.

Bien que la dédicace aille au Prince de Galles sur la page de titre, on remarque surtout ici les multiples possibilités, laissées au choix du compositeur, de la table des «espaces».

TEN LINES PICA.

LEEDS
Hitchin

A

TABLE,

Shewing how the following Pieces of

METAL SPACE-LINES

May be combined to the Length of any Number of Pica m's, from Eleven to Fifty, with only three Pieces in the longeſt Line; and from Fifty to an Hundred, with no more than ſix Pieces in the longeſt Line.

7 4 4 4	4	13 7	7 7	15	9 7	13	9 4	15 7	15 9 4	20	9 7 4 4
11 13 13	12 7	20 7	14 9	15 13	16 7 5	17 13 15	18 15 15 4	19 15 15	20 9 7	21 15 9	22 15 13	23 20 9 7	24 15 15 9	25
26	27	28	29	30 7 4 4	31 15 13	32 13 9 4	33 13 13 7	34 20 9	35 20 15	36 15 13 7	37 20 15 7	38 20 13 4	39 20 15 7	40 20 20 7 7

Many of the Lengths may be made of different Pieces than thoſe in the above TABLE, as for Example, 30 m's may be made not only of two Fifteens, but alſo of 15. 7. 4. 4. (30)—9. 7. 7. 7. (30)—13. 13. 4. (30)—13. 9. 4. 4. (30)—7. 7. 4. 4. 4. (30) and ſo in many others, which is a very conſiderable Advantage.

HAZARD, TYP.

GLOSILLA.

A B C D E F G H I

J K L M N O P Q R

S T U V X Y Z Æ Œ

W Ñ . , : ;

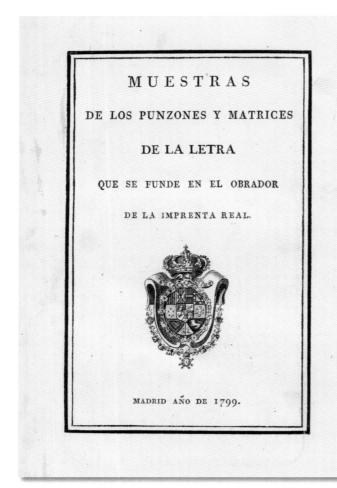

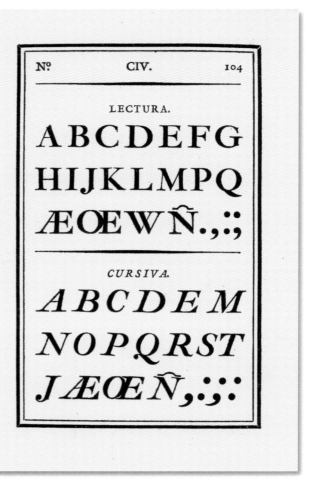

1799, **Muestras de los Punzones y Matrices de la Letra que se funde en el Obrador,** *Imprenta Real,* Madrid

CURSIVA.

A B C D E F G H

I J K L M N O P

Q R S T U V X Y Z

Æ Œ W Ñ , . : ;

ALA DE MOSCA.

ABCDEFGHIJKLMNOP
QRSTUVXYZÆŒÑW.,;:

CURSIVA.

ABCDEFGHIJKLMNOP
QRSTUVXYZÆŒÑW,:;

MIÑONA.

ABCDEFGHIJK
LMNOPQRSTU
VXYZÆŒWÑ.;:,

NOMPAREIL.

ABCDEFGHIJKL
MNOPQRSTUV
XYZÆŒWÑ,.:;

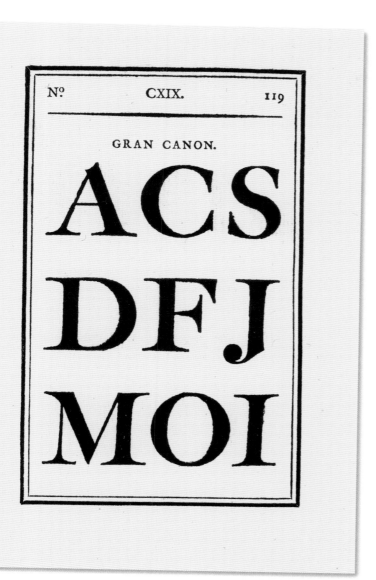

1799, Muestras de los Punzones y Matrices de la Letra que se funde en el Obrador, *Imprenta Real,* Madrid

Wonderful typefaces for missals (misal, in Spanish) and other texts from a royal printer established in 1761 by Carlos III.

Herrliche Schriften für Missalien (spanisch *misal*) und andere Texte, angefertigt von einem 1761 von Carlos III. eingesetzten königlichen Drucker.

De magnifiques caractères pour missels (*misal* en espagnol) et autres textes de l'imprimerie royale fondée en 1761 par Charles III d'Espagne.

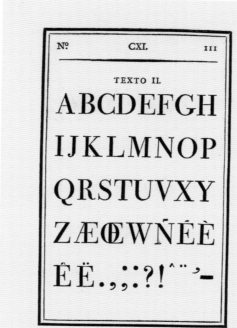

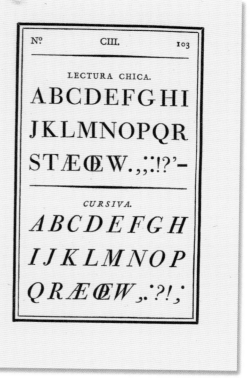

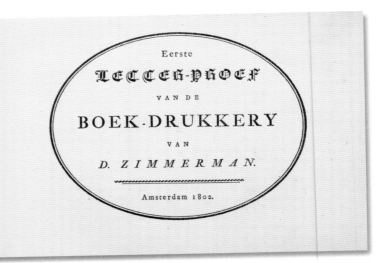

1802, Eerste Letterproef,
D. Zimmerman, Amsterdam

This printer from Amsterdam evidently had a lot of customers in the countryside.

Dieser Drucker aus Amsterdam hatte offenbar viele Kunden auf dem Land.

Cet imprimeur d'Amsterdam avait apparemment de nombreux clients en milieu rural.

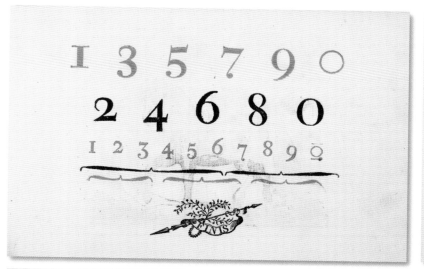

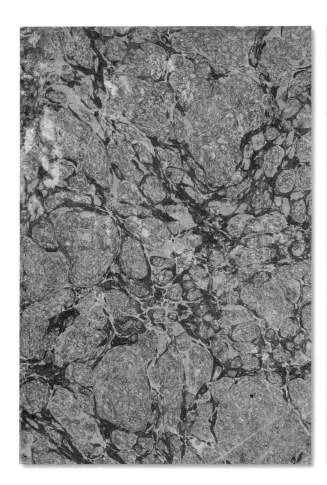

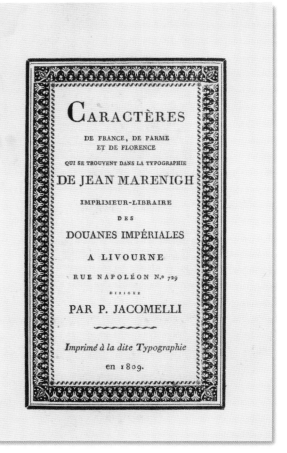

1809, Caractères de France, de Parme et de Florence, *Jean Marenigh,* Livourne

Type specimen from France… and other places. The inclusion of multiple locations on the title page gave clients the idea that this was an international company.

Schriftmuster (nicht nur) aus Frankreich. Die Angabe mehrerer Orte auf der Titelseite vermittelte Kunden den Eindruck, dass es sich um ein internationales Unternehmen handelte.

Des spécimens de caractères de France… et d'ailleurs. L'inclusion, sur la page de titre, de lieux multiples, donnait au client l'idée qu'il s'agissait d'une compagnie internationale.

CAO.

MOYENNES DE FONTE.

MOI.

CAPITALES DE FINANCIERE.

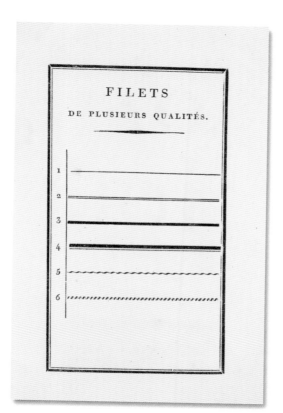

FILETS
DE PLUSIEURS QUALITÉS.

1

2

3

4

5

6

LETTRES DE DEUX POINTS.

NOMPAREILLE.

NAPOLÉON PREMIER.

COURAGE.

PETIT TEXTE.

MAGNIFICENCE.

THÉORIE.

PETIT ROMAIN.

AGRICULTURE.

EUROPE.

PHILOSOPHIE.

ASTRONOMIE.

ÉPREUVES.

CICERO.

FRANÇAISES.

SAINT AUGUSTIN.

EMPEREUR.

GROS TEXTE.

SATURNE.

PALESTINE.

CADMUS.

PETIT CANON.

TARRO.

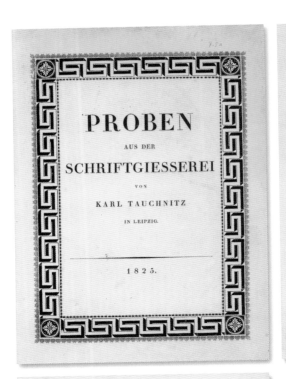

1825, Proben aus der Schriftgiesserei,
Karl Tauchnitz, Leipzig

It is remarkable that a firm from Leipzig had—and apparently used (for the export market)—a Russian and a Greek alphabet.

Interessanterweise gehörten zum Programm dieser Leipziger Firma auch ein russisches und ein griechisches Alphabet, die vermutlich für den Export bestimmt waren.

Il est remarquable qu'une firme de Leipzig ait eu – et apparemment utilisé (pour l'exportation) – des alphabets russe et grec.

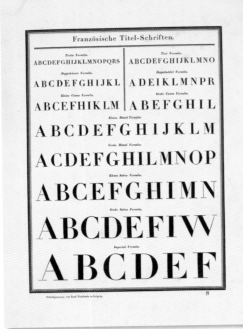

Russische und Griechische Titel-Schriften.

Tertie Russisch, Versalia.

А Г Д Ж З И П Р Ц Ч Ш Ъ

Tertie Griechisch, Versalia.

А В Г Δ Е Θ Λ М N Р Φ Ψ Ω

Text Russisch, Versalia.

А Б Г Д Ж З І И Л Ф Θ

Text Griechisch, Versalia.

А Г Δ Е Z Λ Ξ Р Σ Υ Ω

Doppelmittel Russisch, Versalia.

А Б Г Д Ж И З Л М Р

Doppelmittel Griechisch, Versalia.

А В Δ Θ Е Н Λ N Σ Ω

Kleine Canon Russisch, Versalia.

А Б В Д Ж І К Л Н О П

Kleine Canon Griechisch, Versalia.

А В Г Е Z Λ Р N Φ

Grobe Canon Russisch, Versalia.

А Б Д З И Л М П

Grobe Canon Griechisch, Versalia.

А В Г Δ Λ О Σ Ω

Kleine Missal Russisch, Versalia.

А Б Г Д Ж З

Kleine Missal Griechisch, Versalia.

А Λ М N Σ Ω

Grobe Missal Russisch, Versalia.

А Б Д Ж З

Grobe Missal Griechisch, Versalia.

Г Λ Θ Н П

Kleine Sabon Russisch, Versalia.

А Б Д Ж

Kleine Sabon Griechisch, Versalia.

Δ Г Λ Θ

Grobe Sabon Russisch, Versalia.

А Б Д З

Grobe Sabon Griechisch, Versalia.

Δ Θ І Λ

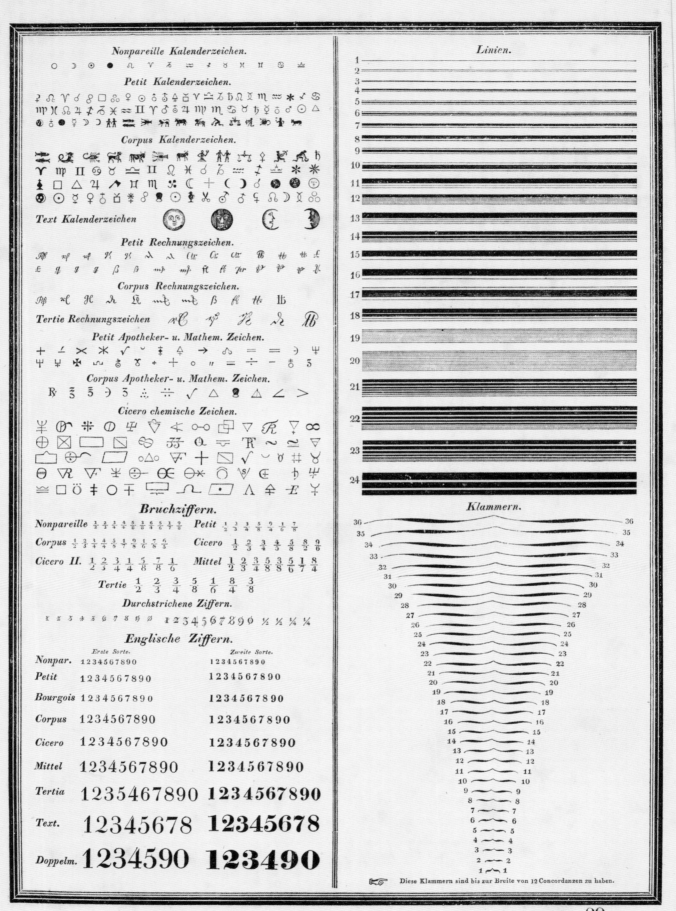

Verzierungen.

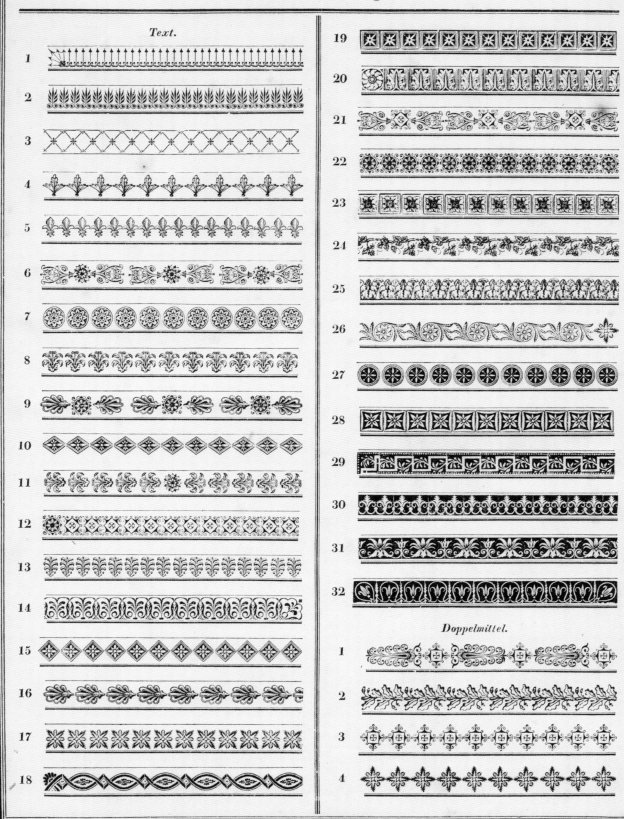

Text.

Doppelmittel.

24

These type specimens, ornaments, and page embellishments were created for various different usages (e. g., for a museum and a theater). The *Journal für Buchdruckerkunst, Schriftgießerei und die verwandten Fächer* (Journal of the Art of Book Printing, Type Founding and Related Fields) was established as a trade journal by the printer and publisher Johann Heinrich Meyer and quickly became the organ of the whole field.

1835, Journal für Buchdruckerkunst, Schriftgießerei und die verwandten Fächer, *Johann Heinrich Meyer,* Braunschweig

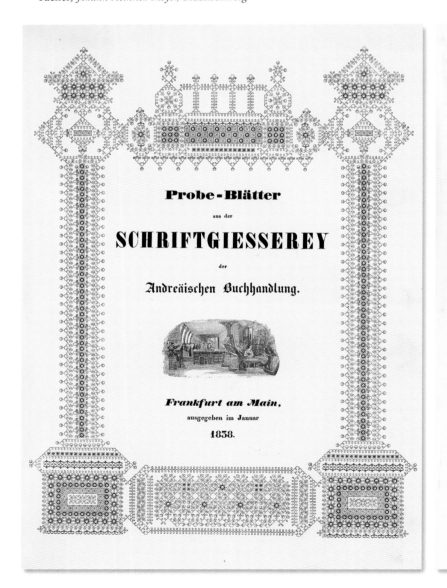

Diese Muster für Schriften, Ornamente und Seitenschmuck wandten sich an unterschiedlichste Adressaten, darunter auch Museen oder Theater. Das *Journal für Buchdruckerkunst, Schriftgießerei und die verwandten Fächer*, gegründet und herausgegeben von dem Drucker und Verleger Johann Heinrich Meyer, wurde schnell zum wichtigsten Organ der Branche.

Ces spécimens de caractères, ornements et vignettes ont été créés pour différentes usages (par exemple, pour un musée ou un théâtre). Le *Journal für Buchdrucker-kunst, Schriftgießerei und die verwandten Fächer*, (Journal de l'imprimerie, des fonderies de caractères et autres sujets analogues), journal spécialisé fondé par l'imprimeur-éditeur Johann Heinrich Meyer, devint rapidement l'organe de toute la profession.

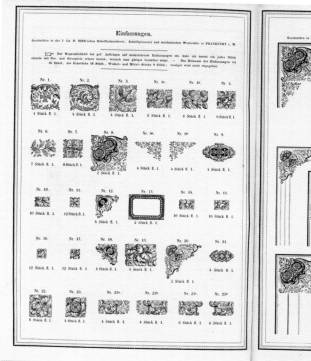

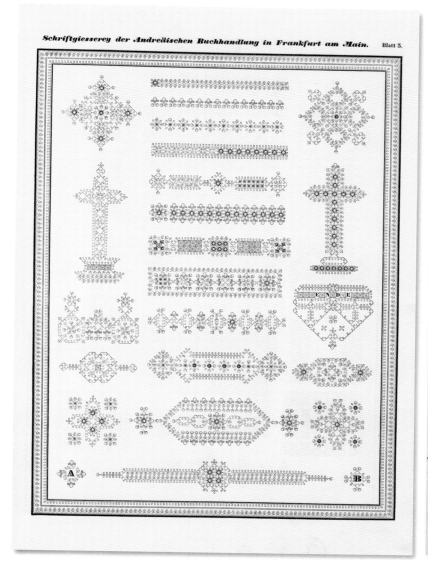

Nro. 1.

PARIS

Nr. 2.

LIEB

Nr. 3.

FURT

Nr. 4.

HAKT

Nr. 5.

KOPF

Nr. 6.

WIEN

Johann Heinrich Meyer

Nr. 7.

Nr. 8.

Nr. 9.

Nr. 10.

Verzierte Antiqua.

10.

DURCHS LEBEN GEHEN, HEISST NICHT UEBER EBEN

11.

ERFINDUNG DER BUCHDRUCKERKUNST,

12.

DIE AUGEN SIND IMMER KINDER.

13.

GESELLIGKEIT.

14.

PRAGENSI

15.

RUHESTEN

Schmale Antiqua-Versalien.

1.

DIE STRENGE ZEIT DER PRUFUNG IST

2.

ENDE GUT ALLES GUT

Moussirte Kanzley.

1.

Erste Größe.

Herr Soll Haben

Zweite Größe.

Herr Soll Haben

Dritte Größe.

Herr Soll Haben

Vierte Größe.

Herr Soll Haben

Schriftgießerei von Gottlieb Haase Söhne in Prag.

Neueste Titelschriften.

Phantasieschrift No. 1.

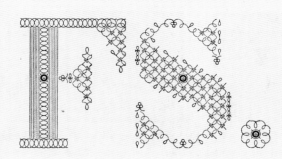

Minimum 10 Pf. pr. Pfund würtbg. Gew. fl. 1. 24 kr.

Phantasieschrift No. 2.

EDINBURG

Minimum 8 Pf. pr. Pfund würtbg. Gew. fl. 1. 24 kr.

Phantasieschrift No. 3.

HAMBURG

Minimum 6 Pf. pr. Pfund würtbg. Gew. fl. 1. 24 kr.

J. Schoch'sche Schriftschneiderei u. Gießerei in Augsburg.

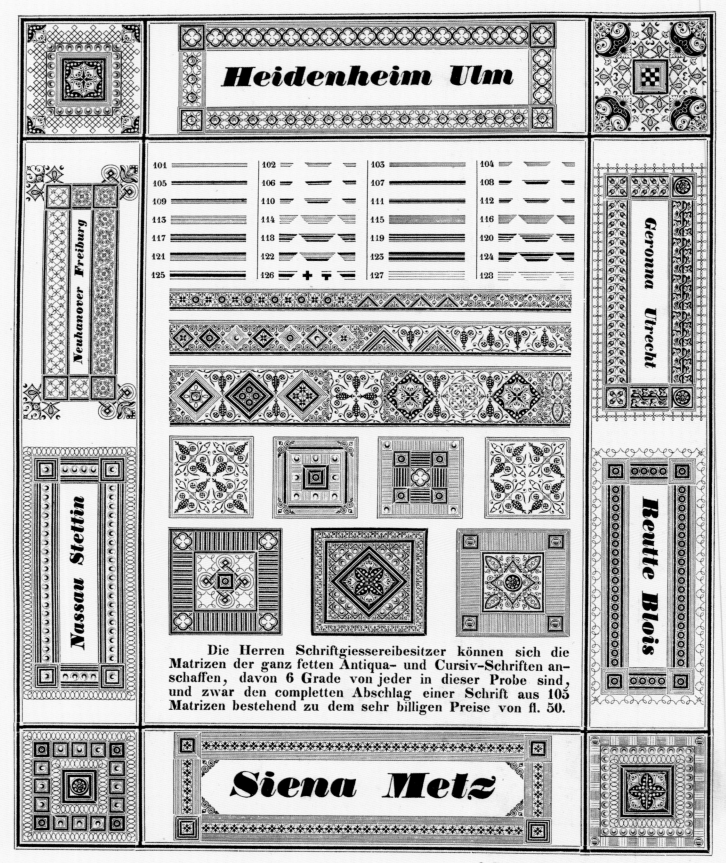

Heidenheim Ulm

Neuhanover Freiburg

Geronna Utrecht

Nassau Stettin

Beutte Blois

Die Herren Schriftgiessereibesitzer können sich die Matrizen der ganz fetten Antiqua- und Cursiv-Schriften anschaffen, davon 6 Grade von jeder in dieser Probe sind, und zwar den completten Abschlag einer Schrift aus 105 Matrizen bestehend zu dem sehr billigen Preise von fl. 50.

Siena Metz

F. Schoch'sche Schriftschneiderei u. Gießerei in Augsburg.

Montabaur Virgin

Antilibanon Cherburg

Dublin Hanau

Pommern Tripoli

Erding Lima

Baden Wien

F. Schoch'sche Schriftschneiderei u. Gießerei in Augsburg.

Englische Linien

aus der

Schriftgiesserey und Schriftschneiderey von Theodor Walbaum in Weimar.

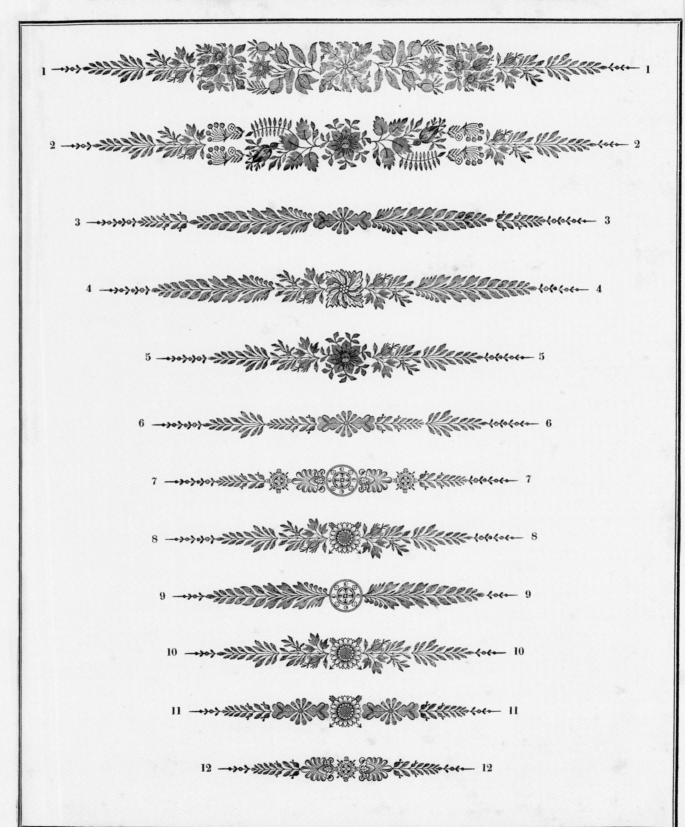

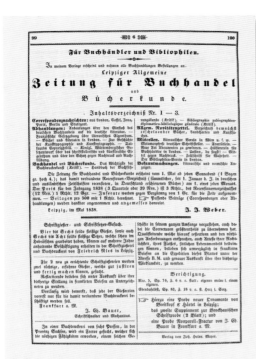

Musirte Antiqua, Zweite Sorte.

Minimum 6 *U. pr. U.* 16 *Gr.*

Doppel Mittel Lapidar Azuré.

Minimum 9 *U. pr. U.* 1 *Rth.*

Musirte Antiqua, Vierte Sorte.

Minimum 9 *U. pr. U.* 14 *Gr.*

Musirte Antiqua, Sechste Sorte.

Minimum 12 *U. pr. U.* 14 *Gr.*

1835, Journal für Buchdruckerkunst, Schriftgießerei und die verwandten Fächer, *Johann Heinrich Meyer,* Braunschweig

Theodor Walbaum was the son of Justus Erich Walbaum, who designed, circa 1800, the famous Walbaum-Antiqua. In 1828, Theodor took over his father's foundry, but then died before him, and Justus Erich Walbaum sold his firm to the company F. A. Brockhaus. The Journal of the Art of Book Printing, Type Founding and Related Fields shows here several of the Walbaum company's products from the 1830s.

Theodor Walbaum war der Sohn jenes Justus Erich Walbaums, der um 1800 die berühmte Walbaum-Antiqua entworfen hatte. 1828 übernahm Theodor die Gießerei des Vaters, verstarb jedoch vor diesem, woraufhin Justus Erich Walbaum den Betrieb an die Firma F. A. Brockhaus verkaufte. Das *Journal für Buchdruckerkunst, Schriftgießerei und die verwandten Fächer* zeigt hier einige Arbeiten der Firma Walbaum aus den 1830er-Jahren.

Theodor Walbaum était le fils de Justus Erich Walbaum, qui grava, vers 1800, le célèbre Walbaum-Antiqua. En 1828, Theodor reprit la fonderie de son père, mais il mourut avant lui, et Justus Erich Walbaum revendit sa maison à la firme F. A. Brockhaus. Le Journal für Buchdruckerkunst, Schriftgießerei und die verwandten Fächer montre ici quelques travaux de la firme Walbaum, datant des années 1830.

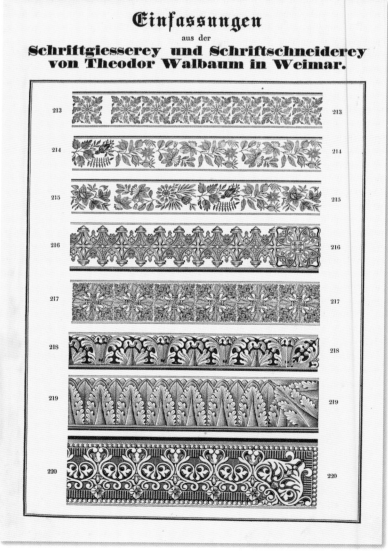

54. 8 ℔

55. 14 ℔

56. 8 ℔

DIEU ET MON DROIT

57. 6 ℔

58. 6 ℔

59. 7 ℔

60. 4 ℔

61. 16 ℔

62. 4 ℔

63. 12 ℔

64. 12 ℔

65. 14 ℔

66. 6 ℔

67. 16 ℔

FEINER AMERIKANISCHER

Tabak

N͞o͞

68. 8 ℔

Zum Buntdruck eingerichtet in zwei Platten 1 rß 12 ℔

Moussirte und Lapidar-Schriften.

Moussirte Schriften.	Lapidar Schriften.

Missal.

PARIS.

Canon.

MÉMOIRE

Doppelmittel. № 1.

HONNEUR.

Doppelmittel.

HANNOVER.

Text. № 1.

HAMBURG.

Tertia.

KOPPENHAGEN.

Tertia. № 1.

BRAUNSCHWEIG.

Mittel.

CONSTANTINOPEL.

Doppelmittel. № 2.

ORATORIU

Doppelmittel Egyptienne.

ERFINDUNG.

Text Lapidar.

ALLGEMEINEN

Tertia.

BRAUCHBARKEIT.

Doppelmittel Egyptienne.

MAGDEBURG

Mittel.

PETERSBURG BRANDENBURG PARIS LONDON KRAKAU.

Text Egyptienne.

CONSTANTINOPEL

Cicero.

NON ENIM RECEPTIS RELIGIONIS. THUCYDIDES. PHILSTRATUS.

Tertia Egyptienne, verziert.

MANCHESTER.

Petit.

NOUS RECONTRIONS CONTINUELLEMENT SUR NOTRE ROUTE DES TRIBUS QUI N'AVAIENT

Fette Tertia Antiqua.

Quousque tandem abutere, Catilina, patientia nostra? quamdiu nos etiam furor iste tuus elu-

Fette Cicero Antiqua.

Quousque tandem abutere, Catilina, patientia nostra? quamdiu nos etiam furor iste tuus eludet? quem ad finem sese effrenata jactabit audatia? nihilne

Fette Corpus Antiqua.

Quousque tandem abutere, Catilina, patientia nostra? quamdiu nos etiam furor iste tuus eludet? quem ad finem sese effrenata jactabit audatia? nihilne te nocturnum præ-

Fette Petit Antiqua.

Quousque tandem abutere, Catilina patientia nostra? quamdiu nos etiam furor iste tuus eludet? quem ad finem sese effrenata jactabit audatia? nihilne te nocturnum præsidium palatii, nihil urbis vigiliæ, nihil timor populi, nihil consensus bonorum

Schrift-Proben

aus der

Schriftgiesserey und Schriftschneiderey von Theodor Walbaum in Weimar.

Musirte Versalien, Erste Sorte.

ABCDEFGH
IJKLMNOP
QRSTUVW
XYZÄÖÜ

Minimum 9 U. per U. 14 Gr.

Musirte Versalien, Zweite Sorte.

ABCDEFGH
IJKLMNOP
QRSTUVW
XYZÄÖÜ

Minimum 9 U. per U. 14 Gr.

Text Blumen-Schrift.

ABCDEFGHIJK
LMNOPQRSTU
VWXYZ.,-
1234567890

Minimum 8 U. per U. 14 Gr.

Doppel Mittel Blumen-Schrift.

ABCDEFGH
IJKLMNOPQ
RSTUVWX
YZ.,-&
1234567890

Minimum 8 U. per U. 14 Gr.

Text verzierte Lapidar.

ABCDEFGHIJ
KLMNOPQRST
UVWXYZ.,-&
1234567890

Minimum 8 U. per U. 14 Gr.

Text schattirte Lapidar.

ABCDEFHIJK
LMNOPQRSTU
VWXYZ.,-&
1234567890

Minimum 8 U. per U. 14 Gr.

Doppel Mittel schattirte Lapidar.

ABCDEFGHIJKLMNOPQ
RSTUVWXYZ.,-&

Minimum 9 U. per U. 14 Gr.

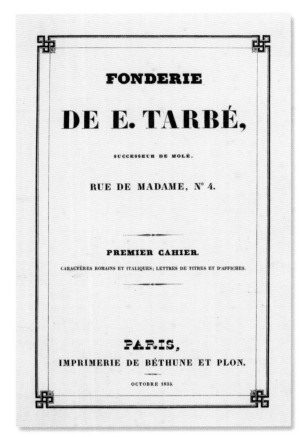

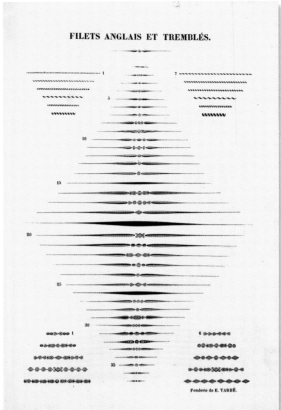

1835, Premier Cahier,
Fonderie de E. Tarbé, Paris

Fine lines, and the large letters of
a so-called slab serif type.

Feine Linien und Versalien einer
serifenbetonten Schrift.

Les lignes fines et les larges
empattements d'une égyptienne.

CORPS CENT-SOIXANTE-CINQ, OU QUINZE CICÉRO.

PARIS, 1835.

CORPS QUATRE-VINGT 8 OU HUIT CICÉRO.

HAVRE

CORPS CENT DIX, OU GROSSE DE FONTE.

SEMER

CORPS CENT TRENTE-QUATRE, OU DOUBLE GROSSE DE FONTE.

RIME.

LETTRES DE DEUX POINTS MAIGRES.

Fonderie de E. TARBÉ

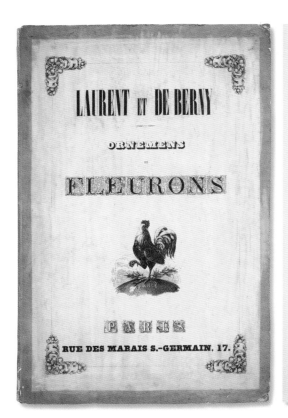

1838, Ornemens et Fleurons,
Laurent et de Berny, Paris

These exuberant letters, with matching ornaments, were created in various shapes and sizes for festive printing.

Lettern wie diese wurden samt passenden Ornamenten in verschiedenen Formen und Größen für Druckwerke mit feierlichem Charakter gestaltet.

Ces lettres exubérantes, avec ornements assortis, étaient gravées sous diverses formes et tailles pour des impressions de fête.

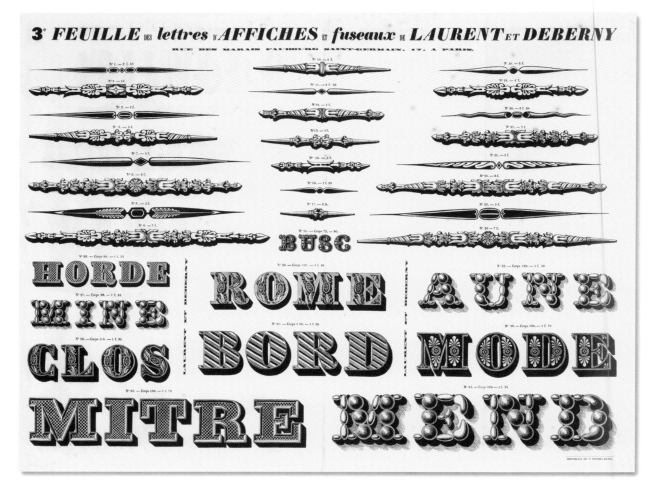

N° 47. — Ornées, C. 76. — 1 fr. 10 la lettre.

ROELE

N° 46. — Ornées, C. 120. — 1 fr. 50 c. la lettre.

BRISE

N° 52. — Profilées, C. 156. — 1 fr. 60 c. la lettre.

MENAGERIE

Fuseau, N° 56. — 7 fr.

N° 54. — Vénitiennes, C. 260. — 2 fr. 25 c. la lettre.

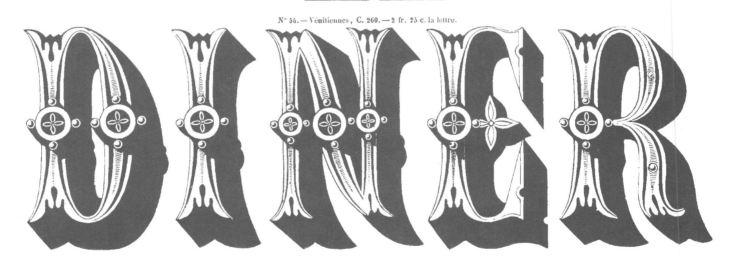

DINER

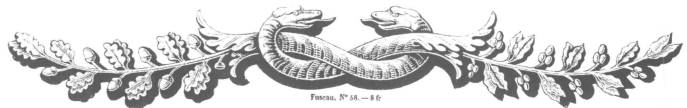

Fuseau, N° 58. — 8 fr

Déposé à la Direction.

1837

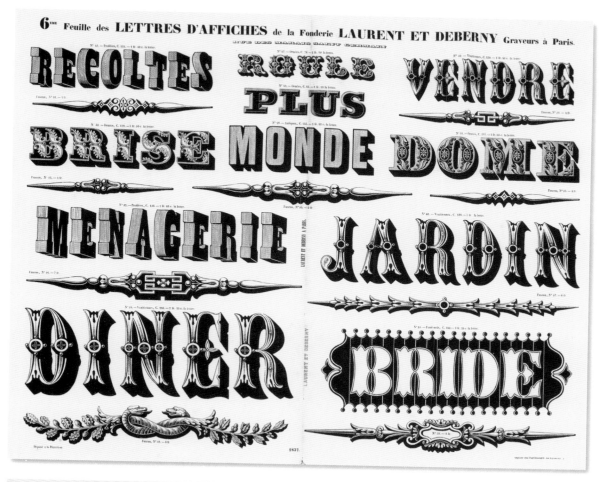

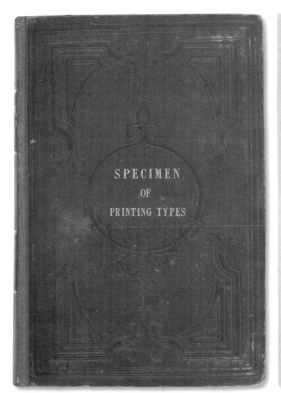

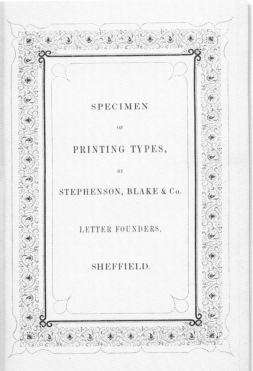

SPECIMEN
OF
PRINTING TYPES,
BY
STEPHENSON, BLAKE & Co.

LETTER FOUNDERS.

SHEFFIELD.

1838, Specimen of Printing Types,
Stephenson, Blake & Company, Sheffield

Seen here are several examples of type-faces and ornaments. In one simple sheet, the letters *RES* are shown in 30-point Condensed Antique—a feast for the eye.

Die Abbildungen zeigen diverse Beispiele für Schriften und Ornamente. In einem Fall die Lettern *RES* in einer fetten Egyptienne-Schrift in 30 Punkt, die ein einzelnes Blatt komplett ausfüllen – eine Augenweide.

Voici plusieurs exemples de caractères et d'ornements. Sur cette feuille-spécimen, les lettres *RES* sont présentées en Antique étroit de 30 points – un régal pour les yeux.

THIRTY LINES CONDENSED ANTIQUE.

RES

EIGHTEEN LINES CONDENSED ANTIQUE.

Grand

BOROUGH

HAUM

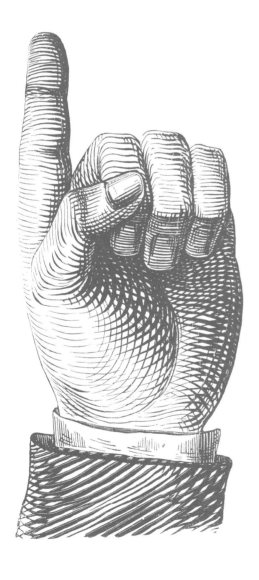

The company Stephenson, Blake & Company was established in 1819, and in 1837, it acquired the famous type foundry H. W. Caslon.

Die Firma Stephenson, Blake & Company öffnete ihre Pforten im Jahr 1819, 1837 wurde sie von der berühmten Schrift-gießerei H. W. Caslon übernommen.

La compagnie Stephenson, Blake & Company, fondée en 1819, racheta la célèbre fonderie de caractères H. W. Caslon en 1837.

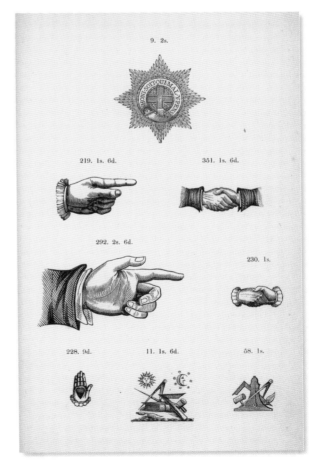

1839, Épreuves des Caractères & Vignettes, *Charles Derriey,* Paris

Majestueuse—suitable not only for a king, but also for ordinary mortals.

Majestueuse – eine angemessene Schrift nicht nur für einen Fürsten, sondern auch für gewöhnliche Sterbliche.

Majestueuse – pour un roi comme pour un simple mortel.

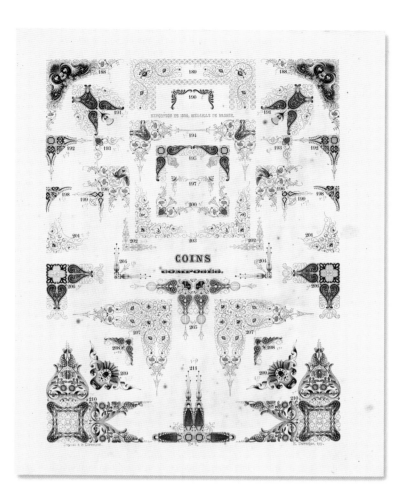

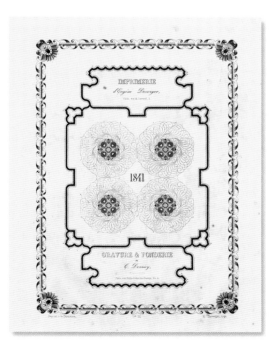

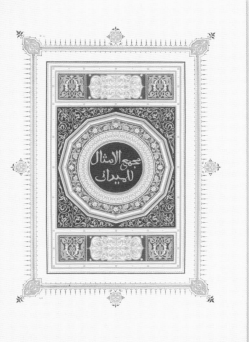

1845, Spécimen Typographique,
Imprimerie Royale, Paris

The French colonies also had a need
for printing work. Remarkably, these
pages were set by hand in lead.

Auch in den französischen Kolonien
gab es Bedarf an Druckerzeugnissen.
Diese beeindruckenden Seiten sind ebenfalls manuell im Bleisatz entstanden.

Les colonies françaises étaient également
en demande de travaux d'impression.
Ces pages remarquables ont été
composées manuellement en plomb.

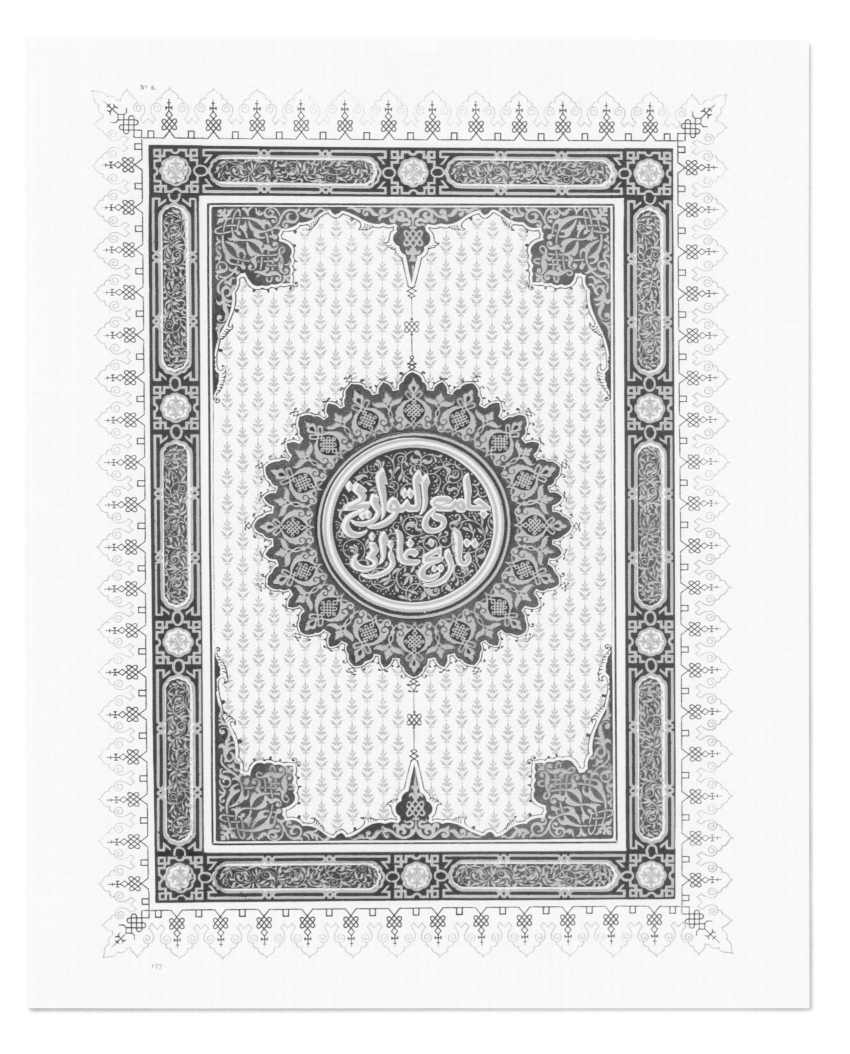

179

FIN

वाल्मीकीयें

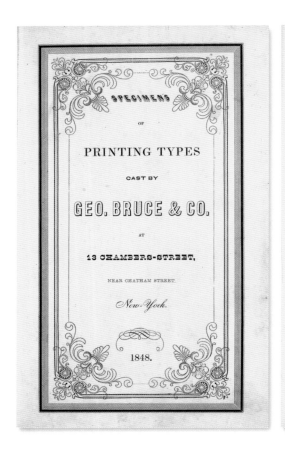

1848, Specimens of Printing Types,
George Bruce & Company, New York

In "Ten-Line Pica Comic," the medium is presumably also the message.

Im Falle der Schriftart „Ten-Line Pica Comic" ist wahrlich das Medium die Botschaft.

En «Pica Comic dix lignes», le moyen d'expression est le message.

TEN-LINE PICA COMIC.

TWO-LINE GREAT-PRIMER ORNAMENTED, NO. 3.

WASHINGTON.

TWO-LINE GREAT-PRIMER SHADED.

DANIEL WEBSTER

DOUBLE ENGLISH ANTIQUE EXTENDED.

STONE bridges,

TWO-LINE ENGLISH ANTIQUE OPEN.

GENERAL SCOTT

TWO-LINE ENGLISH SHADED.

THE PARK FOUNTAIN 18

TWO-LINE ENGLISH ORNAMENTED, NO. 2.

EXTRAORDINARY 18

TWO-LINE ENGLISH ORNAMENTED, NO. 3.

PRESIDENT JACKSON

TWO-LINE PICA GOTHIC.

BOYS WANTED

GEORGE BRUCE & CO.   NEW-YORK.

FIVE-LINE PICA SHADED.

SODA mason

FIVE-LINE PICA EXTRA-CONDENSED.

AMERICANS celebration:

FIVE-LINE PICA ANTIQUE EXTRA-CONDENSED.

ANTIQUE declaration

FIVE-LINE PICA GRECIAN.

ORNAMENTED

GEORGE BRUCE & CO.   NEW-YORK.

FOUR-LINE PICA ORNAMENTED, NO. 3.

CALHOUN

DOUBLE-PARAGON ANTIQUE.

ENGLISH
americans

TWO-LINE PARAGON ORNAMENTED.

BEAUTIFUL 18

TWO-LINE PARAGON ORNAMENTED, NO. 2.

JOHN Q. ADAMS

TWO-LINE GREAT-PRIMER GOTHIC.

MARCHES

TWO-LINE GREAT-PRIMER ORNAMENTED, NO. 1.

TWO-LINE GREAT-PRIMER ORNAMENTED, NO. 2.

ASTOR HOUSE.

GEORGE BRUCE & CO.   NEW-YORK.

EIGHT-LINE PICA ORNAMENTED, NO. 2.

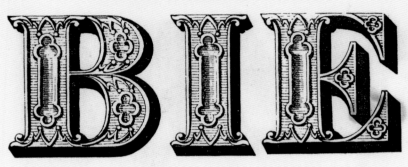

EIGHT-LINE PICA ORNAMENTED, NO. 3.

SEVEN-LINE PICA.

LIS
aim

SEVEN-LINE PICA SHADED.

GEORGE BRUCE & CO.   NEW-YORK.

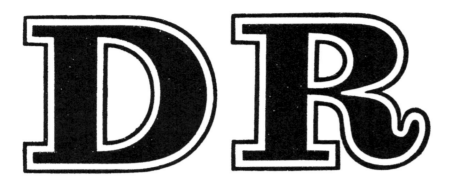

FIVE-LINE PICA CONDENSED, NO. 2.

GERMAN

FIVE-LINE PICA ORNAMENTED.

FIVE-LINE PICA ITALIAN.

BOAT

FIVE-LINE PICA BLACK.

Republic

FIVE-LINE PICA BLACK OPEN.

Republic

FIVE-LINE PICA BLACK OPEN, NO 2.

Republic

GEORGE BRUCE & CO.   NEW-YORK.

TWELVE-LINE PICA GRECIAN.

CHAIR

TEN-LINE PICA GRECIAN.

MARCH

SEVEN-LINE PICA GRECIAN.

PRESIDENT

FIVE-LINE PICA GRECIAN.

ORNAMENTED

FOUR-LINE PICA GRECIAN.

AMERICAN TYPES

GEORGE BRUCE & CO.   NEW-YORK.

802. $0.75.   1227. $1.00.   1246. $1.25.

1536. $3.00.

GEORGE BRUCE & CO.   NEW-YORK.

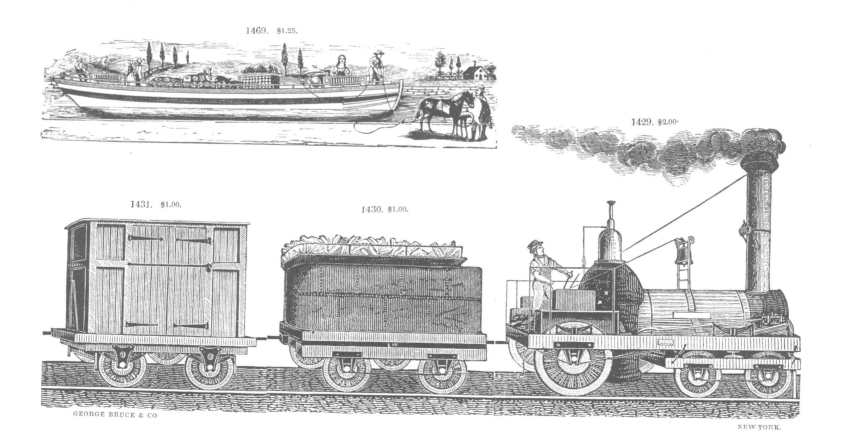

1469. $1.25.

1429. $2.00·

1431. $1.00.   1430. $1.00.

GEORGE BRUCE & CO   NEW-YORK.

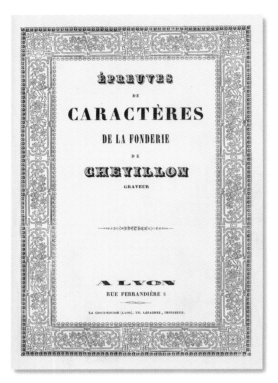

1848, Épreuves de Caractères,
Fonderie de Chevillon, Lyon

Big lines supported the text.

Auffällige Linien zur Unterstützung
des Texts.

Des grandes lignes portaient le texte.

Filets en lames.

1 mètre 20 cent. de longueur.   force de corps très régulière.

CORPS 2

CORPS 3

CORPS 4

CORPS 6

CORPS DIVERS.

FONDERIE DE L. CHEVILLON A LYON.

Lettres demi-grasses pour Titres.

N. 1 CORPS 8.

LES CONNAISSANCES UTILES

N. 2 CORPS 10.

LES MONUMENTS ANCIENS ET MODERNES

N. 3 CORPS 11.

UNE ANTIQUITÉ ROMAINE

N. 4 CORPS 12.

PAQUEBOTS TRANSLANTIQUES

N. 5 CORPS 14.

CONSCIENCIEUSEMENT

N. 6 CORPS 15.

PALAIS DES TUILERIES

N. 7 CORPS 16.

LES PEINTURES

N. 8 CORPS 20.

LES CHEVALIERS

N. 9 CORPS 24.

CATARACTES

N. 10 CORPS 28.

MINISTRES

FONDERIE DE L. CHEVILLON A LYON.

40 GROS CANON.

**Quousque tandem abu-
tere, Catilina, patientia**

Quousque tandem abute

FONDERIE DE L. CHEVILLON A LYON.

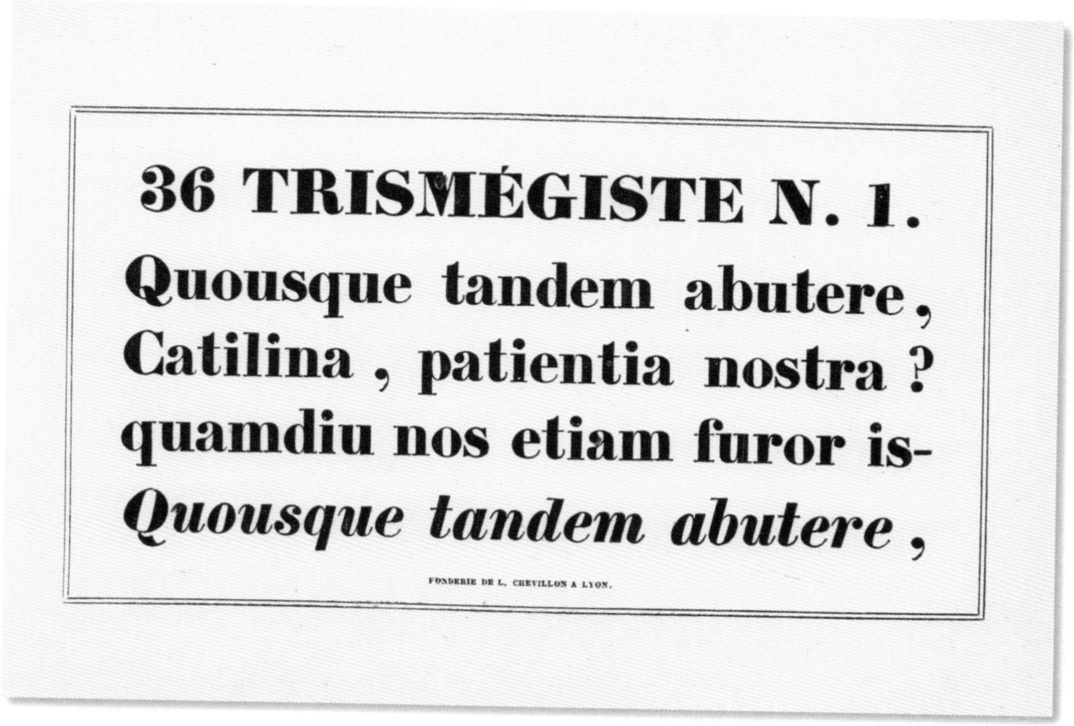

36 TRISMÉGISTE N. 1.

**Quousque tandem abutere,
Catilina, patientia nostra?
quamdiu nos etiam furor is-**

Quousque tandem abutere,

FONDERIE DE L. CHEVILLON A LYON.

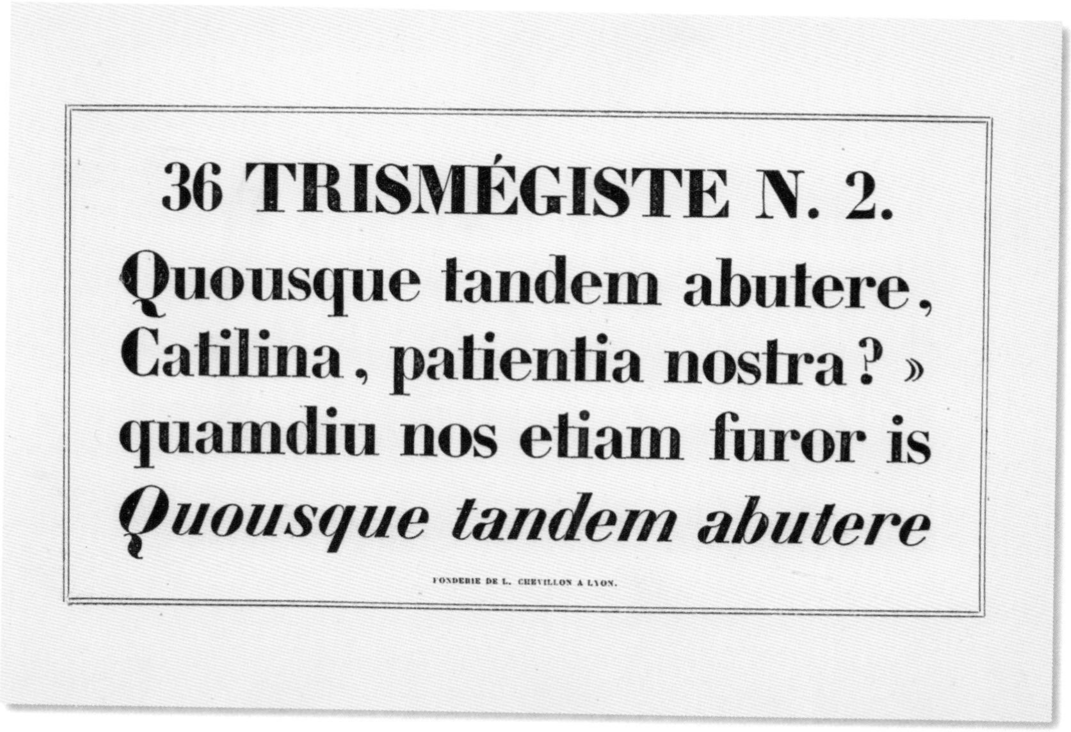

36 TRISMÉGISTE N. 2.

**Quousque tandem abutere,
Catilina, patientia nostra? »
quamdiu nos etiam furor is**

Quousque tandem abutere

FONDERIE DE L. CHEVILLON A LYON.

ACCOLADES.

CORPS 6.

Filets Anglais.

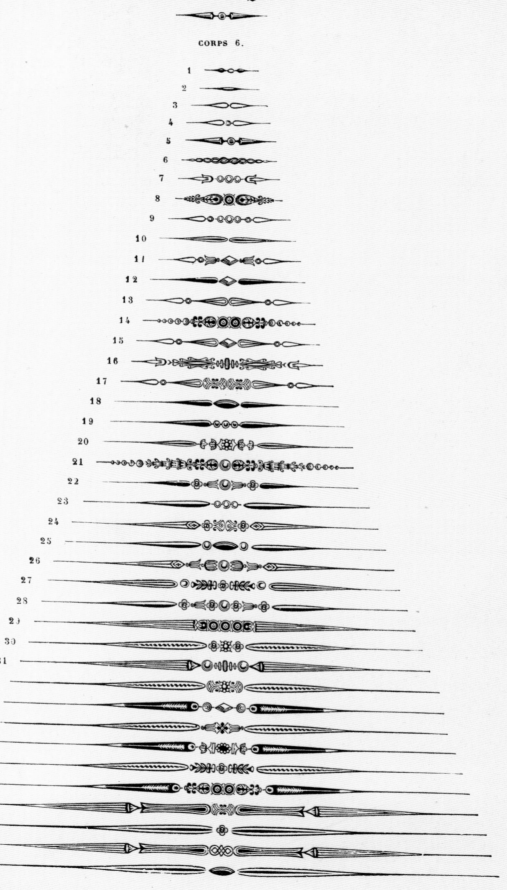

CORPS 6.

1849, Essais Pratiques d'Imprimerie,
Paul Dupont, Paris

It would be a treat to receive such
an invitation.

Eine solche Einladung zu erhalten ist
schon etwas Besonderes.

Quel plaisir ce serait de recevoir
pareille invitation !

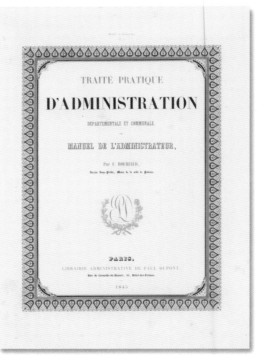

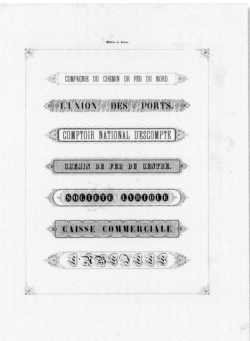

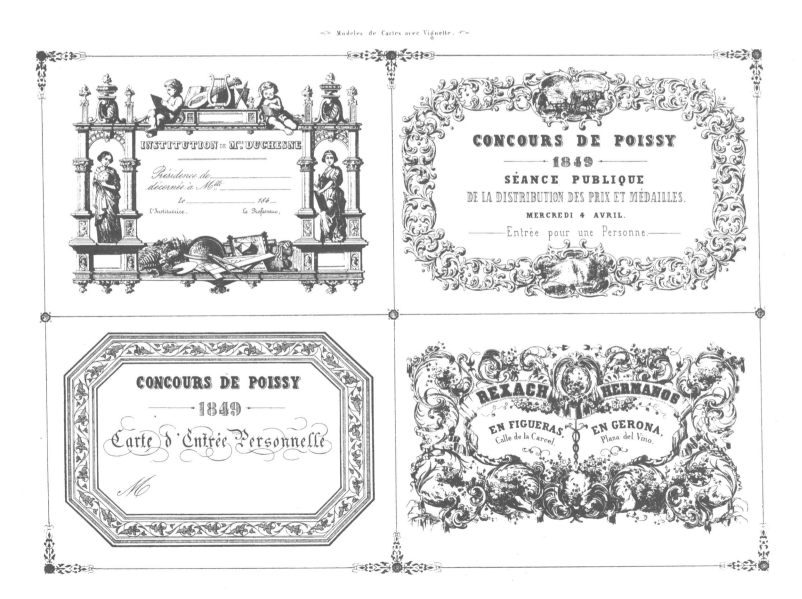

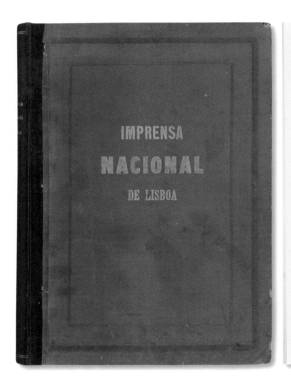

1858, Specimen da Fundição de Typos,
Imprensa Nacional, Lisboa

In 1858, Portugal was connected to the rest of the world. The presentation of these letters speaks for itself.

1858 stand Portugal in engem Austausch mit dem Rest der Welt. Die Präsentation der Schriften spricht für sich.

En 1858, le Portugal était lié au reste du monde. La présentation de ces lettres parle d'elle-même.

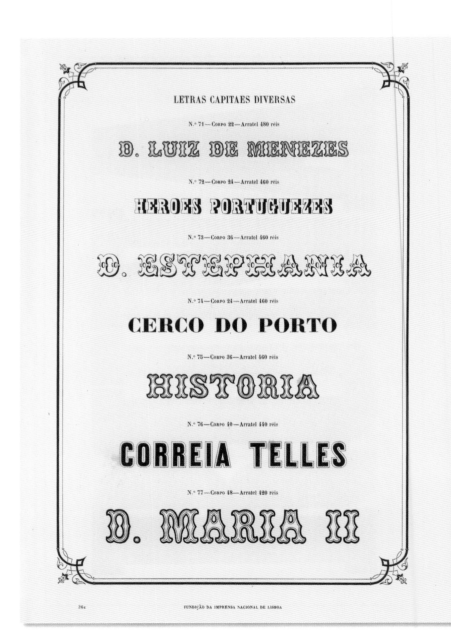

N.º 113 — Corpo 24 — Arratel 460 réis

CABO VERDE

N.º 117 — Corpo 36 — Arratel 440 réis

MOSSAMEDES

N.º 118 — Corpo 52 — Arratel 420 réis

ODEMIRA

N.º 22 — Corpo 20 — Arratel 480 réis

FREI LUIZ DE SOUSA

N.º 23 — Corpo 24 — Arratel 460 réis

DUQUE DE PALMELLA

N.º 24 — Corpo 24 — Arratel 460 réis

VASCO DA GAMA

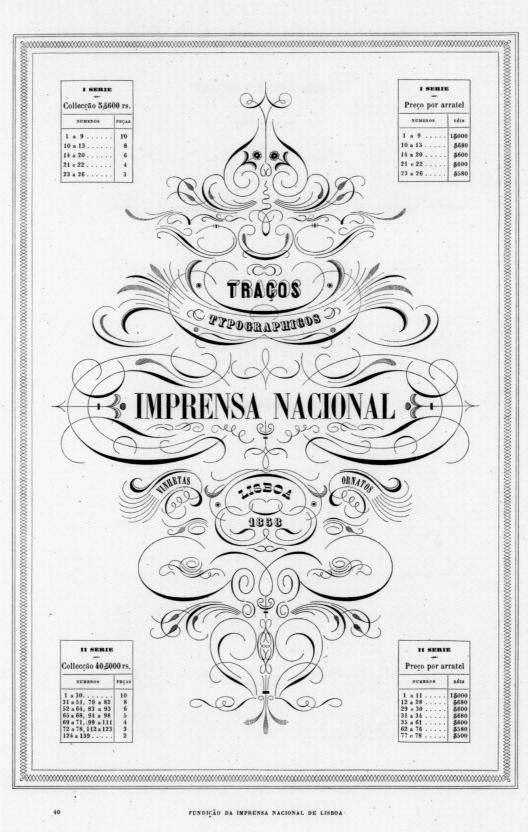

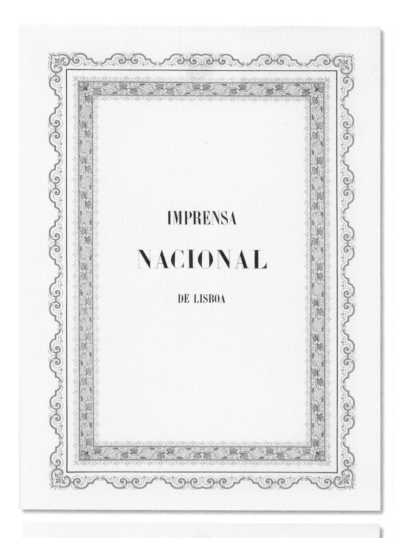

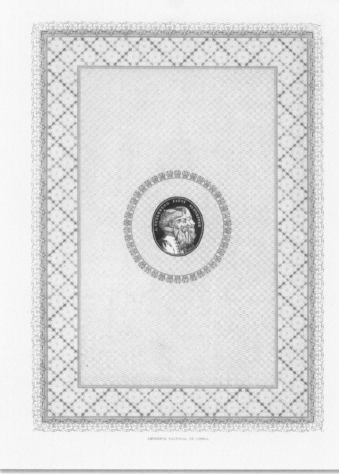

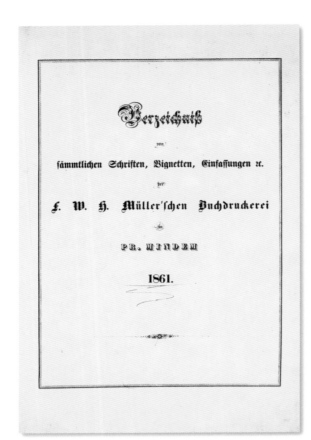

1861, Verzeichniß von sämmtlichen Schriften, Vignetten, Einfassungen, *F. W. H. Müller'sche Buchdruckerei,* Minden

A toothache (Zahnweh, in German), beautifully rendered in words and pictures.

Zahnweh – anschaulich in Wort und Bild überführt.

Un mal de dent (Zahnweh, en allemand), magnifiquement rendu en mots et en images.

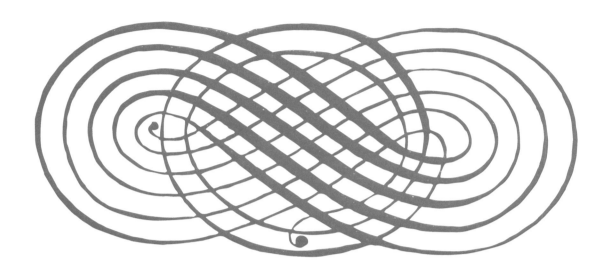

BEINHAUER'S

LONDON   PATENT

STAHLFEDERN

Zahnweh

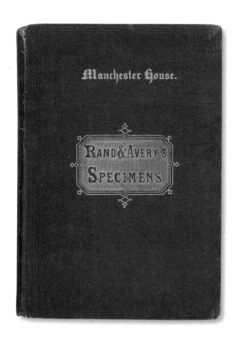

As the world changed, production
and technology were portrayed in contemporary fashion.

Zeitgenössische Darstellungen zum
Wandel von Produktion und Technik.

Dans un monde en changement, la
production et la technologie étaient
représentées de manière contemporaine.

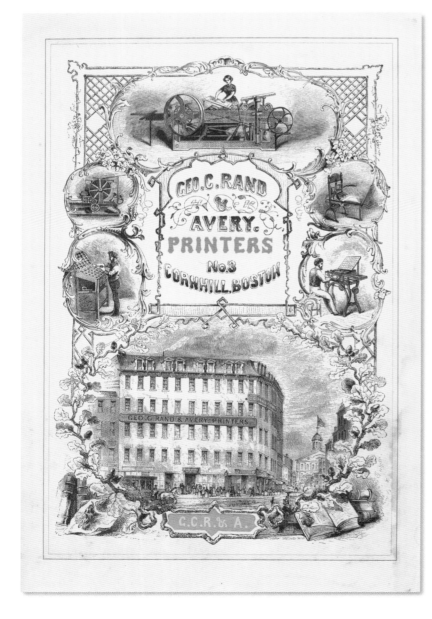

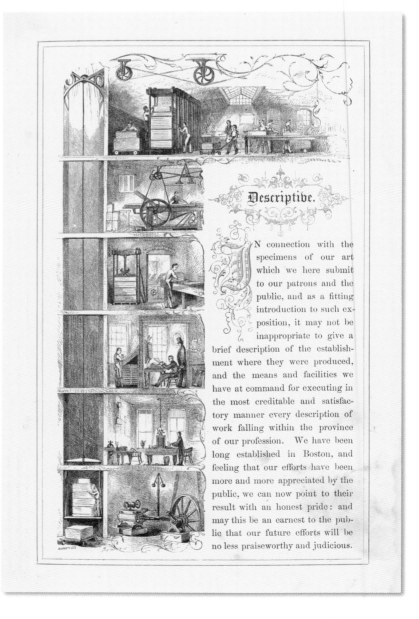

Front on Cornhill.

The block of buildings used by us for a Printing Establishment begins at 13 Washington Street, and extends to 7 Cornhill, comprising the buildings numbered 13, 15, 17, 19, and 21 Washington Street, and 1, 3, 5, and 7 Cornhill, reaching back in each instance to Brattle Street. In the above engraving is seen the Washington-Street and Cornhill Front. It is 125 feet in length on the two streets, and six stories in height, and, though not an architectural model, yet presents an appearance at once solid, substantial, and majestic. No. 3 Cornhill is the main entrance, leading directly to the Counting Room.

We also give a view of the Brattle-Street Front. Here may be seen the entrance for the reception and delivery of merchandise, such as books, paper, ink, and other printing material. The street in front is wide, and not pressed with travel, so that our ingress and egress are not obstructed by the many difficulties that prevail in more crowded thoroughfares. This entrance connects directly with the Elevator, shown in the vignette, and thus with all parts of the building.

In the vignette we present a sectional view of the building and its various departments, which we will enter and examine more closely.

Fireproof Safe, for Plates.

Safe, or Plate Depository, a view of which is given above. It is a large vault of arched masonry, built under the Cornhill and Washington-Street sidewalk, and is probably the most complete work of its kind in our city. It is 90 feet in length, 10 feet wide, and 15 feet high, and is kept thoroughly warm and dry by steam-pipes passing up and down its entire length. Huge shelves line the sides of the vault, and a third tier passes along the centre. On these are stored our Stereotype and Electrotype Plates, as well as Wood Engravings, all of which require great care for their proper preservation. All the shelves are numbered, and so well is everything arranged, and such method is there observed, that notwithstanding the fact that there are

Counting Room.

here deposited more than 200,000 different plates, yet no difficulty is experienced in obtaining immediately any particular one required. A memorandum of all the plates and their location is kept in the Counting Room. This Safe, most judiciously located underground, is built of brick and stone, closed with iron doors, and believed to be in every respect completely fire-proof. And when the value of its contents, and the difficulty, if not impossibility, in many instances, of replacing them, are considered, the importance of having this structure all we have described it cannot be over-estimated. Quitting this subterranean cavern, where part of the time we have been at least twenty feet below the street, we emerge into the light of day, and, making the tour of the building, we pass to

The Counting Room, on the second floor, by the principal entrance, No. 3 Cornhill. We notice that the entire ground-floor and parts of the story above are not used by us for the purposes of our business, but are variously occupied by publishing houses and book-stores. The second story gained, then, we enter the spacious and well-lighted Counting Room, where the proprietors and their head

Composition Room.

centuries ago. On visiting a Printing Office for the first time, and wishing to gain a proper understanding of the most beautiful of arts, this is the point to start from. The first stage of the process is here performed, and the various single letters, under the guiding fingers of skilled compositors, group themselves into words, lines, pages, volumes. From these pages books may be printed directly, or fac-simile plates cast to be used again and again without the preliminary labor and expense of "setting up." Referring to the engraving, ranged down the sides of the room we see rows of stands containing the multitudinous sizes and varieties of book type requisite to this department. In the open space are the Imposing Stones, on which "matter" is imposed, proofs are taken, errors corrected, and the "form" finally made ready for the press. These rooms accommodate some fifty compositors, and possess materials and facilities for letter-press, electrotype, and stereotype composition that we feel assured are unsurpassed in extent and completeness; and we would call the attention of Publishers and Authors to the specimens of the different sizes and faces of book type used in this department.

Job Composition Room.

The Job Department. The specimens of type presented in the following pages of this book, numerous and diverse as they are, convey but an inadequate conception of the vast quantity and assortment daily in use in this department, and we are constantly increasing the variety and amount as new designs make their appearance from the founderies. The field is not limited by "diamond" and "pica," but only by the ingenuity of man. The internal arrangement of the room we are inspecting is similar to that of the Book Composition Room; but the labor performed in it requires quite a different order of talent, and to be a first-class Job Compositor is a high attainment in the art. Whether we have any in our employ who have gained that eminence is for others to decide; and to assist in that decision we present our plea, — this volume, with its specimens of type and of printing, and respectfully solicit for it an impartial examination.

Press Room.

The Proof Readers' Rooms claim a passing notice. They are, as they should be, small, each complete in itself, well lighted, and far removed from the noise and interruptions generally so inseparable from them. The importance of the Proof Reader's part cannot be over-estimated, and these aids to his comfort and success need only be mentioned to be appreciated. Leaving this floor, we pass to

The Book and Job Press Department, occupying the entire fourth and fifth stories, and comprising a series of rooms admirably suited, as the accompanying sketch of one of the floors exhibits, to the interesting and highly artistic labor there performed. It is very essential in this department of our business to have a good and plentiful supply of light, and perhaps nothing will attract the visitor's attention so markedly as the eminent advantages we possess in this respect. The many windows, double frontage, and height above the street and surrounding buildings, secure to us that flood of light so welcome to the pressman. In these several rooms are twenty-one Adams

Dry-Press Room.

Dry-Press Room, where, after being placed between highly-polished pasteboards, they are put into the Hydraulic Presses (Adams' Patent, now Hoe's) capable of exerting a force of five hundred tons' pressure. The simple yet effective arrangement for "filling" these presses is truthfully represented in this engraving. After being thoroughly pressed, the sheets are counted off into quires and dispatched to the bookbinder's, or as may be directed. In this room we have in constant operation one of Buckley's Folders, a very ingenious machine for folding papers, and one well worth the inspection of the curious. The Elevator machinery, placed in this room, is Fox's patent, of admirable design, and of a size capable of lifting two tons.

This completes the survey of our Establishment, and we now commend the following pages to the careful attention of the reader.

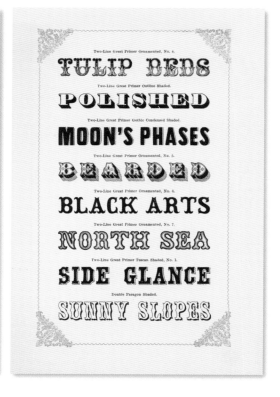

Four-Line Small Pica Condensed Tuscan Shaded.

GROWING PLANTS

Canon Ornamented.

RADIANT

Four Line Pica Ornamented.

SNAKES

Four-Line Pica Italian.

COMIC Tricks

Four-Line Pica Ornamented, No. 1.

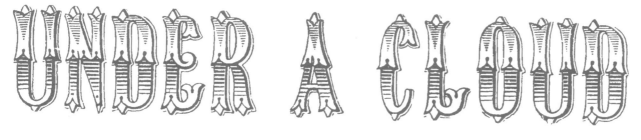

UNDER A CLOUD

Four-Line Pica Ornamented, No. 2.

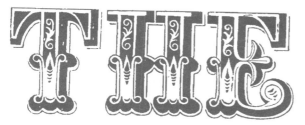

THE END

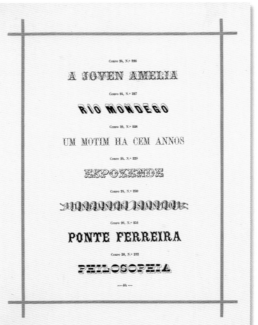

1874, Specimen, *Fundição Typographica Portuense,* Porto

The four red lines in the type area, which just cross, are a unique feature of this layout.

Die sich überschneidenden vier roten Linien verleihen dem Layout einen außergewöhnlichen Charakter.

Les quatre lignes rouges dans la zone du charactère, qui se croisent simplement, sont un trait remarquable de cette mise en page.

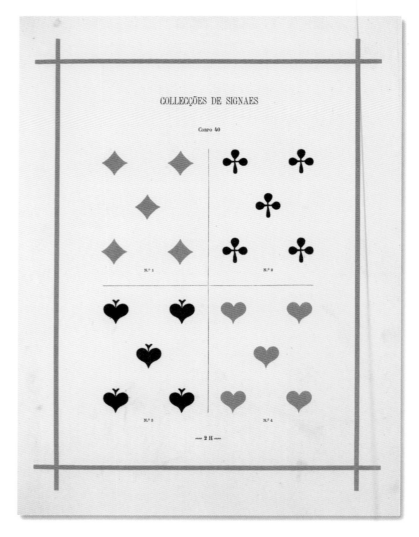

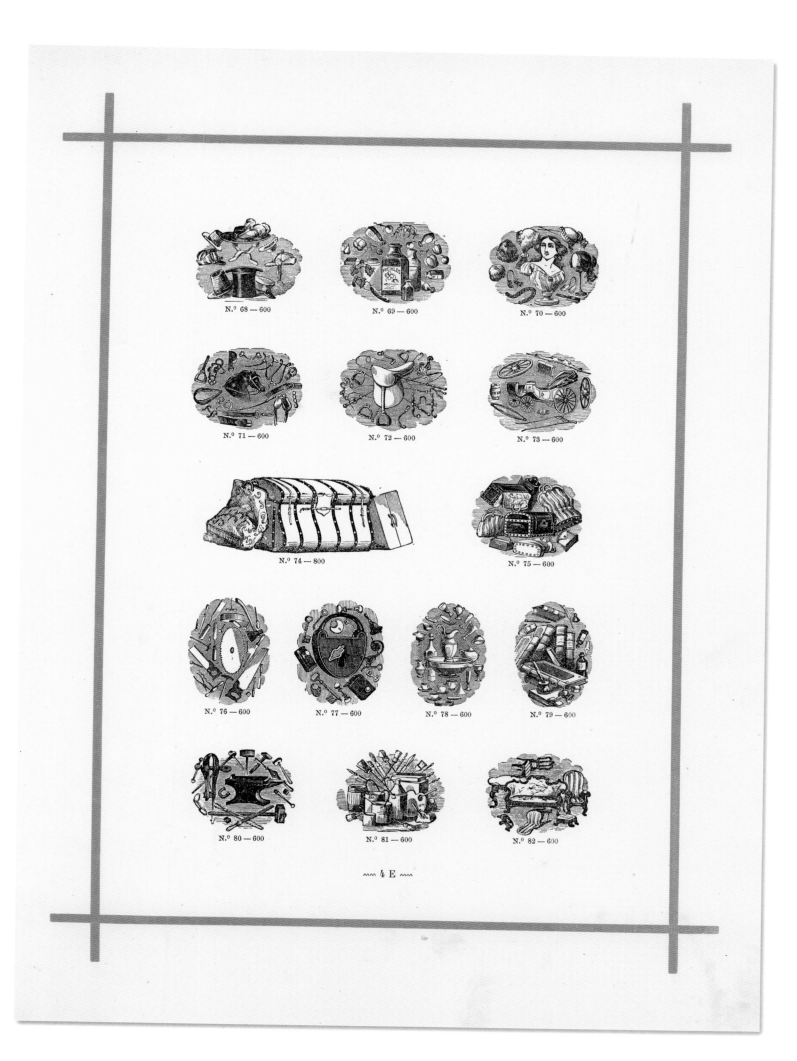

N.º 68 — 600

N.º 69 — 600

N.º 70 — 600

N.º 71 — 600

N.º 72 — 600

N.º 73 — 600

N.º 74 — 800

N.º 75 — 600

N.º 76 — 600

N.º 77 — 600

N.º 78 — 600

N.º 79 — 600

N.º 80 — 600

N.º 81 — 600

N.º 82 — 600

4 E

**1874, The Druggists' Printer, 6,
No. 2,** *United States Label-Printing
Establishment,* Frankford, Philadelphia

These labels for Rye Whiskey and
Jamaica Ginger show the era's version
of niche marketing.

Diese Flaschenetiketten für Rye Whiskey
oder Jamaica Ginger vermitteln einen
Eindruck vom seinerzeitigen Produkt-
marketing.

Ces étiquettes pour le Rye Whiskey
et le Jamaica Ginger montrent la version
de l'époque du marketing de créneau.

NEW, BEAUTIFUL AND CHEAP!

The four new styles shown below are by far the most attractive Shop Labels we have ever produced. They are shown here (for convenience) in but one color of tint, but in filling orders, each 250 Labels will always contain 3 or 4 delicate, pretty shades of assorted tints. These Labels, unlike other styles of Gilt Bordered Labels, will all be *gummed* and *cut*, and furnished at 40 cents for each 250 Labels to a name. Where 500 or 1000 to a name are wanted, the price charged will be at *same rate,* viz : 80 cents for 500, or $1.60 per 1000. Style **A 4** is adapted to articles requiring directions. Special rates given, on application, where 20,000 or upwards are wanted, 1000 or more to a name. In ordering, name the style, with names of articles, and quantities of each.

STYLE A 1.

STYLE A 2.

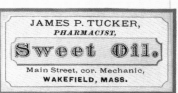

STYLE A 3.

STYLE A 4.

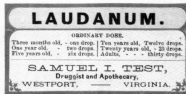

Pattern 2156.

CONCENTRATED EXTRACT OF PINE-APPLE FOR FLAVORING IceCream, Sauces, Jellies, Custards, Pastry &c.

CHAS. JONES,
Druggist,
MAINE, N.Y.

Pattern 2157.

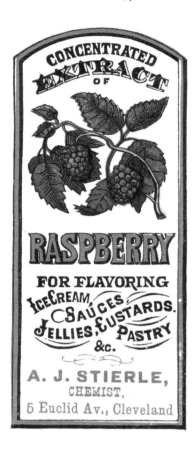

CONCENTRATED EXTRACT OF RASPBERRY FOR FLAVORING IceCream, Sauces, Jellies, Custards, Pastry &c.

A. J. STIERLE,
CHEMIST,
5 Euclid Av., Cleveland

Pattern 2158.

CONCENTRATED EXTRACT OF STRAWBERRY FOR FLAVORING IceCream, Sauces, Jellies, Custards, Pastry &c.

HENRY C. BOWEN,
Druggist,
Sixth & Vine Sts.

Pattern 2159.

CONCENTRATED EXTRACT OF VANILLA FOR FLAVORING IceCream, Sauces, Jellies, Custards, Pastry &c.

—MANGOLD—
Pharmacist,
Trenton, N.J.

Pattern 2160.

CONCENTRATED EXTRACT OF LEMON FOR FLAVORING IceCream, Sauces, Jellies, Custards, Pastry &c.

B. J. STRONG,
Druggist,
WARSAW, ILL.

Pattern 2161.

CONCENTRATED EXTRACT OF LEMON FOR FLAVORING IceCream, Sauces, Jellies, Custards, Pastry &c.

WARRANTED OF SUPERIOR QUALITY

The Labels on this page are furnished without gum, but cut and put in packs—per 1000, $3.00. 500, $2.25. 250, $1.50. When gummed and cut—per 1000, $4.00. 500, $3.00. 250, $2.50. POSTAGE—10 cents per 1000.

Pattern 2113.

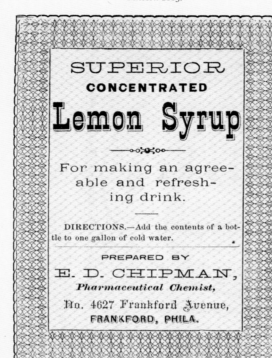

SUPERIOR
CONCENTRATED
Lemon Syrup

For making an agree-
able and refresh-
ing drink.

DIRECTIONS.—Add the contents of a bottle to one gallon of cold water.

PREPARED BY
E. D. CHIPMAN,
Pharmaceutical Chemist,
No. 4627 Frankford Avenue,
FRANKFORD, PHILA.

Pattern 2114.

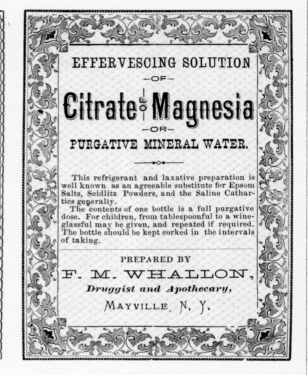

EFFERVESCING SOLUTION
—OF—
Citrate of Magnesia
—OR—
PURGATIVE MINERAL WATER.

This refrigerant and laxative preparation is well known as an agreeable substitute for Epsom Salts, Seidlitz Powders, and the Saline Cathartics generally.
The contents of one bottle is a full purgative dose. For children, from tablespoonful to a wineglassful may be given, and repeated if required. The bottle should be kept corked in the intervals of taking.

PREPARED BY
F. M. WHALLON,
Druggist and Apothecary,
MAYVILLE, N. Y.

Pattern 2115.

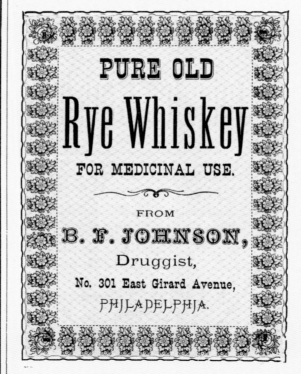

PURE OLD
Rye Whiskey
FOR MEDICINAL USE.

FROM
B. F. JOHNSON,
Druggist,
No. 301 East Girard Avenue,
PHILADELPHIA.

Pattern 2116.

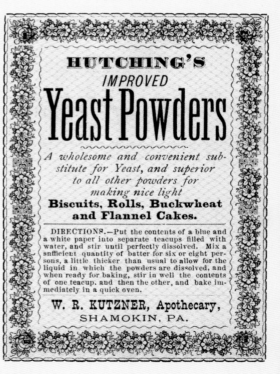

HUTCHING'S
IMPROVED
Yeast Powders

*A wholesome and convenient sub-
stitute for Yeast, and superior
to all other powders for
making nice light*
Biscuits, Rolls, Buckwheat
and Flannel Cakes.

DIRECTIONS.—Put the contents of a blue and a white paper into separate teacups filled with water, and stir until perfectly dissolved. Mix a sufficient quantity of batter for six or eight persons, a little thicker than usual to allow for the liquid in which the powders are dissolved, and when ready for baking, stir in well the contents of one teacup, and then the other, and bake immediately in a quick oven.

W. R. KUTZNER, Apothecary,
SHAMOKIN, PA.

The Labels on this page are furnished without gum, but cut and put in packs—per 1000, $3.00. 500, $2.25. 250, $1.50. When gummed and cut—per 1000, $4.50. 500, $3.00. 250, $2.50. POSTAGE—10 cents per 1000.

Pattern 2110.

FOR MEDICINAL USE.

PURE OLD

Rye Whiskey

B. F. JOHNSON, Druggist,

301 East Girard Ave., Philadelphia.

Pattern 2111.

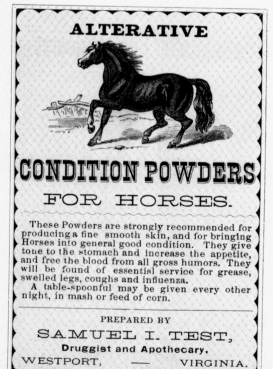

ALTERATIVE

CONDITION POWDERS

FOR HORSES.

These Powders are strongly recommended for producing a fine smooth skin, and for bringing Horses into general good condition. They give tone to the stomach and increase the appetite, and free the blood from all gross humors. They will be found of essential service for grease, swelled legs, coughs and influenza.

A table-spoonful may be given every other night, in mash or feed of corn.

PREPARED BY

SAMUEL I. TEST,

Druggist and Apothecary.

WESTPORT,   —   VIRGINIA.

Pattern 2112.

CONCENTRATED

ESSENCE

OF

Jamaica Ginger

This Essence is warranted to possess in a concentrated form, all the valuable properties of Jamaica Ginger, and will be found on trial an excellent Family Medicine, being a most efficient remedy for

Sick Headache, Indigestion, Colic, Nervous Debility, Cholera Morbus and Cholera.

DIRECTIONS.

A teaspoonful immediately after meals, will most generally relieve Indigestion. In acute cases of pain, or incipient Cholera, a teaspoonful may be given every half hour in sugar and water.

G. R. VERNON, Chemist,

CLIFTON,

DELAWARE CO., PENN'A.

Pattern 2141.

Pattern 2142.

Pattern 2143.

Pattern 2144.

Pattern 2145.

Pattern 2146.

Pattern 2147.

Pattern 2148.

Pattern 2149.

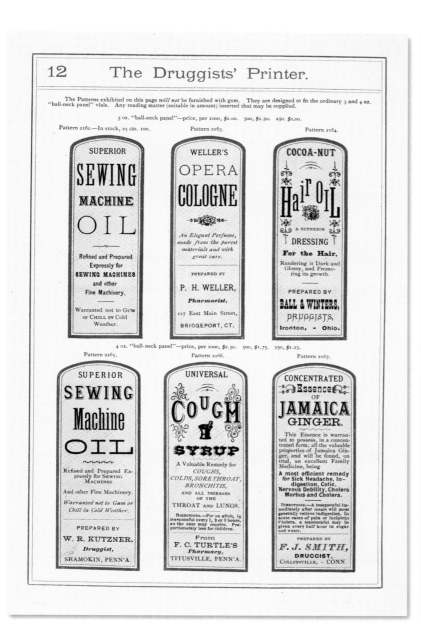

1876, Letterproef, *Algemeene Landsdrukkerij,* The Hague

Algemeene Landsdrukkerij did the typography and printing for the Dutch national telegraph company and national railways.

Die Algemeene Landsdrukkerij übernahm die typografische Gestaltung und den Druck der Publikationen für die staatliche Telegrafenanstalt und die staatliche Eisenbahngesellschaft der Niederlande.

L'Algemeene Landsdrukkerij réalisa la typographie et l'impression pour la compagnie de télégraphe et la compagnie de chemin de fer des Pays-Bas.

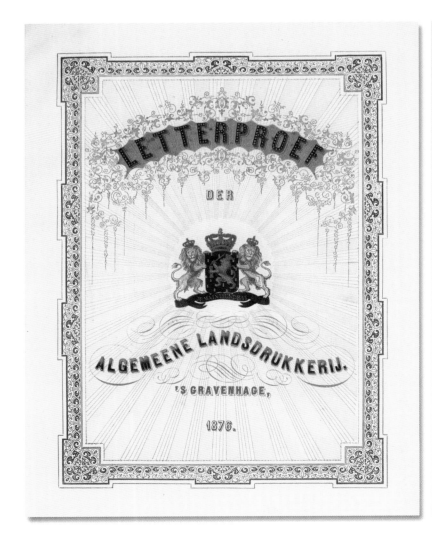

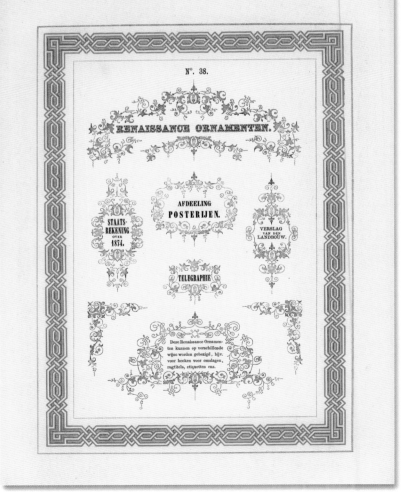

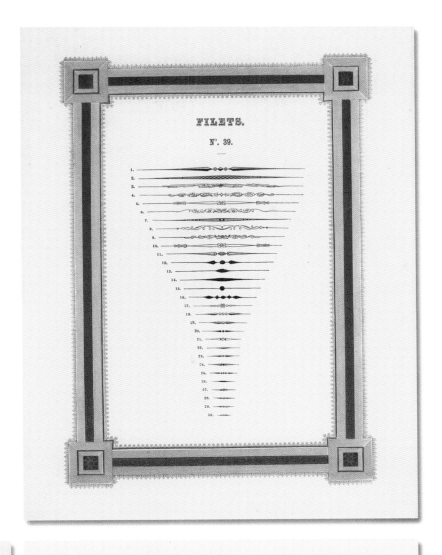

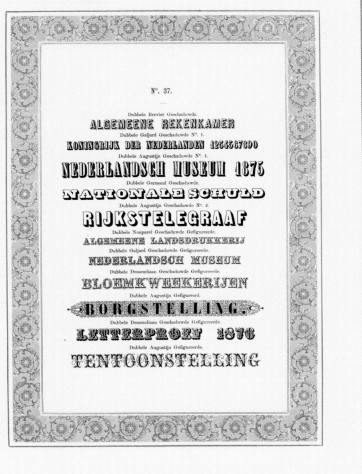

N°. 34.

Dubbele Nonparel Witte Anthieke.

POSTERIJEN WATERSTAAT RIJKSTELEGRAAF 1234567890

Dubbele Nonparel Gefigureerde.

JUSTITIE MARINE OORLOG 1234567890

Dubbele Collonel Gefigureerde.

LANDBOUW EN NIJVERHEID

Dubbele Collonel Hellende.

HANDEL EN SCHEEPVAART 1234567890

Dubbele Collonel Verlengde.

ALMELO ENSCHEDÉ ZAANDAM 1234567890

Dubbele Garmond Verlengde.

ALBLASSERWAARD 1234567890

Dubbele Mediaan Verlengde.

BEETSTERZWAAG 1234567

Dubbele Augustijn Verlengde.

'S HERTOGENBOSCH 2468

Dubbele Tekst Verlengde.

SCHIEDAM 567890

Parijsche Verlengde.

DELFT 1234

N°. 35.

Dubbele Robijn Verlengde Steenkapitalen.

GOES   ZIERIKZEE   GOEDEREEDE   OVERFLAKKEE   1234567890

Dubbele Parel Verlengde Steenkapitalen.

'S GRAVENHAGE   DELFT   ROTTERDAM   SCHIEDAM   1234567890

Dubbele Garmond Verlengde Steenkapitalen.

DEPARTEMENT VAN KOLONIEN

Dubbele Augustijn Verlengde Steenkapitalen.

RIJKSTELEGRAAF

Dubbele Tekst Verlengde Steenkapitalen.

STAATSSPOORWEGEN

Dubbele Nonparel Anthiek N°. 1.

DEPARTEMENT VAN BINNENLANDSCHE ZAKEN

Dubbele Nonparel Anthiek N°. 2.

DEPARTEMENT VAN FINANCIEN

Dubbele Collonel Anthiek.

RIJKSTELERAAF POSTERIJEN WATERSTAAT

Dubbele Garmond Anthiek.

REGISTRATIE EN DOMEINEN

Dubbele Parel Italienne.

MIDDELBURG VLISSINGEN HELDER

Dubbele Parel Verkorte N°. 1.

GOES EDAM 1234567890

Dubbele Parel Verkorte N°. 2.

GOES EDAM PURMER

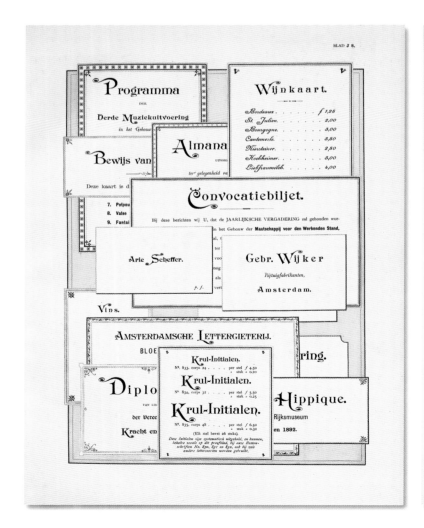

1876, Amsterdamsche Lettergieterij,
Amsterdamsche Lettergieterij, Amsterdam

Everyday, practical printing—from wine lists to visiting cards. In 1851, Nicolaas Tetterode established a type foundry in Rotterdam, which was moved to Amsterdam in 1857. From 1901 on, the foundry was known as N. V. Lettergieterij Amsterdam vorheen N. Tetterode.

Druckerzeugnisse für den Alltagsgebrauch – von Wein- bis zu Visitenkarten. Nicolaas Tetterodes Schriftgießerei war 1851 in Rotterdam gegründet worden, 1857 erfolgte der Umzug nach Amsterdam. Ab 1901 firmierte das Unternehmen als N. V. Lettergieterij Amsterdam vorheen N. Tetterode.

Travaux d'impression pour la vie de tous les jours – des cartes de vins aux cartes de visite. En 1851, Nicolaas Tetterode ouvrit, à Rotterdam, une fonderie de caractères qui fut ensuite transférée à Amsterdam en 1857. À partir de 1901, la fonderie prit le nom de N. V. Lettergieterij Amsterdam vorheen N. Tetterode.

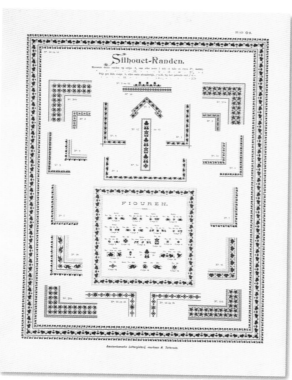

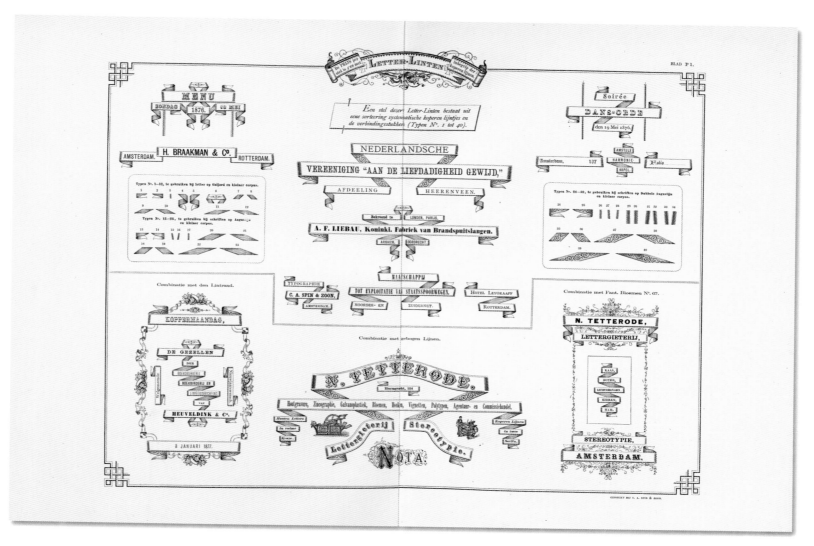

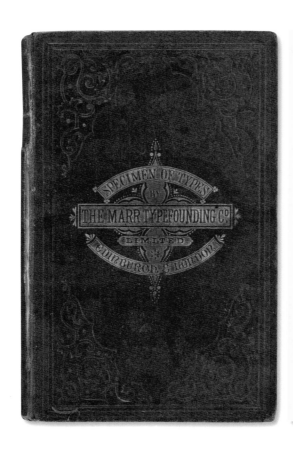

1877, Specimens of Types, *The Marr Typefounding Company*, Edinburgh & London

The texts set in this sample, including "colour printing" and "exhibition of flowers," illustrate daily life in 1877.

Das in diesem Muster vorgestellte Material gibt mit Begrifflichkeiten wie „Farbdruck" und „Blumenschau" einen Einblick in den Alltag des Jahres 1877.

Les textes composés dans cet échantillon, comme «impression en couleur» et «exposition de fleurs» illustrent la vie quotidienne en 1877.

No 306.   3s. 6d.

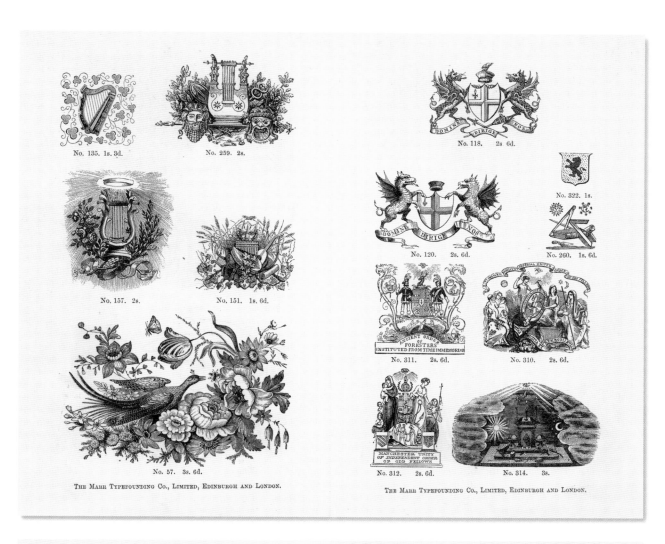

No. 135. 1s. 3d.

No. 259. 2s.

No. 118. 2s 6d.

No. 157. 2s.

No. 151. 1s. 6d.

No. 322. 1s.

No. 120. 2s. 6d.

No. 260. 1s. 6d.

No. 311. 2s. 6d.

No. 310. 2s. 6d.

No. 57. 3s. 6d.

No. 312. 2s. 6d.

No. 314. 3s.

THE MARR TYPEFOUNDING CO., LIMITED, EDINBURGH AND LONDON.

THE MARR TYPEFOUNDING CO., LIMITED, EDINBURGH AND LONDON.

No. 175. 1s. 6d.

No. 224. 1s. 6d.

No. 121. 4/

No. 90. 2s.

No. 184. 1s. 6d.

No. 94. 2s.

No. 117. 4/

No. 82. 2s. 6d.

No. 185. 2/

No. 182. 2/

THE MARR TYPEFOUNDING CO., LIMITED, EDINBURGH AND LONDON.

THE MARR TYPEFOUNDING CO., LIMITED, EDINBURGH AND LONDON.

6 A's, 4 ℔.   TWO LINE GREAT PRIMER FANTASIE.   @ 2/

WANDERER:

6 A's, 3½ ℔.   TWO LINE ENGLISH FANTASIE.   @ 2/

GEOGRAPHICAL

6 A's, 4 ℔.   TWO LINE ENGLISH ORNAMENTED, No. 5.   @ 2/

A CABINET.

6 A's, 2½ ℔.   TWO LINE PICA SANS SERIF OPEN, No. 2.   @ 2/

STEAM NAVIGATION

6 A's, 2½ ℔.   TWO LINE ENGLISH ORNAMENTED, No. 6.   @ 2/

ARCHITECTURE.

6 A's, 2 ℔.   TWO LINE SMALL PICA TUSCAN.   @ 3/

THE MUSICAL MIRROR.

6 A's, 1½ ℔.   TWO LINE BOURGEOIS TUSCAN, No. 3.   @ 3/

FORMER ADMINISTRATIONS.

6 A's, 8 ℔.   TWO LINE ENGLISH ORNAMENTED, No. 7.   @ 2/

GENERAL Leeds, 1867.

N.B.—These Prices are subject to Discount as per list or arrangement.

THE MARR TYPEFOUNDING CO., LIMITED, EDINBURGH AND LONDON.

6 A's, 3 ℔.   TWO LINE PICA ORNAMENTED, No. 5.   @ 2/

MINERALOGY.

6 A's, 2½ ℔.   TWO LINE PICA ORNAMENTED, No. 6.   @ 2/

NEW VOCAL MUSIC.

6 A's, 4 ℔.   TWO LINE PICA ORNAMENTED, No. 7.   @ 2/

ENGRAVINGS ON British.

6 A's, 2½ ℔.   TWO LINE PICA ORNAMENTED, No 8.   @ 2/

COLOUR PRINTING.

6 A's, 11 ℔.   TWO LINE PICA ORNAMENTED, No. 9.   @ 2/

SILK CLOAK Department. 1

TWO LINE SMALL PICA ORNAMENTED, No. 2.

6 A's, 2 ℔.   @ 3/

EXHIBITION OF FLOWERS TICKETS £1234.

TWO LINE SMALL PICA ORNAMENTED, No. 3.

6 A's, 2½ ℔.   @ 3/

ART INSTITUTION.

TWO LINE SMALL PICA ORNAMENTED, No. 4.

6 A's, 2½ ℔.   @ 3/

FLOWER OF MAY.

N.B.—These Prices are subject to Discount as per list or arrangement.

THE MARR TYPEFOUNDING CO., LIMITED, EDINBURGH AND LONDON.

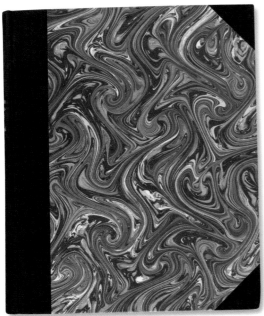

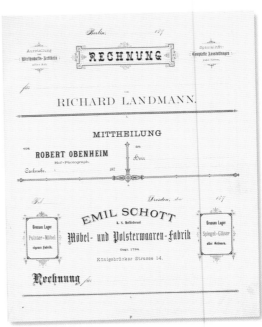

**1878, Archiv für Buchdruckerkunst,
XV. Band,** *Alexander Waldow,* Leipzig

These samples show unprecedented
possibilities. Letterpress technology
now knows no bounds.

Diese Muster demonstrieren typografische Gestaltungsmöglichkeiten,
wie man sie bis dahin noch nie
gesehen hatte. Dem Hochdruck sind
keine Schranken mehr gesetzt.

Ces exemples montrent des possibilités
sans précédent. La technologie typographique ne connaît plus de limites.

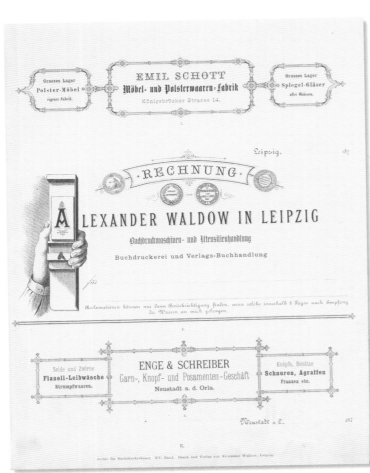

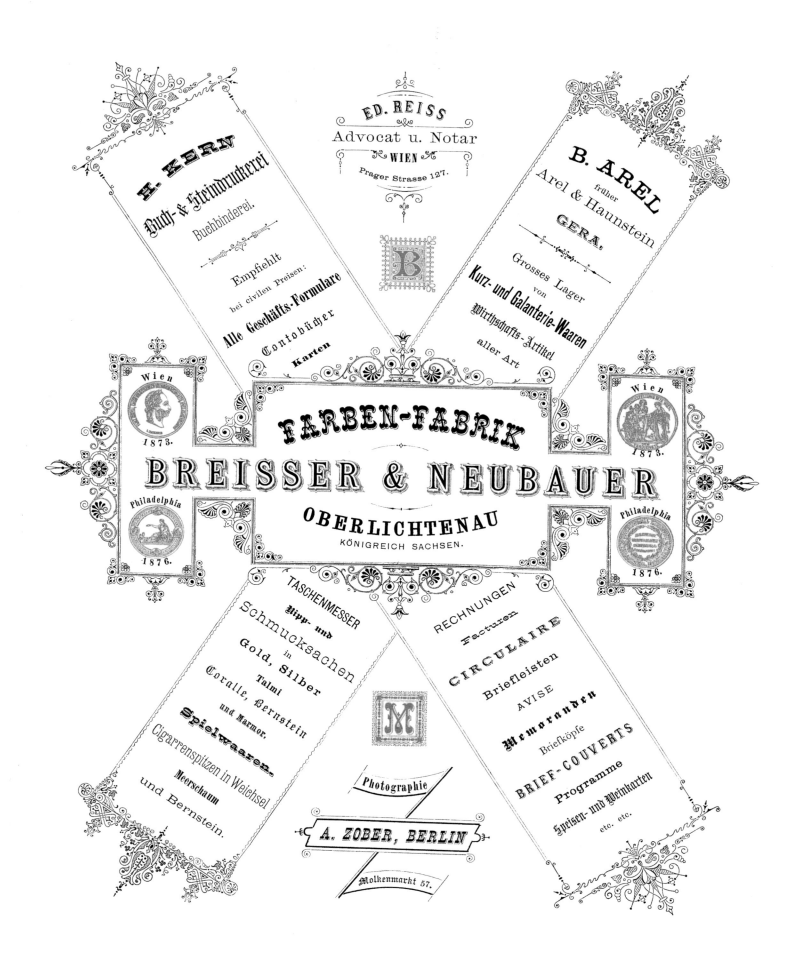

ED. REISS
Advocat u. Notar
WIEN
Prager Strasse 127.

H. KERN
Buch- & Steindruckerei.
Buchbinderei.

Empfiehlt
bei civilen Preisen:
Alle Geschäfts-Formulare
Contobücher
Karten

B. AREL
früher
Arel & Haunstein
GERA,

Grosses Lager
von
Kurz- und Galanterie-Waaren
Wirthschafts-Artikel
aller Art

FARBEN-FABRIK

BREISSER & NEUBAUER

OBERLICHTENAU
KÖNIGREICH SACHSEN.

Wien
1873.

Philadelphia
1876.

Wien
1873.

Philadelphia
1876.

TASCHENMESSER
Nipp- und
Schmucksachen
in
Gold, Silber
Talmi
Coralle, Bernstein
und Marmor,
Spielwaaren.
Cigarrenspitzen in Weichsel
Meerschaum
und Bernstein.

Photographie
A. ZOBER, BERLIN
Molkenmarkt 57.

RECHNUNGEN
Facturen
CIRCULAIRE
Briefleisten
AVISE
Memoranden
Briefköpfe
BRIEF-COUVERTS
Programme
Speisen- und Weinkarten
etc. etc.

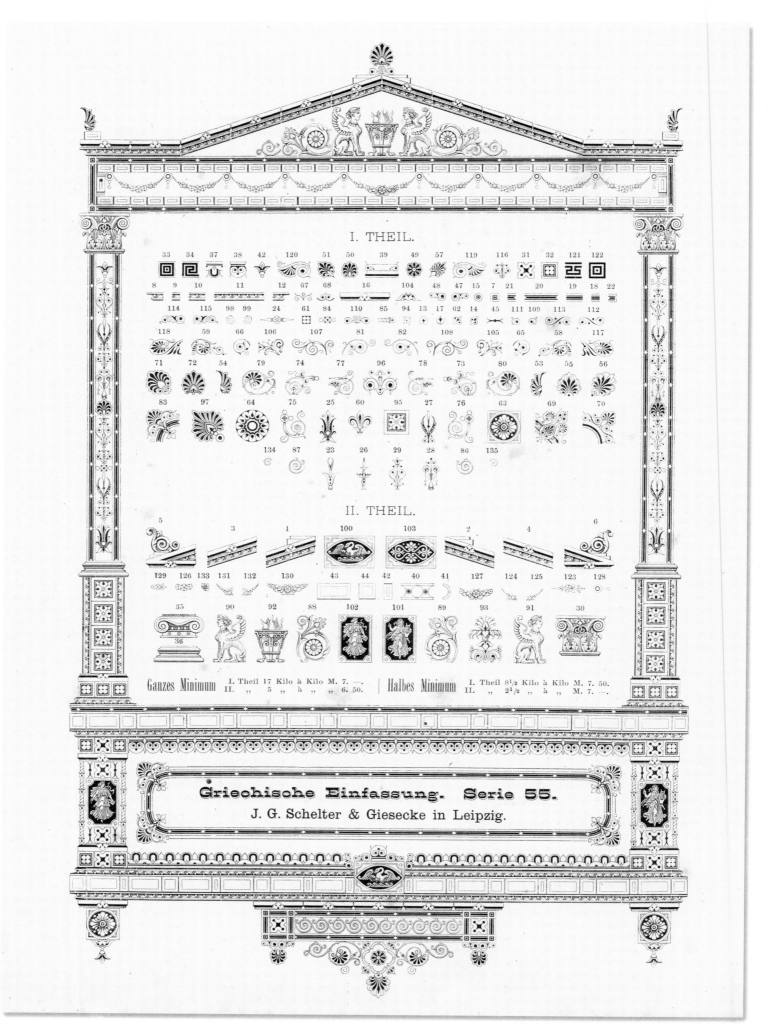

Griechische Einfassung. Serie 55.

J. G. Schelter & Giesecke in Leipzig.

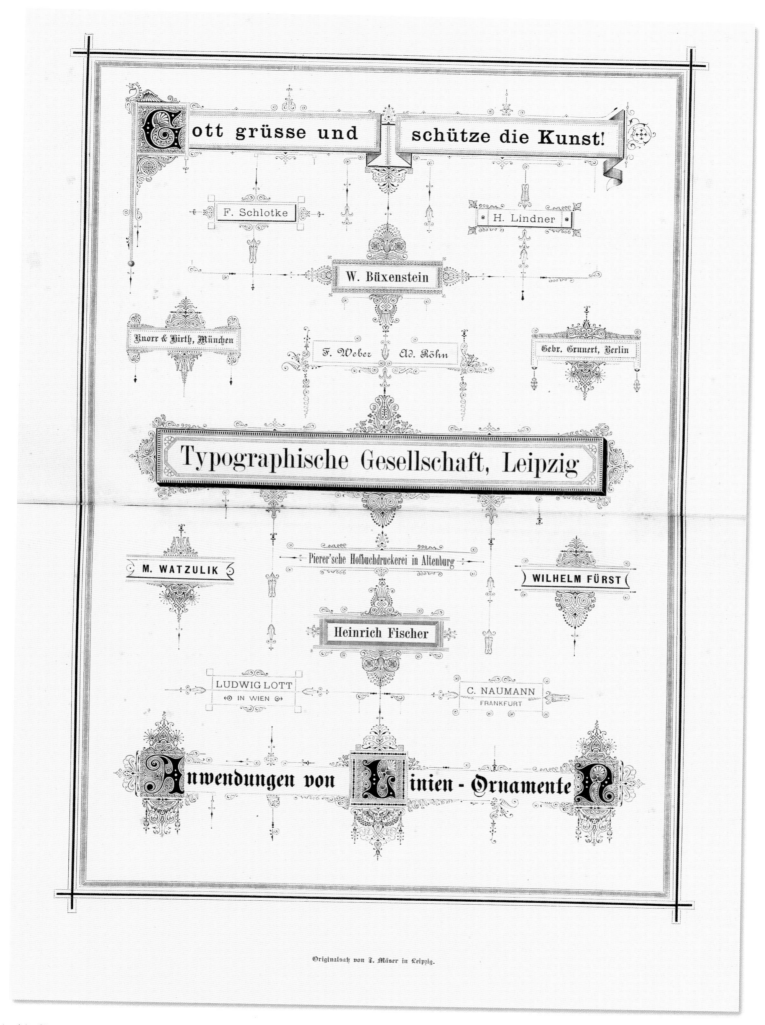

Gott grüsse und schütze die Kunst!

F. Schlotke

H. Lindner

W. Büxenstein

Knorr & Hirth, München

F. Weber   Ad. Röhn

Gebr. Grunert, Berlin

Typographische Gesellschaft, Leipzig

M. WATZULIK

Pierer'sche Hofbuchdruckerei in Altenburg

WILHELM FÜRST

Heinrich Fischer

LUDWIG LOTT
IN WIEN

C. NAUMANN
FRANKFURT

Anwendungen von Linien-Ornamenten

Originalsatz von J. Mäser in Leipzig.

SCHRIFTGIESSEREI

GRAVIR - ANSTALT — MESSINGLINIEN - FABRIK
STEREOTYPIE

JULIUS KLINKHARDT

LEIPZIG

GALVANOPLASTIK — UTENSILIEN - HANDLUNG
XYLOGRAPHIE

1.

Nach einem Original von Julius Klinkhardt in Leipzig.

Productiv-Genossenschaft Deutscher Buchdrucker

2.

Nach einem Original von J. Mäser in Leipzig.

BUCHDRUCKEREI GEBR. GRUNERT

3.

Nach einem Original von Gebr. Grunert in Berlin.

Mendelssohn & Löwenstein, Posen.

4.

Verlagsbuchhandlung.   Leopold Steinhauer, Basel.   Annoncen-Expedition.

5.

I.

Archiv für Buchdruckerkunst. XV. Band. Druck und Verlag von Alexander Waldow, Leipzig.

180 ———— *Alexander Waldow*

1878, Archiv für Buchdruckerkunst,
XV. Band, *Alexander Waldow,* Leipzig

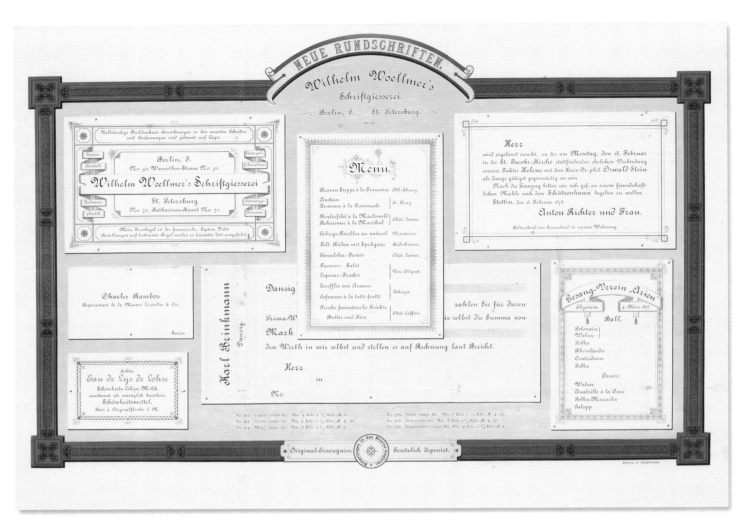

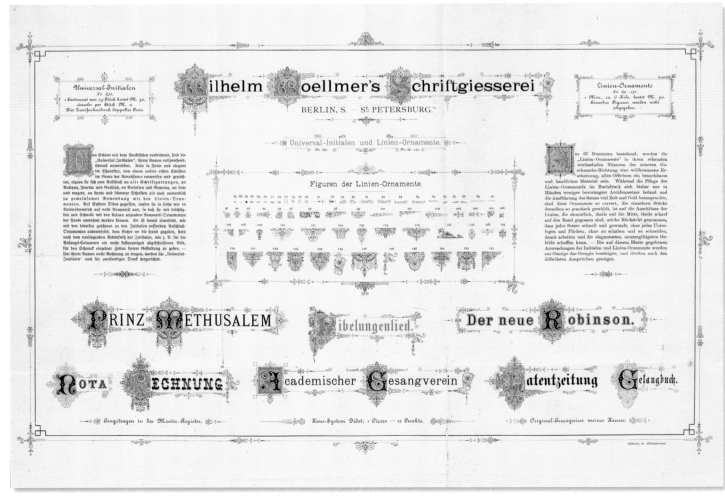

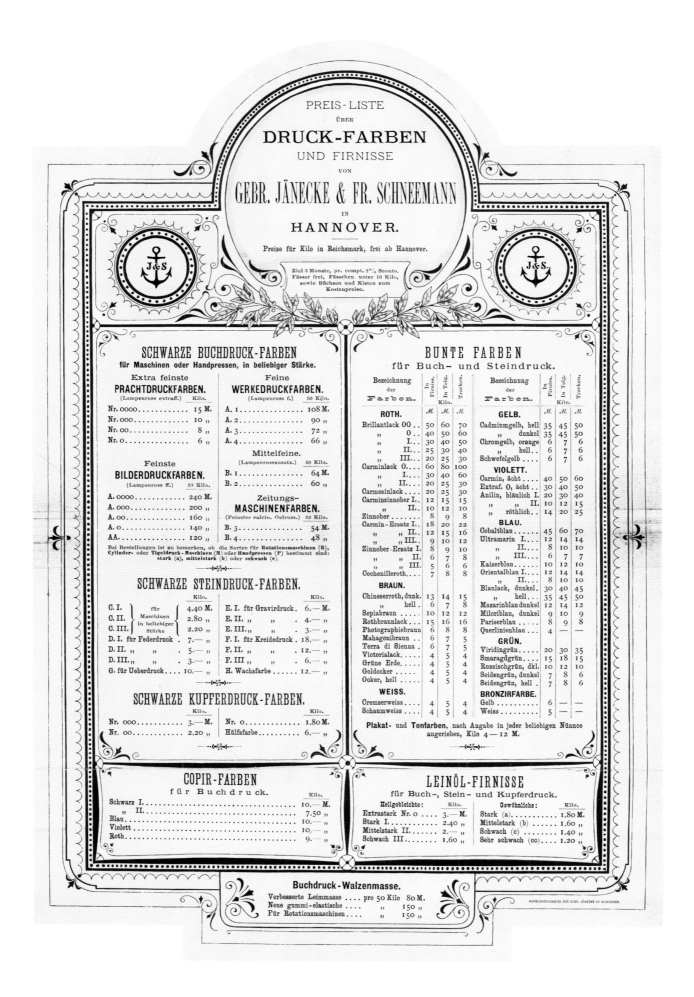

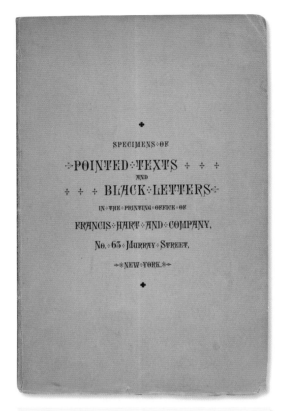

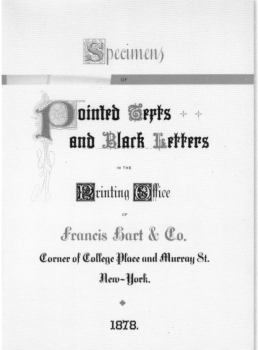

1878, Specimens of Pointed Texts and Black Letters, *Francis Hart & Company,* New York

Black letters, in all shapes and sizes.

Frakturschriften in allen Formen und Größen.

Caractères gothiques, de toutes formes et tailles.

116

RIMMED BLACK.

No Figures.   Double Small-pica.   29½ Ems.

Unto the Noble, Auncient, and Renomed City, the City of London, in Engglond, J, William Caxton, Cytezeyn and Conjurye of the same, and of the Fraternite and Felauship of the Mercerye, owe of right my Servise and

No Figures.   Double Great-primer.   31½ Ems.

Good Wyll, and of very dute am boundin Naturely to Assist, Aide and Counceile, as ferforth as I can

FRANCIS HART & Co. 63 and 65 Murray Street, New-York.

117

BLACK RAY SHADE.

No Figures.   Double Pica.   32 Ems.

to my Power, as to my Moder, of whom I have recevued my Nourcture and Living, and shall Pray for the Good Pros-

No Figures.   Double Great-primer   24½ Ems.

perite and Police of the Same during my life, for as me semith it is of Grete

FRANCIS HART & Co. 63 and 65 Murray Street, New-York.

109

MEDIEVAL.

Figures.   Double English.   24½ Ems.

in these days be neither Usyd ne Understanden: and Furthermore to put it in Enprynte, to thend that it may be had, and the Matters thereof Comprised to be known; for the Book is General, touching

Figures.   Four-line Small-pica.   28½ Ems.

shortly many Notable Matters; and also am avised to make another Book after thys Sayd Werk, whiche shall be

FRANCIS HART & Co. 63 and 65 Murray Street, New-York.

13

8

14

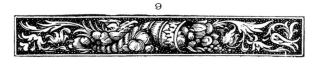

9

15

10

16

11

17

12

130

INITIAL LETTERS.

81

82

83

84

85

86

FRANCIS HART & CO. 63 and 65 Murray Street, New-York.

108

MEDIEVAL.

Figures. Double Pica. 15½ Ems.

sarpe, that I set in following the said
Book, this Book de Amiritia, whiche,
by Goddes Grace, shall plainly folowe.
God be thanked of all his Dedes, this
Translacion is ended on a Thursday,
the Eightenth daye of Aprpll, the xxri.
pere of Kyng Edward the Thyrd, after
the Conquest of England, the pere of
my Lordes Age, Sir Thomas, Lorde
of Berkeley, that made me make this
Translacion, Fyve and Thyrty.

Therefore I, William Cayton, a
Symple Persone, have Endevoyred me
to Wryte fyrst over all the said Book
of Polycronycon, and sommewhat have
chaunged the Rude and Old Englissh,
that is to wete, Certain Words, which

FRANCIS HART & CO. 63 and 65 Murray Street, New-York.

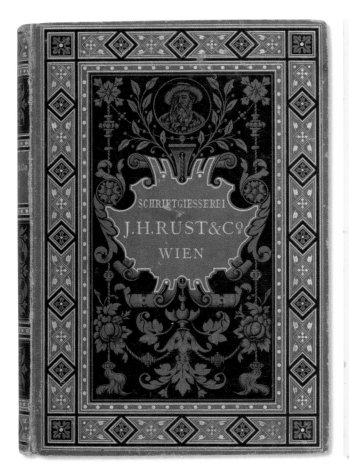

1880, Schriftproben, *Schriftgiesserei J.H. Rust & Co.,* Vienna

In the European market, letters were sold from Vienna to Dresden, Berne, and Bremen.

Auf dem europäischen Markt wurden in Wien hergestellte Schriften an Kunden in Dresden, Bern oder Bremen verkauft.

Sur le marché européen, les lettres étaient vendues de Vienne à Dresde, Berne ou Brême.

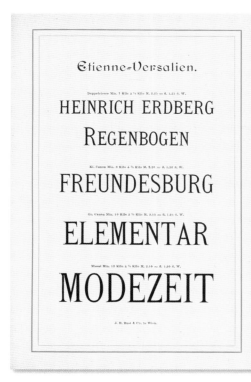

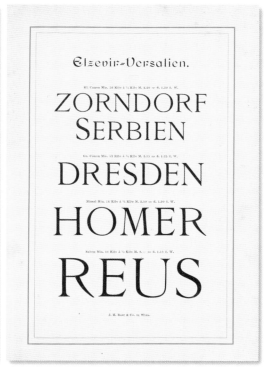

Schatt. Schweifschrift.

Mittel Min. 7 Kilo à ¼ Kilo M. 3.25 = fl. 1.90 ö. W.

Wanderung im Odenwald

Selbstunterricht im Französischen

Hermann Romberg

Tertia Min. 8 Kilo à ¼ Kilo M. 3.05 = fl. 1.80 ö. W.

Abendunterhaltung

Eichenbaum Rebe Buchdrucker

Gumbinnen

Text Min. 9 Kilo à ¼ Kilo M. 2.90 = fl. 1.70 ö. W.

Meisterwerk Hohenheim

Sommervergnügen

Doppelcicero Min. 10 Kilo à ¼ Kilo M. 2.75 = fl. 1.60 ö. W.

Chemnitz Notenbuch

Kundenkreis

J. H. Rust & Co. in Wien.

Schattirte Italienne-Versalien.

Text Min. 5 Kilo à ¼ Kilo M. 2.75 = fl. 1.60 ö. W.

FRANKREICH GEMEINDEN

HOHENSTAUFE

Doppelcicero Min. 6 Kilo à ¼ Kilo M. 2.55 = fl. 1.50 ö. W.

ODER SERBIEN RING

DONAU MINDEN

Doppelmittel Min. 7 Kilo à ¼ Kilo M. 2.40 = fl. 1.40 ö. W.

BREMEN DRUCK

NORMA

Missal Min. 8 Kilo à ¼ Kilo M. 2.20 = fl. 1.30 ö. W.

REICHENAU

J. H. Rust & Co. in Wien.

Zierschriften.

Nr. 215. Min. 4 Kilo à ½ Kilo M. 3.05 = fl. 1.80 ö. W.

DIURNIST HECHT HUNGER

Nr. 220. Min. 5 Kilo à ½ Kilo M. 2.90 = fl. 1.70 ö. W.

REBE GIER

Nr. 216. Min. 4 Kilo à ½ Kilo M. 6.60 = fl. 1.70 ö. W.

MUSE CONCERT OPER

Nr. 219. Min. 4 Kilo à ½ Kilo M. 3.05 = fl. 1.80 ö. W.

DRIESEN COBURG

Nr. 221. Min. 5 Kilo à ½ Kilo M. 2.75 = fl. 1.60 ö. W.

OSTHEIM DRESDEN

KIRCHE

Nr. 218. Min. 3 Kilo à ½ Kilo M. 3.55 = fl. 1.50 ö. W.

GRUND ROMEO

J. H. Rust & Co. in Wien.

Zierschriften.

Nr. 236. Min. 2 Kilo à ½ Kilo M. 6.25 = fl. 3.50 ö. W.

DORAS FREIBURG MAGDAD KONRAD BERLIN
HOCHHEIM BOLLSTEIN

Nr. 240. Min. 4 Kilo à ½ Kilo M. 3.— = fl. 1.75 ö. W.

OESTERREICH ERSCHEINUNG

Nr. 237. Min. 3 Kilo à ½ Kilo M. 3.40 = fl. 2.— ö. W.

HEINRICHSORT

Nr. 241. Min. 5 Kilo à ½ Kilo M. 2.75 = fl. 1.60 ö. W.

KEMBACH JAMAIKA

Nr. 238. Min. 7 Kilo à ½ Kilo M. 2.55 = fl. 1.50 ö. W.

Robert Hermann Conrad

Nr. 242. Min. 10 Kilo à ½ Kilo M. 2.55 = fl. 1.50 ö. W.

Concert Reunion

Nr. 239. Min. 8 Kilo à ½ Kilo M. 2.75 = fl. 1.60 ö. W.

Simon Wendung Emma

J. H. Rust & Co. in Wien.

Zierschriften.

Nr. 243. Min. 7 Kilo à ½ Kilo M. 5.40 = fl. 6.— ö. W.

Thierleben der Gegenwart
NORDERNEY

Nr. 240. Min. 8 Kilo à ½ Kilo M. 3.40 = fl. 1.40 ö. W.

Weimar Neustadt Hansen

Nr. 244. Min. 8 Kilo à ½ Kilo M. 3.05 = fl. 1.80 ö. W.

Handbuch Rübezahl
BAUKUNST

Nr. 247. Min. 6 Kilo à ½ Kilo M. 3.— = fl. 1.75 ö. W.

Hermann Cheruscher

Nr. 245. Min. 9 Kilo à ½ Kilo M. 2.75 = fl. 1.60 ö. W.

Samuel Martha
BERN

J. H. Rust & Co. in Wien.

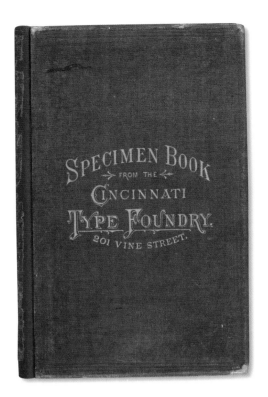

1881, Specimen Book, *Cincinnati Type Foundry,* Cincinnati

The Cincinnati Type Foundry, a big firm established in 1826 by John P. Foote and Oliver Wells as the first manufacturer of typefaces, matrices, and other type-related equipment in Cincinnati, offered a large selection. An extensive range of bill-head logotypes advertised their printing work.

Die Cincinnati Type Foundry, gegründet 1826 von John P. Foote and Oliver Wells als erster Hersteller seiner Art in Cincinnati, bot eine große Auswahl an Lettern, Matrizen und sonstigen typografischen Materialen an. Für ihre Druckerzeugnisse warb die Firma beispielsweise mit einer großen Palette an Schriftzügen für Rechnungsköpfe.

La Cincinnati Type Foundry, grande maison fondée en 1826 par John P. Foote et Oliver Wells et premier fabricant de caractères, matrices et autres équipements relatifs à la typographie de Cincinnati, offrait un large choix. Un vaste éventail de logotypes pour en-tête de facture faisait la réclame de leurs travaux d'impression.

PICA GRAVERS SHADE. 12 A. $3.50

THE NATION. 8

GT. PRIMER GRAVERS SHADE. 10 A. $5.00

FLORIDA 7

TWO-LINE PICA GRAVERS SHADE. 8 A. $6.00

CAMP 2

TWO-L. GT. PRIM. GRAVERS SHADE. 6 A. $8.00

LONG

TWO-L. NONP. RAY SHADE No. 2. 15 A. $4.10

MOUNT VERNON

TWO-L. BOURG. RAY SHADE No. 2. 12 A. $5.65

ORNAMENT

TWO-LINE PICA RAY SHADE No. 2. 10 A. $9.15

BRAND

TWO-L. GT. PRIM. RAY SHADE No. 2. 7 A. $14.25

LINE

TWO-LINE SMALL PICA ORNA. No. 5. 6 A. $2.00 — **REPORTER**

TWO-LINE PICA ORNA. No. 19. 6 A. $2.50 — **SHADOW**

TWO-LINE SM. PICA ORNA. No. 12. 6 A. $2.00 — **CONCERTS**

TWO-LINE PICA ORNA. No. 27. 6 A. $2.50 — **FASHIONS**

TWO-LINE ENGLISH ORNA. No. 13. 4 A. $2.00 — **CHERYMAN**

TWO-LINE GT. PRIMER ORNA. No. 14. 4 A. $3.00 — **CHARM**

FOUR-LINE PICA ORNA. No. 3. 4 A. $2.50 — **SIGHT**

TWO-LINE GT. PRIM. ORNA. No. 13. 6 A. $2.50 — **SENTMINT**

TWO-LINE PICA ORNA. No. 21. 4 A. $2.00 — **TIRES**

TWO-LINE ENGLISH ORNA. No. 14. 4 A. $2.00 — **BLACKING**

TWO-LINE PICA ORNA. No. 30. 6 A. $2.50 — **COUNTRY**

TWO-LINE GT. PRIMER ORNA. No. 18. 4 A. $3.00 — **HERDS**

FOUR-LINE PICA ORNA. No. 1. 4 A. $3.50 — **CORN**

LONG PRIMER RUNIC. 30 A. $1.50 — PUBLIC LIBRARY BUILDINGS.

PICA RUNIC. 18 A. $1.20 — LITERARY COMPOSITOR

GREAT PRIMER RUNIC. 18 A. $2.00 — NONPAREIL PRESS

TWO-LINE LONG PRIMER RUNIC. 12 A. $2.00 — FRENCH POETS

TWO-LINE PICA RUNIC. 12 A. $2.85 — INSTRUCTOR

DBL. PARAGON RUNIC. 4 A, 6 a. $4.00 — American

NONPAREIL SHANGHAI. 40 A. $2.50 — DEVOTED TO COMMERCE AND AGRICULTURE

TWO-LINE NONPAREIL ORNA. No. 15. 20 A. $2.65 — AMERICAN IMPORTATIONS

TWO-LINE BOURGEOIS ORNA. No. 4. 15 A. $2.25 — ENCHANTING SCENERY

TWO-LINE PICA ORNA. No. 25. 12 A. $3.00 — MOUNT HOPE

TWO-LINE GT. PRIM. ORNA. No. 19. 6 A. $3.70 — MONITOR

FOUR-LINE PICA ORNA. No. 21. 4 A. $3.25 — MINOR

DOUBLE PICA FAHNESTOCK. 8 A. $3.00 — PIONEERS

DBL. GT. PRIMER FAHNESTOCK. 6 A. $4.50 — MINER

FOUR-LINE PICA FAHNESTOCK. 4 A. $6.50 — HOM

PICA OLD STYLE SHADED. 18 A, 24 a. $6.60 — Commission House.

GT. PRIM. OLD STYLE SHADED. 15 A, 18 a. $7.25 — Great Eastern 2

DBL. SM. PICA OLD STYLE SHADED. 12 A, 16 a. $7.50 — The Times. 8

TWO-LINE ENGLISH OLD STYLE SHADED. 10 A, 12 a. $8.50 — Comander 6

PICA ROMAN SHADED. 12 A, 12 a. $4.10 — BANKING 25 / MODERN BUILDINGS

GT. PRIMER ROMAN SHADED. 10 A, 10 a. $5.25 — SERIES 18 / CHEAP EDITION

DBL. SM. PICA ROMAN SHADED. 6 A, 6 a. $5.15 — LAWS 8 / BANKRUPTS

TWO-L. BREV. PARALLEL SHADED. 5 A. $2.25 — HIRING GIRLS

TWO-L. BOURG. PARALLEL SHADED. 5 A. $2.55 — OUR POLICE

TWO-L. SM. PICA PARALLEL SHADED. 4 A. $2.75 — REPLEVIN

TWO-L. ENGLISH PARALLEL SHADED. 3 A. $3.05 — LIPEND

TWO-L. GT. PRIM. PARALLEL SHADED. 4 A. $6.10 — BRIMS

PICA CIRCLET. 10 A. $2.75 — CLOSE BANK

GREAT PRIMER CIRCLET. 8 A. $3.25 — REGIONS

DBL. SMALL PICA CIRCLET. 6 A. $3.50 — RID PIN

PICA OLD SHADE EXTEND. 6 A, 8 a. $5.50 — Admired.

PARAGON OLD SHADE EXTEND. 5 A, 6 a. $7.50 — Banner

LG. PRIM. EGYPTIAN SHADED. 20 A, 25 a. $4.50 — AMUSEMENT 16 / Economical Architecture

PICA EGYPTIAN SHADED. 15 A, 20 a. $5.00 — CINCINNATI 16 / Printing Machinery

GT. PRIM. EGYPTIAN SHADED. 10 A, 15 a. $6.00 — BRAZIL 19 / South America

DBL. SM. PICA EGYPT. SHADED. 6 A, 10 a. $5.40 — SIGNS 8 / Lithograph

GT. PRIMER DORIC SHADED. 8 A, 12 a. $5.00 — ELEGANT / Display Lines

DBL. PICA DORIC SHADED. 6 A, 10 a. $6.50 — TYPES / Cincinnati

DBL. GT. PRIMER DORIC SHADED. 5 A, 8 a. $9.00 — Modiste

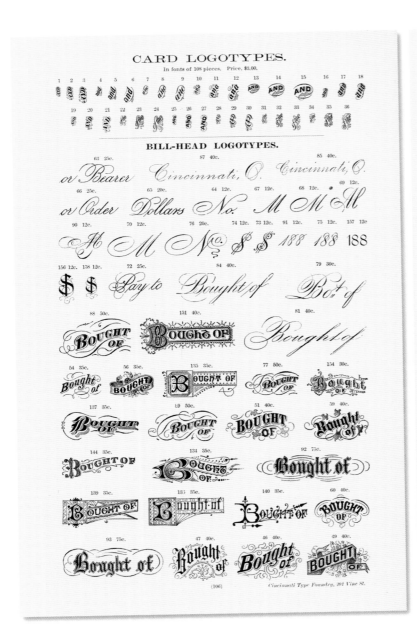

1881, Specimen Book, *Cincinnati Type Foundry,* Cincinnati

TWO-LINE PICA MINSTER.

6 A, 14 a.   Price, $5.75.

CHINESE
Century Pottery

DBL. SM. PICA CELTIC INITIALS. 8 A. $3.50

MNOPRST

7 A, 10 a. Price, $3.65.

ROAST × BEEF
Healthy and Good

TWO-LINE GREAT PRIMER CAMPANILE.
4 A, 6 a. Price, $4.55.

ROVING
Highlanders

DBL. GT. PRIMER CELTIC INITIALS. 6 A. $4.50

ABCDEF

DBL. SM. PICA ARMORIAL. 10 A. $2.50

OF ARMORIAL.

DBL. ENGLISH ARMORIAL. 7 A. $3.00

ELEGANT

DBL. PARAGON ARMORIAL. 5 A. $4.00

DISPLAY

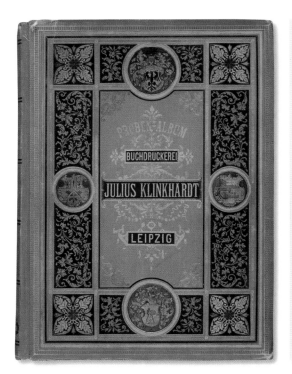

1882, Proben-Album, *Buchdruckerei Julius Klinkhardt,* Leipzig

A different shape for each new color—a perfect example of the art of letterpress. In 1834, Julius Klinkhardt established a bookstore in Leipzig; over the next several years, he expanded his business to include book production, with a printing office, a type foundry, and a bookbindery. Klinkhardt bought the foundry from Gustav Schelter in 1871.

Für jede neue Farbe eine andere Form – ein perfektes Beispiel für die Kunst des Hochdrucks. Nach der Gründung einer Buchhandlung in Leipzig im Jahr 1834 weitete Julius Klinkhardt sein Gewerbe in den folgenden Jahren auf die gesamte Buchproduktion aus, einschließlich Druckerei, Schriftgießerei und Buchbinderei. 1871 erwarb Klinkhardt die Gießerei Gustav Schelters.

Une forme differente pour chaque nouvelle couleur – un exemple parfait de l'art de la typographie. Julius Klinkhardt avait ouvert une librairie à Leipzig, en 1874, et au cours des années suivantes, il agrandit son affaire pour y inclure la production de livres, avec une imprimerie, une fonderie de caractères et un atelier de reliure. En 1871, Klinkhardt acheta la fonderie de Gustav Schelter.

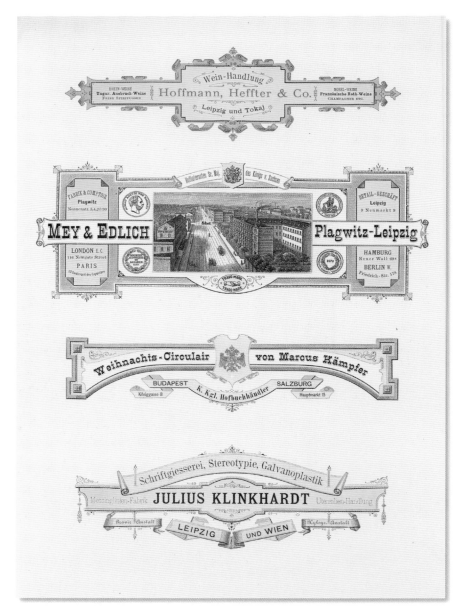

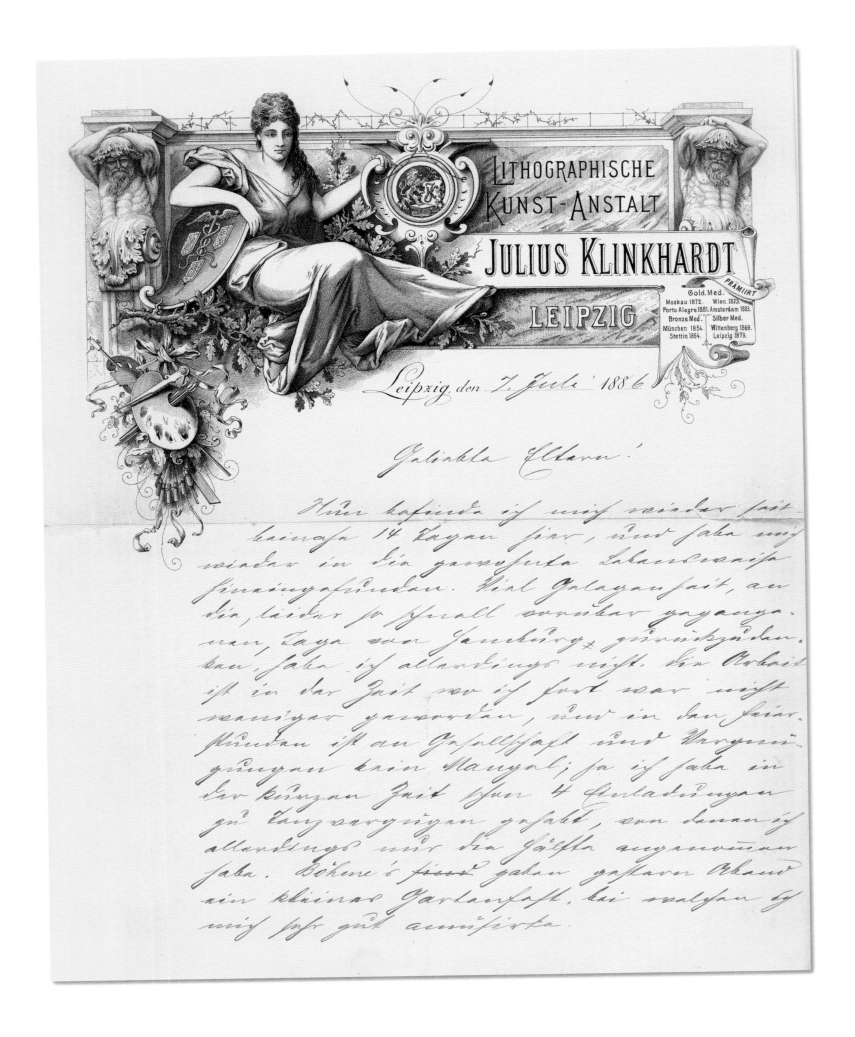

Lithographische Kunst-Anstalt

Julius Klinkhardt

Leipzig

Gold. Med. — PRÄMIIRT
Moskau 1872. Wien 1873.
Porto Alegre 1881. Amsterdam 1883.
Bronze Med. Silber Med.
München 1854. Wittenberg 1869.
Stettin 1864. Leipzig 1879.

Leipzig, den 7. Juli 1886

Geliebte Eltern!

Nun befinde ich mich wieder fast
beinahe 14 Tagen hier, und habe mich
wieder in die gewohnte Lebensweise
hineingefunden. Eine Ferienzeit, an
die, leider so schnell vorüber gegangen.
mein Tage von Hamburg zurückzuden.
ken, habe ich allerdings nicht. Die Arbeit
ist in der Zeit wo ich fort war nicht
weniger geworden, und in den Feier.
stunden ist an Gesellschaft und Vergnü.
gungen kein Mangel; ja ich habe in
der kurzen Zeit schon 4 Einladungen
zu Tanzvergnügen gehabt, von denen ich
allerdings nur die Hälfte angenommen
habe. Böhme's haben gestern Abend
ein kleines Gartenfest, bei welchen ich
mich sehr gut amüsirte.

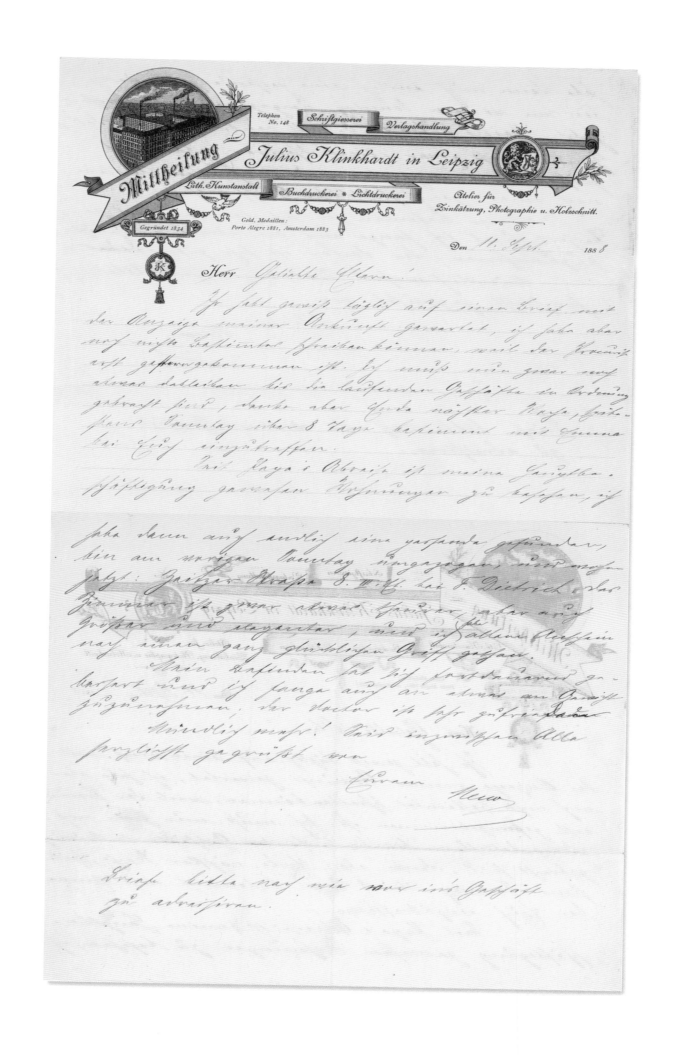

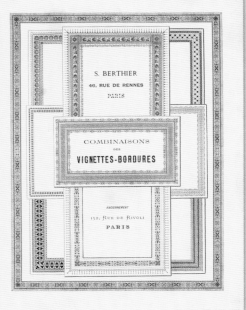

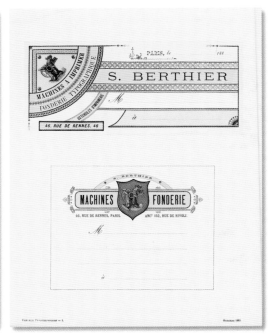

1883, Specimens de Travaux Typographiques en noir et en couleurs, *Imprimerie et Fonderie S. Berthier,* Paris

This is letterpress, not lithography, with hand setting and layout. In letterpress, or relief, printing, individual blocks of raised type make an impression on paper. In lithography, chemicals are placed on a smooth stone or plate to create an image.

Sämtliche dieser Muster sind im Hochdruckverfahren entstanden, manuell gesetzt und gelayoutet. Beim Hoch- oder Reliefdruck wird der Abdruck mittels einzelner erhabener Lettern auf das Papier gebracht. Bei der Lithografie dagegen entsteht das Bild mithilfe von Chemikalien, die auf einen glatten Stein oder eine Platte aufgetragen werden.

Ceci est de l'impression typographique, non lithographique, avec composition et mise en page manuelle. Dans l'impression typographique ou en relief, des blocs individuels de caractères surélevés impriment le papier. En lithographie, l'image est créée à partir de produits chimiques sur une pierre ou une plaque lisse.

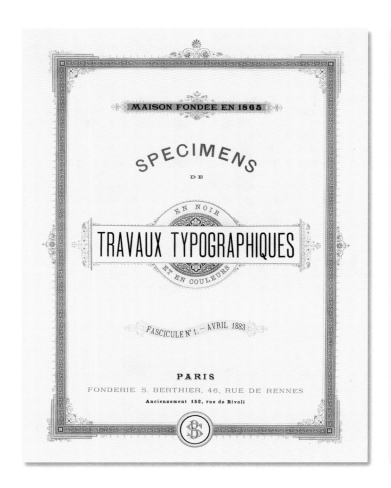

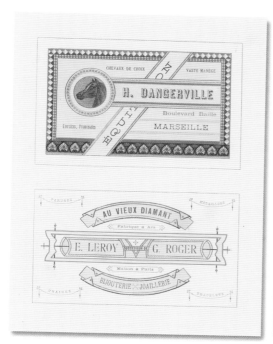

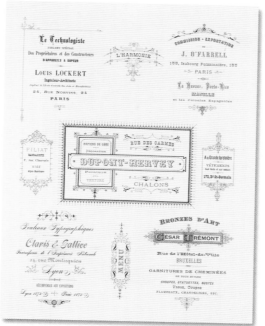

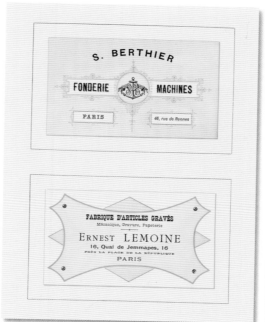

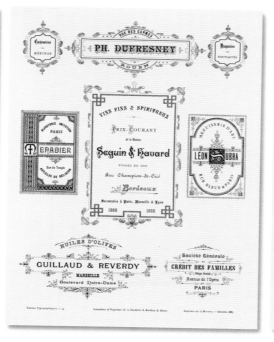

Specimens de Travaux Typographiques en noir et en couleurs, 1883

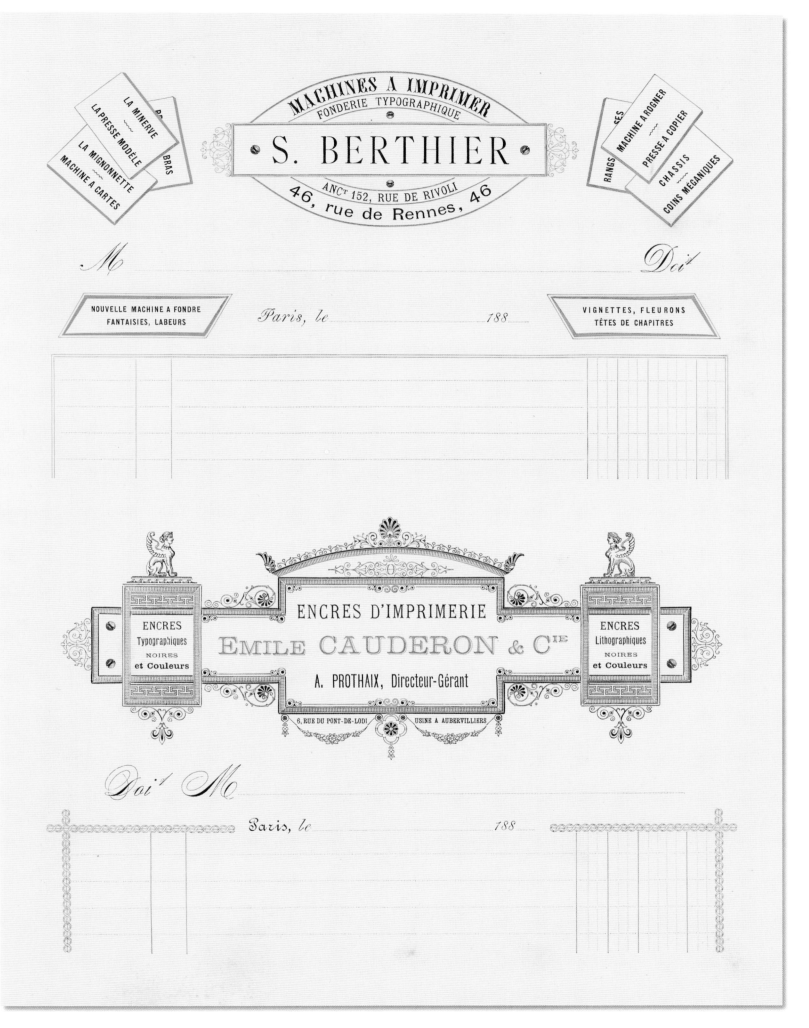

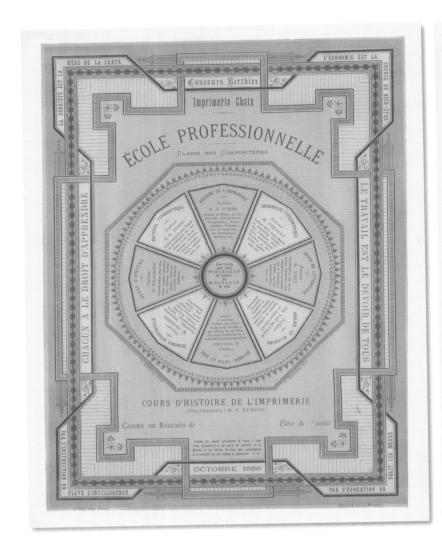

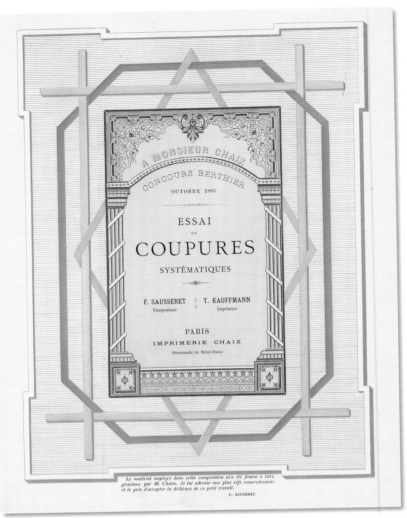

1883, Specimens de Travaux Typographiques en noir et en couleurs, *Imprimerie et Fonderie S. Berthier,* Paris

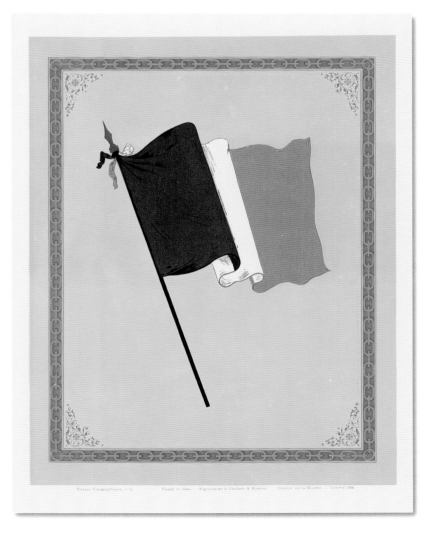

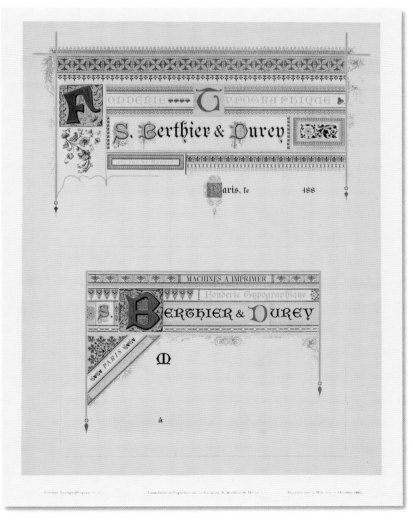

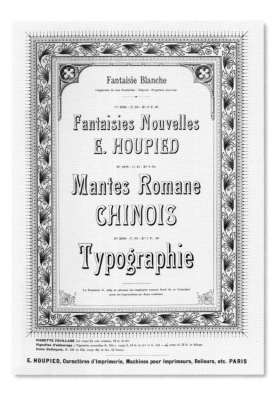

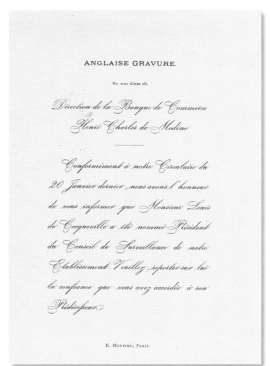

1883, Anglaise Gravure,
E. Houpied, Paris

Is the foreign product always superior?
Anglaise Gravure was all the rage in Paris.

Sind ausländische Produkte grundsätz-
lich besser? In Paris war die Anglaise
Gravure ein großer Renner.

Le produit venu de l'étranger est-il toujours supérieur? Anglaise Gravure faisait
fureur à Paris.

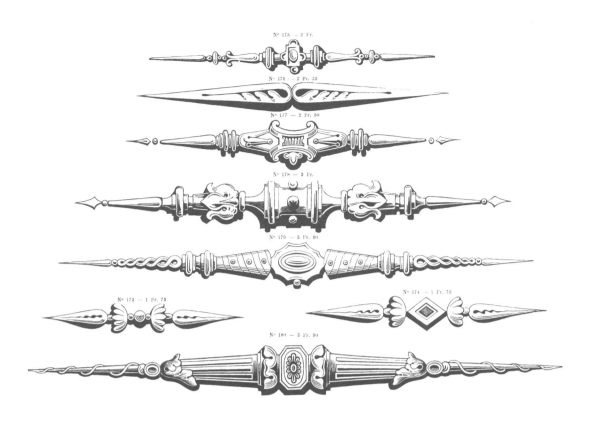

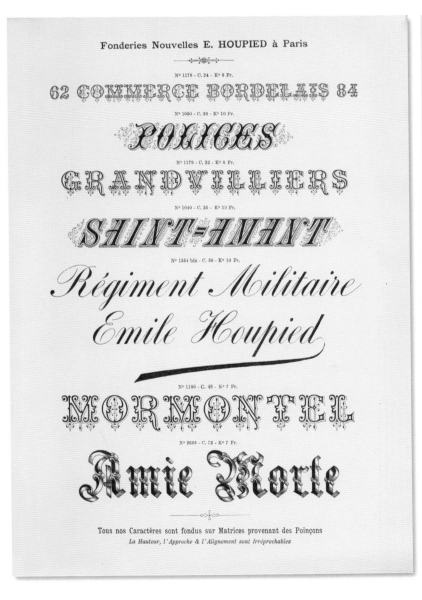

Fonderies Nouvelles E. HOUPIED à Paris

N° 1178 - C. 24 - K° 9 Fr.

62 COMMERCE BORDELAIS 84

N° 1030 - C. 36 - K° 10 Fr.

POLICES

N° 1179 - C. 32 - K° 8 Fr.

GRANDVILLIERS

N° 1040 - C. 36 - K° 10 Fr.

SAINT-AMANT

N° 1354 bis - C. 56 - K° 10 Fr.

Régiment Militaire

Emile Houpied

N° 1180 - C. 48 - K° 7 Fr.

MORMONTEL

N° 2695 - C. 72 - K° 7 Fr.

Amie Morte

Tous nos Caractères sont fondus sur Matrices provenant des Poinçons

La Hauteur, l'Approche & l'Alignement sont irréprochables

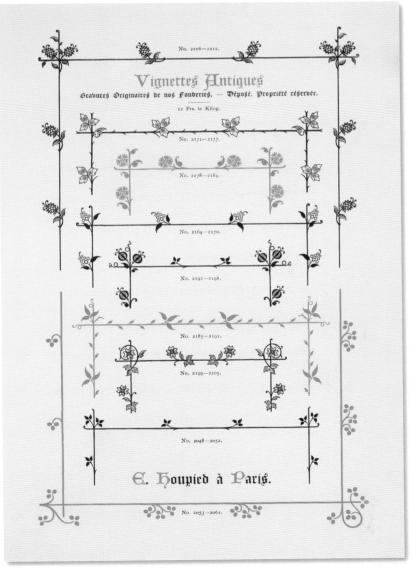

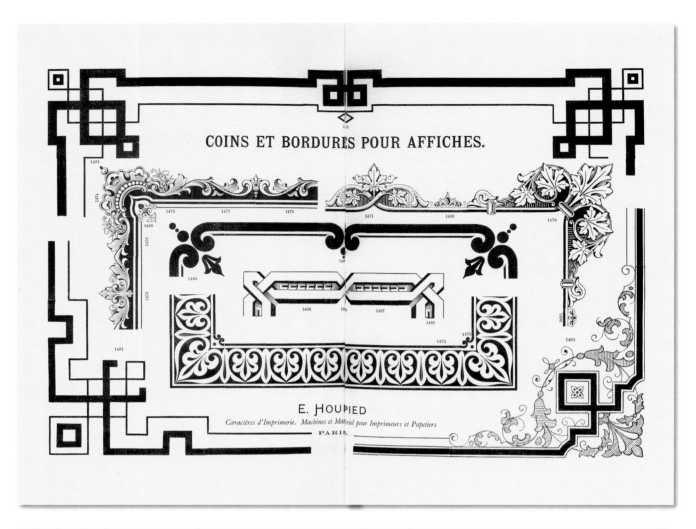

COINS ET BORDURES POUR AFFICHES.

E. HOUPIED

Caractères d'Imprimerie. Machines et Matériel pour Imprimeurs et Papetiers

PARIS

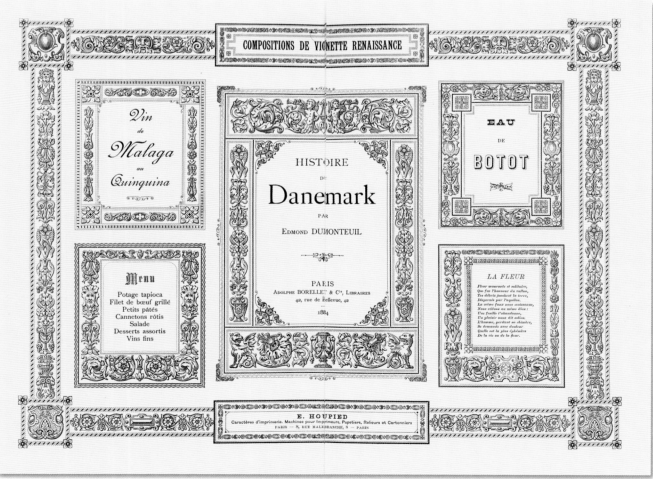

COMPOSITIONS DE VIGNETTE RENAISSANCE

Vin de Malaga au Quinquina

Menu

Potage tapioca
Filet de bœuf grillé
Petits pâtés
Cannetons rôtis
Salade
Desserts assortis
Vins fins

HISTOIRE DE

Danemark

PAR

Edmond DUMONTEUIL

PARIS

Adolphe BORELLE & Cⁱᵉ, Libraires

42, rue de Bellevue, 42

1884

EAU DE BOTOT

LA FLEUR

E. HOUPIED

Caractères d'imprimerie. Machines pour Imprimeurs, Papetiers, Relieurs et Cartonniers

PARIS — 8, RUE MALEBRANCHE, 8 — PARIS

No. 726. Corps 18.

NOUVELLES MACHINES DES BATEAUX
98 MULHOUSE 56

No. 727. Corps 24.

DIRECTION 2 IMPRIMERIE

No. 728. Corps 36.

VOIE DE NARBONNE

No. 695. Corps 24.

L'INDUSTRIE FRANÇAISE

No. 729. Corps 36.

DANUBE 8 TAMISE

1883, Anglaise Gravure,
E. Houpied, Paris

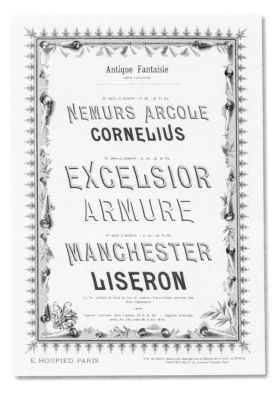

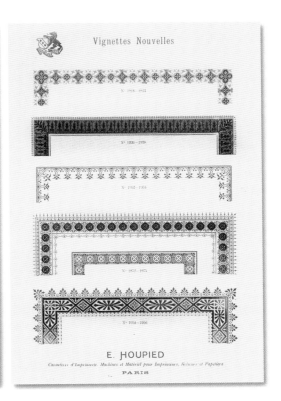

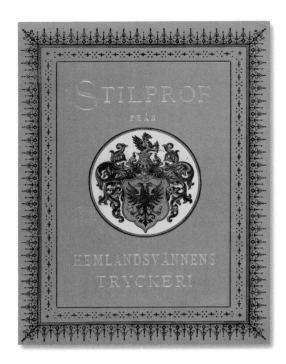

1883, Stilprof,
Hemlandsvånnens Tryckeri

The 19th Century was marked by both eclecticism and simplicity of style.

Eklektizismus und stilistische Schlichtheit waren gleichermaßen für das 19. Jahrhundert kennzeichnend.

Le XIXᵉ siècle a été marqué à la fois par un certain éclectisme et une simplicité de style.

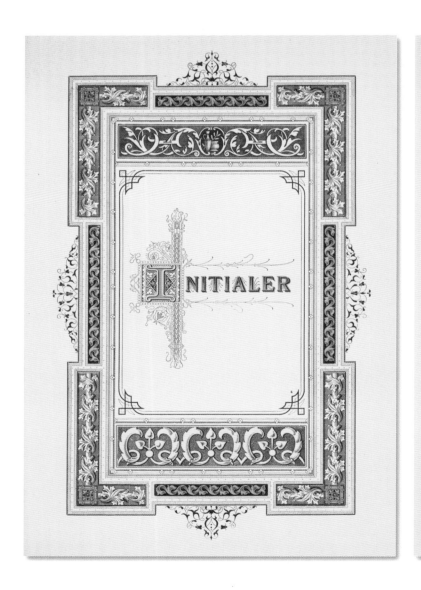

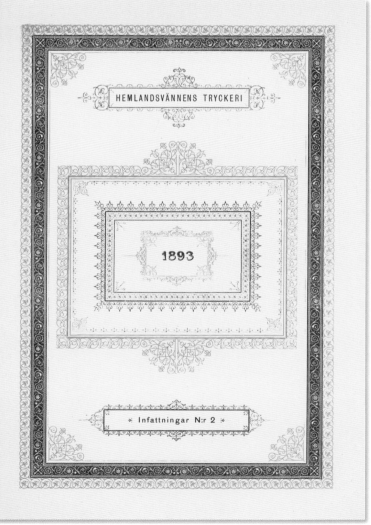

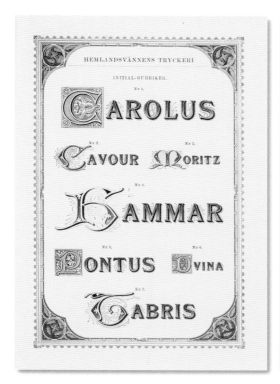

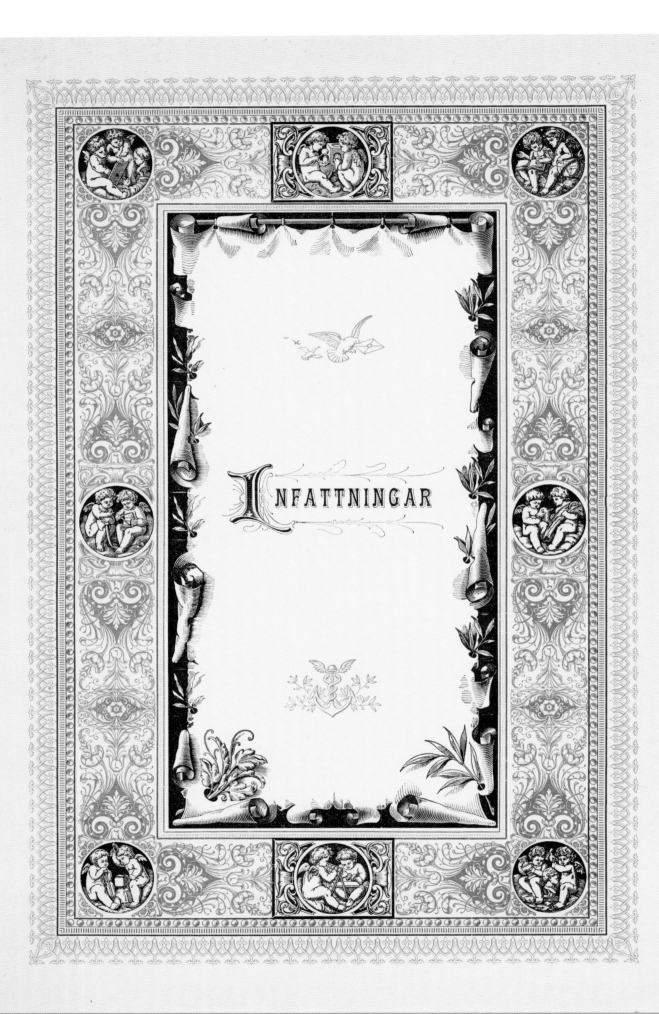

Infattningar

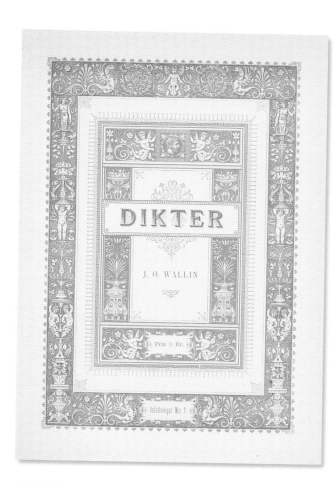

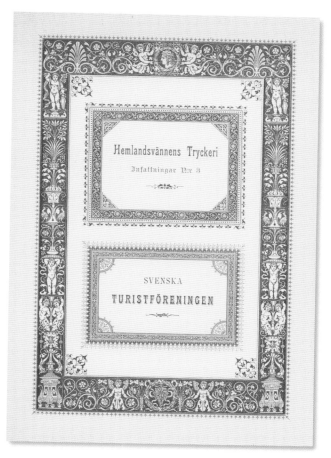

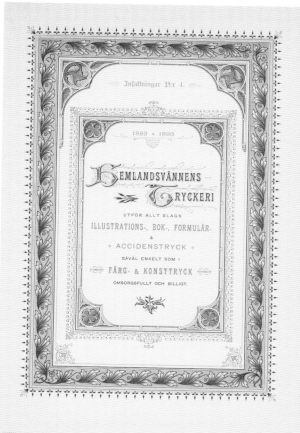

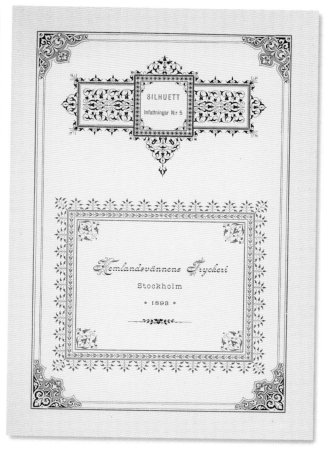

1884, Proben, *Schriftgiesserei Flinsch,* Frankfurt am Main & St. Petersburg

A customer faced with this sample, which offered so many choices, was bound to place an order for printing. In 1859, Heinrich Friedrich Gottlob Flinsch bought the Dreslersche Gießerei (established in 1827). In 1865, an agency in Saint Petersburg was founded, and in 1916 Bauersche Gießerei took over the foundry.

Beim Anblick eines Musters mit einer derart großen Auswahl musste ein Kunde einfach einen Druckauftrag erteilen. 1859 kaufte Friedrich Gottlob Flinsch die 1827 gegründete Dreßlersche Gießerei, 1865 eröffnete er eine Zweigstelle in Sankt Petersburg. 1916 wurde die Firma von der Bauerschen Gießerei übernommen.

Face à un tel assortiment, le client n'avait d'autre choix que de passer commande d'une impression. En 1859, Heinrich Friedrich Gottlob Flinsch acheta la Dreslersche Gießerei (fondée en 1827). En 1865, une succursale fut créée à Saint-Petersbourg, et, en 1916, la fonderie fut reprise par la Bauersche Gießerei.

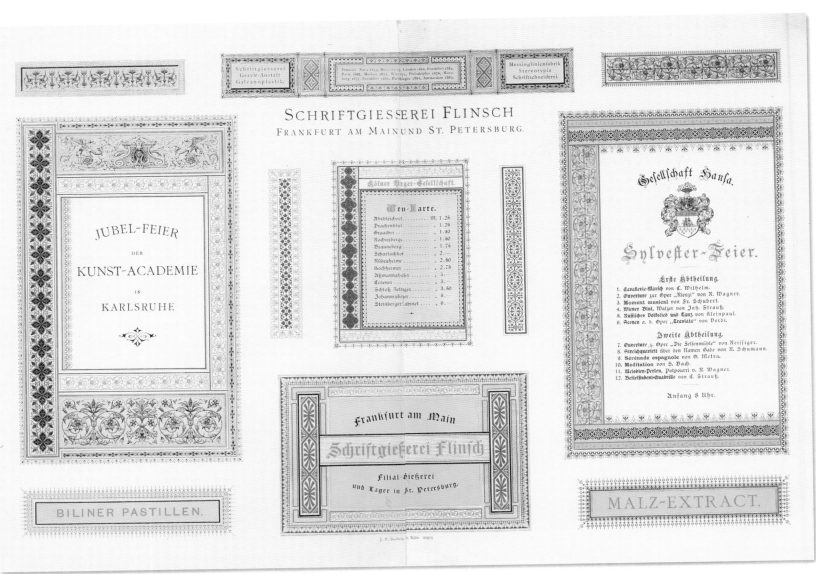

SCHRIFTGIESSEREI FLINSCH

Schriftgiesserei ✳ Schriftschneiderei   Messinglinien-Fabrik ✳ Stereotypie
Galvanoplastik   Gravir-Anstalt

FRANKFURT A. M. ✳ ST. PETERSBURG

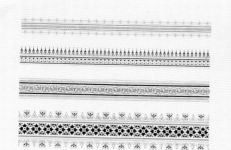

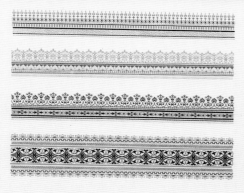

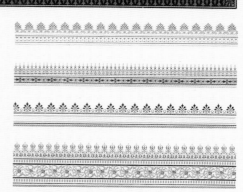

Prämiirt auf 12 Ausstellungen, dabei goldene Medaillen der Ausstellungen zu Nürnberg 1877, Frankfurt a. M. 1881, Porto-Alegre 1881.

MINIMA UND PREISE

1814—1814½	Min.	1½	Pfd.	pr.	Pfd.	M.	4.50	1910—1911	Min.	3	Pfd.	pr. Pfd. M.	4.—
1815—1815½	»	1½	»	»	»	»	4.50	1912—1917	»	8	»	» » »	4.50
1816—1816½	»	2	»	»	»	»	4.50	1918—1923	»	10	»	» » »	4.—
1817—1819	»	3	»	»	»	»	4.50	1924—1925	»	3	»	» » »	4.50
1820—1821	»	4	»	»	»	»	4.50	1926—1927	»	3	»	» » »	4.50
1896—1897	»	2	»	»	»	»	4.50	1928—1929	»	4	»	» » »	4.50
1898—1899	»	2	»	»	»	»	4.50	1930—1931	»	3	»	» » »	4.50
1900—1902	»	3	»	»	»	»	4.—	1932—1933	»	4	»	» » »	4.50
1903—1904	»	3	»	»	»	»	4.—	1934—1935	»	6	»	» » »	4.—
1905—1907	»	3	»	»	»	»	4.—	1936—1939	»	10	»	» » »	4.—
1908—1909	»	3	»	»	»	»	4.—	1940—1941	»	4	»	» » »	4.—

Tanz-Ordnung

1. Walzer
1. Rheinländer
1. Schottisch
Contredanse
1. Mazurka
2 Walzer
Quadrille à la cour
2. Mazurka
3. Walzer
2. Rheinländer
2. Schottisch
4. Walzer

Ed. Schlau

Permanente

Kunst-Ausstellung

Mainz

Gutenbergplatz

1814 1814½ 1815 1815½ 1816 18
1908 1909 1900 1901 1902
1820 1821 1957 1958
1966 1967 1932 1933
1952 1953 19

NEUE EI

Eingetrag

Entworfen und g

1950 1951
1976 1977 1978
1963
1918 1919 1920 192
1912 1913 1914 191
1960 1960a

J.

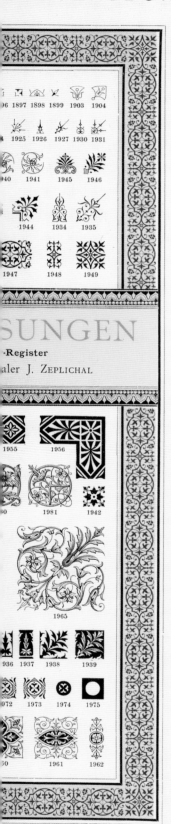

Prämiirt auf der Internationalen Ausstellung zu Amsterdam 1883 mit dem Ehren-Diplom, der höchsten ertheilten Auszeichnung.

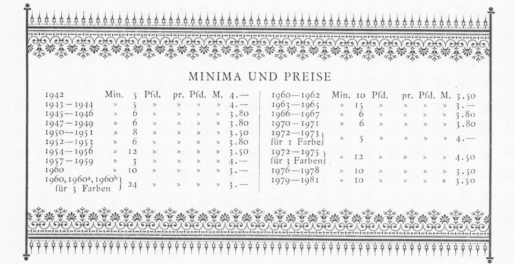

MINIMA UND PREISE

1942	Min.	5	Pfd.	pr. Pfd.	M.	4.—	1960—1962	Min.	10	Pfd.	pr. Pfd.	M.	3.50
1943—1944	»	5	»	»	»	4.—	1963—1965	»	15	»	»	»	3.—
1945—1946	»	6	»	»	»	3.80	1966—1967	»	6	»	»	»	3.80
1947—1949	»	6	»	»	»	3.80	1970—1971	»	6	»	»	»	3.80
1950—1951	»	8	»	»	»	3.50	1972—1973 für 1 Farbe	»	5	»	»	»	4.—
1952—1953	»	6	»	»	»	3.80							
1954—1956	»	12	»	»	»	3.50	1972—1975 für 3 Farben	»	12	»	»	»	4.50
1957—1959	»	3	»	»	»	4.—							
1960	»	10	»	»	»	3.—	1976—1978	»	10	»	»	»	3.50
1960, 1960ᵃ, 1960ᵇ für 3 Farben	»	24	»	»	»	3.—	1979—1981	»	10	»	»	»	3.50

MASTIX

SAYETTE

Spinnerei A. Berg

BONN

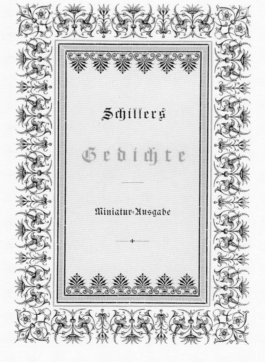

Schillers

Gedichte

Miniatur-Ausgabe

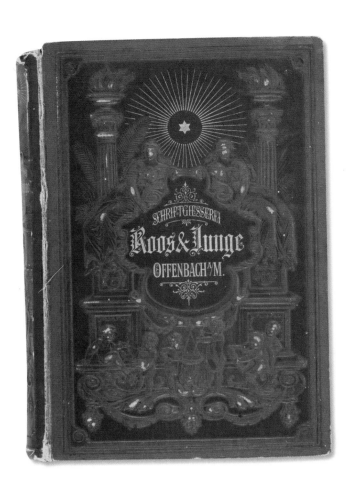

1885, Probe, *Schriftgiesserei Roos & Junge,* Offenbach am Main

Fraktur, Vignet, Antiqua, italic, decorative letter, handwriting and round-hand initial, symbol, line: Choose them and use them. The foundry was established in 1868 by Jakob Roos and Ernst Ludwig Junge. In 1917, it was taken over by D. Stempel AG, whose founder, David Stempel, had worked for Roos and Junge from 1888.

Fraktur-, Vignetten-, Antiqua-, Kursiv- und Zierschriften, Schreibschriften und Initialen in „round hand", Symbole und Linien: eine riesige Auswahl, zum Einsatz bereit. Jakob Roos und Ernst Ludwig Junge hatten ihre Gießerei im Jahr 1868 ins Leben gerufen. 1917 übernahm sie die D. Stempel AG, deren Gründer, David Stempel, von 1888 an für Roos and Junge gearbeitet hatte.

Fraktur, Antique, vignettes, italiques, lettres décoratives, lettrines anglaises, symboles, lignes : il n'y a que l'embarras du choix. La fonderie fut créée en 1868 par Jakob Roos et Ernst Ludwig Junge. En 1917, elle fut reprise par la D. Stempel AG, dont le fondateur David Stempel avait travaillé pour Roos et Junge à partir de 1888.

Messing-Einfassungs-Linien.

No.	2b	3b	4b	5b	8b	22b	23b	24b	25b	28b	42b	43b	44b	45b	48b
Per Ko. ℳ.	21	18	17	17	17	21	18	17	17	17	21	18	17	17	17
No.	53b	54b	55b	56b	59b	75b	76b	77b	78b	81b	86b	87b	88b		
Per Ko. ℳ.	21	18	17	17	17	21	18	17	17	17	21	21	21		
No.	90b	91b	98b	101b	116b	117b	118b	120b	121b						
Per Ko. ℳ.	21	21	21	21	24	21	21	21	21						
No.	2c	3c	4c	5c	8c	11c	12c	16c	17c	18c	19c	22c	25c	26c	
Per Ko. ℳ.	21	18	17	17	17	16	21	18	17	17	17	17	16		
No.	30c	31c	32c	33c	36c	41c	42c	43c	44c	47c	52c	53c	54c		
Per Ko. ℳ.	21	18	17	17	17	21	18	17	17	17	21	18	17		
No.	55c	58c	63c	64c	65c	66c	69c	117c	118c	121c	122c	125c			
Per Ko. ℳ.	17	17	17	18	17	17	21	18	17	21	21	21			
No.	127c	129c	131c	133c	135c	137c	138c	141c	142c	162c	166c				
Per Ko. ℳ.	20	21	20	21	20	21	20	21	18	21	21				
No.	167c	168c	172c	173c	189c	190c	192c	193c	194c	195c	196c				
Per Ko. ℳ.	21	21	21	21	21	21	21	21	21	21	21				
No.	205c	206c	212c	218c	81d	82d	100d	114d	115d	127d	128d				
Per Ko. ℳ.	21	21	21	21.50	21.80	21.80	20.—	19.90	20.—	19.90					
No.	137d	142d	143d	187d	189d	201d	202d	203d	204d	216d	253d				
Per Ko. ℳ.	19.90	20.—	19.90	22.80	22.90	22.80	23.—	22.90	22.—	23.—	23.—				
No.	254d	44e	80e	81e	83e	88e	244	245	268	280	281	288			
Per Ko. ℳ.	22.90	21.50	22.90	21.—	21.—	21.50	17.10	16.70	17.10	16.70	16.70	16.70			

Messing-Ecken.

No.	1	2	3	4	5	6	7	8	9	10	11	12
Per Stück ℳ.	—.30	—.30	—.50	—.60	—.50	—.75	—.90	—.80	—.90	—.90	—.90	—.90
No.	13	15	16	18	20	21	22	23	24	25	26	27
Per Stück ℳ.	1.25	—.60	1.75	2.50	1.75	2.—	2.50	3.—	2.75	3.50	4.50	
No.	28	29	30	31	32	33	34	35	36	38	39	42
Per Stück ℳ.	4.50	3.—	3.50	4.—	4.—	4.—	3.75	3.—	4.50	5.—	1.10	5.50

Messing-Kreise und Ovale.

Kreise No.	6	7	8	9	11	12	13	14	17	18	19	21	22
Per Stück ℳ.	1.25	1.25	1.25	2.—	1.25	1.25	1.50	2.—	1.25	1.50	2.—	1.25	1.25
Kreise No.	23	24	25	26	27	28	29	30					
Per Stück ℳ.	3.75	2.—	5.10	1.25	1.25	1.50	1.75	5.10					
Ovale No.	1	3	5	13	14	15	17	18	21				
Per Stück ℳ.	2.—	4.20	2.—	2.—	2.—	7.30	2.—	2.—	2.—				

Messing-Zierlinien.

No.	82	131	133	136	138	147	151	158	178	182
Per Stück ℳ.	1.—	2.—	2.50	3.—	1.70	3.50	6.—	5.—	5.50	5.—

No. 202—211 per Stück ℳ. —.25	No. 252—262 per Stück ℳ. —.75
" 212—224 " " " —.30	" 263—270 " " " 1.—
" 225—243 " " " —.40	" 271—276 " " " 1.25
" 244—251 " " " —.50	" 277—282 " " " 1.50

Moderne Italienne.

No. 794. Nonpareille (Corps 6). Min. 3 Kilo.

Hundertjährige Geburtstagsfeier Aufnahme-Prüfung
Fürst von Bulgarien Herzog von Cambridge Prinzessin von Wales
Auswanderer aus dem russischen Reiche

No. 795. Petit (Corps 8). Min. 4 Kilo.

Petition um Aufhebung der Getreidezölle
Quadrille Polka-Mazurka Rheinländer Damen-Schottisch
Versailles Rom Florenz Athen Lissabon Madrid

No. 796. Garmond (Corps 10). Min. 5 Kilo.

Bruchsal Darmstadt Osnabrück Rastatt
Lohnbewegung der Schuhmacher Deutschlands
Moment-Aufnahmen Photographie

No. 797. Cicero (Corps 12). Min. 6 Kilo.

Erste Quartett-Soirée
Hôtel-Restaurant zum Petersburger Hof
Sänger-Gesellschaft CONCORDIA

No. 798. Tertia (Corps 16). Min. 8 Kilo.

Undine Die Hugenotten Rheingold
Marbach Ems Barmen

No. 799. Text (Corps 20). Min. 9 Kilo.

Madeira Burgunder
Italien Schweiz Holland

Schriftgiesserei ROOS & JUNGE, Offenbach a. M.

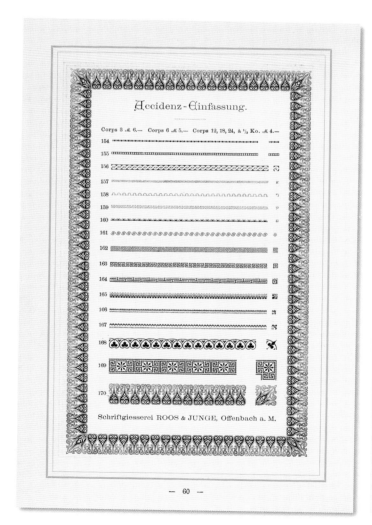

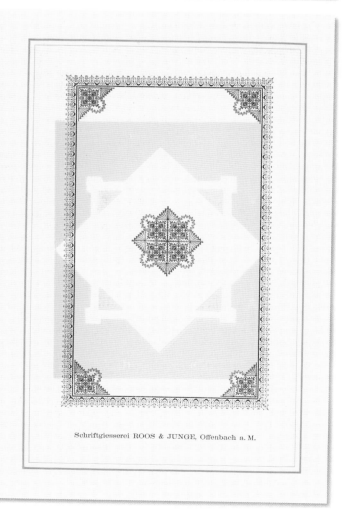

Schriftgiesserei ROOS & JUNGE, Offenbach a. M.

ANTIQUA-
UND CURSIV-
SCHRIFTEN

Zierschriften, Schreib= und Rund=schriften etc. Initialen, Zeichen und Linien.

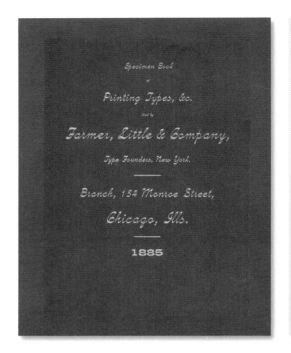

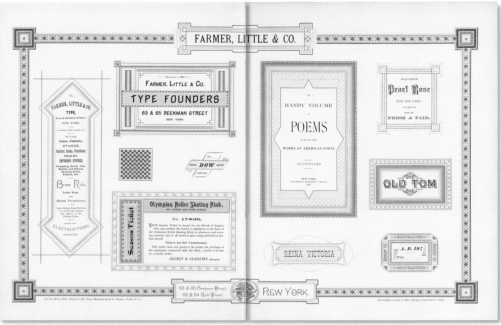

1885, Specimen book of Printing Types, *Farmer, Little & Company,* New York

Hand setters and typographers had no trouble finding all of these type specimens, preparing them for print, and using them. A. D. Farmer emerged from White's Type Foundry (1804–62), the name of which was later changed to Farmer, Little & Co. In 1909, American Type Founders acquired this foundry. Scottish founders exerted a strong influence on the development of "transitional" types, the bridge from "old style" faces like Jenson and Garamond to "modern" designs like Bodoni and Didot.

Bei dieser Schriftmusterauswahl fanden Setzer und Typografen problemlos ihr gewünschtes Material. A. D. Farmer ging aus White's Type Foundry (1804–1862) hervor und wurde später Farmer, Little & Co. 1909 übernahmen die American Type Founders die Gießerei. Schottische Gießer hatten großen Einfluss auf die Entwicklung von „Übergangsschriften" zwischen den Schriften „alten Stils", etwa den Schriften Jensons oder Garamonds, und „modernen" Entwürfen wie den Schriften Bodonis und Didots.

Les compositeurs manuels et les typographes n'avaient aucun mal à trouver tous ces spécimens de caractères. A. D. Farmer émergea de White's Type Foundry (1804–1862), dont le nom se transforma plus tard en Farmer, Little & Co. En 1909, American Type Founders acheta cette fonderie. Les fondeurs écossais exercèrent une forte influence sur la mise au point de caractères de «transition» entre des caractères «à l'ancienne» comme Jenson ou Garamond et des graphismes «modernes» comme Bodoni ou Didot.

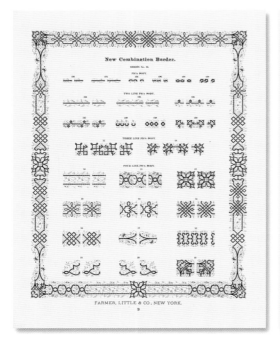

8 A	Two Line Pica Ornamented No. 12.	$6 00

BROKLYN

8 A	Two Line Pica Ornamented No. 14.	$4 50

DRIVES 2

12 A	Two Line Pica Ornamented No. 15.	$4 50

STATEMENT 4

12 a 8 A	Two Line Pica Orn. No. 22.	$8 00

Northern 27

6 A		

8 A	Two Line Pica Double Shade.	$6 00

FINE SCENE

12 A	Two Line Pica Grecian Shade.	$4 00

INTELLIGENT POETS. 23

12 A	Two Line Pica Rustic.	$5 00

WALDERMERE 2

6 A	Two Line Pica Shade No. 1.	$6 00

PUND 1

8 A	Two Line English Ornamented No. 3.	$6 00

ALL RUST 5

8 A	Two Line English Ornamented No. 4.	$6 00

IN CAMP

6 A	Two Line English Ornamented No. 5.	$5 00

MONTH

	Four Line Pica Ornamented No. 1.	$10 00

MENTION 85

8 A	Two Line English Ornamented No. 6.	$5 00

NO NAIL

6 A	Two Line English Ornamented No. 7.	$4 25

FORGE

8 A	Two Line English Orn. No. 8.	$6 00

HEN BIRD

8 A	Two Line English Orn. No. 9.	$5 50

MINORY

6 A		

8 A	Two Line English Orn. No. 10.	$6 00

ARMENIAN

6 A	Two Line English Ornamented No. 12.	$5 00

RAWEST 8

12 A	Two Line English Orn. No. 13.	$5 00

WORKER 5

12 a 8 A	Two Line English Orn. No. 15	$7 50

Temperance 5

8 A	Two Line English Ornamented No. 16.	$6 00

SUPER GOOD

8 A	Two Line English Ornamented No. 17.	$6 00

TAR CODE

6 A	Two Line English Ornamented No. 18.	$5 00

IN RANK

8 A	Two Line English Ray Shade.	$7 00

BROWNS

	Four Line Pica Ornamented No. 4.	$7 75

FLORAL FESTIVAL

6 A	Two Line Great Primer Orn. No. 1.	$5 00

SHINE ON

6 A	Two Line Great Primer Orn. No. 2.	$5 00

MUSET

6 A	Two Line Great Primer Orn. No. 3.	$7 00

HONOR

6 A	Two Line Great Primer Orn. No. 4.	$6 50

STRIFE

6 A	Two Line Great Primer Orn. No. 5.	$5 50

FAT NAG

8 A	Two Line Great Primer Orn No. 7.	$6 50

RANG 5

12 a 3 A	Two Line Gt. Pr. Orn. No. 13.	$7 25

Palestine HILL 5

8 A	Two Line Great Pr. Orn. No. 15.	$6 00

LOATHE

8 A	Two Line Gt. Pr. Cond. Shade.	$5 50

SAME VOTE

FARMER, LITTLE & CO., NEW YORK.

CCXV

18 A	Two Line Nonpl. Orn. No. 12.	$5 30

THE LAST WAR NARRATIVE 8

18 A	Great Primer Outline.	$4 50

MEMOIR OF MADISON

12 A	Two Line Pica Outline.	$5 50

ORIGINAL STONE

6 A	Double Paragon Outline.	$6 25

NEIN SCALP

6 A	Two Line Paragon Ornamented No. 6.	$6 00

STEAK

6 A	Two Line Paragon Orn. No. 9.	$6 00

SMILE

6 A	Two Line Paragon Shade.	$6 00

ACKTORS 8

6 A	Two Line Paragon Orn. No. 3.	$6 50

RATE

6 A	Two Line Paragon Ornamented No. 4.	$6 50

MAINE 2

6 A	Two Line Paragon Ornamented No. 5.	$6 00

BLINDS

6 A	Four Line Pica Condensed Open Gothic.	$7 00

THE PRINTING HOUSE

8 A	Two Line English Scroll.	$6 00

WAVES

12 A	Two Line Pica Ornamented No. 18.	$5 00

NEW TELEGRAPH

18 A	English Scroll.	$3 00

NATIONAL SIGN

12 A	Two Line Lg. Primer Black Ground.	$5 00

PIANO MANUFACTURER 18

12 A	Two Line Lg. Primer Orn. No. 1.	$5 00

HISTORIC

12 A	Two Line Pica Ornamented No. 19.	$5 50

FAT MEN

12 A	Two Line Pica Shade in Relief.	$5 50

MAGAZINE

8 A	Two Line English Ornamented No. 22.	$6 25

THE MARCH 7

8 A	Two Line Great Primer Ornamented No. 14.	$6 75

HEMPEN 97

6 A	Four Line Pica Ornamented No. 9.	$10 25

TERMINATION

24 A	Long Primer Ornamented No. 9.	$3 50

MEMORY OF THE PAST

24 A	Two Line Nonpl. Orn. No. 19.	$4 50

AUTHORS DUSTING

12 A	Great Primer Ornamented No. 7.	$3 75

CONSTITUTION.

8 A	Two Line Pica Ornamented No. 16.	$5 25

RANTER 68

24 a 12 A	Great Primer Rimmed Gothic.	$5 00

Universal Attention 187

20 a 10 A	Two Line Sm. Pica Rim'd Gothic.	$6 00

Her Reminiscence 18

18 A	Long Primer Tuscan Shade.	$2 00

ANNUAL MEETING 57

18 A	Pica Tuscan Shade.	$3 80

MUSIC ACADEMY

24 A	Pica Tuscan No. 1.	$3 50

CALM STAR OBSERVATIONS

18 A	Great Primer Tuscan No. 1.	$4 00

DOMESTIC MANAGER

24 A	Long Primer Tuscan No. 2.	$3 00

ENGLISH GRAMMAR. 851

18 A	Two Line Nonpl. Ornamented No. 4.	$3 00

PUSHING HOUSES 34

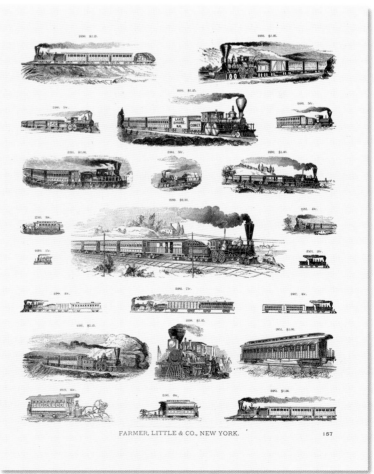

New Combination Borders.

SERIES 19

7 LB. FONTS, $5.00.

SERIES 27

$1.28 PER FONT.

SERIES 28

$1.44 PER FONT.

SERIES 29.

$2.56 PER FONT.

SERIES 30.

$4.25 PER FONT.

FARMER, LITTLE & CO., NEW YORK.

13

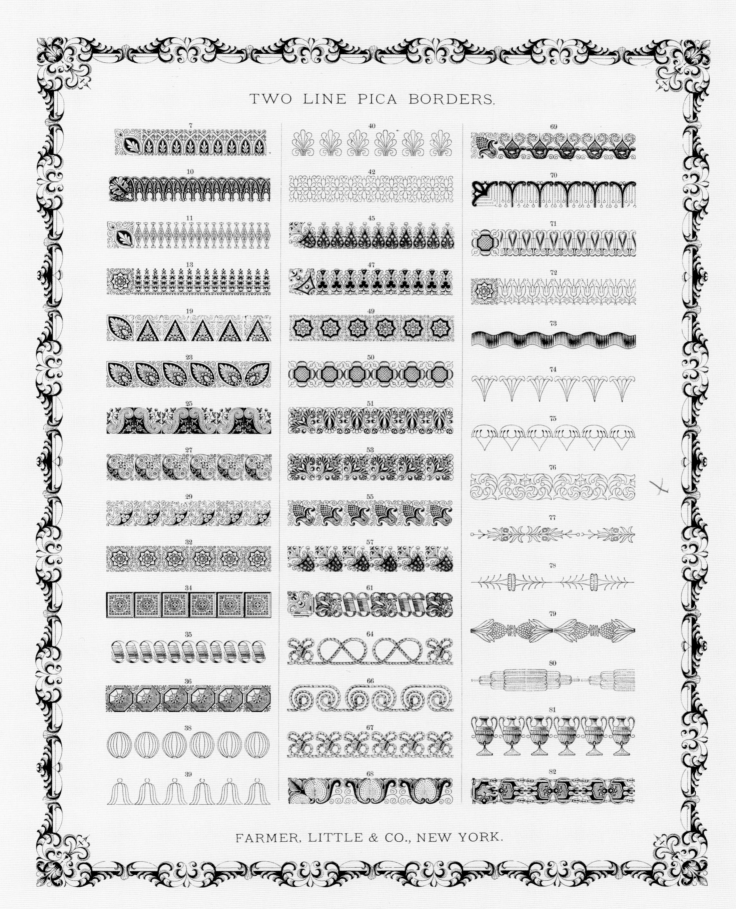

TWO LINE PICA BORDERS.

FARMER, LITTLE & CO., NEW YORK.

25

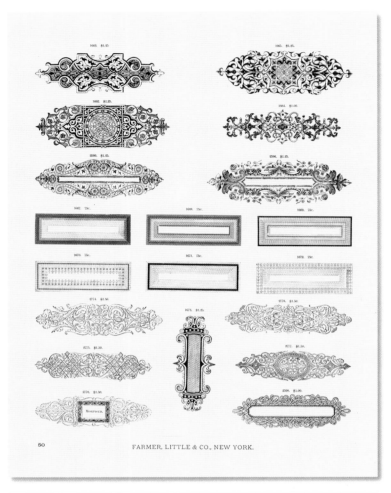

FARMER, LITTLE & CO., NEW YORK.

50

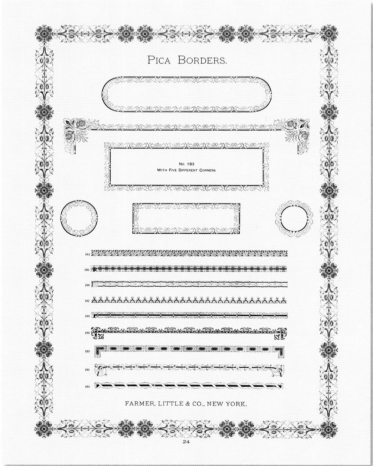

PICA BORDERS.

No. 183
WITH FIVE DIFFERENT CORNERS

FARMER, LITTLE & CO., NEW YORK.

24

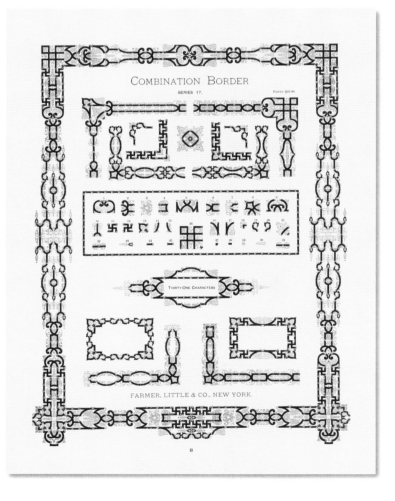

COMBINATION BORDER
SERIES 17.

THIRTY-ONE CHARACTERS

FARMER, LITTLE & CO., NEW YORK.

8

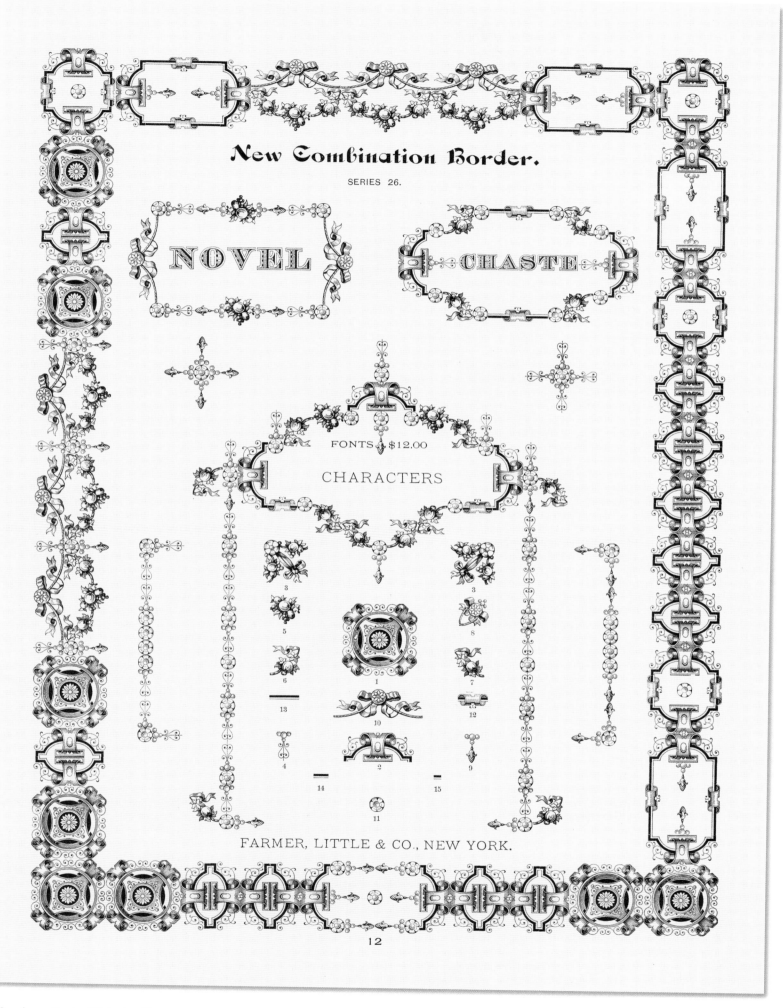

New Combination Border.

SERIES 26.

NOVEL

CHASTE

FONTS $12.00

CHARACTERS

FARMER, LITTLE & CO., NEW YORK.

12

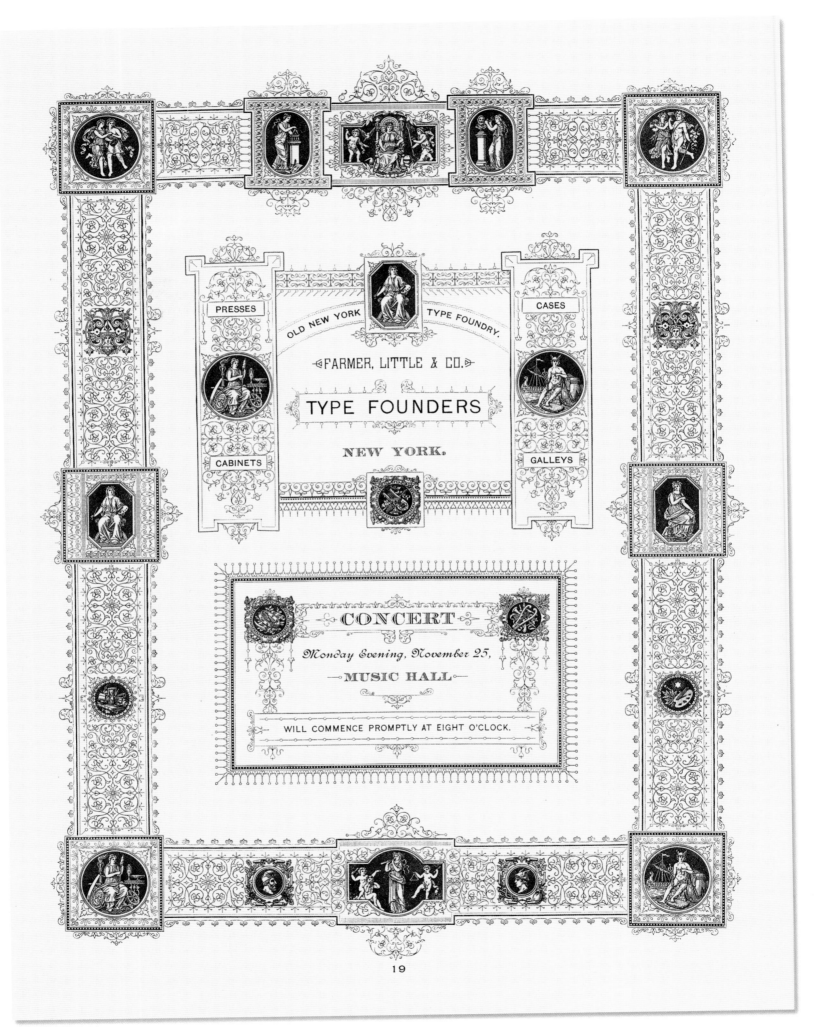

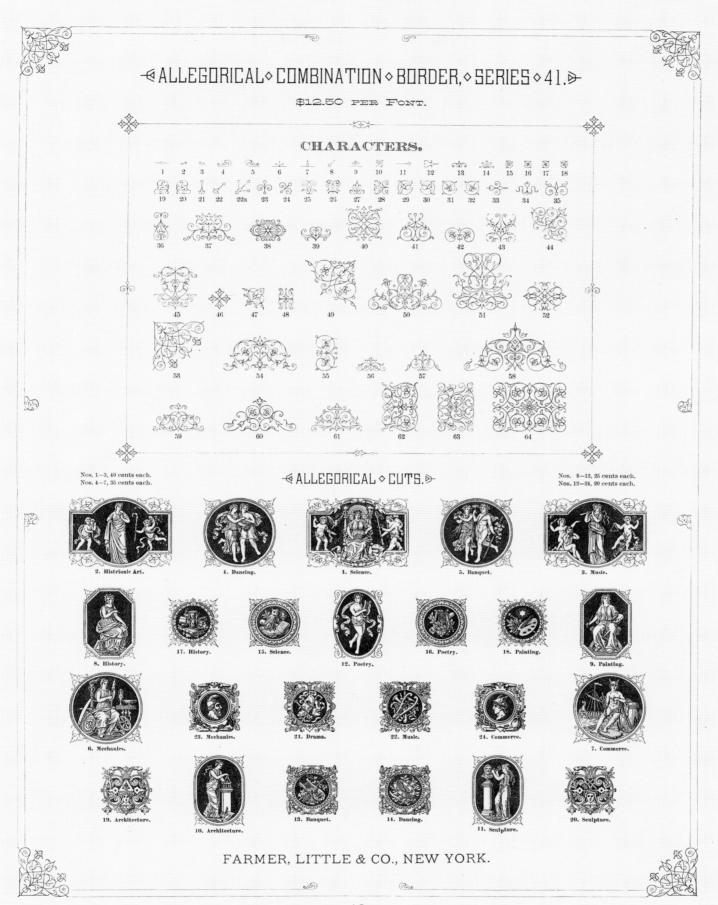

⊲ALLEGORICAL ◇ COMBINATION ◇ BORDER, ◇ SERIES ◇ 41.▷

$12.50 PER FONT.

CHARACTERS.

1 2 3 4 5 6 7 8 9 10 11 12 13 14 15 16 17 18

19 20 21 22 22a 23 24 25 26 27 28 29 30 31 32 33 34 35

36 37 38 39 40 41 42 43 44

45 46 47 48 49 50 51 52

53 54 55 56 57 58

59 60 61 62 63 64

Nos. 1—3, 40 cents each.
Nos. 4—7, 35 cents each.

⊲ALLEGORICAL ◇ CUTS.▷

Nos. 8—12, 25 cents each.
Nos. 12—24, 20 cents each.

2. Histrionic Art.　4. Dancing.　1. Science.　5. Banquet.　3. Music.

17. History.　15. Science.　12. Poetry.　16. Poetry.　18. Painting.

8. History.　9. Painting.

23. Mechanics.　21. Drama.　22. Music.　24. Commerce.

6. Mechanics.　7. Commerce.

19. Architecture.　10. Architecture.　13. Banquet.　14. Dancing.　11. Sculpture.　20. Sculpture.

FARMER, LITTLE & CO., NEW YORK.

18

1885, Verzameling van Lettersoorten, Versieringen & Vignetten, *Drukkerij C.A. Spin & Zoon,* Amsterdam

Verzameling van Lettersoorten was so successful that it was reprinted multiple times. This is the seventh edition.

Aufgrund seines großes Erfolges erlebte der Schriftmusterkatalog *Verzameling van Lettersoorten* zahlreiche Neuauflagen. Hier ist die siebte Auflage abgebildet.

Verzameling van Lettersoorten connut un tel succès qu'il fut réimprimé maintes fois. Il s'agit ici de la septième édition.

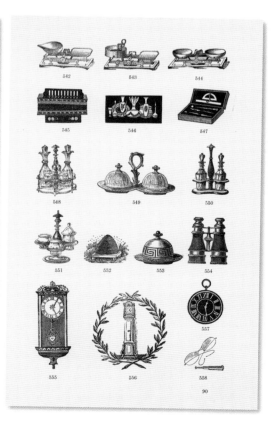

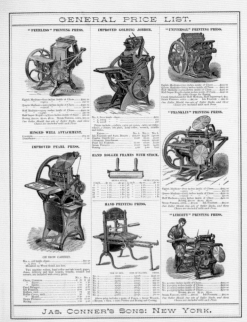

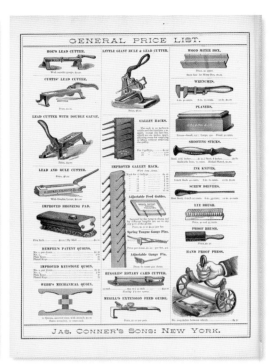

1888, Type Specimens,
James Conner & Sons, New York

American Romance, literally
and figuratively.

Romantische Americana in Wort
und Bild.

American Romance, au propre
comme au figuré.

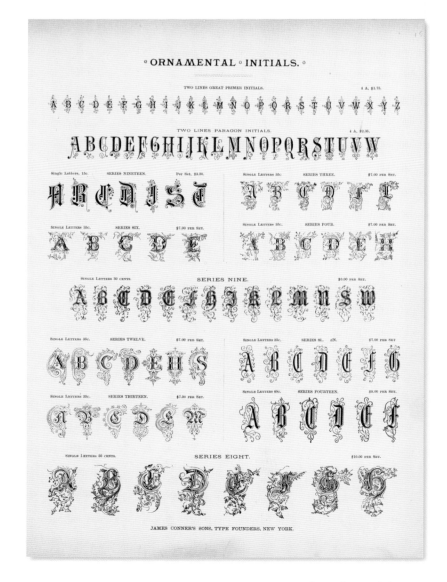

SEVEN-LINE PICA MODERN TEXT.

The Journal

SEVEN-LINE PICA MODERN TEXT OPEN.

Daily Herald

SEVEN-LINE PICA MODERN TEXT SHADED.

Home News

SEVEN-LINE PICA MODERN TEXT DOUBLE SHADED.

Weekly Star

EIGHT-LINE PICA MODERN TEXT SHADED.

Messenger

EIGHT-LINE PICA MODERN TEXT DOUBLE SHADED.

Washington

TEN-LINE PICA MODERN TEXT SHADED

American

TEN-LINE PICA MODERN TEXT DOUBLE SHADED.

Romance

JAMES CONNER'S SONS, TYPE FOUNDERS, NEW YORK.

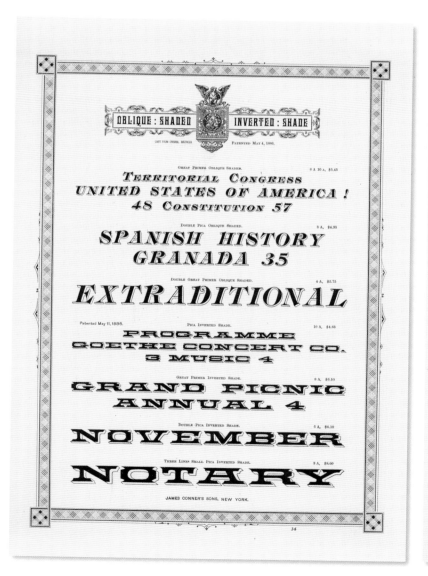

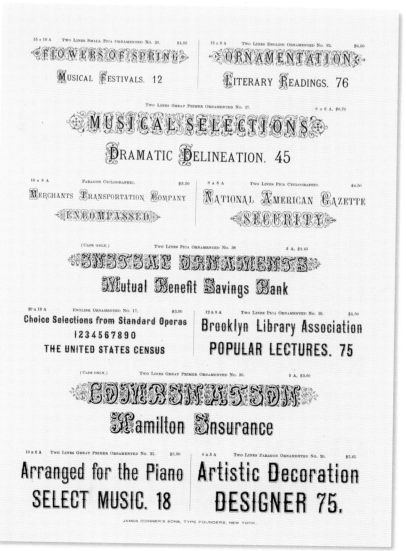

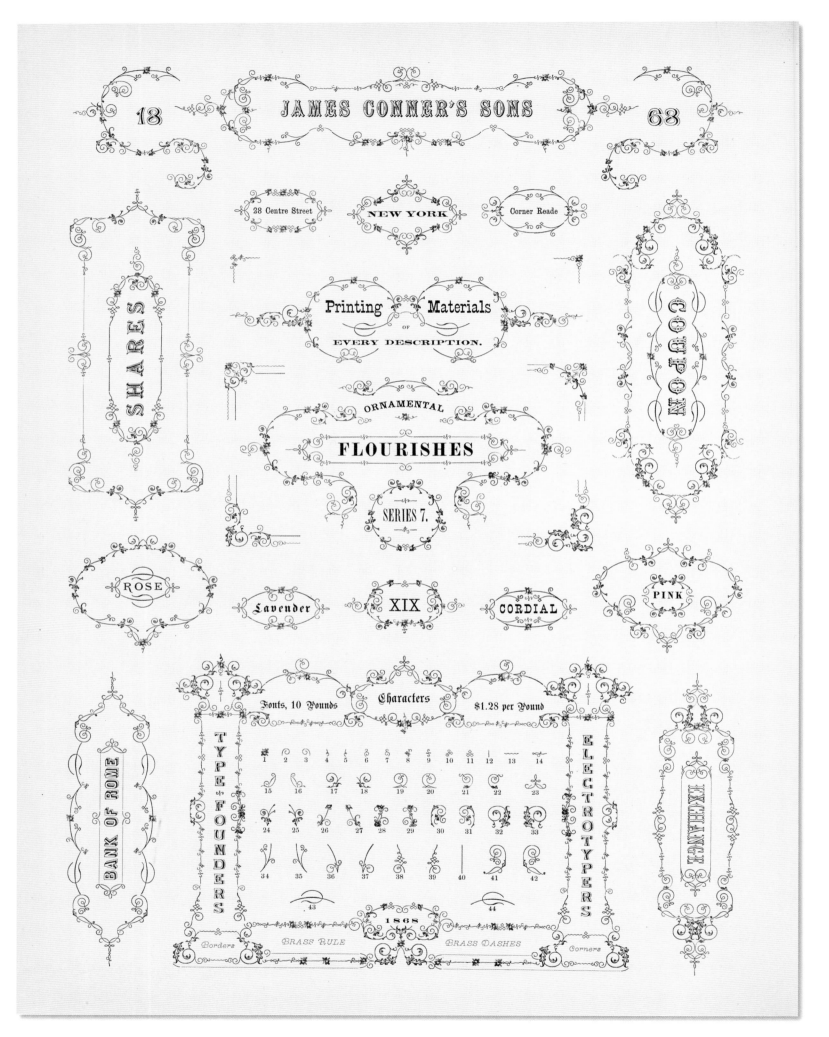

18 JAMES CONNER'S SONS **68**

28 Centre Street

NEW YORK

Corner Reade

SHARES

COUPON

Printing Materials

OF

EVERY DESCRIPTION.

ORNAMENTAL

FLOURISHES

SERIES 7.

ROSE

Lavender

XIX

CORDIAL

PINK

Fonts, 10 Pounds — Characters — $1.28 per Pound

BANK OF ROME

TYPE FOUNDERS

ELECTROTYPERS

EXCHANGE

1868

Borders — BRASS RULE — BRASS DASHES — *Corners*

| 20 A | LONG PRIMER ORNAMENTED NO. 11.* | $2.90. |

ORNAMENTAL TYPOGRAPHY

| 20 A | PICA ORNAMENTED NO. 31.* | $3.50 |

FURNITURE WAREHOUSE.

| 10 A | GREAT PRIMER ORNAMENTED NO. 18.* | $3.25 |

COMMEMORATORY

| 10 A | TWO LINES SMALL PICA ORN. NO. 22.* | $4.95 |

TUSCALOOSA

| | TWO LINES ENGLISH ORNAMENTED NO. 27. | | 8 A, $5.80 |

CALIFORNIA MINES 18

| 20 A | LONG PRIMER ORNAMENTED NO. 10.* | $3.00 |

ILLUSTRATED MAGAZINES.

| 20 A | PICA ORNAMENTED NO. 30.* | $3.50 |

INTERCOMMUNICATION

| 10 A | GREAT PRIMER ORNAMENTED NO. 17.* | $3.25 |

PHOSPHORESCENT

| 10 A | TWO LINES SMALL PICA ORN. NO. 21.* | $4.50 |

WASHINGTON

| | TWO LINES ENGLISH ORNAMENTED NO. 26. | | 6 A, $4.50 |

CUMBERLAND BANK 1586

| | TWO LINES PARAGON ORNAMENTED NO. 18. | | 5 A, $5.85 |

SIDEROGRAPHIC

| 25 a 20 A | PICA ORNAMENTED NO. 32. | $5.80 |

Brooklyn Safe Deposit Co.

TRANSPORTATION 75

| 20 a 15 A | TWO LINES BREVIER ORNAMENTED NO. 5. | $6.40 |

Typographic Messenger

ORNAMENTATION 18

| | PARAGON ORNAMENTED NO 16. | | 15 a 10 A, $6.60 |

The Hamilton Fire Insurance Company

NATIONAL NASSAU BANK 25

PATENTED JULY 18TH, 1881.

| | GREAT PRIMER ORNAMENTED NO. 41. | | 12 a 8 A, $3.80 |

2 ~BANQUET·OF·THACKERANIAN·TITBITS~ 3

Delightful Essays and Incisive Bits of Humor and Satire

| | TWO LINES PICA ORNAMENTED NO. 46. | | 10 a 6 A, $6.00 |

6 UNDISCOVERED·COUNTRIES 5

Beautiful Imagination Exquisite Humor

| | TWO LINES GREAT PRIMER ORNAMENTED NO. 42. | | 6 a 4 A $6.75 |

2 ~SUMMER·EXCURSION~ 8

Foreign Countries

* With Figures.

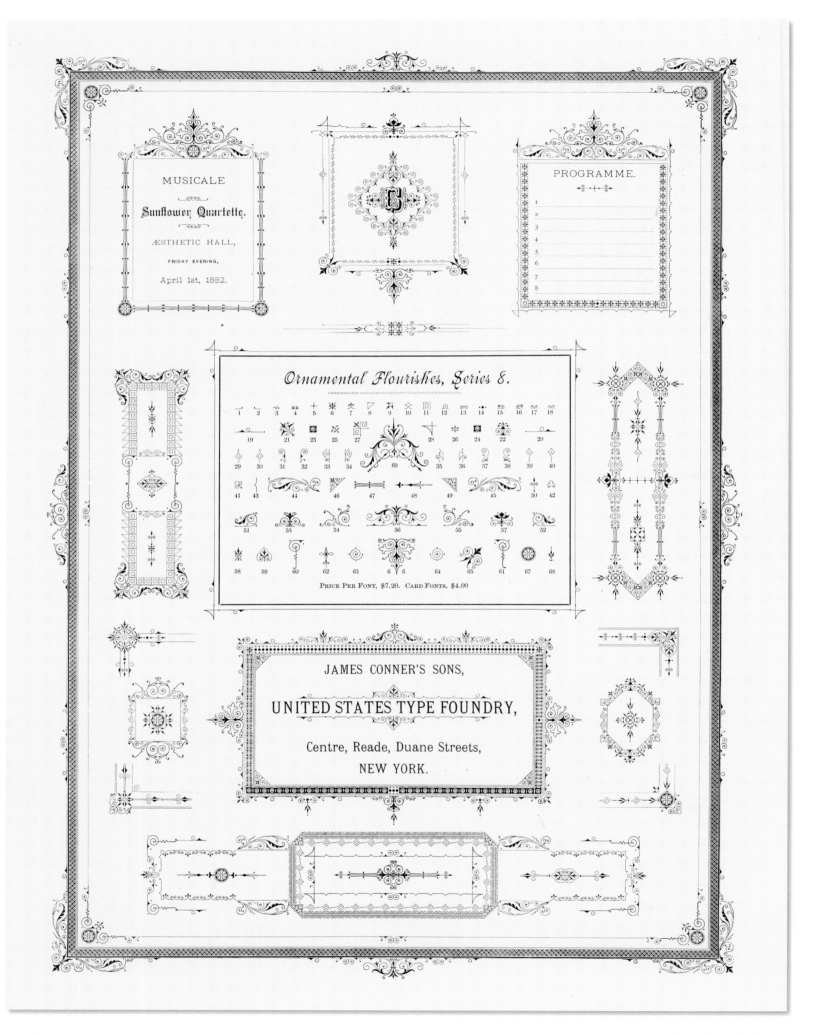

MUSICALE

Sunflower Quartette.

ÆSTHETIC HALL,

FRIDAY EVENING,

April 1st, 1882.

PROGRAMME.

1
2
3
4
5
6
7
8

Ornamental Flourishes, Series 8.

PRICE PER FONT, $7.20. CARD FONTS, $4.00

JAMES CONNER'S SONS,

UNITED STATES TYPE FOUNDRY,

Centre, Reade, Duane Streets,

NEW YORK.

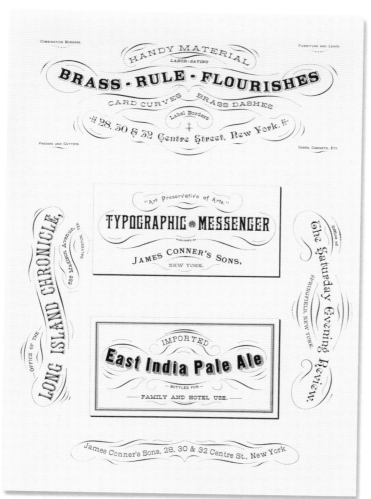

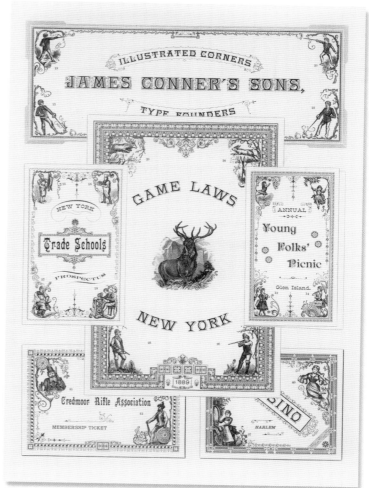

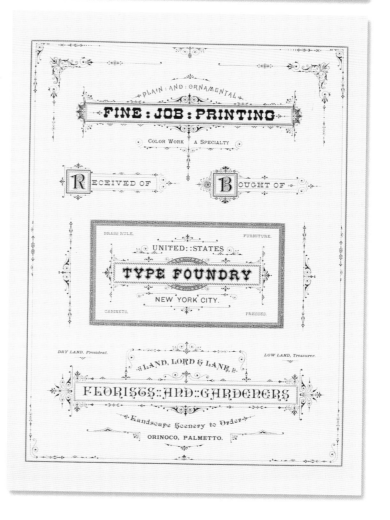

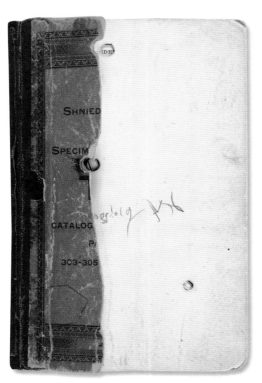

1888, Specimen Book and Price List of Type, *Shniedewend & Lee Company,* Chicago

This price list shows a number of lovely serif and sans serif examples. The "handsome satyrs" cost $1.95.

Die Preisliste hält eine Reihe reizvoller Beispiele für Schriften mit und ohne Serifen bereit. Die „hübschen Satyren" kosten 1,95 Dollar.

Cette liste de prix montre plusieurs jolis exemples de caractères avec ou sans empattements. Les « beaux satyres » coûtent 1,95 $.

Franklin Shaded, Minaret and Byzantine.

Patented Jan. 3, 1871.

GREAT PRIMER FRANKLIN SHADED.
10 A, 14 a. $5.50

LOVING WIFE
123456

TWO-LL SM. PICA FRANKLIN SHADED.
8 A, 10 A. $6.20

KIND MAID
12345

7 A, 8 A.   TWO-LINE ENGLISH FRANKLIN SHADED. $8.40

52 NEAT WAITERS

TWO-LINE SMALL PICA MINARET.
10 A, 14 a. $5.50

LIGHTS
6 Candelabra

Patented Dec. 1, 1868.

TWO-LINE ENGLISH MINARET.
7 A, 12 a. $6.90

DARK
4 Lanterns

7 A, 10 a.   TWO-LINE GREAT PRIMER MINARET. $8.05

MOIST Distillery 12

5 A, 6 a.   CANON MINARET. $10.35

9 White HUTS

5 A, 7 a.   TWO-LINE GREAT PRIMER BYZANTINE. $7.35

PURE Wines 81

JAPANESQUE.

Patented Feb. 6, 1877.

PICA JAPANESQUE, No. 2.
12 A. $2.30

RARE BIRDS
12345

GREAT PRIMER JAPANESQUE, No. 2.
8 A. $2.75

TICKLER
1234

6 A.   TWO-LINE PICA JAPANESQUE, No. 2. $3.70

COURTESIES

PICA JAPANESQUE, No. 3.
12 A. $2.30

KIND MOODS
12345

GREAT PRIMER JAPANESQUE, No. 3.
8 A. $2.75

CARTOON
1234

6 A.   TWO-LINE PICA JAPANESQUE, No. 3. $3.70

MONUMENT

PICA JAPANESQUE.
12 A. $2.30

WILD DUCKS
12345

GREAT PRIMER JAPANESQUE.
8 A. $2.75

CONTEST
1234

6 A.   TWO-LINE PICA JAPANESQUE. $3.70

CONSOLATION

ALL COMPLETE WITH FIGURES.

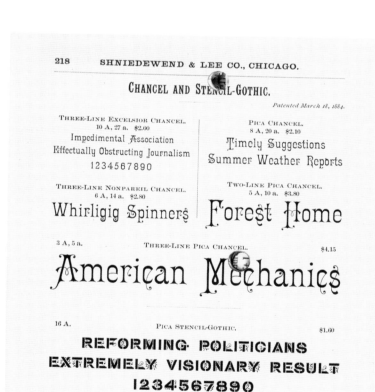

218 SHNIEDEWEND & LEE CO., CHICAGO.

CHANCEL AND STENCIL-GOTHIC.

Patented March 18, 1884.

THREE-LINE EXCELSIOR CHANCEL.
10 A, 27 a. $2.00

Impedimental Association
Effectually Obstructing Journalism
1234567890

PICA CHANCEL.
8 A, 20 a. $2.10

Timely Suggestions
Summer Weather Reports

THREE-LINE NONPAREIL CHANCEL.
6 A, 14 a. $2.80

Whirligig Spinners

TWO-LINE PICA CHANCEL.
5 A, 10 a. $3.80

Forest Home

3 A, 5 a.   THREE-LINE PICA CHANCEL. $4.15

American Mechanics

16 A.   PICA STENCIL-GOTHIC. $1.60

REFORMING POLITICIANS
EXTREMELY VISIONARY RESULT
1234567890

16 A.   PICA STENCIL-GOTHIC, No. 2. $1.95

HANDSOME SATYRS
FINELY ATTIRED GOBLINS

12 A.   THREE-LINE NONPAREIL STENCIL-GOTHIC. $2.65

RETROGRADE
WAVERING TROOPS

ALL COMPLETE WITH FIGURES.

SHNIEDEWEND & LEE CO., CHICAGO. **219**

RELIEVO.

Patented April 15, 1879.

14 A.   GREAT PRIMER RELIEVO, No. 2. $3.70

IMPROVISED COLLECTIONS.
1234567890

5 A.   DOUBLE PARAGON RELIEVO, No. 2. $6.30

35 LAMPS

10 A.   TWO-LINE PICA RELIEVO, No. 2. $4.55

CABLE COMPANY 0

Patented March 12, 1878.

10 A.   TWO-LINE PICA RELIEVO. $4.80

129 DARK HOURS

TWO-LINE GREAT PRIMER AND TWO-LINE PICA RELIEVO IN COMBINATION.

TEXTURE

5 A.   TWO-LI. GREAT PRIMER RELIEVO. $5.35

BENDING 4

Mortised, No. 2.
Patented Nov. 18, 1884.
Mechanical Patent, Mar. 31, 1885.

3 A.   FOUR-LINE PICA MORTISED, NO. 2. $6.00

This type will give a new idea to the printer, and add to his facilities for varying the style of his work. Types of numerous faces can be easily and accurately fitted into the slotted sides, and the extension pieces, being cast on Pica bodies, added without justification.

ORNAMENTAL INITIAL LETTERS.
FORTY-THIRD SERIES.
Patent Pending.
Mechanical Patent, March 31, 1885.   Price, per Set, $4.00.   Single Letter, 40 cts.

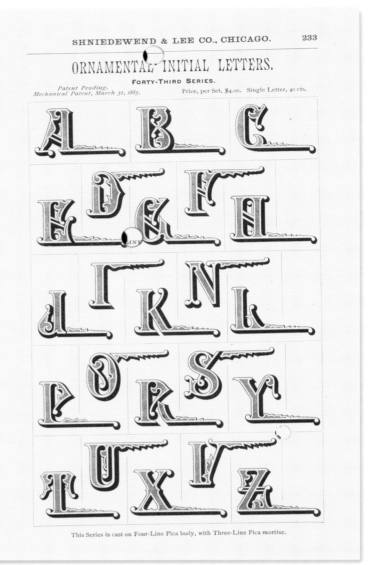

This Series is cast on Four-Line Pica body, with Three-Line Pica mortise.

CHARCOAL SKETCHES.
COPYRIGHTED.

Single cut, 20 cts.; 30 cuts or over, 18 cts. each; 50 cuts or over, 15 cts. each.
Complete set, cuts 1 to 122, $10.00.

CHARCOAL SKETCHES.
COPYRIGHTED.

Single cut, 20 cts.; 30 cuts or over, 18 cts. each; 50 cuts or over, 15 cts. each.
Complete set, cuts 1 to 122, $10.00.

PAPER KNIVES.

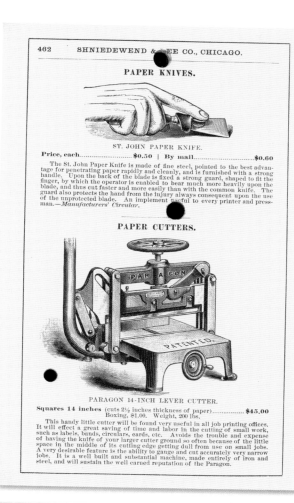

ST. JOHN PAPER KNIFE.

Price, each.........................$0.50 | By mail.........................$0.60

The St. John Paper Knife is made of fine steel, pointed to the best advantage for penetrating paper rapidly and cleanly, and is furnished with a strong handle. Upon the back of the blade is fixed a strong guard, shaped to fit the finger, by which the operator is enabled to bear much more heavily upon the blade, and thus cut faster and more easily than with the common knife. The guard also protects the hand from the injury always consequent upon the use of the unprotected blade. An implement useful to every printer and pressman.—*Manufacturers' Circular.*

PAPER CUTTERS.

PARAGON 14-INCH LEVER CUTTER.

Squares 14 inches (cuts 2½ inches thickness of paper).................$45.00
Boxing, $1.00. Weight, 200 lbs.

This handy little cutter will be found very useful in all job printing offices. It will effect a great saving of time and labor in the cutting of small work, such as labels, bands, circulars, cards, etc. Avoids the trouble and expense of having the knife of your larger cutter ground so often because of the little space in the middle of its cutting edge getting dull from use on small jobs. A very desirable feature is the ability to gauge and cut accurately very narrow jobs. It is a well built and substantial machine, made entirely of iron and steel, and will sustain the well earned reputation of the Paragon.

PAPER CUTTERS.

THE FRANKLIN PAPER CUTTER.

30 Inch, with movable head......**$50.00** | **30 Inch,** without movable head, **$45.00**

It has a movable head, which travels above the paper, across the board, so that the paper can be cut one way as many times as desired without being disturbed. The head is worked by a small crank at side of cutter, by a simple arrangement, and is easily operated.—*Mfrs' Circular.*

PAPER COUNTER.

Patented Nov. 15, 1877.

PATENT PAPER COUNTER.

Price (sent by mail).........................**$1.00**

For bookbinders, printers, lithographers, paper mailers and general office use; counting paper, making tablets, weighing paper, gauging paper, etc.

PAPER CUTTERS.

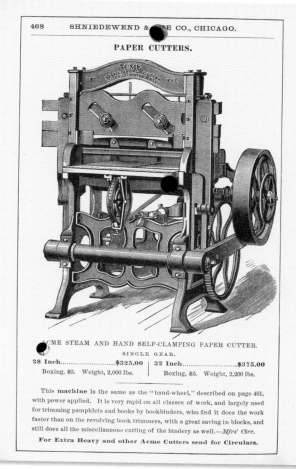

ACME STEAM AND HAND SELF-CLAMPING PAPER CUTTER.

SINGLE GEAR.

28 Inch.........................**$325.00** | **32 Inch**.........................**$375.00**
Boxing, $5. Weight, 2,000 lbs. | Boxing, $5. Weight, 2,200 lbs.

This **machine** is the same as the "hand-wheel," described on page 461, with power applied. It is very rapid on all classes of work, and largely used for trimming pamphlets and books by bookbinders, who find it does the work faster than on the revolving book trimmers, with a great saving in blocks, and still does all the miscellaneous cutting of the bindery as well.—*Mfrs' Circ.*

For Extra Heavy and other Acme Cutters send for Circulars.

PAPER CUTTERS.

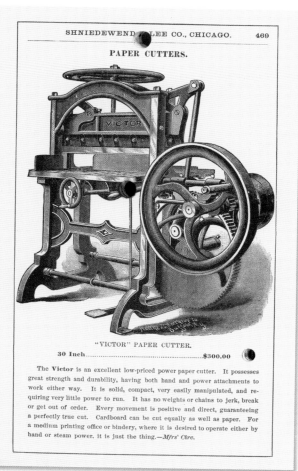

"VICTOR" PAPER CUTTER.

30 Inch.........................**$300.00**

The **Victor** is an excellent low-priced power paper cutter. It possesses great strength and durability, having both hand and power attachments to work either way. It is solid, compact, very easily manipulated, and requiring very little power to run. It has no weights or chains to jerk, break or get out of order. Every movement is positive and direct, guaranteeing a perfectly true cut. Cardboard can be cut equally as well as paper. For a medium printing office or bindery, where it is desired to operate either by hand or steam power, it is just the thing.—*Mfrs' Circ.*

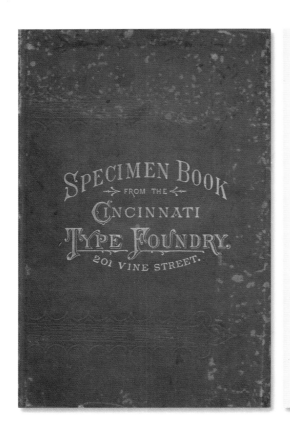

Pica (12 Points) Card Line.

THE CINCINNATI SOUTHERN RAILROAD
Most Advantageous Route for Transportation of Freight, 345
GARDEN CITY 17489 BIRMINGHAM

Three-Line Nonpareil (18 Points) Card Line.

ARTISTIC EUROPEAN PRODUCTIONS
Beautiful Monuments of Grecian Architecture, $284
GRANITE AND MARBLE WORKS

ROBINSON & COMSTOCK,
STATIONERS,
COMMERCIAL PRINTERS,
AND
Blank Book Manufacturers.
No. 26 Spring Lane,   SANDUSKY, OHIO.

The Small Caps of Three-Line Nonpareil and Two-Line Pica sizes line by placing Nonpareil quads or triplets at the top.

BOUGHT OF   THIRD NATIONAL BANK.   RECEIVED

Two-Line Pica (24 Points) Card Line.

MODERN 25 DESIGNS
CARD ORNAMENTS AND FLOURISHES
SPECIMEN SHEETS, 873

Quads and Spaces extra.   86   *Cincinnati Type Foundry, 201 Vine St.*

Ornamental Type.

Two-Line Nonpareil (22 Points) Orna. No. 22.   Two-Line Minion (14 Points) Orna. No. 5.

SONGS AND DANCES 26   PRINTING INKS 5

Three-Line Nonp. (18 Points) Orna. No. 11.   Two-Line Pica (24 Points) Ornamented No. 36.

EXHIBITS 6   BRIDAL 7

Two-Line Long Primer (20 Points) Ornamented No. 15.

PERFECT CHROMOTYPE 7

Two-Line Pica (24 Points) Orna. No. 6.

OUR TYPOGRAPHIC CHARMS

Five-Line Nonpareil (30 Points) Ornamented No. 26.

NONPAREIL PRESS
Combination of Excellences 47

Two-Line Long Primer (20 Points) Ornamented No. 9.

AESTHETIC METHODS

Two-Line Pica (24 Points) Ornamented No. 18.

IMPORTED CIGARS 50

Two-Line Pica (24 Points) Orna. No. 22.   Two-Line Minion (14 Points) Orna. No. 18.

Five-Line Nonpareil (30 Points) Ornamented No. 16.

Five-Line Nonpareil (30 Points) Ornamented No. 38.

SPECIMEN SHEET

Four-Line Pica (48 Points) Ornamented No. 1.

CHOICE BUDS

Quads and Spaces extra.   87   *Cincinnati Type Foundry, 201 Vine St.*

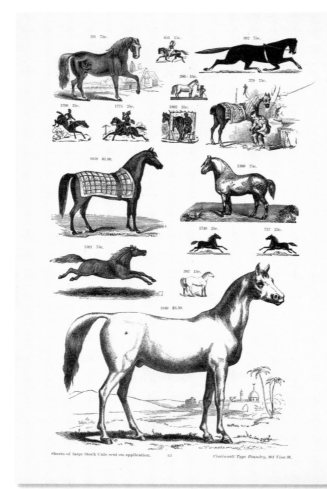

sheets of large Stock Cuts sent on application.   62   *Cincinnati Type Foundry, 201 Vine St.*

sheets of large Stock Cuts sent on application.   63   *Cincinnati Type Foundry, 201 Vine St.*

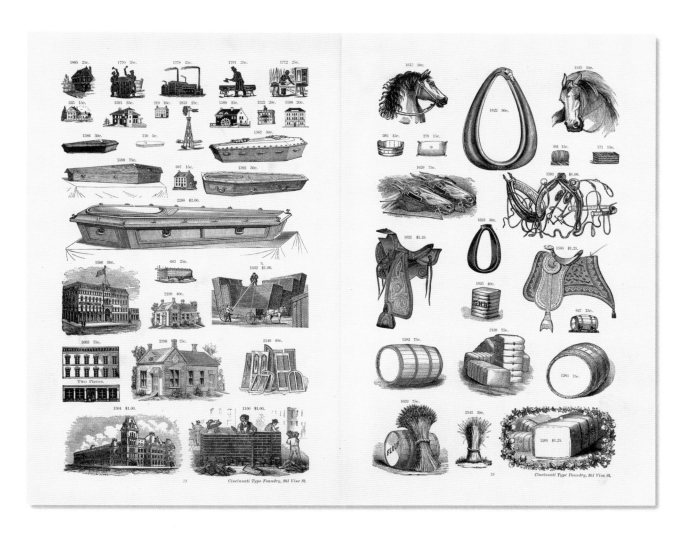

1888, The 17th Book of Specimens,
Cincinnati Type Foundry, Cincinnati

Back in time! Two lines, two different typefaces in a fantasy world.

Zurück in die Vergangenheit! Zwei Zeilen, zwei unterschiedliche Schriften in einer Welt voller Fantastik.

Retour vers le passé ! Deux lignes, deux caractères différents dans un monde imaginaire.

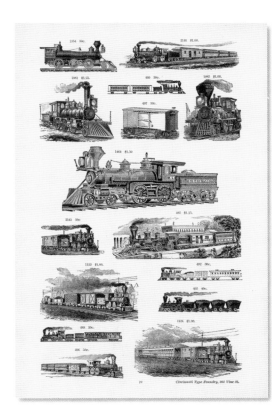

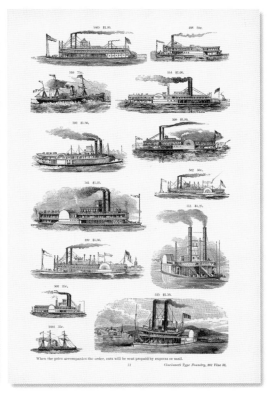

1706 75c.   763 15c.   762 15c.   634 20c.   632 20c.   787 30c.

1702. 40c.

1680   40c   1681.   40c.

631 50c.   633 $1.00.   1814 25c.   1355 40c.

1679. 40c.   739 15c.   1716 $1.00.   1709 40c.

682 40c.

1707 50c.   1708 50c.

1337 40c.

1721. $1.00   1720 $1.00

776 50c.　779 50c.　778 50c.　774 50c.　773 50c.

617 40c.　1807 25c.　1699 50c.　786 25c.　640 40c.

1710 40c.　1781 25c.　1704. 40c.　1779 25c.　775 50c.

1788 25c.　1782 25c.

785 40c.　1698 $1.00.　777 40c.

1762 25c.　1763 25c.

1722 75c.　1726 $1.50.

27

Cincinnati Type Foundry, 201 Vine St.

N° 1271 Par. Kanon (36 p.) Min. 6 kilo

BRANDENBURG

N° 1284 Par. Kanon (36 p.) Min. 6 kilo

23 DELFZIJL 45

N° 2505 Sabon (48 p.) Min. 7 kilo

LEIDEN ONTZET

N° 2055 Op 52 punten. Min. 10 kilo

CONCERT

N° 1274 Sabon (48 p.) Min. 7 kilo

SCHIEDAM BREDA

1889, Letterproef, Deel II, Fantaisie-Letter, *Joh. Enschedé & Zonen,* Haarlem

Design knows no borders. Seen here are fantasy letters from Netherlands-based Enschedé & Zonen.

Design ohne Schranken, hier in Form von Zierschriften der niederländischen Firma Enschedé & Zonen.

Le graphisme ne connaît pas de frontières. Voici des caractères fantaisie de la fonderie néerlandaise Enschedé & Zonen.

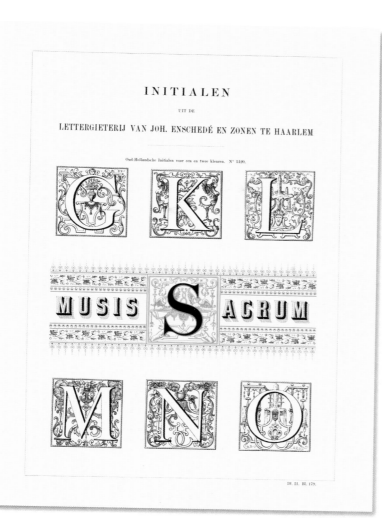

INITIALEN

UIT DE

LETTERGIETERIJ VAN JOH. ENSCHEDÉ EN ZONEN TE HAARLEM

Oud-Hollandsche Initialen voor een en twee kleuren. N°. 1420.

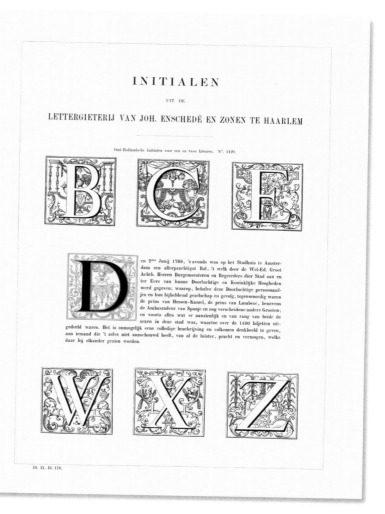

INITIALEN

UIT DE

LETTERGIETERIJ VAN JOH. ENSCHEDÉ EN ZONEN TE HAARLEM

Oud-Hollandsche Initialen voor een en twee kleuren. N°. 1420.

en 2den Junij 1768, 's avonds was op het Stadhuis te Amsterdam een allerprachtigst Bal, 't welk door de Wel-Ed. Groot Achtb. Heeren Burgemeesteren en Regeerders dier Stad aan en ter Eere van hunne Doorluchtige en Koninklijke Hoogheden werd gegeven; waarop, behalve deze Doorluchtige persoonaadjes en hun bijhebbend gezelschap en gevolg, tegenwoordig waren de prins van Hessen-Kassel, de prins van Lambesc, benevens de Ambassadeur van Spanje en nog verscheidene andere Grooten; en voorts alles wat er aanzienlijk en van rang van beide de sexen in deze stad was, waartoe over de 1400 bijetten uitgedeeld waren. Het is onmogelijk eene volledige beschrijving en volkomen denkbeeld te geven, aan iemand die 't zelve niet aanschouwd heeft, van al de luister, pracht en vermogen, welke daar bij elkander gezien werden.

Initialen N° 1423

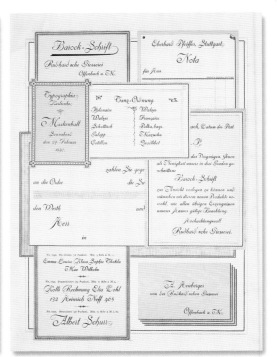

1890, Buch- und Zeitungs-schriften, *Rudhard'sche Giesserei,* Offenbach am Main

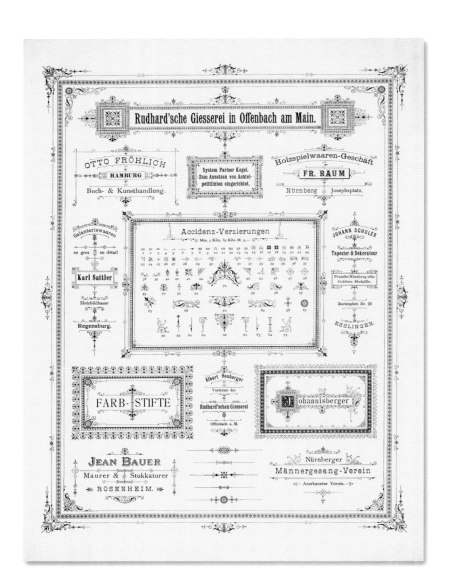

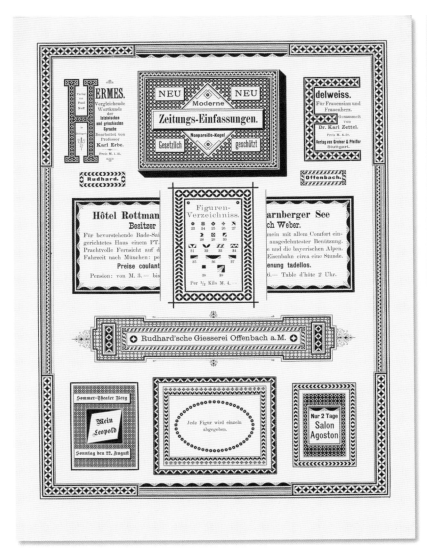

For everyday newspaper advertising, a vendor could simply choose the layout and typeface and deliver the copy.

Anzeigenverkäufer von Tageszeitungen konnten einfach ein Layout samt passender Schrift als Vorlage auswählen.

Pour la publicité quotidienne dans les journaux, un marchand n'avait qu'à choisir la mise en page et les caractères, et livrer le message.

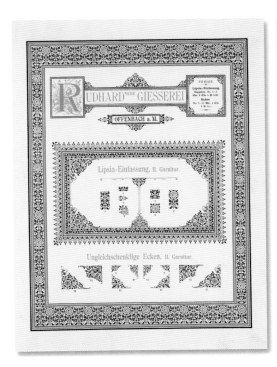

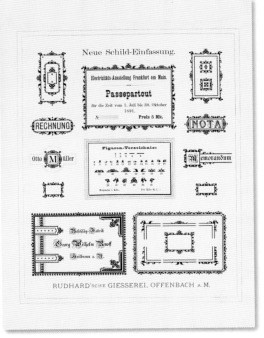

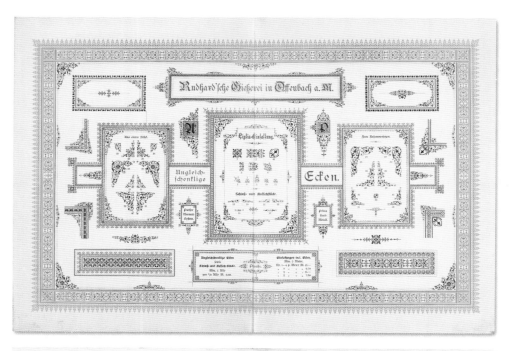

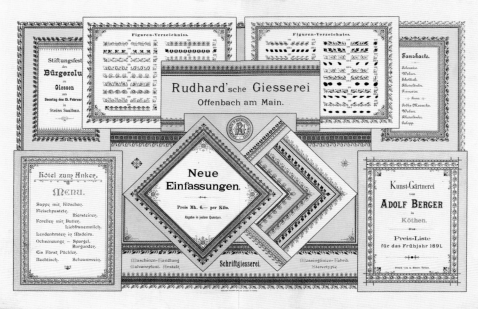

1890, Buch- und Zeitungs-schriften, *Rudhard'sche Giesserei,* Offenbach am Main

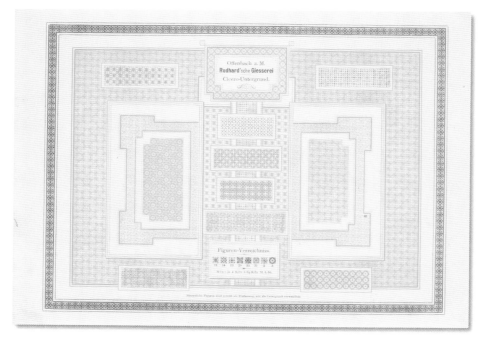

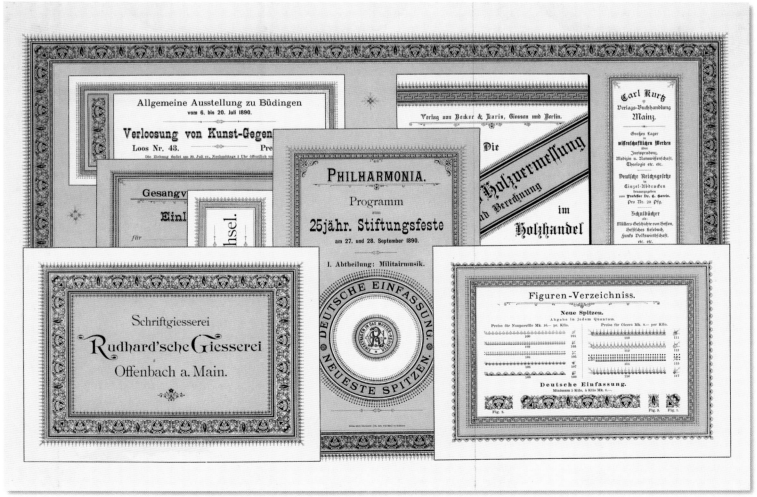

Radfahr-Verein D

Sonntag den 24. J

FEST-B

in der

Altgothisch.

Nr. 1138. Cicero (Corps 12).
Minimum 6 Kilo à ½ Kilo ℳ 2.80

Die Antiquaschrift ist entstander
eine Vereinigung des Alphabets
83 NIEDERWALD. Fest

Nr. 1139. Tertia (Corps 16).
Minimum 8 Kilo à ½ Kilo ℳ 2.65.

Förderung nützlicher Künste
Eisenbahn-Verwaltung Rom
23 GUTENBERG. 60

Nr. 1140. Text (Corps 20).
Minimum 10 Kilo à ½ Kilo ℳ 2.45.

Gesellschafts-Zimmer.
Orchester. Wiesbaden.
45 BANKET 78

Zum bevorstehenden Jahreswechsel
erlauben wir uns, Ihnen die besten
Glückwünsche
darzubringen und bitten, uns Ihr werth-
geschätztes Wohlwollen auch fernerhin
zu erhalten.

Brühl'sche Druckerei.

Giessen.

Hermann El

Giessen.

Alexander Kramer
Vertreter der Rudhard'schen Giesserei
in Offenbach a. M.

RUDHARD'

OFFE

ALTG

u

DER

Berlin.

HEILIG

Expedition des Giessener In

Brühl'sche Druckerei.

Fol.

Giessen, den

RECHNUNG

für

Karl Bleibtreu
Eleonore Wohlgem

Verlobte.

Borsdorf

Ch

August 1891.

ik

r & Co.

GEBRÜDER ZEIG
NAUMBURG
Holzcommissions- und Incasso-Geschäft.

Herren Heimann & Comp.
Dampf-Sägewerk

den

Lahn-Kalk-Industrie Rodheim
Station Giessen (M. W. B.)

1872er.

Herr

ER

inz.

GIESSEREI
M.

Altgotische Versalien.

Nr. 1141. Mittel (Corps 14).
Minimum 4 Kilo à ½ Kilo M. 2.75.

FRIEDRICH DER GROSSE

Nr. 1142. 1½ Cicero (Corps 18).
Minimum 5 Kilo à ½ Kilo M. 2.65.

AUSSTELLUNG.

Nr. 1143. Doppelcicero (Corps 24).
Minimum 6 Kilo à ½ Kilo M. 2.40.

JUGENHEIM

ISCH

handlung.

ANOPLASTIK.

ompte Lieferung.

en-Karte.

ebs-Suppe.

Lendenbraten.

t Kartoffel.

ehziemer.

Pastete in Würzbrühe.

Gefrorenes.

Käse und Butter.

Nr. 1144. 2½ Cicero (Corps 30).
Minimum 7 Kilo à ½ Kilo M. 2.40.

CAMBERG

Nr. 1145. Canon (Corps 36).
Minimum 8 Kilo à ½ Kilo M. 2.25.

RHEIN

Coupon.

Anfang 8 Uhr.

MADEIRA

FONDERIE G. RENAULT

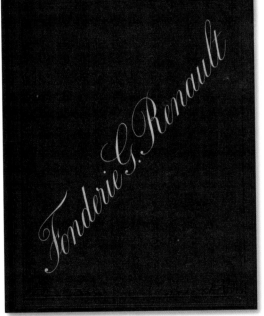

1890, Spécimen,
Fonderie G. Renault Fils, Paris

Typography is anything but boring
in these prints, created in Paris for
the Folies-Bergère.

Die Typografie dieser für die Folies-
Bergère in Paris entstandenen Drucke
ist alles anderes als einfallslos.

La typographie de ces impressions
réalisées pour les Folies-Bergère à Paris
est tout sauf ennuyeuse.

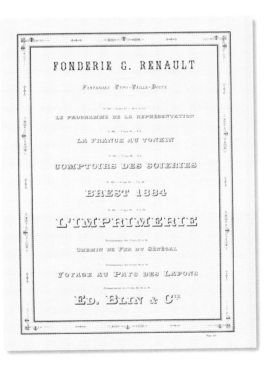

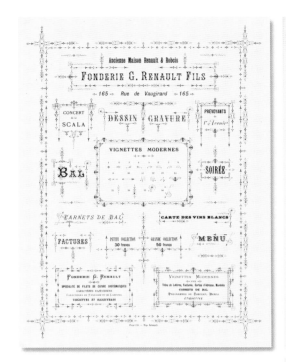

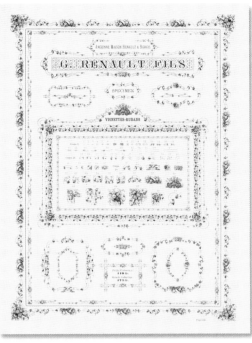

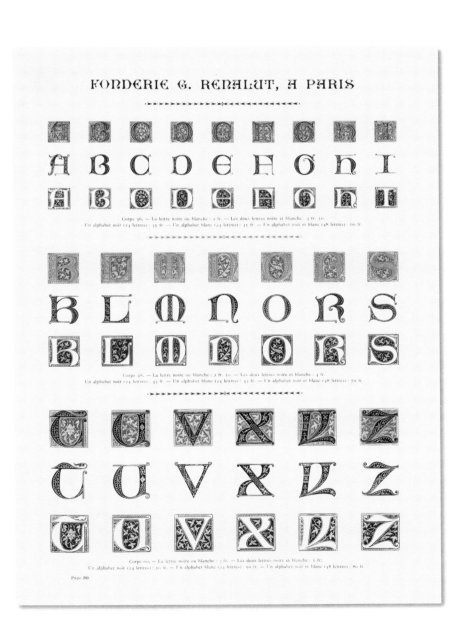

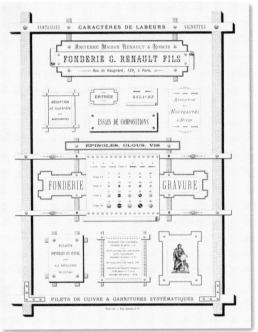

FONDERIE G. RENAULT FILS

✦ Blanches Ombrées ✦

Nº 636. — Corps 16. — 9 fr. le kil.

GRANDE FÊTE DE BIENFAISANCE
1234567890

Nº 637. — Corps 24. — 8 fr.

THÉATRE FRANÇAIS
RUY-BLAS

Nº 638. — Corps 36. — 7 fr.

FOLIES-BERGÈRE
1875

Parangonnage des corps 16 et 24.

GRAND CONCERT PARISIEN

Parangonnage des corps 24 et 36.

MOREL & Cᴵᴱ

Page 157. — Typ. Schmidt.

VIGNETTES-RUBANS

ANCIENNE MAISON RENAULT & ROBCIS

G. RENAULT FILS

ESSAIS DE COMPOSITIONS

FONDERIE

G. RENAULT FILS

A PARIS

ALBUM

Page 129.

IMPRIMERIE
des
SCIENCES & ARTS
PARIS
Avenue Victor-Hugo, 15

VOITELAIN

Paris, le

Serrurerie Artistique

44

rue Richelieu

Paris, le

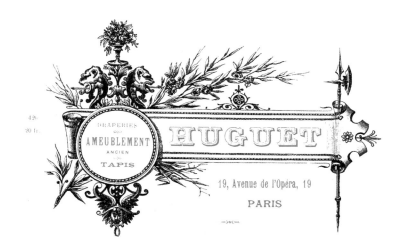

DRAPERIES
AMEUBLEMENT
ANCIEN
TAPIS

HUGUET

19, Avenue de l'Opéra, 19

PARIS

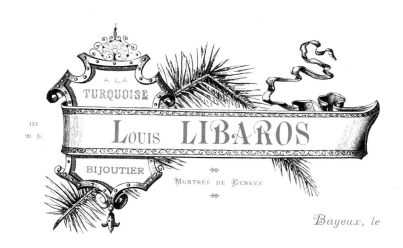

A LA
TURQUOISE

Louis LIBAROS

BIJOUTIER

MONTRES DE GENÈVE

Bayeux, le

AU VASE ETRUSQUE

Galerie Vivienne

PALAIS-ROYAL

165, rue de Vaugirard, 165

Labeurs
Fantaisies
Vignettes
Filets de cuivre

G. RENAULT

1890, Spécimen,
Fonderie G. Renault Fils, Paris

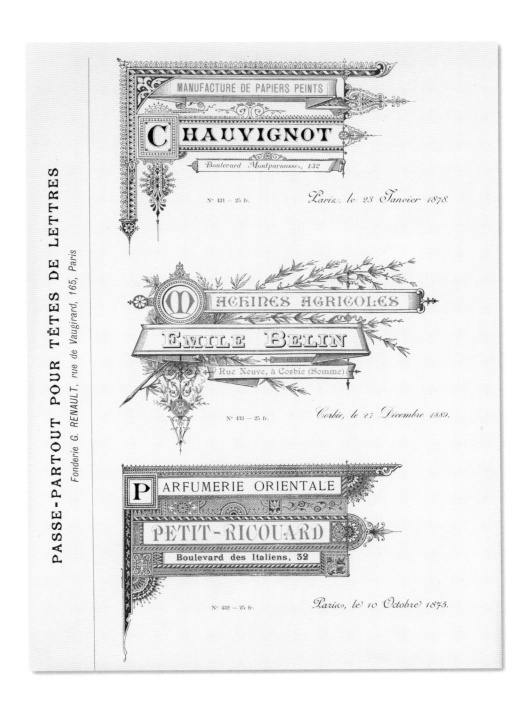

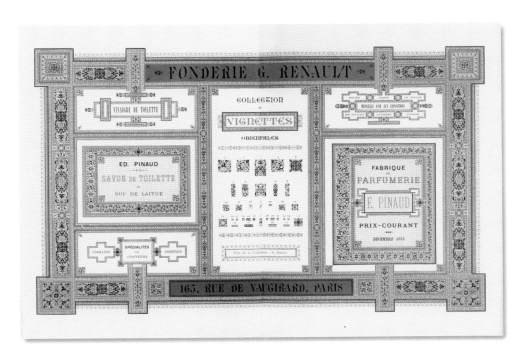

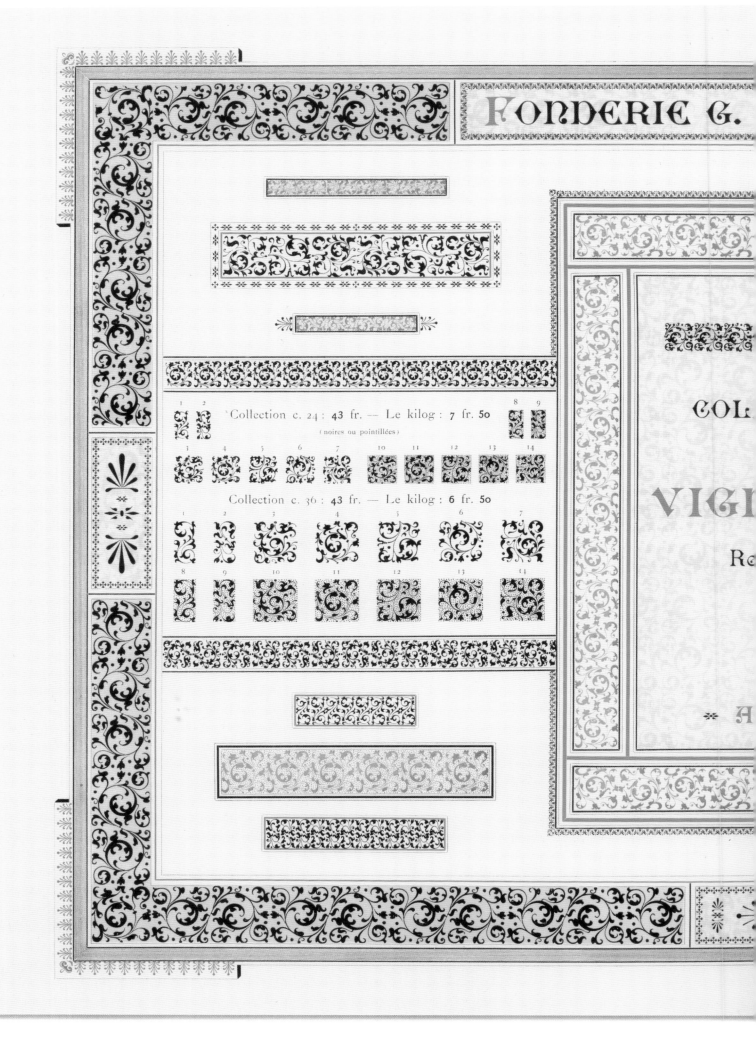

FONDERIE G.

Collection c. 24 : **43** fr. — Le kilog : **7** fr. **50**
(noires ou pointillées)

Collection c. 36 : **43** fr. — Le kilog : **6** fr. **50**

COL

VIGI

Re

Collection c. 48 : **45** fr. — Le kil. : 5 fr. 5o

(noires ou pointillées)

1890, Specimen,
S. Berthier & Durey, Paris

Every picture was custom-designed and
produced according to the customer's
specifications.

Entwurf und Herstellung jedes einzelnen
Bildes waren auf die speziellen Wünsche
des Kunden abgestimmt.

Chaque image était dessinée et réalisée
sur commande selon les stipulations du
client.

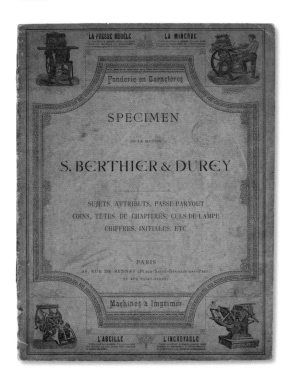

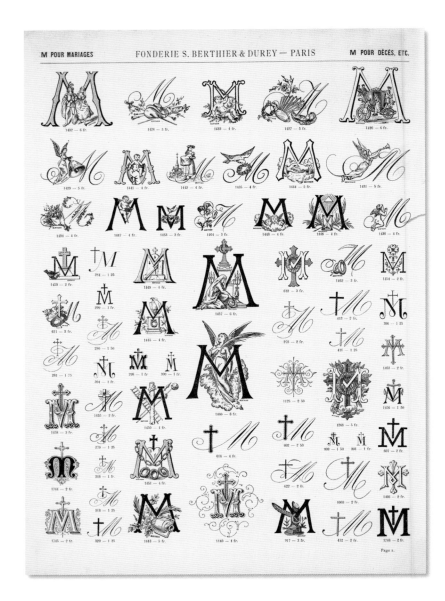

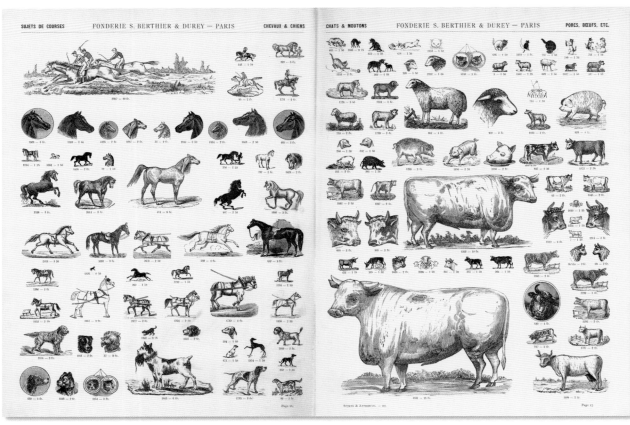

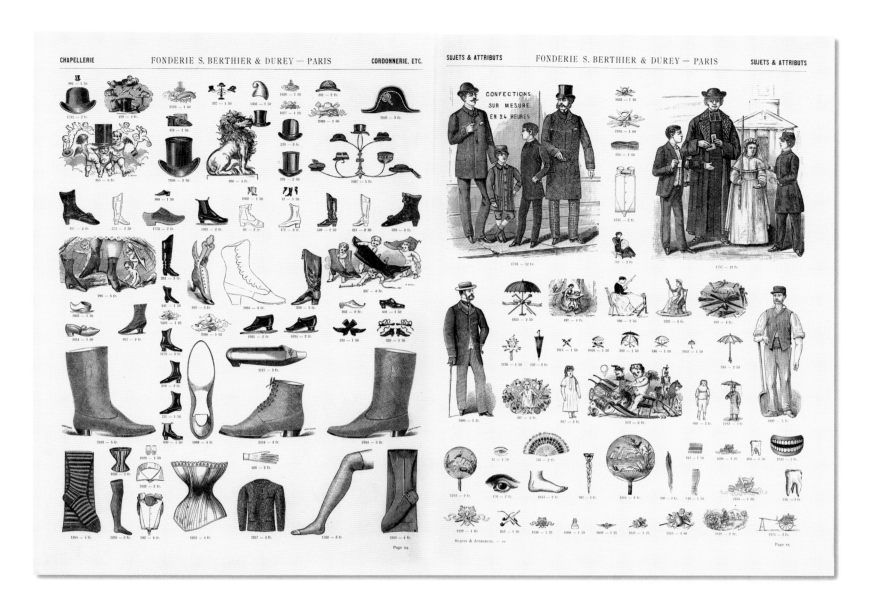

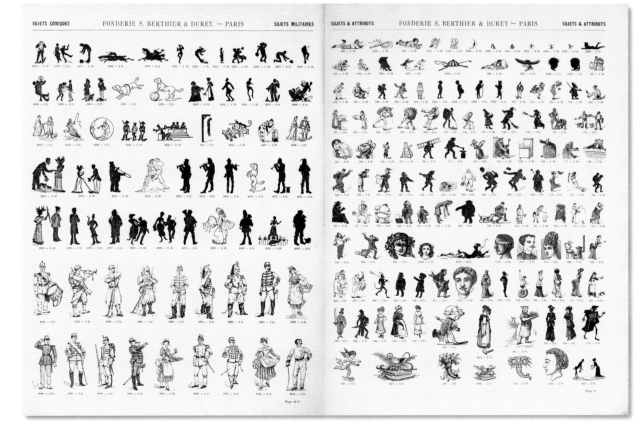

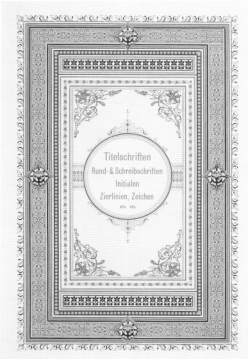

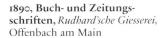

1890, Buch- und Zeitungs-schriften, *Rudhard'sche Giesserei,* Offenbach am Main

An abundance of beautiful newspaper headlines and book titles. In 1892, Carl Klingspor acquired Rudhard'sche Giesserei in Offenbach am Main. He conferred the administration on his son Karl, who managed the firm with his brother Wilhelm from 1895 on. In 1906, the foundry's name was changed to Gebrüder Klingspor to reflect the brothers' ownership.

Eine Fülle an herrlichen Zeitungsüber-schriften und Titeln – viel zu viele und viel zu schöne, um sich entscheiden zu können. 1892 hatte Carl Klingspor die Rudhard'sche Giesserei in Offenbach am Main erworben. Die Verwaltung über-trug er seinem Sohn Karl, der das Unter-nehmen ab 1895 gemeinsam mit seinem Bruder Wilhelm führte. Von 1906 an firmierte es unter dem Namen Gebrüder Klingspor.

Une quantité de magnifiques gros titres de journaux et titres de livres. En 1892, Carl Klingspor acheta la fonderie Rud-hard'sche Giesserei à Offenbach-sur-le-Main. Il en confia la gestion à son fils Karl qui dirigea la firme avec son frère Wilhelm à partir de 1895. En 1906, la fonderie devint la Gebrüder Klingspor pour refléter le partenariat des deux frères.

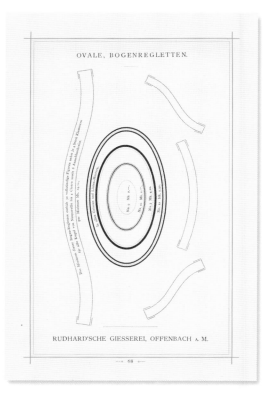

CIRCULAIR-SCHRIFTEN.

Preise nach Tabelle C, Colonne 10 des Preis-Courantes.

No. 978. Garmond (10 Punkte). Min. 5 Kilo. No. 979. Cicero (12 Punkte). Min. 6 Kilo.

Auf die Verschiedenheit der
Zwecke, welchen das Gewerbe
der Buchdruckerei dient, gründet
sich Prosperität derselben.

Von allen Ländern der
Welt erzeugt Italien infolge
der geographischen Lage
und klimatischen

No. 980. Cicero (12 Punkte). Min. 6 Kilo.

Werthere Leiden Die Franzosen in Tonking
Pauvre jeune idolâtre, s'écria-t-elle, tu me fais réellement pitie
123 Socialpolitik der Gegenwart 456

EXTENDED-CURSIV.

Preise nach Tabelle C, Colonne 10 des Preis-Courantes.

No. 997. Garmond (10 Punkte). Min. 6 Kilo.

Bei dem Satz von guten Accidenzen hat
meistens die Phantasie mitzuwirken, weil es sich
dabei um richtige Anwendung des

No. 998. Cicero (12 Punkte). Min. 6 Kilo.

Bei dem Satz von guten Accidenzen hat
meistens die Phantasie mitzuwirken, weil
es sich dabei um richtige Auswahl

No. 999. Tertia (16 Punkte). Min. 8 Kilo.

Turn- und Fecht-Club
2 UNTERRICHTS-MITTEL
Gabelsberger Stenographie

No. 1000 a. Text (20 Punkte). Min. 9 Kilo.

Buch- und Steindruckfarben
PHILIPPI BEIT

RUDHARD'SCHE GIESSEREI, OFFENBACH A. M.

VERZIERTE ITALIENNE-CURSIV.

Preise nach Tabelle C, Colonne 9 des Preis-Courantes.

No. 646. Petit (8 Punkte). Min. 5 Kilo. No. 647. Garmond (10 Punkte). Min. 6 Kilo.

Panorama von Freudenberg und Umgegend
Alexander von Humboldt Kölner Dombau-Loose
Um ihr Haupt reiht sich die Familie

Ansichten von der Sächsischen Schweiz
Die Zerstörung der Tuilerien in Paris 1871
Der Corrector in der Thurmstube

No. 648. Cicero (12 Punkte). Min. 6 Kilo.

Die Botschaft hör' ich wohl, allein mir fehlt der Glaube
Die Rache ist keine Zierde für eine grosse Seele

No. 649. Tertia (16 Punkte). Min. 7 Kilo.

Anistenes, der Stifter der cynischen Secte, war zu

No. 650. Text (20 Punkte). Min. 8 Kilo.

Schriftgiesserei Rudhard, Offenbach a. M.

No. 651. Doppelmittel (28 Punkte). Min. 10 Kilo.

Mittelrheinisches Turnfest 1890

ZIERSCHRIFTEN.

Preise nach Tabelle C, Colonne 13 des Preis-Courantes.

No. 428 a. Tertia (16 Punkte). Min. 3 Kilo.

SCHATTENBILDER EHRENZEICHEN MARIENBURG ARABER

No. 423 a. Text (20 Punkte). Min. 4 Kilo.

12345 ERINNERUNGS-BLÄTTER LUTHER-DENKMAL ZU 67890
WORMS SCHLACHT BEI KÖNIGSGRÄTZ

RUDHARD'SCHE GIESSEREI, OFFENBACH A. M.

ZIERSCHRIFTEN.

Preise nach Tabelle C, Colonne 13 des Preis-Courantes.

No. 230. Petit (8 Punkte). Min. 1½ Kilo. No. 409. Cicero (12 Punkte). Min. 6 Kilo.

HERMANNSSCHLACHT
ORIGINALKREIDEZEICHNUNGEN
HELDENTHATEN

Sommernachtstraum
PANTOMIME

No. 430. Mittel (14 Punkte). Min. 7 Kilo.

Eintritts-Karte Preciosa Stiftungs-Fest
ORANGERIE PALMENGARTEN

No. 431. Tertia (16 Punkte). Min. 7 Kilo.

ST. GOTTHARDT-BAHN BASEL
Exposition universelle à Paris Louvre

No. 432. Text (20 Punkte). Min. 8 Kilo.

Der Liebe Lenz Töchteralbum
DECORATIONS-MALER

No. 226. Text (20 Punkte). Min. 3 Kilo.

MONUMENTALE BAUTEN
DICHTERGRUSS

No. 153. 2 Cicero (24 Punkte). Min. 3 Kilo.

HOTEL GOLDENE ROSE
MANNHEIM

No. 122. 2 Cicero (24 Punkte). Min. 4 Kilo.

NIBELUNGEN-RING
2 WALKÜRE 4

RUDHARD'SCHE GIESSEREI, OFFENBACH A. M.

ZIERSCHRIFTEN.

Preise nach Tabelle C, Colonne 13 des Preis-Courantes.

No. 133. Mittel (14 Punkte). Min. 2 Kilo. No. 235. Tertia (16 Punkte). Min. 2 Kilo.

BARCELONA HEIDELBERG
DIE HUGENOTTEN

REGENSBURG IN BAYERN
NORDAMERIKA

No. 362. Cicero (12 Punkte). Min. 2 Kilo.

GUTENBERG-DENKMAL IN FRANKFURT
INDUSTRIE- UND HANDELS-BANK

No. 216. Cicero (12 Punkte). Min. 2 Kilo.

GIESSEREI RUDHARD, OFFENBACH
REGENSBURG AMBERG

No. 238. Text (20 Punkte). Min. 3 Kilo.

CHOPIN RICHARD WAGNER MOZART
HERMANN UND DOROTHEA

No. 224. Text (20 Punkte). Min. 3 Kilo.

ARIADNE AUF NAXOS
REGENSBURG

No. 220. 2 Cicero (24 Punkte). Min. 4 Kilo.

HANAUER ACTIEN-BRAUEREI
NATHAN DER WEISE

No. 227. 2 Cicero (24 Punkte). Min. 4 Kilo.

RECHNUNG MEMORANDUM
TANZUNTERRICHT

RUDHARD'SCHE GIESSEREI, OFFENBACH A. M.

ZIERSCHRIFTEN.

Preise nach Tabelle C, Colonne 13 des Preis-Courantes.

No. 233. Cicero (12 Punkte). Min. 9 Kilo.   No. 234. Cicero (12 Punkte). Min. 2 Kilo.

AUCH DAS UNSCHEINBARE   KUNSTAUSSTELLUNG ZU
29 HAT BEDEUTUNG 48   BRAUNSCHWEIG

No. 256. Tertia (16 Punkte). Min. 3 Kilo.

MALERISCHE GEGENDEN
AN DER DONAU

No. 129. Text (20 Punkte). Min. 4 Kilo.

DAS BUCH DER NATUR LIEGT SEIT
239 JAHRTAUSENDEN 571

No. 217. Tertia (16 Punkte). Min. 3 Kilo.   No. 218. Tertia (16 Punkte). Min. 3 Kilo.

BERLIN MONARCHIE   DAS TREUE HERZ
NORD-AMERIKA   LIEDERHAIN

No. 224. 2 Cicero (24 Punkte). Min. 3 Kilo.

CONCERT JUBEL-FEIER THEATER

No. 208. 2 Cicero (24 Punkte). Min. 8 Kilo.

Schiller 3 Rom 8 Lessing

No. 357. 3 Cicero (36 Punkte). Min. 5 Kilo.

KOMPONIST

No. 242. 3 Cicero (36 Punkte). Min. 5 Kilo.

MOSKAU AMBERG

RUDHARD'SCHE GIESSEREI, OFFENBACH A. M.

— 118 —

ZIERSCHRIFTEN.

Preise nach Tabelle C, Colonne 13 des Preis-Courantes.

No. 1131. Cicero (12 Punkte). Min. 3 Kilo.

ROM LESSING SCHILLER EMS
BERG THEATER-VERBAND THAL
891 KONSTANTINOPEL 180

No. 1132. Tertia (16 Punkte). Min. 4 Kilo.

HOTEL GOLDENER ADLER
3 MEMORANDUM 4

No. 1133. 2 Cicero (24 Punkte). Min. 5 Kilo.

27 MONUMENTE 51

No. 1134. 3 Cicero (36 Punkte). Min. 5 Kilo.

8 WECHSEL 5

No. 1135. 1½ Cicero (18 Punkte). Min. 8 Kilo.

RHEIN DONAU MAIN
SALAMANDER

No. 1136. 2 Cicero (24 Punkte). Min. 5 Kilo.

BLUMEN REIGEN
PROGRAMM

No. 1137. 3 Cicero (36 Punkte). Min. 6 Kilo.

M URANUS K

RUDHARD'SCHE GIESSEREI, OFFENBACH A. M.

— 119 —

ZIERSCHRIFTEN.

Preise nach Tabelle C, Colonne 13 des Preis-Courantes.

No. 75. Tertia (16 Punkte). Min. 8 Kilo.

Damen-Garderobe-Magazin
Mannheim 48 Preis-Liste 92 Darmstadt
Museum in Dresden

No. 207. 4 Cicero (48 Punkte). Min. 14 Kilo.

2 Barcelona 8

No. 381. Text (20 Punkte). Min. 8 Kilo.

623 Schwerin Stralsund Triest 145

No. 384. Doppelmittel (28 Punkte). Min. 9 Kilo.

47 Regensburg Würzburg 56

No. 387. Kleine Kanon (32 Punkte). Min. 10 Kilo.

3 Hessische Ludwigsbahn 5

No. 401. 4 Cicero (48 Punkte). Min. 15 Kilo.

Romeo und Julia

RUDHARD'SCHE GIESSEREI, OFFENBACH A. M.

— 120 —

ZIERSCHRIFTEN.

Preise nach Tabelle C, Colonne 13 des Preis-Courantes.

No. 406. Tertia (16 Punkte). Min. 7 Kilo.

Frühjahrsversammlung im landwirthschaftlichen
Bezirksverein Frankfurt

No. 388. 2 Cicero (24 Punkte). Min. 8 Kilo.

London Petersburg Berlin Emden

No. 290. Doppelmittel (28 Punkte). Min. 9 Kilo.

Niederrhein Welle Ankerkette

No. 291. Kleine Kanon (32 Punkte). Min. 11 Kilo.

Zeus Mittelfranken Amor

No. 354. 2 Cicero (24 Punkte). Min. 8 Kilo.

Bruchsal Magdeburg Genf

No. 355. Grosse Kanon (40 Punkte). Min. 12 Kilo.

Frankfurt Main

No. 607. 2 Cicero (24 Punkte). Min. 9 Kilo.

Mailand Wien Florenz

No. 608. 3 Cicero (36 Punkte). Min. 10 Kilo.

Merseburg Rom

RUDHARD'SCHE GIESSEREI, OFFENBACH A. M.

— 121 —

No. 358. 9½ Cicero. à 40 Pfg.

No. 39. 6½ Cicero. Fette Antiqua. à 25 Pfg.

Bomb

No. 350. 16 Cicero. à 50 Pfg.

No. 37. 9 Cicero. Fette Antiqua. à 30 Pfg.

Mut

No. 347. 8 Cicero. Egyptienne. à 25 Pfg.

MAST

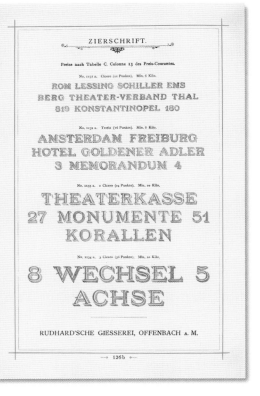

MEDIAEVAL-ANTIQUA U. -CURSIV.

3 Cicero (36 Punkte) No. 361.

Marie Humbert Laura

Laura Deutschland *Marie*

78 Ball HEBEL Fest 59

3 Cicero (36 Punkte) No. 362.

Schiller Lessing Goethe

Briefe aus Italien

RUDHARD'SCHE GIESSEREI, OFFENBACH A. M.

— 32 —

HALBFETTE KANZLEI

Preise nach Tabelle C. Colonne 3 des Preis-Courantes.

No. 409. Nonpareille (6 Punkte). Min. 4 Kilo.
Die Mode ist keine Zierde für eine große Seele
Verschwiegenheit ist eine der vornehmsten Tugenden
210 Band für Handel und Industrie 436

No. 410. Petit (8 Punkte). Min. 5 Kilo.
Keine Großmuth will mit Zingern ge-
wiesen sein Victor von Scheffel's Gedichte
5 Weinfelden Frauenfeld Zürich 6

No. 411. Garmond (10 Punkte). Min. 6 Kilo.
Naturwissenschaftliche Studien
Heribert Rau's sämtliche Gedichte
Die Forstwirthschaft

No. 411. Cicero (12 Punkte). Min. 6 Kilo.
Zeitschrift für Geflügelzucht
Agentur u. Speditionsgeschäft
Luftkurort Königstein

No. 413. Mittel (14 Punkte). Min. 7 Kilo.
Elektrotechnische Ausstellung zu Frankfurt a. M. 1891
Die Ereignisse in Bulgarien Tägliche Rundschau

No. 414. Tertia (16 Punkte). Min. 8 Kilo.
Durch Kampf zum Sieg Abend-Unterhaltung
3 Beschreibung der Erlebnisse in Afrika 5

No. 415. Text (20 Punkte). Min. 9 Kilo.
Hero und Leander Gerichtliche Anzeigen
33 Bycicle-Club zu Potsdam 76

No. 416. Doppelmittel (28 Punkte). Min. 10 Kilo.
9 Mittelrheinisches Turnfest 7
Ariadne auf Naxos

No. 417. 3 Cicero (36 Punkte). Min. 11 Kilo.
Schriftgießerei Rudhard

RUDHARD'SCHE GIESSEREI, OFFENBACH A. M.

— 50 —

ZIERSCHRIFT.

Preise nach Tabelle C. Colonne 13 des Preis-Courantes.

No. 1131 a. Cicero (12 Punkte). Min. 6 Kilo.
ROM LESSING SCHILLER EMS
BERG THEATER-VERBAND THAL
819 KONSTANTINOPEL 180

No. 1131 a. Tertia (16 Punkte). Min. 8 Kilo.
AMSTERDAM FREIBURG
HOTEL GOLDENER ADLER
3 MEMORANDUM 4

No. 1133 a. 2 Cicero (24 Punkte). Min. 10 Kilo.
THEATERKASSE
27 MONUMENTE 51
KORALLEN

No. 1134 a. 3 Cicero (36 Punkte). Min. 10 Kilo.
8 WECHSEL 5
ACHSE

RUDHARD'SCHE GIESSEREI, OFFENBACH A. M.

— 126b —

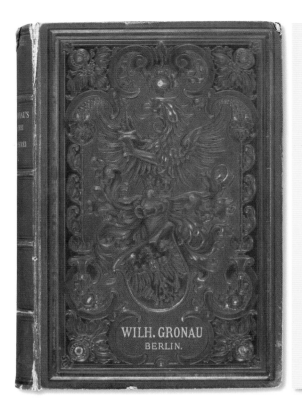

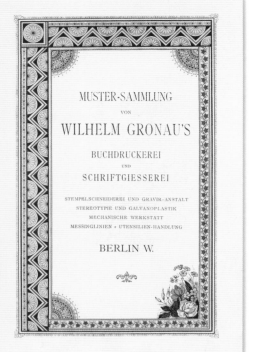

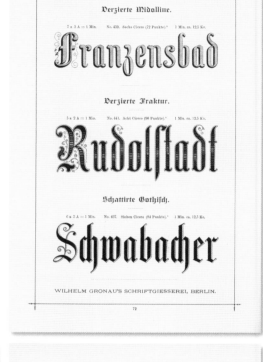

1891, Muster-Sammlung,
Buchdruckerei und Schriftgiesserei
Wilhelm Gronau, Berlin

Large and small type sizes, indicated
in ciceros and points.

Große und kleine Schriftgrade,
angegeben in Cicero und Punkten.

Des tailles de caractères, petites et
grandes, définies en cicero et en points.

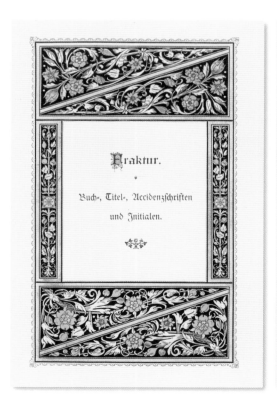

5 A = 1 Min. No. 428. Drei Cicero (36 Punkte). 1 Min. ca. 6 Ko.

RHEIN

4 A = 1 Min. No. 33. Grobe Canon (44 Punkte). 1 Min. ca. 5 Ko.

MINISTER

4 A = 1 Min. No. 236. Sechs Cicero (72 Punkte). 1 Min. ca. 7,5 Ko.

MERINO

7 A = 1 Min. No. 22. Vier Cicero (48 Punkte). 1 Min. ca. 7 Ko.

BUCHBINDER

Altgothische Initialen.

Sämmtliche fünf Grade werden für einfarbigen oder zweifarbigen Druck geliefert.

Zweiunddreissigste Sorte. No. 769. Text (20 Punkte).*

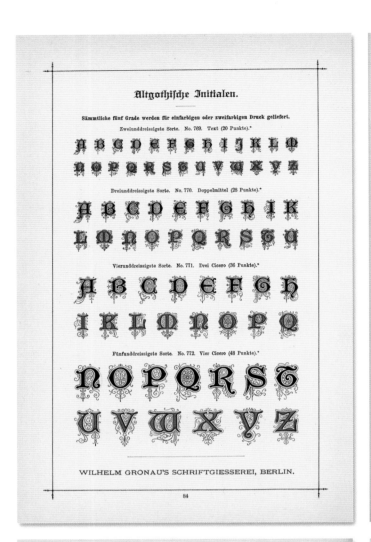

Dreiunddreissigste Sorte. No. 770. Doppelmittel (28 Punkte).*

Vierunddreissigste Sorte. No. 771. Drei Cicero (36 Punkte).*

Fünfunddreissigste Sorte. No. 772. Vier Cicero (48 Punkte).*

WILHELM GRONAU'S SCHRIFTGIESSEREI, BERLIN.

84

Altgothische Initialen.

Sechsunddreissigste Sorte. No. 773. Sechs Cicero (72 Punkte).*

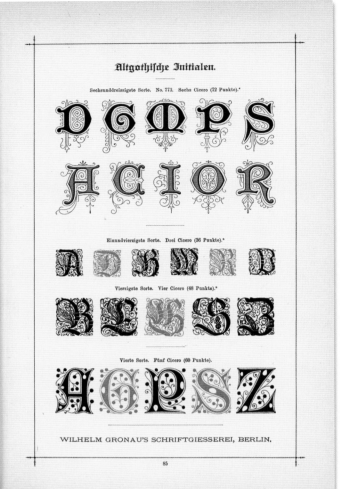

Einundvierzigste Sorte. Drei Cicero (36 Punkte).*

Vierzigste Sorte. Vier Cicero (48 Punkte).*

Vierte Sorte. Fünf Cicero (60 Punkte).*

WILHELM GRONAU'S SCHRIFTGIESSEREI, BERLIN.

85

Altgothische Versalien.

Petit (8 Punkte).*

A B C D E F Gewinnliste Programm Mittheilung N O U W X Z
Lyon Regensburg Kreuznach Tübingen Stockholm Hamm

Corpus (10 Punkte).*

Gunzenhausen Breslau H I K L M N O Forbach Constantinopel
Stiftungsfest der Berliner Turnerschaft, Corporation

Cicero (12 Punkte).*

A B C D Telegramm Menu Fahrschein S U W Z

Tertia (16 Punkte).*

Linz Hamburg M N O P Arnheim Rom

Text (20 Punkte).*

E K M Dresden London N Q U

Doppelmittel (28 Punkte).*

Stolp B F K P Z Gotha

Drei Cicero (36 Punkte).*

G M Adolphine W S

Vier Cicero (48 Punkte).*

Arad Wien R

WILHELM GRONAU'S SCHRIFTGIESSEREI, BERLIN.

86

Verzierte Initialen.

Sechsundzwanzigste Sorte. No. 3315—3339.*

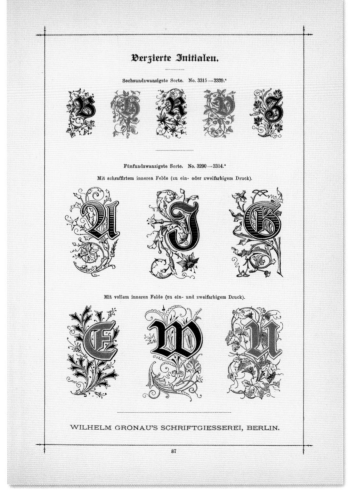

Fünfundzwanzigste Sorte. No. 3290—3314.*
Mit schraffirtem inneren Felde (zu ein- oder zweifarbigem Druck).

Mit vollem inneren Felde (zu ein- und zweifarbigem Druck).

WILHELM GRONAU'S SCHRIFTGIESSEREI, BERLIN.

87

1891, Muster-Sammlung,
*Buchdruckerei und Schriftgiesserei
Wilhelm Gronau*, Berlin

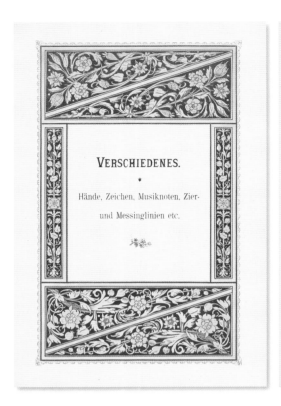

WILHELM GRONAU'S SCHRIFTGIESSEREI, BERLIN.

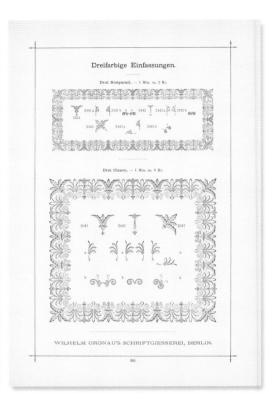

WILHELM GRONAU'S SCHRIFTGIESSEREI, BERLIN.

1891, Muster-Sammlung,
Buchdruckerei und Schriftgiesserei
Wilhelm Gronau, Berlin

2649 (Auch Polnisch vorhanden.)

2766

2991

3375
(Auch Schwedisch und Dänisch vorhanden.)

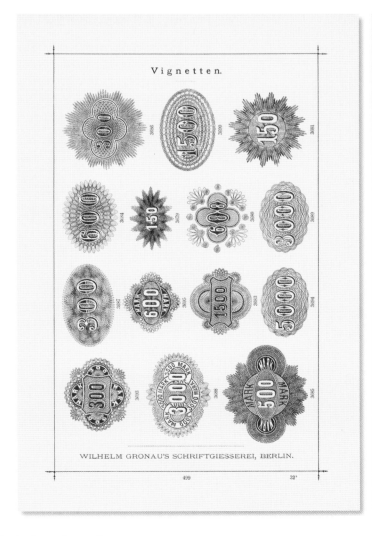

Vignetten.

WILHELM GRONAU'S SCHRIFTGIESSEREI, BERLIN.

Vignetten.

ACTIE
3123

ACTIE
3124

ACTIE
3130

ACTIE
3128

ACTIE
3129

ACTIE
3131

ACTIE
3126

WILHELM GRONAU'S SCHRIFTGIESSEREI, BERLIN.

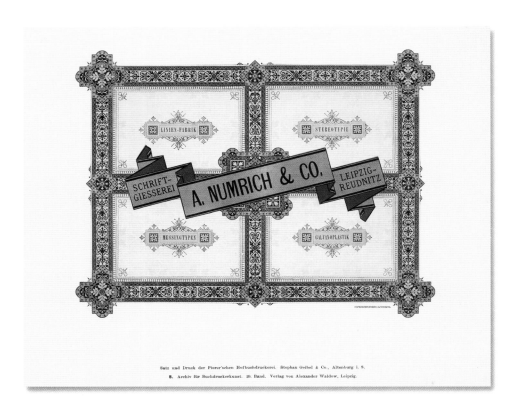

1892, Archiv für Buchdruckerkunst, 29. Band, Heft 2, *Alexander Waldow,* Leipzig

This sample highlights diverse fantasy typefaces and ornaments.

Highlights unterschiedlicher Zierschriften und -ornamente.

Cet échantillon met l'accent sur divers caractères et ornements fantaisie.

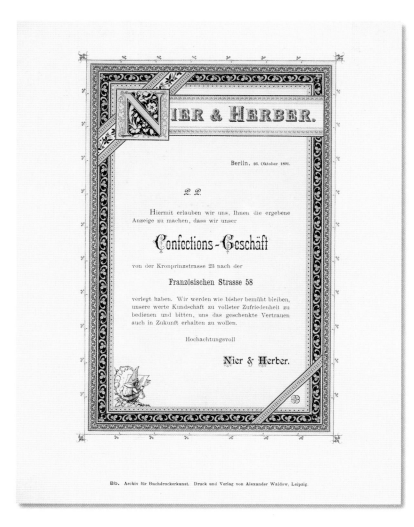

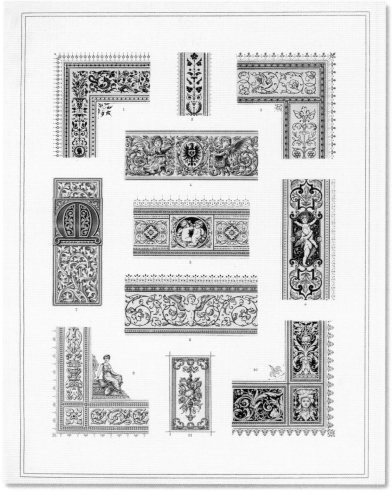

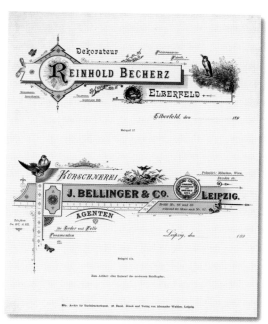

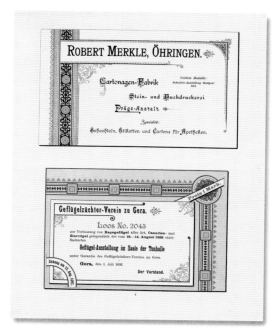

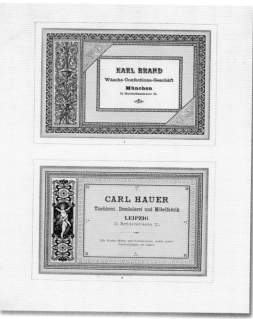

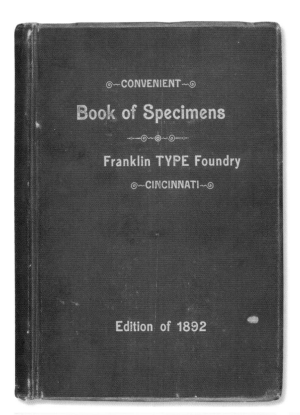

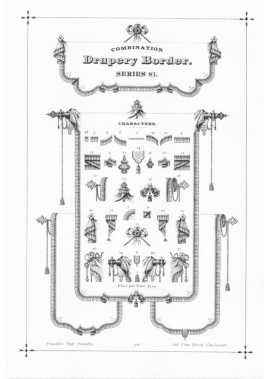

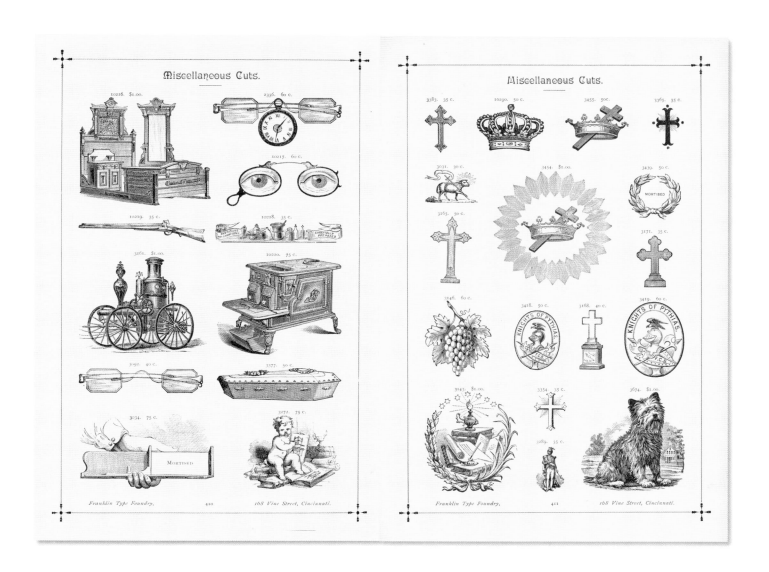

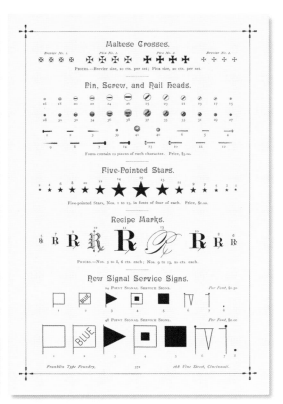

14 A. 18 Point Relievo, No. 2.—*Great Primer.* $3.70

10 A. 24 Point Relievo, No. 2.—*2 line Pica.* $4.55

5 A. 40 Point Relievo, No. 2.—*Double Paragon.* $6.30

24 POINT RELIEVO.—*2 line Pica.* $4.80

5 A.   36 POINT RELIEVO.—*2 line Great Primer.* $5.35

24 POINT AND 36 POINT RELIEVO IN COMBINATION.

Franklin Type Foundry,   223   *168 Vine Street, Cincinnati.*

Department Headings.

No. 19. 50 C.

No. 20. 50 C.

No. 21. 50 C.

No. 22. 50 C.

No. 23. 50 C.

No. 24. 50 C.

No. 25. 50 C.

No. 26. 50 C.

No. 27. 50 C.

No. 28. 50 C.

No. 29. 50 C.

No. 30. 50 C.

No. 31. 50 C.

No. 32. 50 C.

No. 33. 50 C.

No. 34. 50 C.

These "department headings" could be
used to catalog content into different
groups: religious news, poetry, Masonic …

Rubrizierungen wie die hier abgebildeten
ließen sich zum Ordnen verschiedener
Inhalte verwenden: Religiöses, Nachrich-
ten, Dichtung, Logentum …

Ces « têtes de rubrique » pouvaient être
utilisées pour répertorier le contenu
selon différents groupes : nouvelles
religieuses, poésie, franc-maçonnerie…

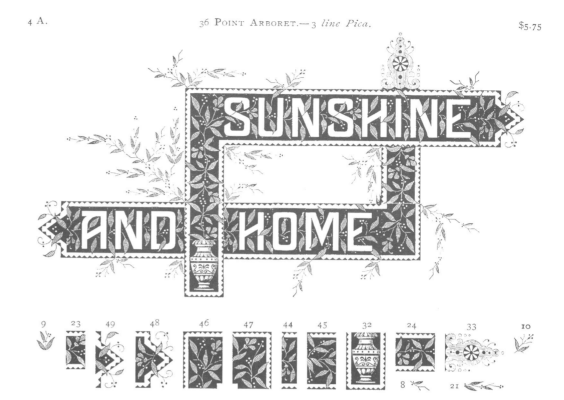

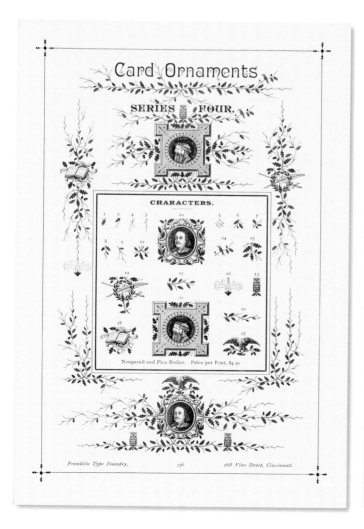

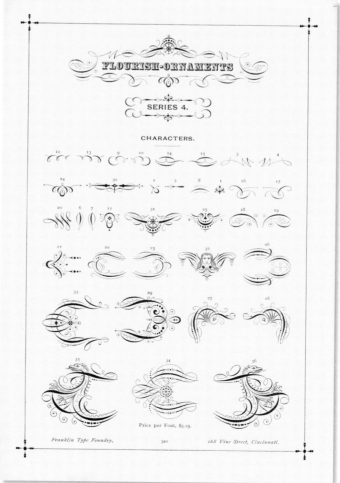

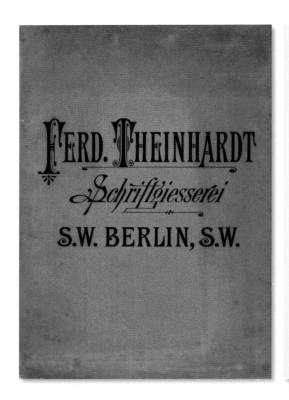

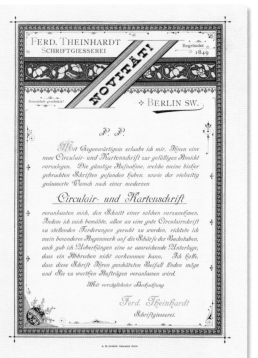

1892, Proben,
Schriftgiesserei Ferd. Theinhardt, Berlin

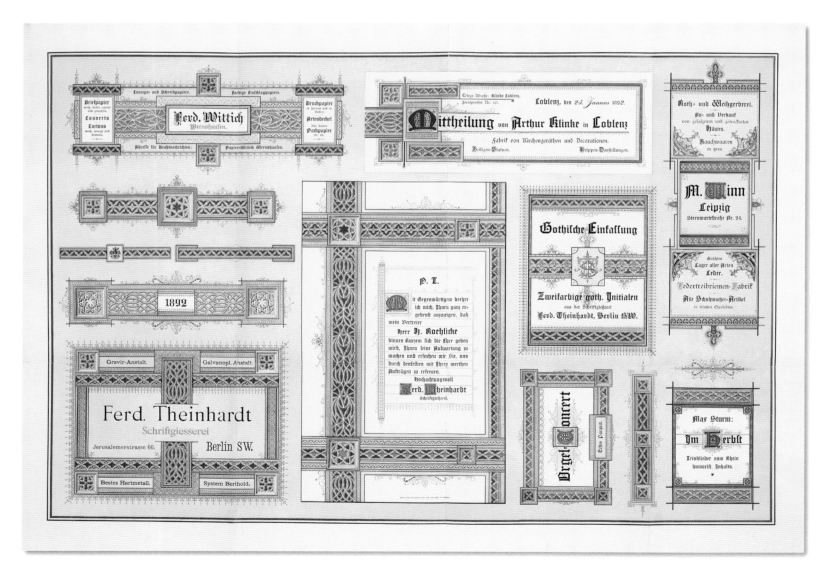

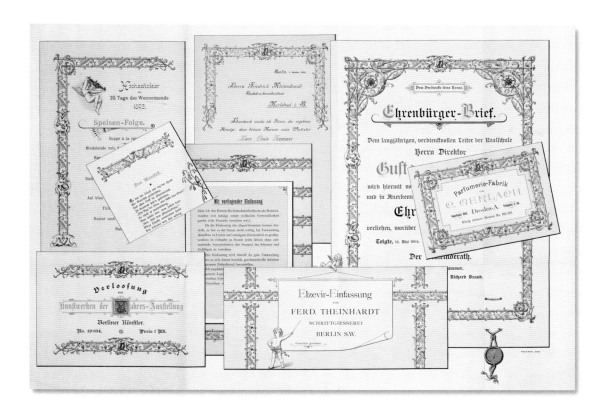

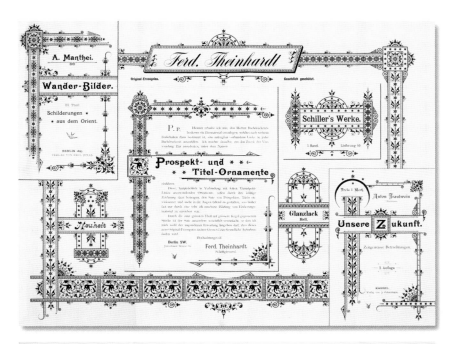

There was no lack of craftsmanship or creativity in Berlin. Ferdinand Theinhardt was a German typographer, Orientalist, and "Royal Prussian Type Designer." He created the Royal Grotesk in four font styles and made the Grotesk socially acceptable in Berlin. In 1908, the H. Berthold AG foundry absorbed the Ferd. Theinhardt Schriftgießerei, and in 1918 the Royal Grotesk was sold under the name Akzidenz Grotesk.

An Kreativität und Kunstfertigkeit herrschte in Berlin kein Mangel. Der deutsche Typograf, Orientalist und „Königlich-Preußische Schriftentwerfer" Ferdinand Theinhardt entwarf seine Royal-Grotesk in vier verschiedenen Schriftschnitten und machte damit die Grotesk in Berlin salonfähig. 1908 wurde die Schriftgießerei Ferd. Theinhardt in die H. Berthold AG integriert, welche die Royal Grotesk ab 1918 als Teil der Akzidenz-Grotesk-Familie vertrieb.

L'art et la créativité n'étaient pas en reste à Berlin. Ferdinand Theinhardt était un typographe allemand, orientaliste et « graveur de caractères de la Prusse royale ». Il grava le Royal-Grotesk dans quatre styles de fontes de caractères et rendit le Grotesque socialement acceptable à Berlin. En 1908, la fonderie H. Berthold AG absorba la Schriftgießerei Ferd. Theinhardt et, en 1918, le Royal-Grotesk était vendu sous le nom d'Akzidenz Grotesk.

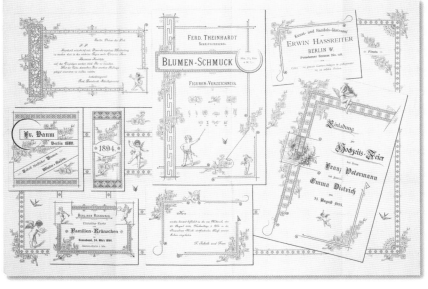

Original-Erzeugniss.　　　　　　　　Gesetzlich geschützt.

Figuren-Verzeichniss der Italienischen Einfassung.

Kleines Minimum:	Grosses Minimum:
zweifarbig: 30 Pfd. à Pfd. Mk. 3,50.	zweifarbig: 50 Pfd. à Pfd. Mk. 3,50.
dreifarbig: 45 Pfd. à Pfd. Mk. 3,50.	dreifarbig: 75 Pfd. à Pfd. Mk. 3,50.

1 a b　　2 a b　　3 a b　　4 a b

5 a b　　6 a b　　7 a b　　8 a b

9 a b　　10 a b　　11 a b　　12 a b　　13 a b

14 a b　　15 a b　　20 a b　　16 a b　　17 a b

18 a b　　19 a b　　21 a b　　22 a b　　23 a b　　24 a b

25 a b　　26 a b　　27 a b　　28 a b　　29 a b　　30 a b

Ferd. Theinhardt, Schriftgiesserei.

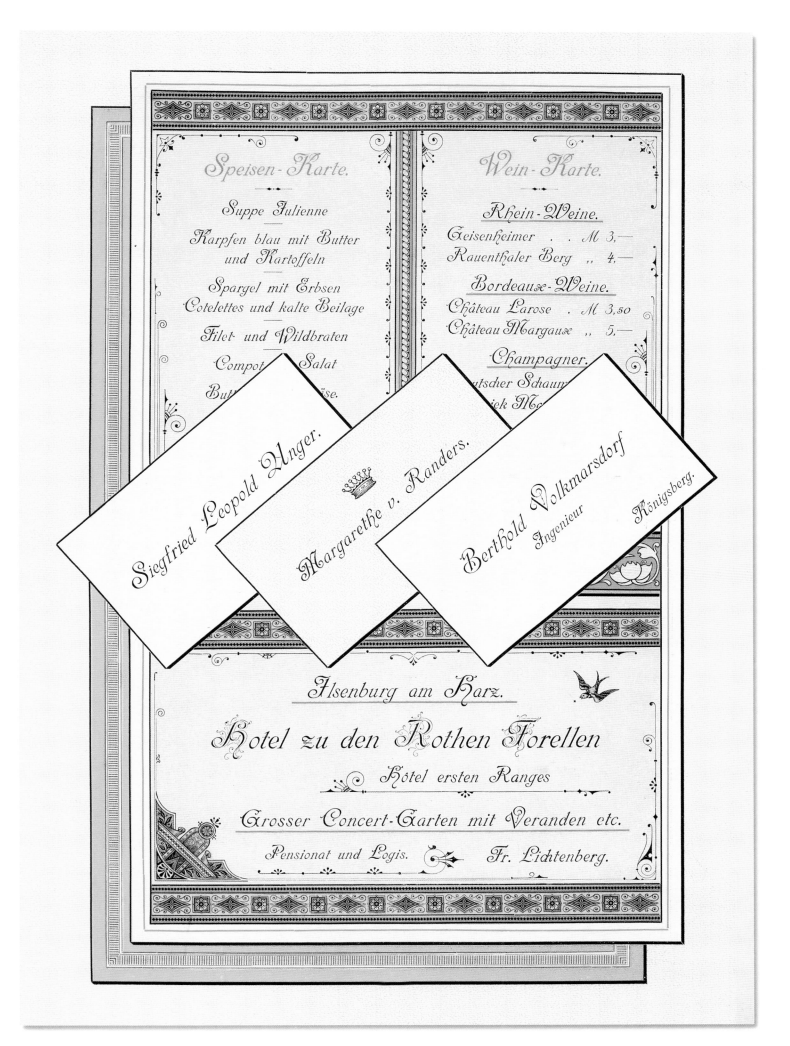

Speisen-Karte.

Suppe Julienne

Karpfen blau mit Butter
und Kartoffeln

Spargel mit Erbsen
Cotelettes und kalte Beilage

Filet- und Wildbraten

Compot   Salat

Butt   äse.

Wein-Karte.

Rhein-Weine.

Geisenheimer . . M 3,—
Rauenthaler Berg ,, 4,—

Bordeaux-Weine.

Château Larose . M 3,50
Château Margaux ,, 5,—

Champagner.

utscher Schaum
iek Ma

Siegfried Leopold Unger.

Margarethe v. Randers.

Berthold Volkmarsdorf
Ingenieur   Königsberg.

Ilsenburg am Harz.

Hotel zu den Rothen Forellen

Hôtel ersten Ranges

Grosser Concert-Garten mit Veranden etc.

Pensionat und Logis.   Fr. Lichtenberg.

1892, Schriftproben, *Aktiengesellschaft für Schriftgiesserei und Maschinenbau,* Offenbach

The title page of this 19th-Century type specimen offered a variety of Neoclassical styles.

Die Haupttitelseite dieses Schriftmusters aus den 1890er-Jahren präsentiert sich mit gleich mehreren neoklassizistischen Schriftarten.

La page de titre de ce spécimen de caractères du XIXe siècle offrait une variété de styles néo-classiques.

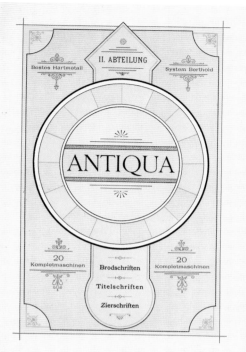

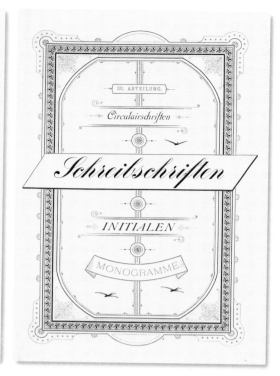

Monogramme.

Serie II.

AKTIENGESELLSCHAFT FÜR SCHRIFTGIESSEREI UND MASCHINENBAU
OFFENBACH AM MAIN.

246

1892, Schriftproben, *Aktiengesellschaft für Schriftgiesserei und Maschinenbau,* Offenbach

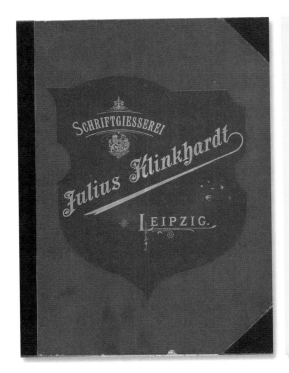

1893, Proben, *Schriftgiesserei Julius Klinkhardt,* Leipzig

Klinkhardt's samples always have their own signature, which makes them immediately recognizable.

Die einzelnen Seiten der Klinkhardt-Muster waren problemlos zuzuordnen, da sie stets den Namenszug der Gießerei trugen.

Les échantillons de Klinkhardt possèdent toujours leur propre signature qui les rend immédiatement reconnaissables.

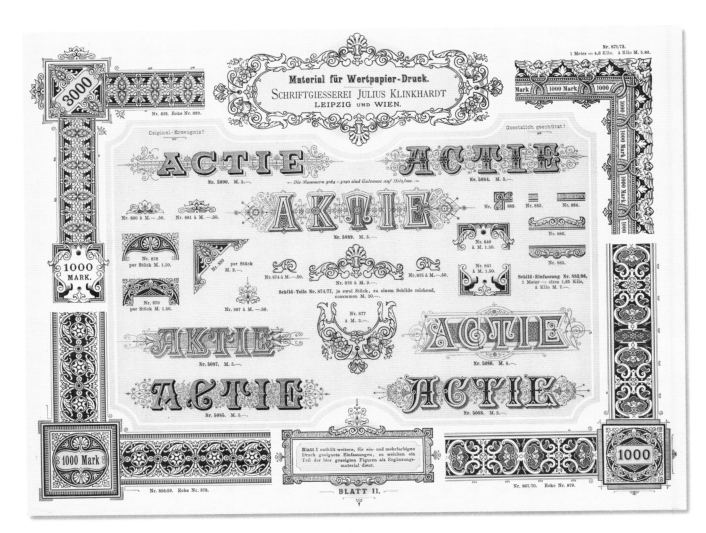

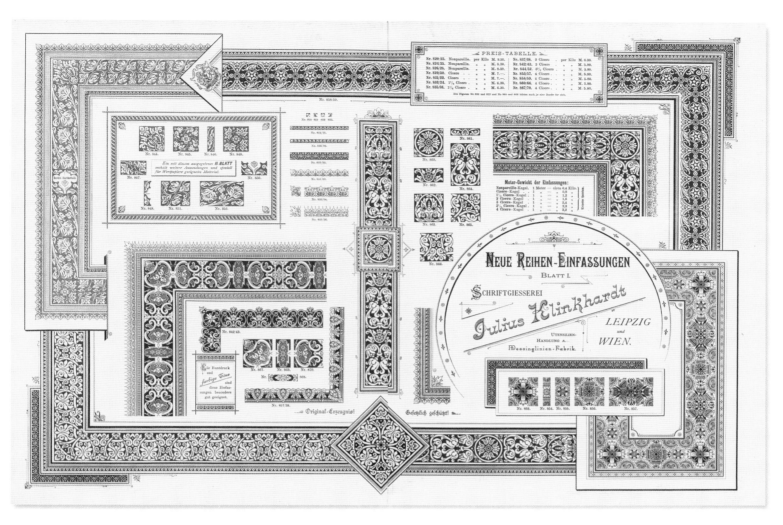

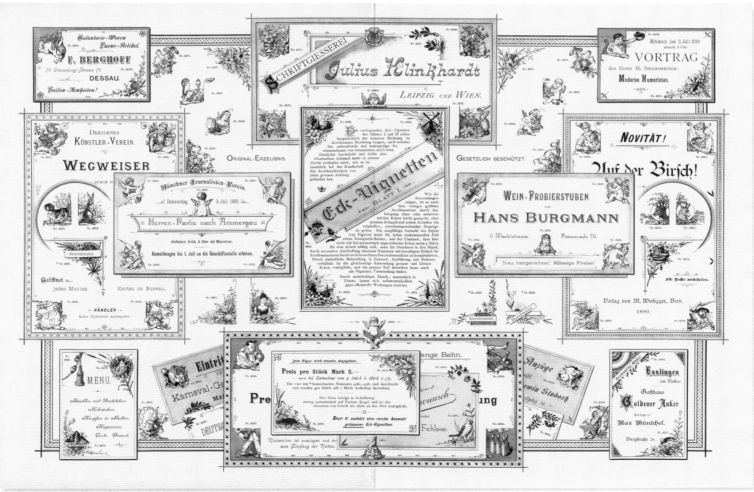

Mikado-Dekoration

Schriftgiesserei Julius Klinkhardt

Leipzig · Wien

Extrafeine Pfirsich-Seife
Preis pro Stück
10 Pfennige.

NOVITÄT

Paul Raisa

Galant...

sowie

Figuren, Attrappen...
etc. etc.

Meining...

Lindenstrasse 66, Ecke der Wi...

BALL-ORDNUNG.
Polonaise
Walzer
Quadrille à la cour
Polka

PAUSE.

Rheinländer
Française
Walzer
Galopp

Keine Extra-Touren!

KUNST-HANDLUNG

GEGRÜNDET
1840.

VICTOR BERENDS

Dom-Strasse 46

FRANKFURT AM MAIN.

Geschäft

Abteilung für JAPAN-WAREN.

Reimann & Kröner

...strasse, Ecke der Mohrenstrasse. BERLIN W.

TELEPHON 2216 Amt I.

Heinrich Schmid

LEIPZIG

Spezial-Geschäft für

Chinesische Thees

japanische Lackwaren

etc.

Im fernen Osten

Reisebilder.

WIEN und MÜNCHEN, Verlag von Feodor Ackermann.

MENU

Austern-Suppe
Roastbeef à la Jardinière
Kapaun mit Kompot
Rheinlachs
Pfirsich-Auflauf
Dessert.

Herzlichen Glückwunsch

zum

Jahreswechsel!

...Waren

Chocoladen
Thee, Cacaos
Waffeln
aus der FABRIK
Hartwig & Vogel.

SCHUTZ-MARKE.

SERIE 69

Min. 8 Ko. à Mark 8.—.

Die mit * bezeichneten Figuren werden auch als Reihen-Einfassungen, jedoch nicht unter 1 Mtr., zum Kilopreise von M. 8.50 für Nonpareille- und M. 7.— für Cicero-Kegel, einzeln abgegeben.

Original-Erzeugnis meines Hauses. Gesetzlich geschützt.

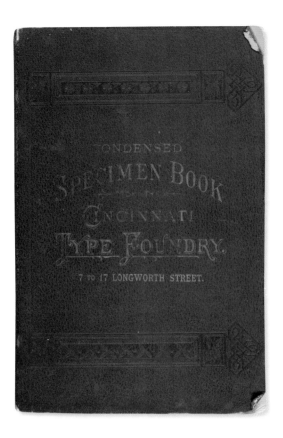

1893, Condensed Specimen Book,
Cincinnati Type Foundry, Cincinnati

This was the foundry's 18th book of
specimens; 17 other specimen books had
previously been issued.

Das hier abgebildete war bereits das
18. Schriftmusterbuch der Cincinnati
Type Foundry.

C'était le dix-huitième ouvrage de
spécimens de caractères de la fonderie;
dix-sept autres avaient déjà été publiés.

SERIES No. 57.
Single Letters, 50 cents; per set of 25 Letters, $6.00.

SERIES No. 58.
Single Letters, 50 cents; per set of 24 Letters, $6.00.

SERIES No. 59.
Single Letters, 40 cents; per set of 25 Letters, with Ornaments, $4.50.

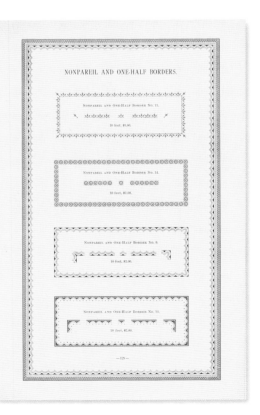

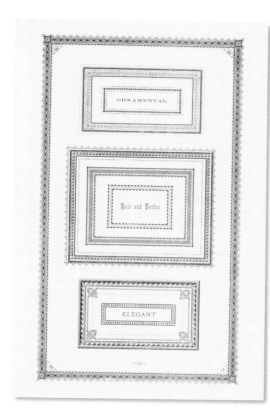

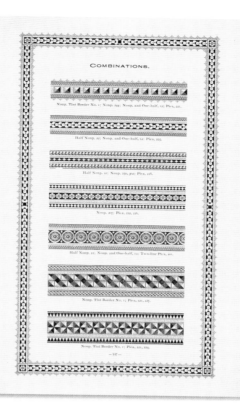

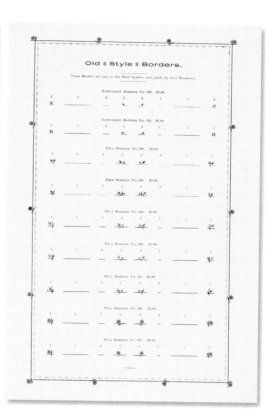

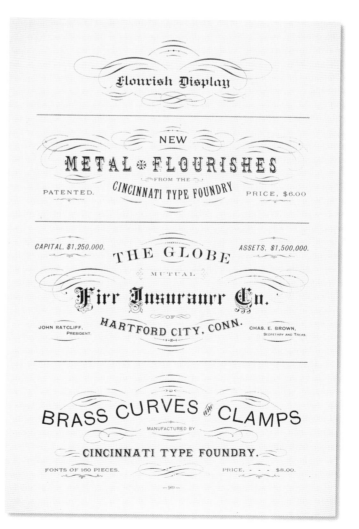

Zweifarbenschrift Alexandra.

SARAGOSSA HEIDELBERG
HABSBURG MEISSEN BRADBURY
HARICH & REIMER
ARCONA VENEDIG
MERAN DENIS REGEN
EMAR & BERIG
ROM HOMER EMS
KISSINGEN

Schriftgiesserei H. Berthold Berlin SW. Messinglinienfabrik.

1894, Probenbuch, *H. Berthold Messing-linienfabrik und Schriftgiesserei,* Berlin

The illustration at the bottom of page 297 shows the work of the Gustav Reinhold type foundry, which was taken over by Berthold AG—the first of a series of numerous strategic company take-overs—one year before this type specimen was produced.

Die Abbildung auf Seite 297 unten zeigt die Arbeit der Gießerei Gustav Reinhold, die ein Jahr vor der Entstehung dieses Musters von der Berthold AG erworben worden war – die erste in einer Reihe von mehreren strategischen Firmenüber-nahmen.

L'illustration de la page 297 en bas montre le travail de la fonderie Gustav Reinhold, rachetée par Berthold AG un an avant la publication de ce spécimen. C'était, pour Berthold AG, le premier d'une série de rachats stratégiques.

Neue Hände.
(Gesetzlich geschützt.)
1 Sortiment No. 40–53 M. 14.—, einzeln à Stück M. 1.50

44

45

Gustav Reinhold

BERLIN.

50

40

Kleider-Magazin
von
Hermann Winkler, Leipzig
Katharinenstrasse 25.

Reichhaltiges Lager aller Bekleidungsgegenstände
für Herren.

Auf Wunsch Anfertigung nach Maass.
• Preise niedrig, aber fest. •

47

46

Der ergebenst Unterzeichnete gestattet sich hiermit, seine verehrlichen Kunden

zur Besichtigung seiner in Anger-Crottendorf, an der Zweinaundorfer Strasse, gelegenen

Rosen-Gärtnerei

49

einzuladen. Dieselbe umfasst alle Sorten von den einfachsten bis zu den edelsten. Gerade

jetzt gewähren die Stöcke, da sie alle in voller Entfaltung stehen, einen reizenden Anblick.

Recht zahlreichem Besuche entgegensehend, zeichne

hochachtungsvoll

Leipzig, den 1. Juli 1890.

J. C. Hanisch.

52

53

48

43

42

51

41

Rokoko-Initialen Serie XXIV (8 Cicero), das Sortiment M. 28.—, einzeln bezogen das Stück M. 1.50.

Rokoko-Initialen Serie XXIII (10 Cicero), das Sortiment M. 35. , einzeln bezogen das Stück M. 2.

Berlin W.
Lützow-Strasse No. 6.

Schriftgiesserei Gustav Reinhold.
(Haussystem Didot.)

Berlin W.
Lützow-Strasse No. 6.

Breite umzogene Italienne.

No. 364. Corpus (Corps 10). Min. 6 Kilo à ½, Kilo Mk. 4.—

Carthäuser Cabale und Liebe Max Geibel
12 NARSDORF PLAU 34

No. 365. Cicero (Corps 12). Min. 6 Kilo à ½, Kilo Mk. 3.80.

Martin Luthers Rede in Worms
34 REICHSTAG 89

No. 366. Tertia (Corps 16). Min. 8 Kilo à ½, Kilo Mk. 3.60.

Kalden Halle Nole Fest
32 MOSES 41

No. 367. Text (Corps 20). Min. 10 Kilo à ½, Kilo Mk. 3.40.

Arcona Galveston
5 MUSEUM 6

No. 368. Doppelmittel (Corps 28). Min. 12 Kilo à ½, Kilo Mk. 3.30.

Trogen Dernis
2 BERN 3

No. 369. Kl. Canon (Corps 32). Min. 12 Kilo à ½, Kilo Mk. 3.20.

Mondhafen
BURG

No. 370. Canon (Corps 36). Min. 14 Kilo à ½, Kilo Mk. 3.00.

Stuttgart
EGER

Zierschriften.

No. 2000. Cicero (Corps 12). Min. 6 Kilo à ½, Kilo Mk. 3.80.

München Geschichte des Kaiserreichs Dresden
234 BREMEN CHEMNITZ 569

No. 2001. Mittel (Corps 14). Min. 7 Kilo à ½, Kilo Mk. 3.60.

Bamberg Griesbach Uttenreuth Zeulenroda

No. 3002. Tertia (Corps 16). Min. 8 Kilo à ½, Kilo Mk. 3.60.

Amerikanische Schiffahrts-Gesellschaft

No. 3003. Text (Corps 20). Min. 10 Kilo à ½, Kilo Mk. 3.40.

Kassel Charlottenburg Hildsbach

No. 3004. Doppelcicero (Corps 24). Min. 10 Kilo à ½, Kilo Mk. 3.35.

Kronstadt Gorze Frankfurt

No. 3005. Doppelmittel (Corps 28). Min. 12 Kilo à ½, Kilo Mk. 3.30.

München Berlin Dresden

No. 510. Tertia (Corps 16). Min. 8 Kilo à ½, Kilo Mk. 3.60.

Kaufmann von Venedig
42 RECHNUNG 83

No. 511. Doppelcicero (Corps 24). Min. 10 Kilo à ½, Kilo Mk. 3.35.

Kursaal von Baden
35 NOTEN 26

No. 512. Kl. Canon (Corps 32). Min. 12 Kilo à ½, Kilo Mk. 3.20.

Bremen Eilsen

No. 500. Text (Corps 20). Min. 10 Kilo à ½, Kilo Mk. 3.40.

Gustav Adolph König von Schweden
23 BUCHDRUCKEREI 45

No. 501. Doppelmittel (Corps 28). Min. 12 Kilo à ½, Kilo Mk. 3.30.

Eisleben Dirnbach Potsdam
23 MERSEBURG 45

No. 502. Canon (Corps 36). Min. 14 Kilo à ½, Kilo Mk. 3.20.

Nordpol-Expedition

No. 503. Kl. Missal (Corps 48). Min. 16 Kilo à ½, Kilo Mk. 2.75.

Eintritts-Karte

No. 413. Mittel (Corps 14). Min. 7 Kilo à ½, Kilo Mk. 3.60.

Die Erstürmung der Düppler Schanze
67 WIESBADEN 98

No. 514. Text (Corps 20). Min. 10 Kilo à ½, Kilo Mk. 3.40.

Glückliche Meerfahrt

No. 515. Doppelmittel (Corps 28). Min. 12 Kilo à ½, Kilo Mk. 3.30.

Eisenach Frankfurt

No. 516. Gr. Canon (Corps 42). Min. 14 Kilo à ½, Kilo Mk. 3.—

Berliner Thor

No. 517. Gr. Missal (Corps 60). Min. 18 Kilo à ½, Kilo Mk. 2.75.

Dielsdorf

No. 507. Tertia (Corps 16). Min. 8 Kilo à ½, Kilo Mk. 3.60.

Musikalische Unterhaltungen
65 MONTENEGRO 90

No. 508. Text (Corps 20). Min. 10 Kilo à ½, Kilo Mk. 3.40.

Hermann und Dorothea
32 RECHNUNG 54

No. 509. Doppelmittel (Corps 28). Min. 12 Kilo à ½, Kilo Mk. 3.30.

Erfurt ROM Berlin

No. 518. Tertia (Corps 16). Min. 8 Kilo à ½, Kilo Mk. 3.60.

Sonne Mond und Sterne
23 CONCERT 41

No. 519. Text (Corps 20). Min. 10 Kilo à ½, Kilo Mk. 3.40.

Blätter Blüthen
53 PERU 37

No. 520. Doppelcicero (Corps 24). Min. 10 Kilo à ½, Kilo Mk. 3.35.

STOCKHEIM
3 EBRO 4

No. 521. Canon (Corps 36). Min. 14 Kilo à ½, Kilo Mk. 3.20.

CARMEN

No. 522. Kl. Missal (Corps 48). Min. 16 Kilo à ½, Kilo Mk. 2.75.

DIJON

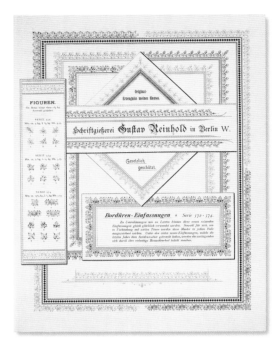

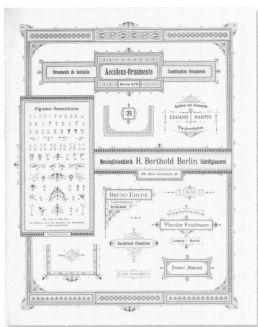

1894, Probenbuch, *H. Berthold Messing-linienfabrik und Schriftgiesserei,* Berlin

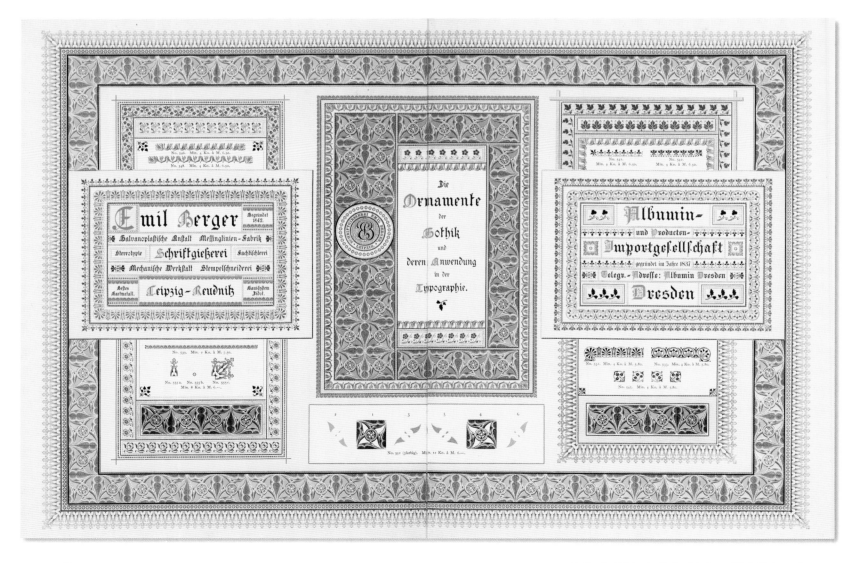

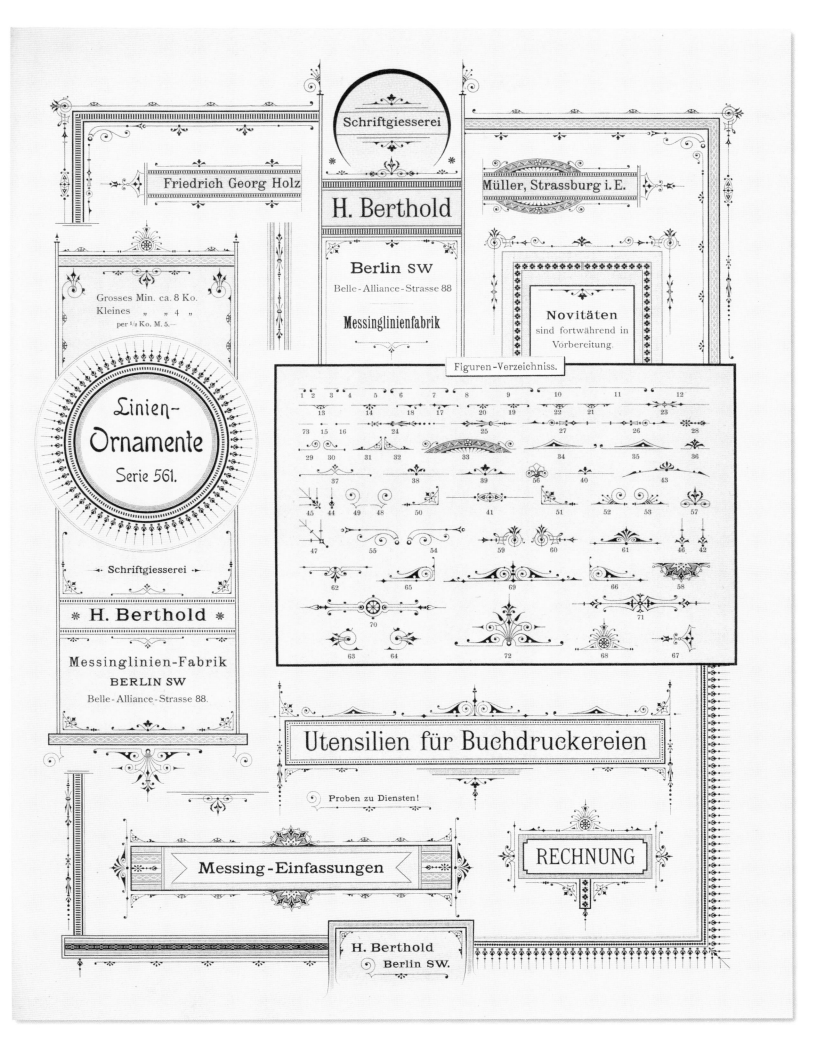

Schriftgiesserei

Friedrich Georg Holz

H. Berthold

Berlin SW
Belle-Alliance-Strasse 88

Messinglinienfabrik

Müller, Strassburg i. E.

Grosses Min. ca. 8 Ko.
Kleines „ „ 4 „
per ½ Ko. M. 5.—

Novitäten
sind fortwährend in
Vorbereitung.

Linien-
Ornamente
Serie 561.

Figuren-Verzeichniss.

Schriftgiesserei

* H. Berthold *

Messinglinien-Fabrik
BERLIN SW
Belle-Alliance-Strasse 88.

Utensilien für Buchdruckereien

Proben zu Diensten!

Messing-Einfassungen

RECHNUNG

H. Berthold
Berlin SW.

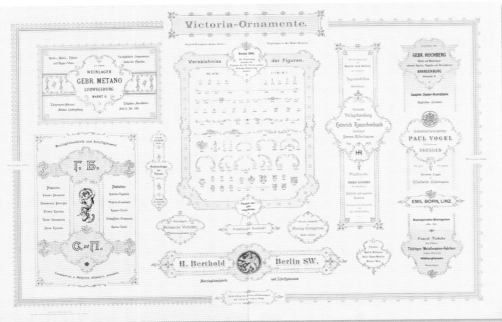

1894, Probenbuch, *H. Berthold Messing-*
linienfabrik und Schriftgiesserei, Berlin

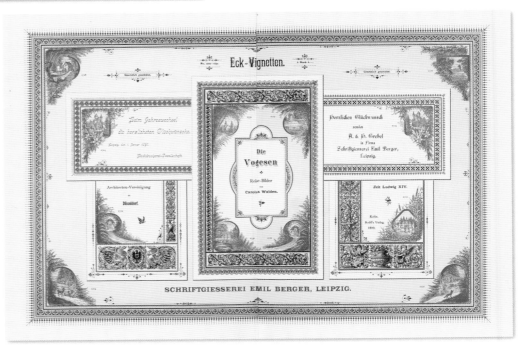

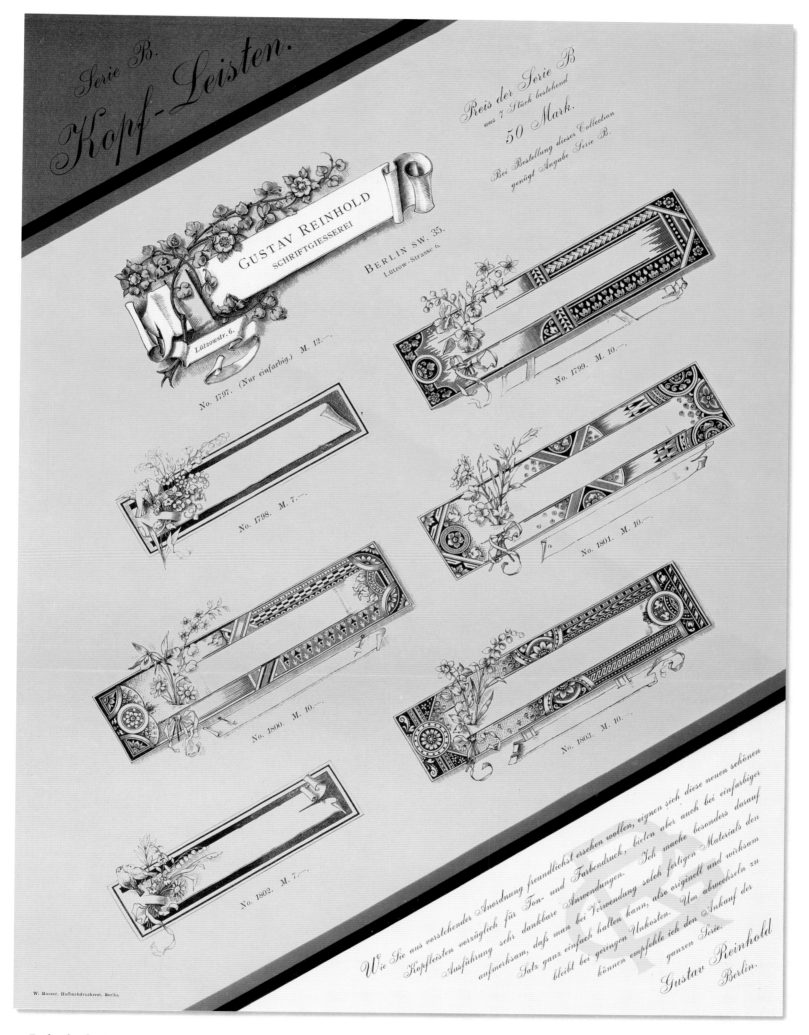

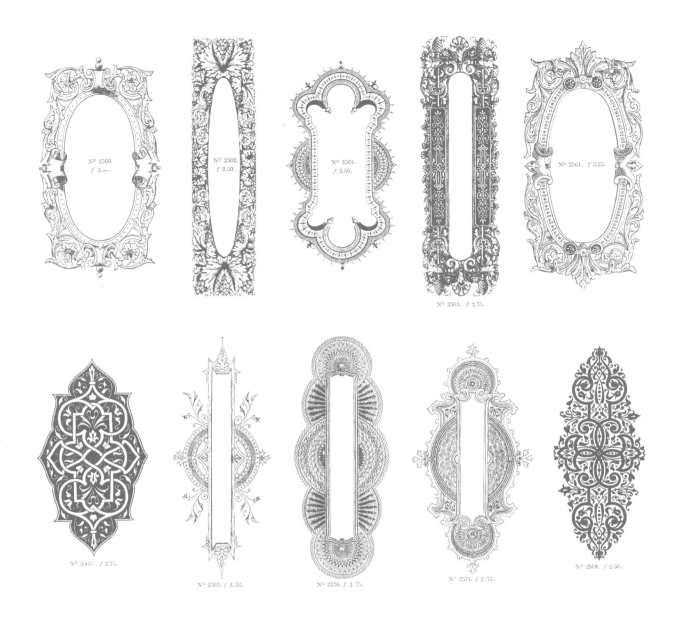

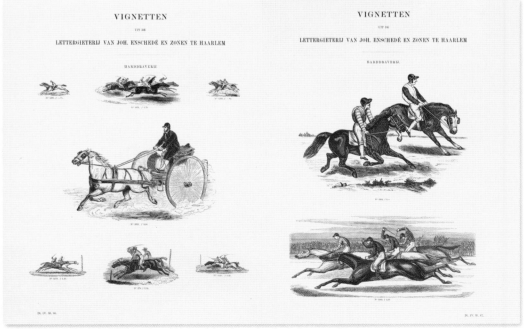

VIGNETTEN

UIT DE

LETTERGIETERIJ VAN JOH. ENSCHEDÉ EN ZONEN TE HAARLEM

GARNITUREN.

VIGNETTEN

UIT DE

LETTERGIETERIJ VAN JOH. ENSCHEDÉ EN ZONEN TE HAARLEM

GARNITUREN (Vervolg).

1894, Letterproef, Deel IV, Vignetten,
Joh. Enschedé & Zonen, Haarlem

This black hand is another beautiful vignette, this time from Haarlem.

Weitere schwarze Hände als hübsche Ornamente, dieses Mal aus Haarlem.

Voici encore une magnifique vignette, une main noire en provenance, cette fois, de Harlem.

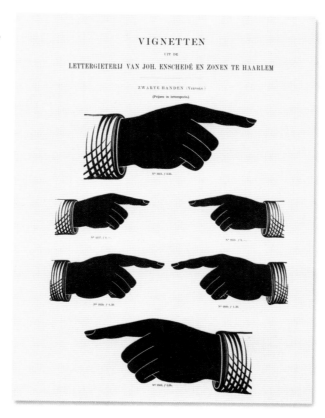

1895, Die Graphischen Künste der Gegenwart, *Theodor Goebel*, Stuttgart

A message that started with initial letters like these would leave little doubt as to the writer's amorous intentions.

Wer seine Botschaft mit einer solchen Initiale schmückt, signalisiert dem Adressaten gleich seine amourösen Absichten.

Un message commençant avec une lettrine de ce genre laissait peu de doutes sur les intentions amoureuses de son auteur.

Amoretten-Initialen.

SCHRIFTGIESSEREI BENJAMIN KREBS NACHFOLGER
FRANKFURT AM MAIN.

**1895, Internationaler
Grafischer Muster-Austausch,**
Deutscher Buchdrucker-Verein,
Leipzig

These experiments in typography, design,
and printing show the state of the arts
at the German Society of Printers
(Deutscher Buchdrucker-Verein) in 1895.
This society was founded in 1866 as the
first trade union in the printing industry
and remained active until the suppression
of trade unions in 1933.

Typografische, gestalterische und druckkünstlerische Experimente wie die abgebildeten demonstrieren den hohen
Standard des Deutschen Buchdrucker-
Vereins im Jahr 1895. Gegründet 1866 als
erste gewerkschaftliche Vereinigung des
Buchdruckgewerbes, war der Verein bis
zur Zerschlagung der Gewerkschaften im
Jahr 1933 aktiv.

Ces expérimentations en typographie,
graphisme et impression reflètent l'état
des arts à la société allemande des imprimeurs (Deutscher Buchdrucker-Verein)
en 1895. Cette société, fondée en 1866,
fut le premier syndicat de l'industrie du
graphisme et fonctionna jusqu'à la suppression des syndicats en 1933.

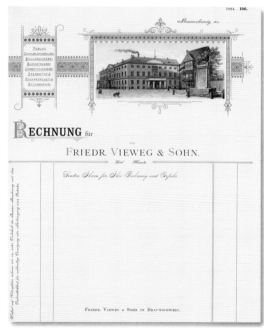

GESELLSCHAFT "TYPOGRAPHIA" LEIPZIG

Ausgeführt vom Gesangverein
Typographia
Fritz Schmidt
Dirigent.

Heitere

Abend-Unterhaltung

im

Etablissement „Battenberg"

am

3. Februar 1894.

Glückliche Heimfahrt!

Frankenstein & Wagner, Leipzig.

**1895, Internationaler
Grafischer Muster-Austausch,**
Deutscher Buchdrucker-Verein,
Leipzig

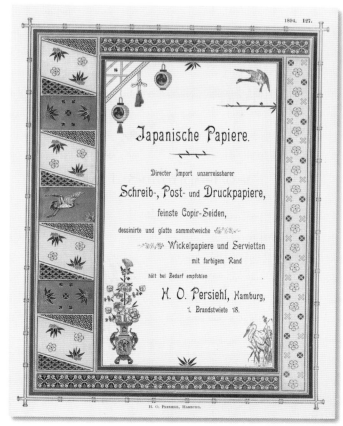

1895, Probe, *Schriftgiesserei Julius Klinkhardt,* Leipzig and Vienna

The presentation here is overwhelming—
a feast for the eyes.

Schriftmuster von überwältigender
Wirkung – eine wahre Augenweide.

La présentation est ici extrêment réjouis-
sante, un vrai régal pour les yeux.

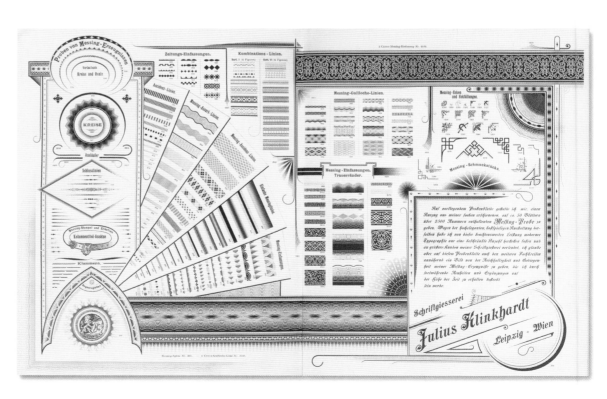

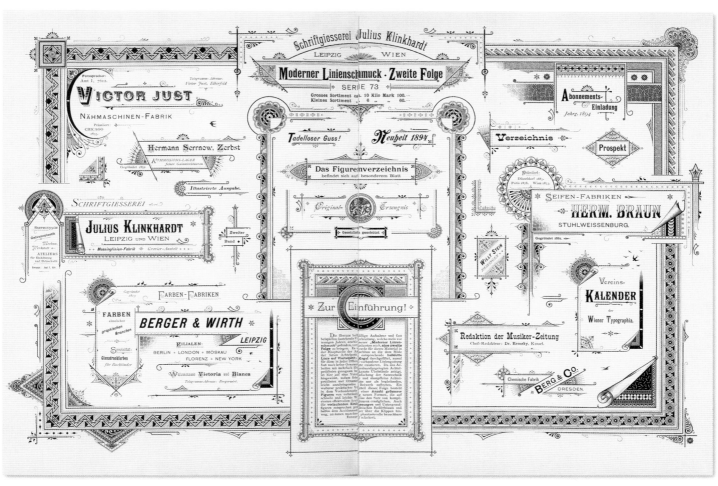

ZIERSCHRIFT „ELEGANT"

für ein- und zweifarbigen Druck.

Nr. 498. Text (20 Punkte) zweifarbig. Min. 10 Ko., ½ Min. 5 Ko. à Mark 5.50.
Nr. 498a einfarbig. Min. 5 Ko. à Mark 6.20.

SCHULFEST GYMNASIUM
SPEISENFOLGE
VOLKSLIEDER DEUTSCHLAND
GRAZ UNGARN SUHL

Nr. 499. Doppelmittel (28 Punkte) zweifarbig. Min. 12 Ko., ½ Min. 6 Ko. à Mark 5.20.
Nr. 499a einfarbig. Min. 6 Ko. à Mark 6.—.

ORATORIUM
GESANG 83 PAULUS
HARMONIE

Nr. 500. 3½ Cicero (42 Punkte) zweifarbig. Min. 15 Ko., ½ Min. 8 Ko. à Mark 5.—.
Nr. 500a einfarbig. Min. 8 Ko. à Mark 5.70.

5 MODE BERN 2
RECHNUNG

Zu grösseren Anfangsbuchstaben ist der nächstfolgende Schriftgrad zu verwenden.

— ► Schriftgiesserei Julius Klinkhardt in Leipzig und Wien. ◄ —

Zierschrift Brillant *für ein- und zweifarbigen Druck.*

Original- Erzeugnis.
Gesetzlich geschützt.

Nr. 504a. Tertia (16 Punkte) **einfarbig.** Min. 4 Ko. à M. 6.50.

OPUS MUSIK VOSS
PADUA EMS DESSAU

Nr. 505a. 2 Cicero (24 Punkte) **einfarbig.** Min. 5 Ko. à M. 6.10.

TRISTAN ISOLDE
STRALSUND

Nr. 506a. 3 Cicero (36 Punkte) **einfarbig.** Min. 7 Ko. à M. 5.80.

DAHOME

Nr. 507a. 4 Cicero (48 Punkte) **einfarbig.** Min. 8 Ko. à M. 5.—.

HEIM KADEN

Nr. 505. 2 Cicero (24 Punkte) **zweifarbig.**
Min. 10 Ko., ½ Min. 5 Ko. à M. 6.10.

REINHOLD DROBNER
RITTERSHAUS

Nr. 504. Tertia (16 Punkte) **zweifarbig.**
Min. 8 Ko., ½ Min. 4 Ko. à M. 6.50.

SEUME HOMO SUM
KAUKASUS SIAM DAMASKUS

Nr. 507. 4 Cicero (48 Punkte) **zweifarbig.** Min. 16 Ko., ½ Min. 8 Ko. à M. 5.—.

AMBROSIA

Nr. 506. 3 Cicero (36 Punkte) **zweifarbig.**
Min. 14 Ko., ½ Min. 7 Ko. à M. 5.80.

SERBIEN
OKARINA

Nr. 504b. Tertia (16 Punkte) **einfarbig.** Min. 4 Ko. à M. 6.50.

SODOM MISSISSIPPI HUSUM
VESUV DUMAS

Nr. 505b. 2 Cicero (24 Punkte) **einfarbig.** Min. 5 Ko. à M. 6.10.

KREISAU FREIBURG

HOMER QUISISANA

Nr. 506b.
3 Cicero (36 Punkte) **einfarbig.**
Min. 7 Ko. à M. 5.80.

Aus den zweifarbigen Schriften Nr. 504—507 ergeben sich die Nr. 504a und b bis 507a und b für einfarbigen Druck, so dass also die Abnehmer der Zweifarbenschrift gleichzeitig die beiden Garnituren für einfarbigen Druck erhalten.

Schriftgiesserei Julius Klinkhardt
LEIPZIG UND WIEN.

Nr. 507b. 4 Cicero (48 Punkte) **einfarbig.** Min. 8 Ko. à M. 5.—.

MEMOIREN

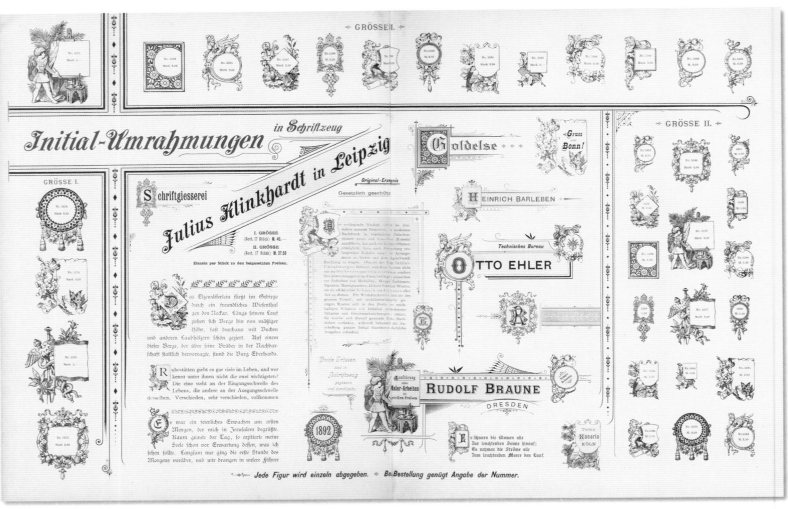

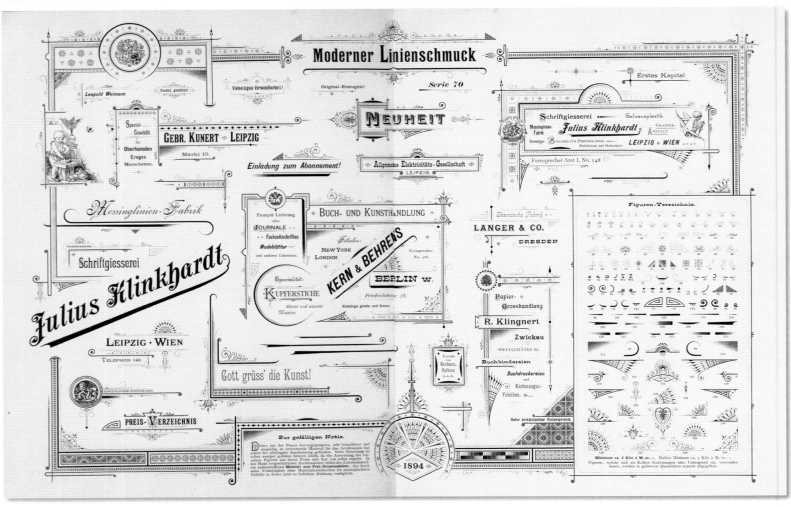

5426.   Mk. 1.50.

5430.   75 Pf.

5431.   Mk. 1.50.

5432.   75 Pf.

5436.   Mk. 1.50.

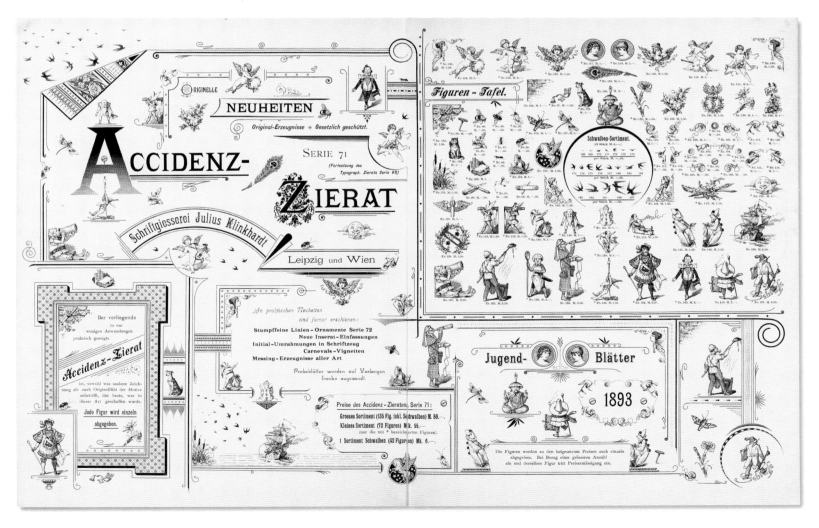

1895, Probenfolge Erstes Heft,
*H. Berthold Messinglinienfabrik
und Schriftgiesserei,* Berlin

Letters, initials, vignettes, frames, and lines combine to convey the message. H. Berthold AG was established in 1858 by Hermann Berthold as an "Institute for Galvanotypie," a company that produced copper printing plates and traded under the name of H. Berthold Messinglinienfabrik und Schriftgiesserei until 1896. After acquiring numerous other companies, by around 1900, H. Berthold AG was the biggest and most famous type foundry. The company remained in business until 1993.

Gekonnt kombiniert ergeben Lettern, Initialen, Vignetten, Rahmen und Linien eine überzeugende Botschaft. Die spätere H. Berthold AG war 1858 von Hermann Berthold als „Institut für Galvanotypie" – als Betrieb zur Herstellung von Kupfer-druckplatten – gegründet worden und firmierte bis 1896 als H. Berthold Messinglinienfabrik und Schriftgiesserei. Nach der Übernahme mehrerer anderer Firmen war die H. Berthold AG um 1900 die größte und bekannteste Schrift-gießerei. Das Unternehmen bestand bis ins Jahr 1993.

Lettres, lettrines, vignettes, cadres et lignes s'associent pour faire passer le message. La future H. Berthold AG, fon-dée en 1858 par Hermann Berthold comme « Institut de galvanotypie », fabri-quait des plaques de cuivre pour impres-sion. Elle porta le nom de H. Berthold Messinglinienfabrik und Schriftgießerei jusqu'en 1896. Après avoir racheté plu-sieurs autres compagnies, H. Berthold AG devint, aux alentours de 1900, la fonderie de caractères la plus importante. La com-pagnie resta en activité jusqu'en 1993.

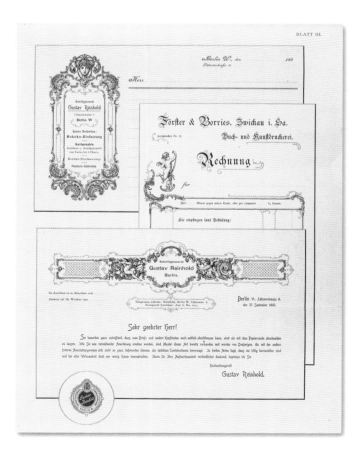

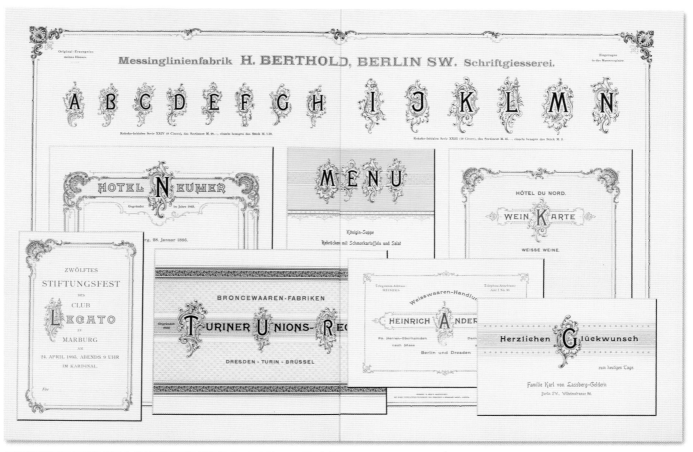

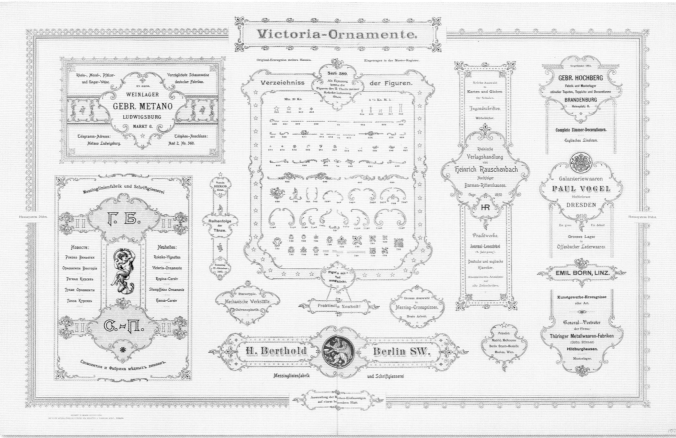

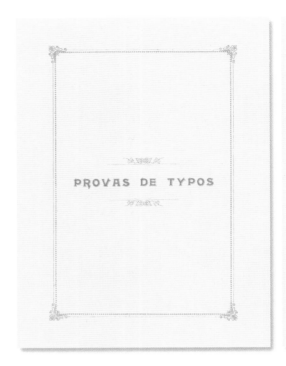

PROVAS DE TYPOS

CAPITAES ANTIGAS

N.º 44   Corpo 10
ARCO TRIUMPHAL DA PRAÇA DO COMMERCIO DE LISBOA

N.º 45   Corpo 12
FRANCISCO MANUEL TRIGOSO DE ARAGÃO MORATO

N.º 46   Corpo 16
ALDEIA GALLEGA DO RIBATEJO

N.º 47   Corpo 18
Administração Geral da Casa da Moeda e Papel Sellado
CURSO SUPERIOR DE LETRAS

N.º 48   Corpo 20
A RAINHA SANTA

N.º 49   Corpo 32
Supremo Tribunal de Justiça
ILHA DE BOLAMA

N.º 50   Corpo 48
CAMPO GRANDE

N.º 51   Corpo 64
S. THOMÉ

ANTIGAS COMPACTAS

N.º 52   Corpo 6
CORTES GERAES EXTRAORDINARIAS E CONSTITUINTES DA NAÇÃO PORTUGUEZA

N.º 53   Corpo 10
CHRONICA DA COMPANHIA DE JESUS NA PROVINCIA DE PORTUGAL

N.º 54   Corpo 12
MONUMENTO DE LUIZ DE CAMÕES INAUGURADO A 9 DE OUTUBRO 1866

N.º 55   Corpo 18
CAMINHO DE FERRO DE LOANDA A AMBACA

N.º 56   Corpo 24
FRANCISCO ALEXANDRE LOBO, BISPO DE VIZEU

N.º 57   Corpo 32
DR. SOUSA MARTINS

N.º 58   Corpo 48
PASSEIO DA ESTRELLA

N.º 59   Corpo 96
COIMBRA

1895, Provas de Typos,
M.A. Branco & CA., Lisboa

"Capitaes Diversas"—samples of various capital letters: Porto, Sines, Luz.

„Capitaes Diversas" – Muster von verschiedenen Versalschriften: Porto, Sines, Luz.

«Capitaes Diversas» – des échantillons de plusieurs lettres capitales: Porto, Sines, Luz.

CLICHÉS

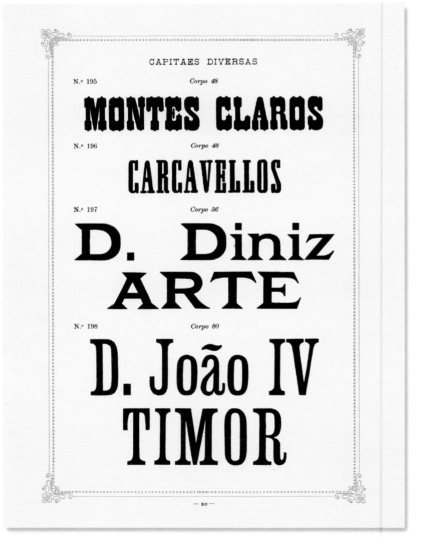

CAPITAES DIVERSAS

N.º 195   Corpo 48
MONTES CLAROS

N.º 196   Corpo 48
CARCAVELLOS

N.º 197   Corpo 56
D. Diniz
ARTE

N.º 198   Corpo 80
D. João IV
TIMOR

N.º 199   *Corpo 80*

PORTO

N.º 200   *Corpo 96*

SINES

N.º 201   *Corpo 96*

1895, Ultime Novità
Nebiolo & Comp., Torino

Trade and distribution by type foundries
was an international affair, as evidenced
by the involvement of Torino-based
Nebiolo & Comp.

Schriftgießereien hatten beim Verkauf
und Vertrieb ihrer Produkte den internationalen Markt im Auge, so auch die
in Turin ansässigen Nebiolo & Comp.

Le commerce et la distribution par les
fonderies de caractères étaient une affaire
internationale, comme en témoigne
l'implication de la fonderie Nebiolo &
Comp., basée à Turin.

ATTESTATO

FONDERIA **NEBIOLO & COMP.** TIPOGRAFICA

MAC LEAN

DIPLOMA

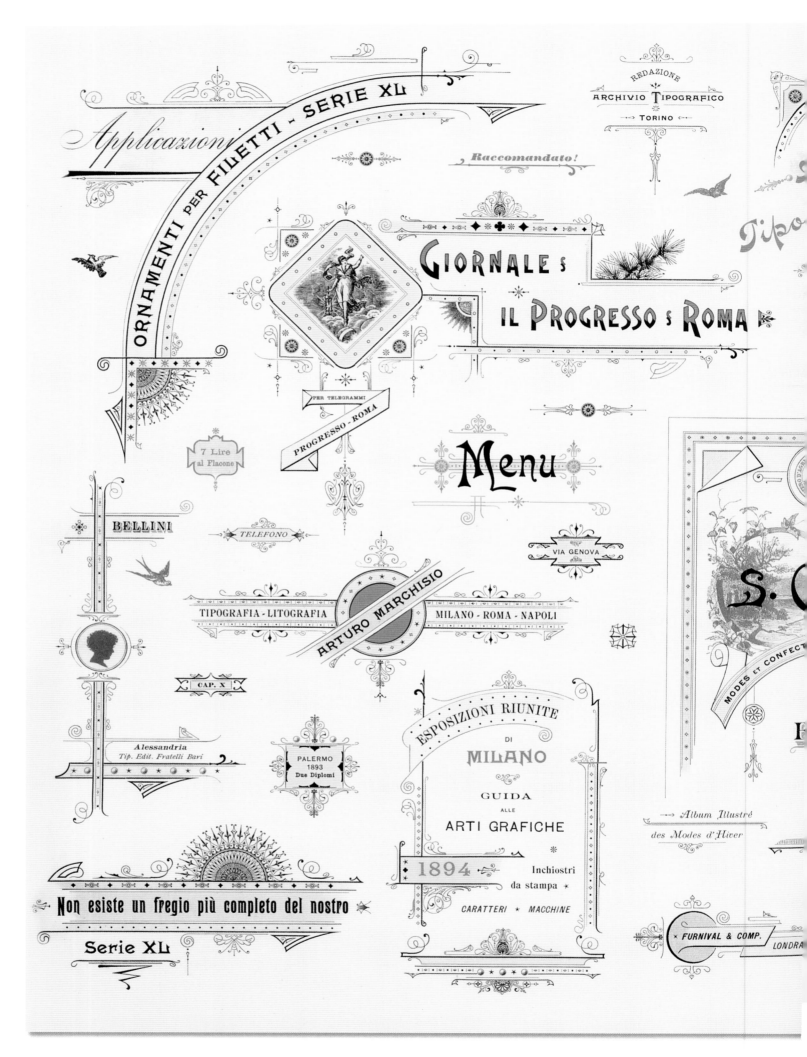

Applicazioni

ORNAMENTI PER FILETTI - SERIE XL

REDAZIONE
ARCHIVIO TIPOGRAFICO
TORINO

Raccomandato!

GIORNALE s
IL PROGRESSO s ROMA

PER TELEGRAMMI
PROGRESSO - ROMA

7 Lire
al Flacone

Menu

BELLINI

TELEFONO

VIA GENOVA

ARTURO MARCHISIO

TIPOGRAFIA - LITOGRAFIA

MILANO - ROMA - NAPOLI

CAP. X

Alessandria
Tip. Edit. Fratelli Bari

PALERMO
1893
Due Diplomi

ESPOSIZIONI RIUNITE
DI
MILANO

GUIDA
ALLE
ARTI GRAFICHE

1894

Inchiostri
da stampa

CARATTERI ✶ MACCHINE

Album Illustré
des Modes d'Hiver

S. C

MODES ET CONFECT

Non esiste un fregio più completo del nostro

Serie XL

FURNIVAL & COMP.

LONDRA

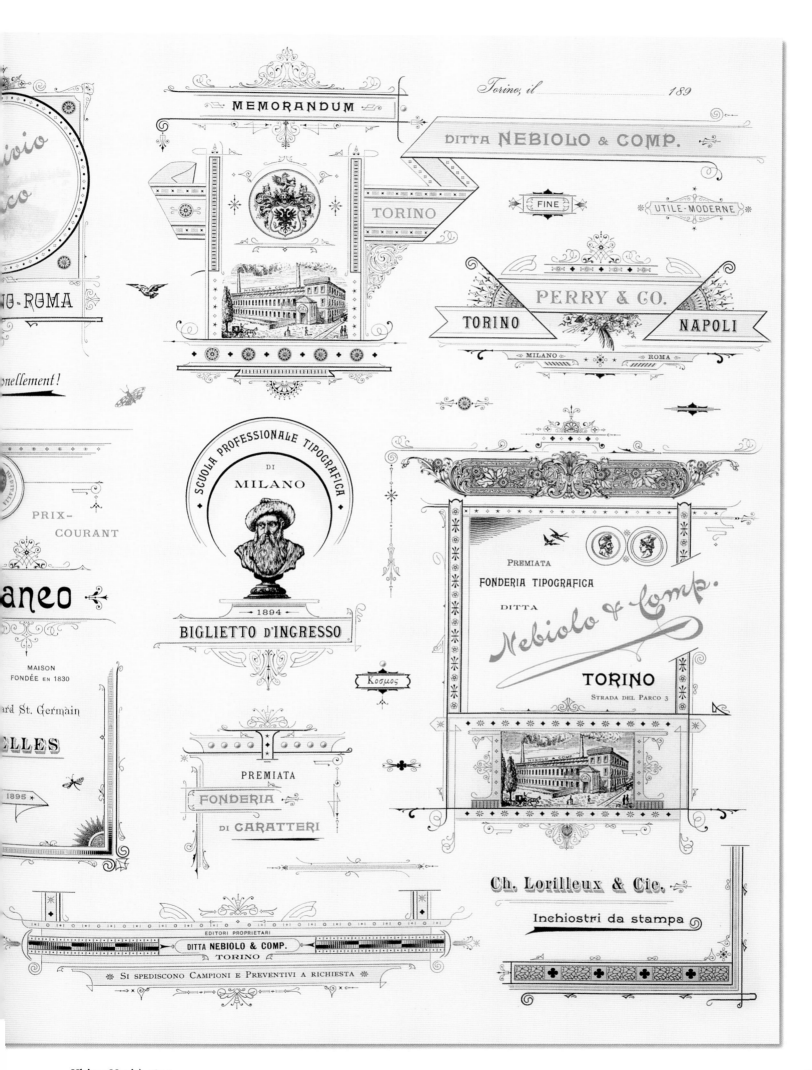

MEMORANDUM

Torino, il _____ *189*

DITTA NEBIOLO & COMP.

TORINO

FINE · UTILE-MODERNE

PERRY & CO.

TORINO · NAPOLI

MILANO · ROMA

SCUOLA PROFESSIONALE TIPOGRAFICA
DI
MILANO

1894

BIGLIETTO D'INGRESSO

Κοσμος

PREMIATA
FONDERIA TIPOGRAFICA
DITTA
Nebiolo & Comp.

TORINO
STRADA DEL PARCO 3

PREMIATA
FONDERIA
DI CARATTERI

Ch. Lorilleux & Cie.

Inchiostri da stampa

EDITORI PROPRIETARI
DITTA NEBIOLO & COMP.
TORINO

Si spediscono Campioni e Preventivi a richiesta

PRIX-
COURANT

MAISON
FONDÉE EN 1830

O-ROMA

PRIX-
COURANT

aneo

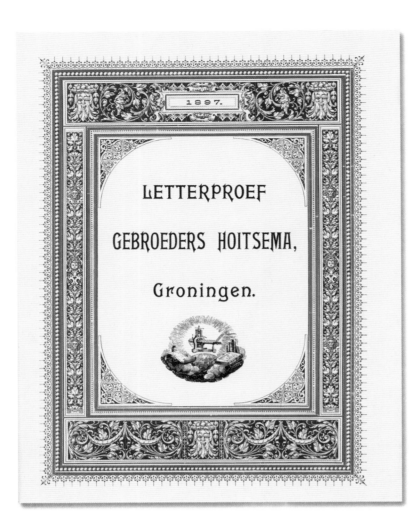

1897, Letterproef, *Gebr. Hoitsema,* Groningen

Groningen, in the northern part of the Netherlands, did not escape late 19th-Century Romanticism.

Groningen in den nördlichen Niederlanden war noch der Romantik des späten 19. Jahrhunderts verhaftet.

Groningue, dans le nord des Pays-Bas, n'échappa pas au romantisme de la fin du XIXᵉ siècle.

BENAMING.	Lettersoorten aanwezig ter Book-, Muziek- en Handelsdrukkerij van GEBROEDERS HOITSEMA te Groningen.	Regual.	Aantal kasten.	Hoeveelheid gewicht in Kilo's.	Jaar van aankoop.	LEVERANCIER.
Tertia Aurora.	ZIJN LICHAAM IS KR 3 6 7	Q	1	2.75	1892	Schelter & Giesecke. Tertia Aurora No. 1327.
Laureata No. 446.	ZIJN LICHAAM IS KRACH 3 6 8	Q	1	1.65	1888	Krebs Nachfolger. Corpus 12. Laureata No. 446.
Laureata No. 447.	ZIJN LICHAAM IS 6 9 4	Q	1	2.85	1888	Krebs Nachfolger. Corpus 18. Laureata No. 447.
Laureata No. 443.	ZIJN LICHAAM 16	Q	1	3.70	1888	Krebs Nachfolger. Corpus 24. Laureata No. 448.
Pretiosa.	ZIJN LICHAAM 2 9 4	Z	1	2.30	1884	Schelter & Giesecke. Schildschrift Preciosa No. 567 A.
Talonletter.	ZIJN LICHAAM IS 95	Q	1	4.55	1886	Flinschgiesserei. Corpus 36. Talonschrift No.731.
Antiqua Zierschrift.	ZIJN LICH 2 5 6	Q	1	5.10	1881 1882	Schelter & Giesecke. Corpus 36. Zierschrift No.146.
Kl. Kan. Witte.	ZIJN LICHAAM 2 9 4	Q	1			Flinschgiesserei. Corpus 24. Zierschrift No. 875 en 876.
Kl. Kan. Zwarte.	ZIJN LICHAAM 2 9 4	Q	1	3.40	1870	
Lichte Bont-drukletter.	Zijn lichaam is 4 1 6	Q	1			Flinschgiesserei. Ruetdruckschrift No.1867.
Zwarte Bont-drukletter.	Zijn lichaam is 4 1 6	Q	1	6.30	1896	

BLAD 63.

BENAMING.	Lettersoorten aanwezig ter Book-, Muziek- en Handelsdrukkerij van GEBROEDERS HOITSEMA te Groningen.	Regual.	Aantal kasten.	Hoeveelheid gewicht in Kilo's.	Jaar van aankoop.	LEVERANCIER.
Mediaan Gefigureerde.	ZIJN LICAAM IS KRACHTIG GEBOUWD, DE BEHARI	DD	1			Inventaris 1864.
Tertia Schattirte.	ZIJN LICHAAM IS KRACHTIG 1897	DD	1	4.30	1883	Schelter & Giesecke. Tertia Schattirte Egyptienne No. 613.
3 Mediaan Titelkapitalen	ZIJN LICHAAM IS KRAC 8 6 4	DD	1	3.65	1874	Enschedé & Zonen. Titelkapitalen No. 2111.
Kanon Zierschrift.	Zijn lichaam is krac 2 5 8	DD	1	5.50	1882	Wilh Woellmer. Corpus 36. Canon Zierschrift No. 150.
Zierschrift No.1463.	Zijn lichaam is krachtig gebouwd, de 1 8 9 7	SS	1	6.45	1885	Flinschgiesserei. Corpus 14. Zierschrift No.1463.
Text Zierschrift.	Zijn lichaam is krachti 1 2 3	SS	1	5.40	1885	Van Dijk. Text Zierschrift No. 952.
Doppelmittel Zierschrift.	Zijn lichaam is 2 9 4	SS	1	6.50	1885	Van Dijk. Zierschrift No. 953.
Paragon Geschaduwde.	Zijn lichaam is krach 2 9 4	DD	1	6.30	1868	Flinschgiesserei. Zierschrift No. 733.
Versierde No. 186.	Zijn lichaam is 4 5 6	SS	1	5.70	1881	G. W. v. d. Wiel. Versierde No. 186.
Versierde No. 187.	Zijn lichaa 1 6 9	SS	1	8.70	1892	G. W. v. d. Wiel. Versierde No. 187.
Geschaduwde Fantasie No.2927.	Zijn lic 4 5 6	SS	1	10.50	1893	Enschedé & Zonen. Corpus 48. Gesch. Fantasie-schrift No. 2927.
Antiqua Zierschrift.	ZIJN LICHA	A	1	6.90	1888	Schelter & Giesecke. Corpus 54. Antiqua Zierschrift No. 380.
Cicero Zierschrift.	Zijn lihaam is krachtig gebouw 2 0 4	DD	1	3.70	1889	Schelter & Giesecke. Cicero breite Schattirte Italienne No. 474.
Text Zierschrift.	Zijn lichaam is kracht 4 6 7	DD	1	6.90	1882	Flinschgiesserei. Corpus 16. Zierschrift No. 1121.
Paragon Versierde.	ZIJN LICHAAM IS 2 9 4	DD	1	3.20	1865	Onnes, de Boer & Coers. Versierde No. 149.

BLAD 61.

ZN

Beh

HI

Zijn

BLAD 135.

BLAD 140.

Billetletter.	**ZIJN LIC** (31)	W				No. 31. 88 stuks houten letters, kapitalen.
	Zijn 53 (32)	W				No. 32. 191 stuks houten letters met 35 cijfers.
	I (33) **H** (34)	II				No. 33. 66 stuks houten letters, kapitalen.
	E S	A				No. 34. Tweemaal het woord Het Schoolblad één in spetie en één in hout.

BLAD 144.

Benaming.	Lettersoorten aanwezig ter Boek-, Muziek- en Handelsdrukkerij van *GEBROEDERS HOITSEMA te Groningen.*	Regaal.	Aantal kastjen.	Hoeveelheid gewicht in Kilo's.	Jaar van aankoop.	LEVERANCIER.

Billetletter.	**ZIJN LICHAAM** (1)	JJ				No. 1. 6¼ kilo Kapitalen (specie.)
	ZIJN LICHAAM IS 1960 (2)	JJ				No. 2. 6¼ kilo Kapit. met cijfers (specie.)
	ZIJN L (3)	JJ				No. 3. 17 kilo Kapitalen (specie.)
	ZIJN LICHAA (4)	JJ				No. 4. 11 kilo Kapitalen (specie.)
	Zijn (5)	II				No. 5. 17 kilo Kapit. en onderkast (specie.)
	ZIJ (6)	II				No. 6. 66 stuks opgeslagen Kapitale letters.

BLAD 133.

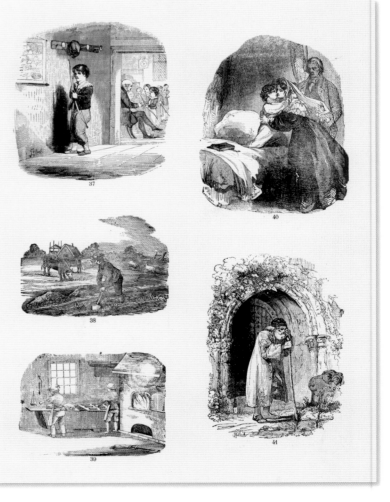

48

19

27

24

25

1897, Letterproef, Deel V, Titel- & Biljetletter, *Joh. Enschedé & Zonen,* Haarlem

A visual treat: Uppercase and lowercase letters and types with special accents, decorated, in perspective, with shadows.

Ein visuelles Vergnügen: Groß- und Kleinbuchstaben mit besonderen Akzenten, verziert, dreidimensional, schattiert.

Un régal pour les yeux : des lettres et caractères de haut et de bas de casse spécialement accentués, décorés, en perspective, ombrés.

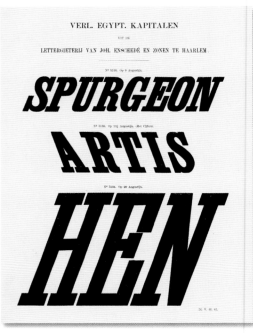

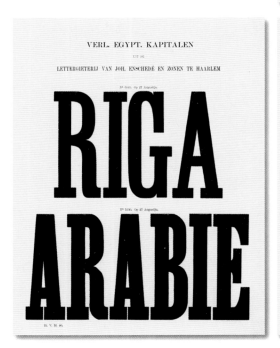

N° 5170. Op 11 Augustijn.

HAARLEM

N° 5168. Op 11 Augustijn.

ITALIE

N° 5031. Op 102 Punten.

GRAFT

N° 5040. Op 10½ Augustijn.

MARS

Dl. V. Bl. 123.

GESCHAD. FANTAISIE KAPITALEN

UIT DE

LETTERGIETERIJ VAN JOH. ENSCHEDÉ EN ZONEN TE HAARLEM

Nº 5013. Op 84 Punten.

ALPHEN

Nº 5010. Op 72 Punten.

LEXMOND

Nº 5033. Op 9 Augustijn.

ZEIST

Nº 5063. Op 15 Augustijn.

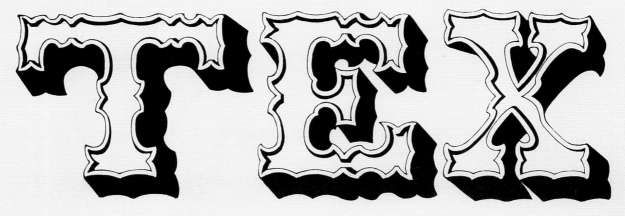

TEX

Dl. V. Bl. 118.

Nº 5166. Op 96 Punten.

Nº 5030. Op 9 Augustijn.

Nº 5169. Op 10½ Augustijn.

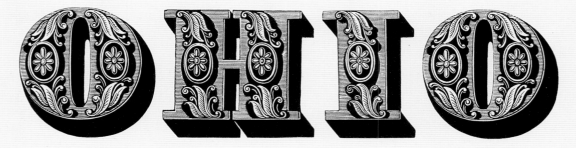

Nº 5044. Op 11 Augustijn.

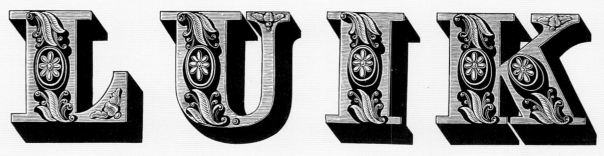

Dl. V. Bl. 121.

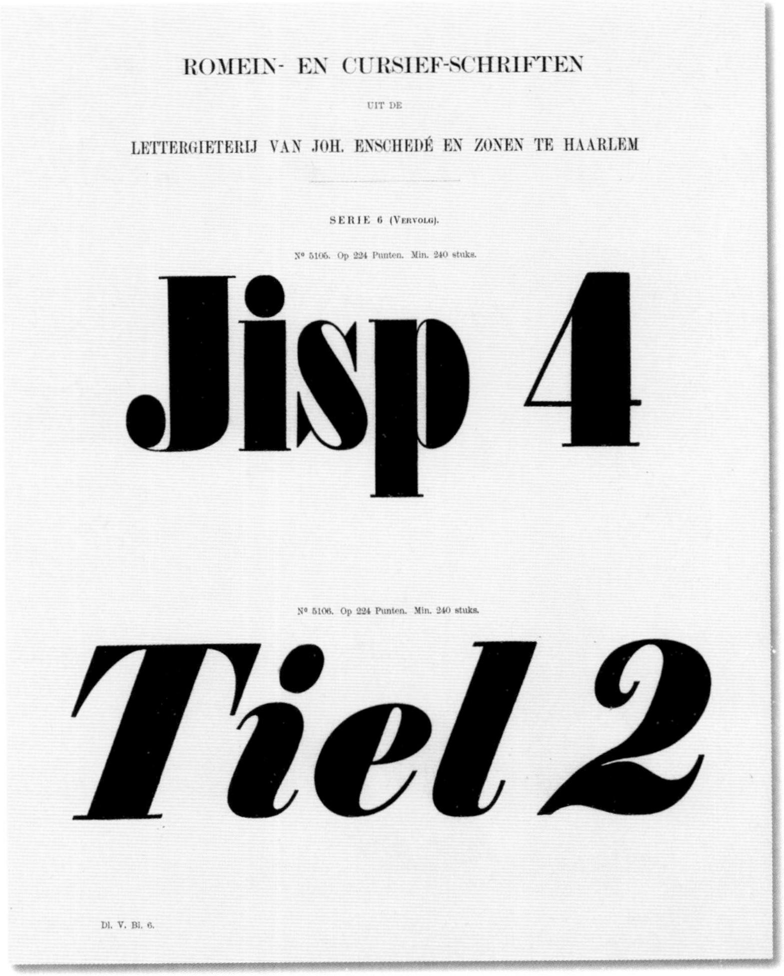

**1897, Letterproef, Deel V, Titel- &
Biljetletter,** *Joh. Enschedé & Zonen,*
Haarlem

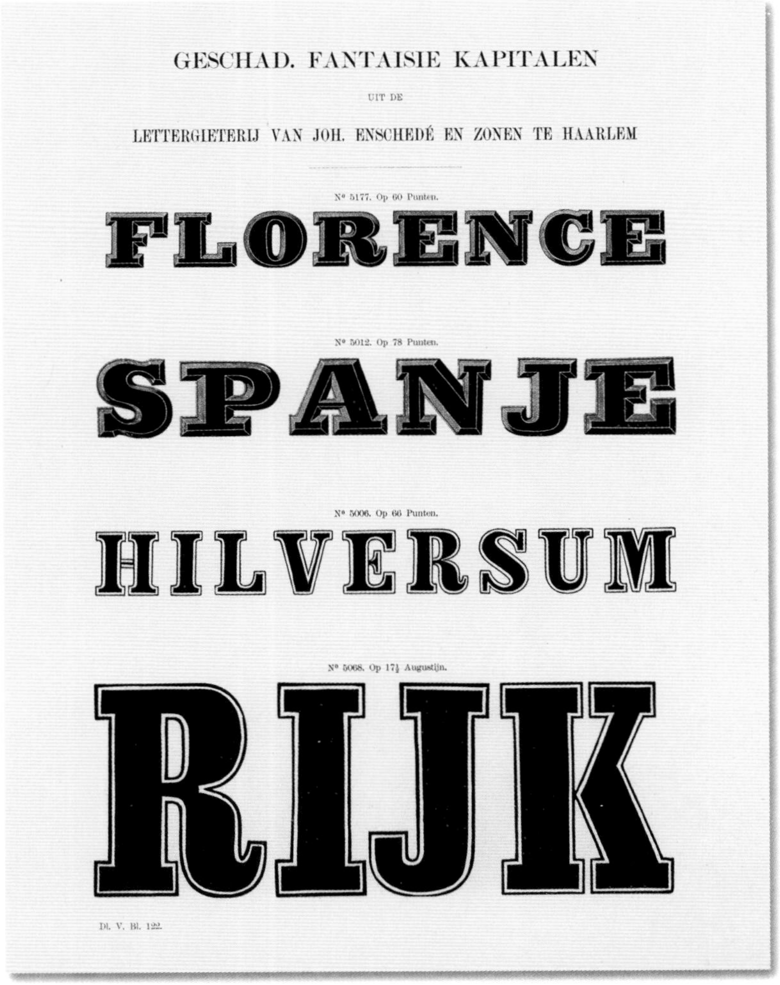

ROMEIN- EN CURSIEF-SCHRIFTEN

UIT DE

LETTERGIETERIJ VAN JOH. ENSCHEDÉ EN ZONEN TE HAARLEM

SERIE 6 (VERVOLG).

Nº 5106. Op 224 Punten. Min. 240 stuks.

Jisp 4

Nº 5106. Op 224 Punten. Min. 240 stuks.

Tiel 2

Dl. V. Bl. 6.

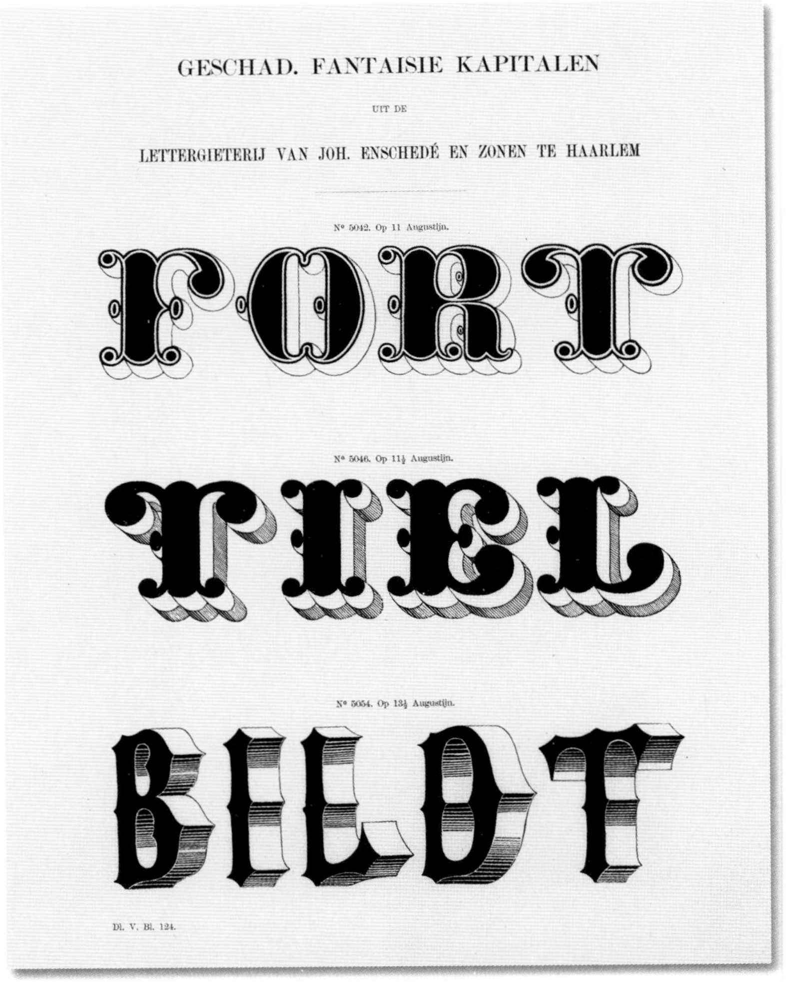

GESCHAD. FANTAISIE KAPITALEN

UIT DE

LETTERGIETERIJ VAN JOH. ENSCHEDÉ EN ZONEN TE HAARLEM

Nº 5042. Op 11 Augustijn.

FORT

Nº 5046. Op 11½ Augustijn.

TIEL

Nº 5054. Op 13½ Augustijn.

BILDT

Dl. V. Bl. 124.

GESCHAD. FANTAISIE KAPITALEN

UIT DE

LETTERGIETERIJ VAN JOH. ENSCHEDÉ EN ZONEN TE HAARLEM

Nº 5177. Op 60 Punten.

FLORENCE

Nº 5012. Op 78 Punten.

SPANJE

Nº 5006. Op 66 Punten.

HILVERSUM

Nº 5058. Op 17½ Augustijn.

RIJK

Dl. V. Bl. 122.

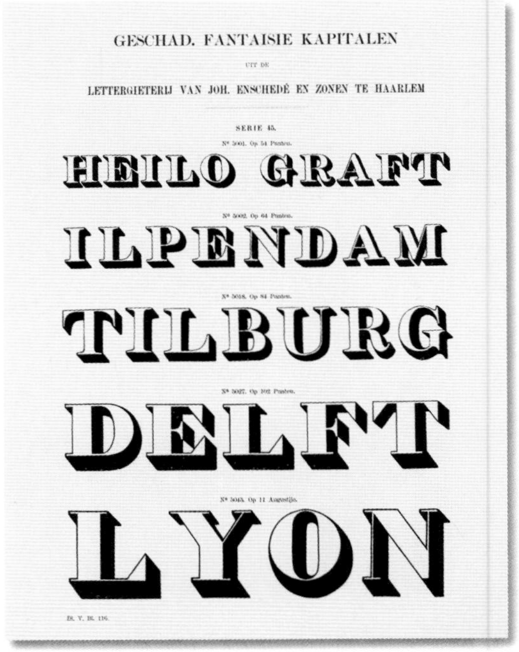

GESCHAD. FANTAISIE KAPITALEN

UIT DE

LETTERGIETERIJ VAN JOH. ENSCHEDÉ EN ZONEN TE HAARLEM

SERIE 45.

HEILO GRAFT

ILPENDAM

TILBURG

DELFT

LYON

Dl. V. Bl. 126.

AMERIKA

Nº 5164. Op 80 Punten.

BASTILLE

Nº 5165. Op 84 Punten.

VOSMAER

Nº 5175. Op 9 Augustijn.

HEKLA

Nº 5167. Op 102 Punten.

BERG

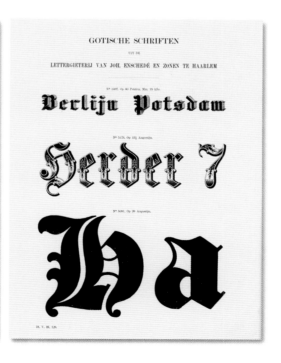

GOTISCHE SCHRIFTEN

UIT DE

LETTERGIETERIJ VAN JOH. ENSCHEDÉ EN ZONEN TE HAARLEM

Nederland Amerika Afrika   Stoombaart-Maatschappij

123 Factory der Staats-Spoorwegen 890

18 Lettergietery 94

1 Nederland 3

Harlingen 42

GOTISCHE SCHRIFTEN

UIT DE

LETTERGIETERIJ VAN JOH. ENSCHEDÉ EN ZONEN TE HAARLEM

Berlijn Potsdam

Herder 7

Ha

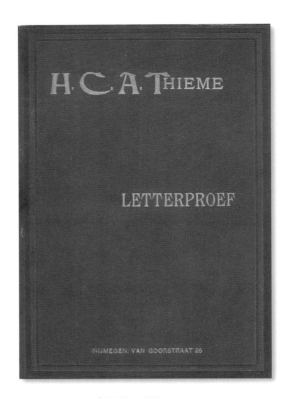

1898, Letterproef, *H. C. A. Thieme,*
Nijmegen

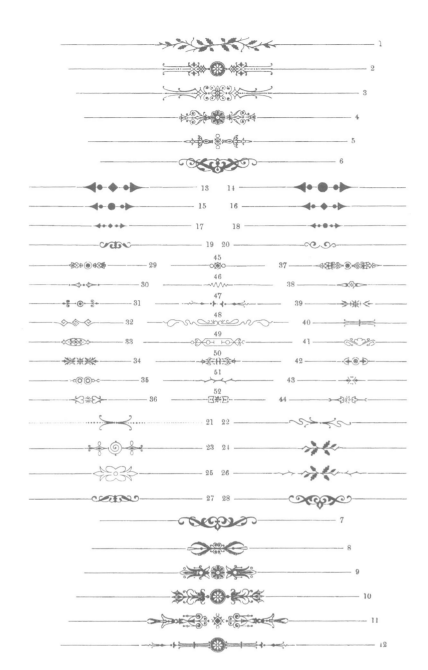

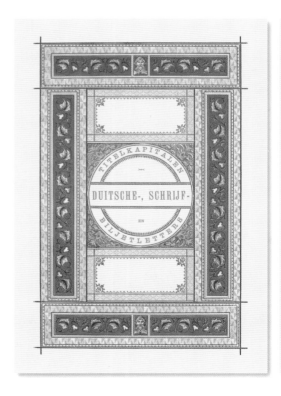

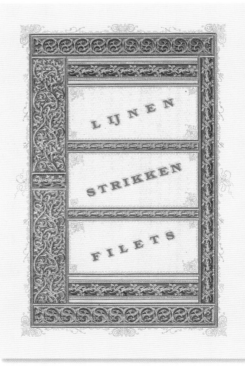

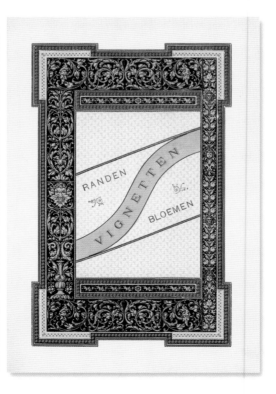

In this type-specimen proof, notice the page containing a single, large capital *M*. Set among many other pages featuring dazzling fantasy letters, ornaments, and different colors, this is real letterpress.

Ein Schriftmuster, das eindrucksvoll die vielfältigen Möglichkeiten des Hochdrucks präsentiert: Faszinierende Zierschriften, Ornamente, verschiedene Farben – und plötzlich ein ganzseitiges großes *M*.

Sur cette épreuve de spécimen de caractères, on remarquera la page qui ne contient qu'un grand *M* en capitale. Disposée au milieu de nombreuses autres pages présentant des caractères fantaisie éblouissants, des ornements et différentes couleurs, c'est de la vraie typographie.

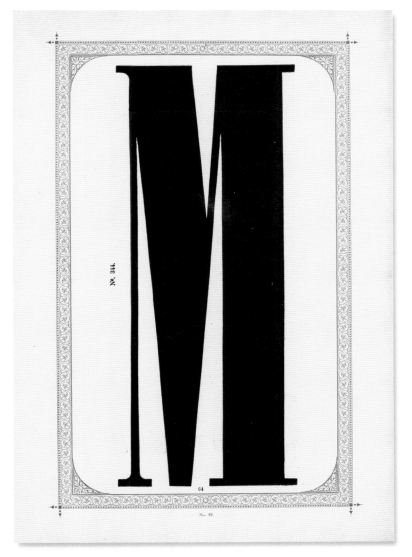

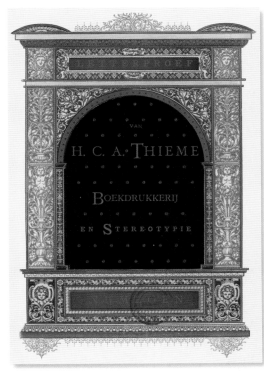

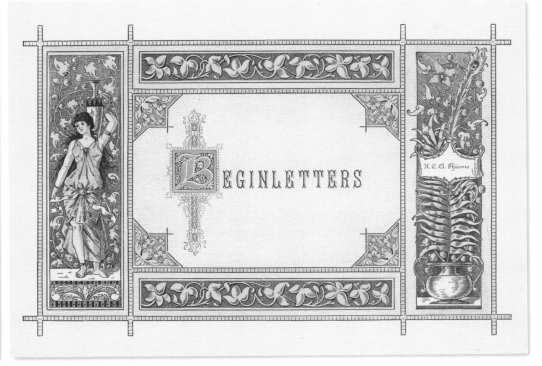

АБВГДЕЖ
ЗІЙКЛМН

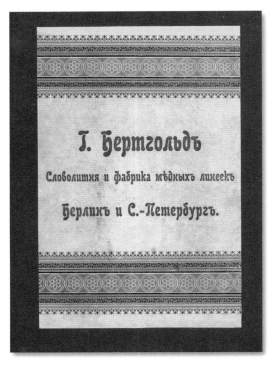

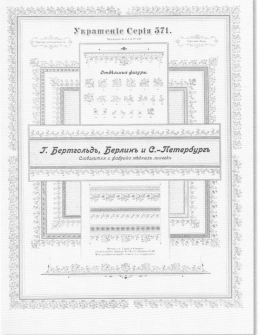

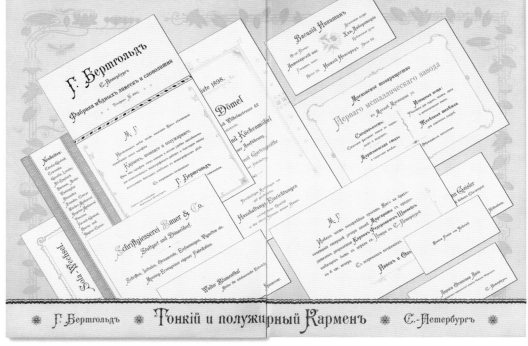

1898, Russische Letterproef,
H. Berthold AG, Berlin

Berthold exported a lot to Russia and held a significant market share there.

Ein wichtiger Exportmarkt für die H. Berthold AG war Russland, wo die Firma einen bedeutenden Marktanteil besaß.

Berthold exportait beaucoup vers la Russie et y tenait une part de marché importante.

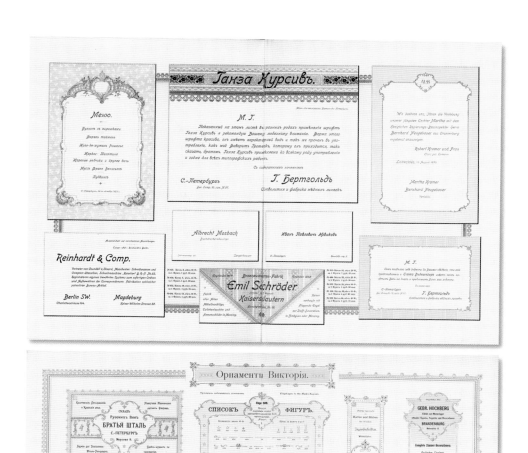

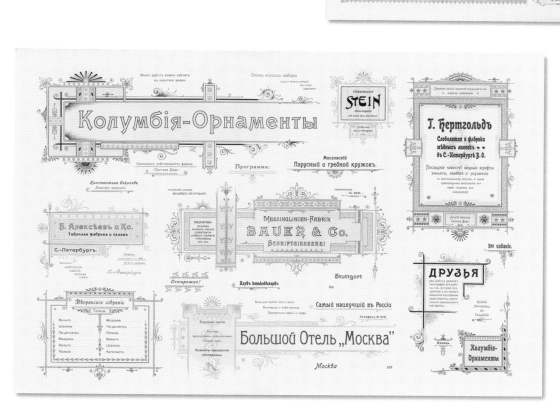

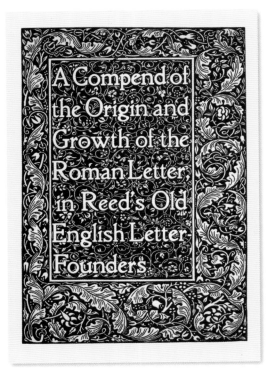

1900, Jenson Old Style,
American Type Founders, Boston

American Type Founders (ATF) was created in 1892 by the merger of 23 type
foundries, including the Boston Type
Foundry, the Cincinnati Type Foundry,
and Farmer, Little & Co. From its beginning until the 1940s, ATF was one of the
dominant manufacturers of metal type.

Die American Type Founders (ATF)
gründeten sich 1892 als Zusammen-
schluss von 23 Schriftgießereien, unter
ihnen die Boston Type Foundry, die
Cincinnati Type Foundry und Farmer,
Little & Co. Von ihren ersten Tagen
bis in die 1940er Jahre gehörten die
ATF zu den führenden Herstellern von
Metall-Lettern.

American Type Founders (ATF) est née
en 1892 de la fusion de 23 fonderies de
caractères dont Boston Type Foundry,
Cincinnati Type Foundry et Farmer,
Little & Co. De ses débuts jusque dans
les années 40, ATF a été l'un des plus
gros fabricants de caractères métalliques.

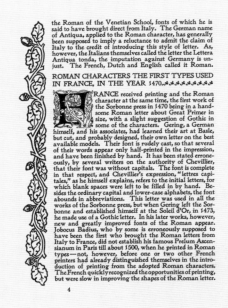

4275

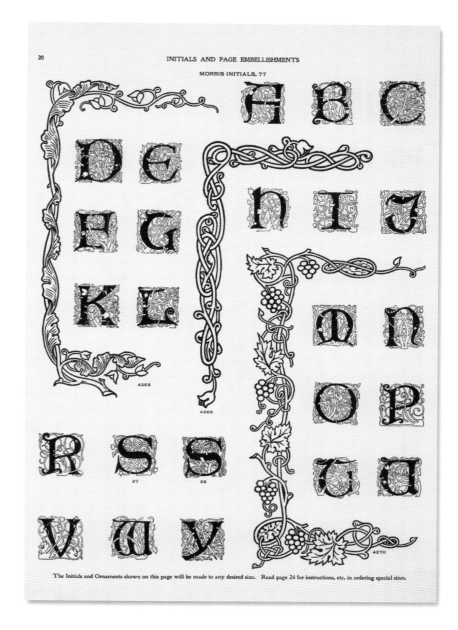

MORRIS INITIALS, 77

ABC
De
FG
hIJ
KL
nn
RSS
OP
VWY
UU

4268

4269

37

38

4270

The Initials and Ornaments shown on this page will be made to any desired size.   Read page 24 for instructions, etc. in ordering special sizes.

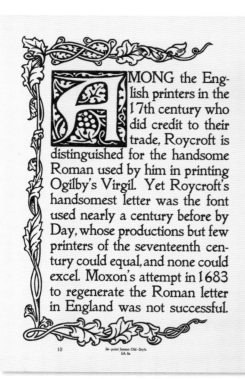

AMONG the English printers in the 17th century who did credit to their trade, Roycroft is distinguished for the handsome Roman used by him in printing Ogilby's Virgil. Yet Roycroft's handsomest letter was the font used nearly a century before by Day, whose productions but few printers of the seventeenth century could equal, and none could excel. Moxon's attempt in 1683 to regenerate the Roman letter in England was not successful.

10   36-point Jenson Old-Style
5A 8a

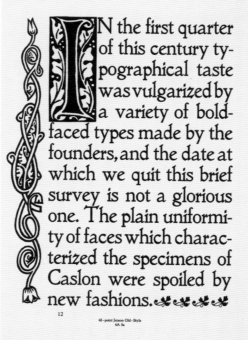

IN the first quarter of this century typographical taste was vulgarized by a variety of bold-faced types made by the founders, and the date at which we quit this brief survey is not a glorious one. The plain uniformity of faces which characterized the specimens of Caslon were spoiled by new fashions. ❧ ❧ ❧

12   48-point Jenson Old-Style
4A 5a

PRICES AND DIRECTIONS WHEN ORDERING SPECIAL NEW SIZES.

THE Page Embellishments and Initials shown in this specimen will be made to any required dimensions. When ordering Page Embellishments give the exact height in inches wanted, on inside, from top to bottom. All new sizes will be charged by the square inch over all, as measured by the square of the blocking trimmed close to the plate, including mortise. Special sizes of initials will be made to order, and charged according to size, etc., and will be mounted on wood unless otherwise ordered. Fresh designs in Initials and Page Ornaments and Embellishments will follow these specimens. Our arrangements contemplate the best work in black and white by leading artists in Europe and America, and we expect to show early proofs of their drawings. ❧ ❧

4299

1900, **Schriftproben,** *Buchdruckerei*
H. Keller, Luzern

Zeit ist Geld
3 Poseidon 4

"Zeit ist Geld" (Time is money)—
appropriate copy to illustrate commercial
printing.

„Zeit ist Geld" – eine passende Losung
für das Druckgewerbe.

« Zeit ist Geld » (Le temps, c'est de
l'argent) – un texte approprié pour
illustrer l'impression publicitaire.

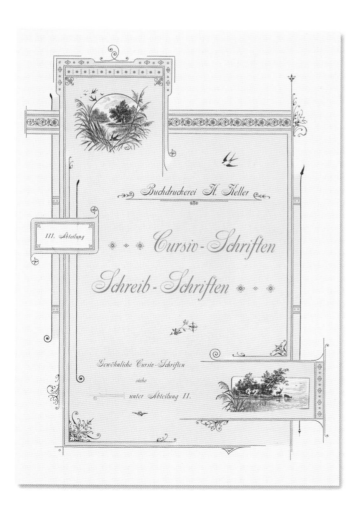

Schweiz

Inseraten-Schreibschrift.

Wer gar zu viel bedenkt,
2 wird wenig leisten 3

FONDERIE & GRAVURE ▷

TYPOGRAPHIQUES

A. VANDERBORGHT

& DUMONT

RUE VERTE, 154, BRUXELLES ✦ ✦ ✦

ANCIENNE FIRME

A. & F. VANDERBORGHT ✦

IMPRIMÉ SUR LA PÉDALE « LIBERTY »

1900, Spécimen Album, *Fonderie & Gravure A. Vanderborght & Dumont,* Bruxelles

These samples reflect both a return to Neoclassical roots and the contemporary influence of Art Nouveau.

Die abgebildeten Muster lassen sowohl eine Rückbesinnung auf neoklassizistische Wurzeln als auch den Einfluss des Art Nouveau erkennen.

Ces échantillons reflètent à la fois un retour vers des racines néo-classiques et l'influence contemporaine de l'Art Nouveau.

PLANTIN A ANVERS

É à Saint-Avertin en 1473, Plantin vint s'installer à Anvers en 1549, à côté de plusieurs imprimeurs établis depuis longtemps dans cette ville, et réussit à conquérir la première place parmi ces redoutables émules.

L'origine de l'imprimerie qui devait illustrer le nom de Plantin est assez singulière. Au début de son installation, Plantin n'avait pas d'atelier, il avait ouvert une échoppe et il y vendait des livres. Attaqué pendant une nuit de carnaval par des individus masqués, il fut grièvement blessé, mais il put retrouver la

ELZÉVIR ITALIQUE

Philippe II éleva Christophe Plantin à la dignité d'archi-typographe, en récompense des

PEUT ÊTRE FONDU SUR DIX-HUIT DIDOT.

LES HOMMES DE L'IMPRIMERIE

Jean Gutenberg.

UTENBERG naquit à Mayence un peu avant l'an 1400. Il est nommé, tantôt Gensfleisch de Sorgenloch, et tantôt de Gutenberg; mais c'est ce dernier nom que la renommée a retenu. Gutenberg n'avait guère plus de quinze ans lorsqu'il perdit son père, et sa mère ne jouissait que d'une aisance relative. Il commença donc sans plus attendre son apprentissage d'orfèvre-bijoutier. La famille Gensfleisch habitait à Mayence la *Maison du Taureau noir*; sur la porte d'entrée on avait sculpté une tête de taureau. Elle portait cette inscription : *Rien ne me résiste,* que Gutenberg prit pour devise. Presque toujours les hommes de génie se sont formés d'eux-mêmes. Franklin en fut un exemple remarquable. D'abord simple ouvrier en Angleterre, il devint un des écrivains, un des législateurs, un des savants dont s'honore le plus l'Amérique, sa patrie. Jean

Ce caractère peut être fondu sur 14 Didot.

LA GRAVURE SUR BOIS

Note historique.

ES origines de la gravure sur bois sont entourées d'obscurité tout comme celles de l'Imprimerie. Les Chinois gravaient sur bois avant le XVᵉ siècle, et il est à supposer que cet art fut introduit en Europe par des marchands vénitiens. Marco Polo, en décrivant la fabrication du papier-monnaie, dit que celle-ci avait lieu en marquant le papier au moyen d'un sceau couvert de vermillon; mais cet art si simple ne fut même guère admis en Europe que vers la fin du XIVᵉ siècle. Beaucoup d'ouvrages imprimés en Italie, en Allemagne et en Angleterre, pendant la dernière partie du quinzième siècle, sont ornés de gravures grossières formées de lignes épaisses et lourdes. Exercée jusqu'alors par des mains inha-

Ce caractère peut se fondre sur 16 Didot.

ELZÉVIR 2ᵉ SÉRIE, C. 18.   A. & F. VANDERBORGHT.

LOUIS ELZEVIER

APRÈS les Alde et les Estienne, une autre grande famille d'imprimeurs a été l'honneur des Pays-Bas durant près d'un siècle. Le nom de ces imprimeurs s'écrivait en latin *Elzevirius*. Le chef de la famille, Louis Elzevier, naquit à Louvain, vers 1540. Il se maria en 1563, avec Marie Duverdyn, dont il eut cinq fils : Mathieu, Josse, Bonaventure, Louis et Gilles. Louis Elzevier n'imprima pas lui-même : il s'installa libraire à Leyde.

Isaac, fils de Mathieu Elzevier

ELZÉVIR 2ᵉ SÉRIE, C. 22.   A. & F. VANDERBORGHT.

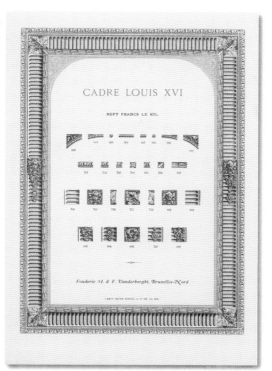

CADRE LOUIS XVI

SEPT FRANCS LE KIL.

Fonderie A. & F. Vanderborght, Bruxelles-Nord.

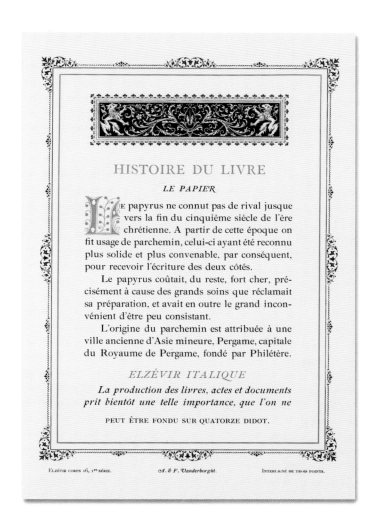

HISTOIRE DU LIVRE

LE PAPIER

LE papyrus ne connut pas de rival jusque vers la fin du cinquième siècle de l'ère chrétienne. A partir de cette époque on fit usage de parchemin, celui-ci ayant été reconnu plus solide et plus convenable, par conséquent, pour recevoir l'écriture des deux côtés.

Le papyrus coûtait, du reste, fort cher, précisément à cause des grands soins que réclamait sa préparation, et avait en outre le grand inconvénient d'être peu consistant.

L'origine du parchemin est attribuée à une ville ancienne d'Asie mineure, Pergame, capitale du Royaume de Pergame, fondé par Philétère.

ELZÉVIR ITALIQUE

La production des livres, actes et documents prit bientôt une telle importance, que l'on ne

PEUT ÊTRE FONDU SUR QUATORZE DIDOT.

ELZÉVIR CORPS 16, 1ʳᵉ SÉRIE.   A. & F. Vanderborght.   INTERLIGNÉ DE TROIS POINTS.

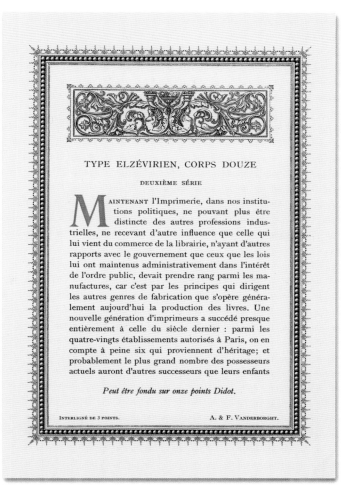

TYPE ELZÉVIRIEN, CORPS DOUZE

DEUXIÈME SÉRIE

MAINTENANT l'Imprimerie, dans nos institutions politiques, ne pouvant plus être distincte des autres professions industrielles, ne recevant d'autre influence que celle qui lui vient du commerce de la librairie, n'ayant d'autres rapports avec le gouvernement que ceux que les lois lui ont maintenus administrativement dans l'intérêt de l'ordre public, devait prendre rang parmi les manufactures, car c'est par les principes qui dirigent les autres genres de fabrication que s'opère généralement aujourd'hui la production des livres. Une nouvelle génération d'imprimeurs a succédé presque entièrement à celle du siècle dernier : parmi les quatre-vingts établissements autorisés à Paris, on en compte à peine six qui proviennent d'héritage; et probablement le plus grand nombre des possesseurs actuels auront d'autres successeurs que leurs enfants

Peut être fondu sur onze points Didot.

INTERLIGNÉ DE 3 POINTS.   A. & F. VANDERBORGHT.

VIGNETTES ESTHÉTIQUES

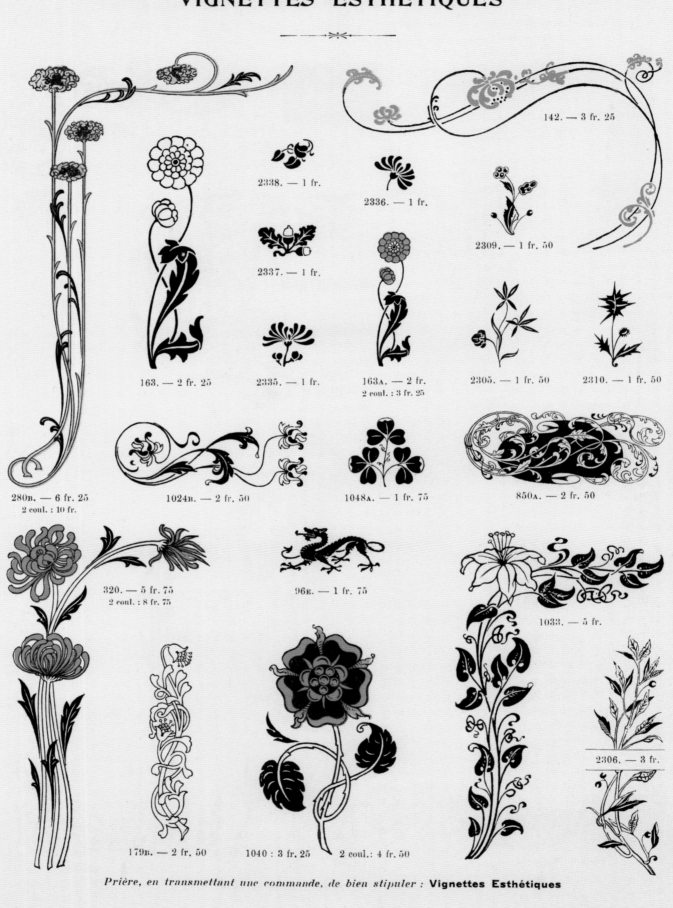

142. — 3 fr. 25

2338. — 1 fr.

2336. — 1 fr.

2337. — 1 fr.

2309. — 1 fr. 50

163. — 2 fr. 25

2335. — 1 fr.

163A. — 2 fr.
2 coul. : 3 fr. 25

2305. — 1 fr. 50

2310. — 1 fr. 50

280B. — 6 fr. 25
2 coul. : 10 fr.

1024B. — 2 fr. 50

1048A. — 1 fr. 75

850A. — 2 fr. 50

320. — 5 fr. 75
2 coul. : 8 fr. 75

96E. — 1 fr. 75

1033. — 5 fr.

179B. — 2 fr. 50

1040 : 3 fr. 25

2 coul.: 4 fr. 50

2306. — 3 fr.

Prière, en transmettant une commande, de bien stipuler : **Vignettes Esthétiques**

Fonderie & Gravure A. Vanderborght & Dumont

Fonderie et Gravure A. & F. Vanderborght

7A. — 4 fr. 50
2 coul. : 7 fr. 50

356. — 3 fr. 25

144AR. — 3 fr. 75
2 coul. : 5 fr. 75

2303. — 2 fr.   2302. — 2 fr.   1040A. — 2 fr. 25   2304. — 2 fr.   2301. — 2 fr.

Vignettes & Esthétiques

190A. — 2 fr.   348. — 5 fr. 25   1049C. — 1 fr.

140R. — 3 fr. 75
2 coul. : 5 fr. 75

139. — 5 fr. 75
2 coul. : 8 fr.

1027B. — 2 fr.

840A. — 2 fr. 50   1027BR. — 2 fr.   846A. — 2 fr. 50

261C. — 2 fr.   1041A : 4 fr. 50 — 2 coul. : 7 fr.   261D. — 2 fr.

Prière, en transmettant une commande, de bien stipuler : **Vignettes Esthétiques**

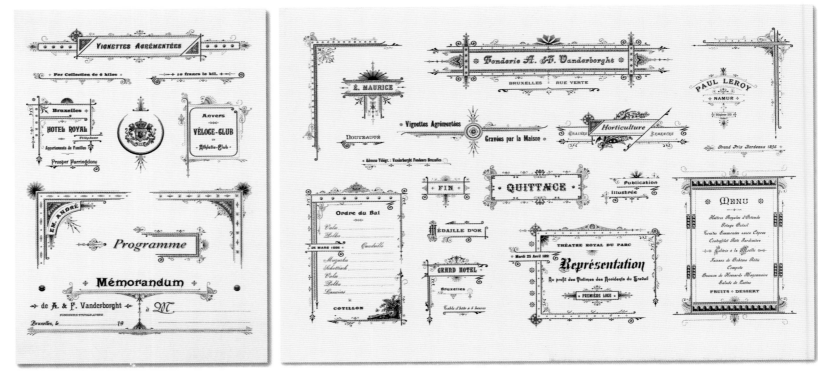

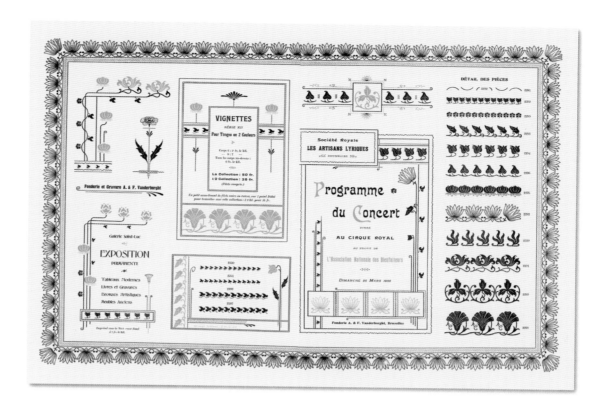

1900, Spécimen Album, *Fonderie*
& Gravure A. Vanderborght & Dumont,
Bruxelles

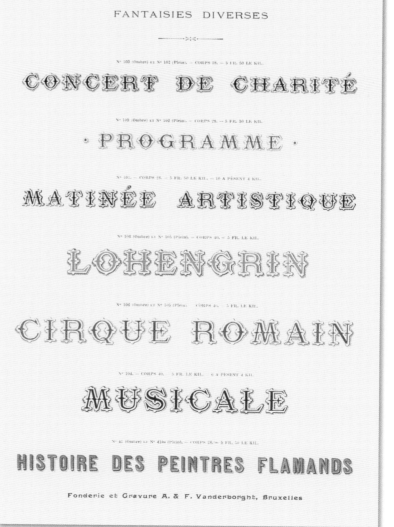

1900, Spécimen Album, *Fonderie Gustave Mayeur,* Paris

The first in a series of initials. Letterpress representations of the bicycle (see page 352)—a new product at the time.

Das erste aus einer Reihe von Blättern mit Initialen. Ferner im Hochdruck-verfahren entstandene Abbildungen eines damals noch jungen Produkts: des Fahrrads (siehe Seite 352).

La première d'une série de lettrines. Des représentations typographiques de la bicyclette (voir page 352), une nouveauté de l'époque.

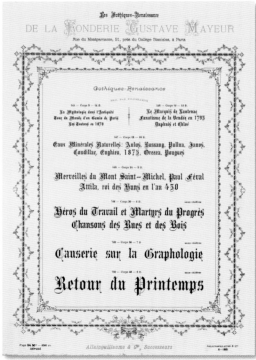

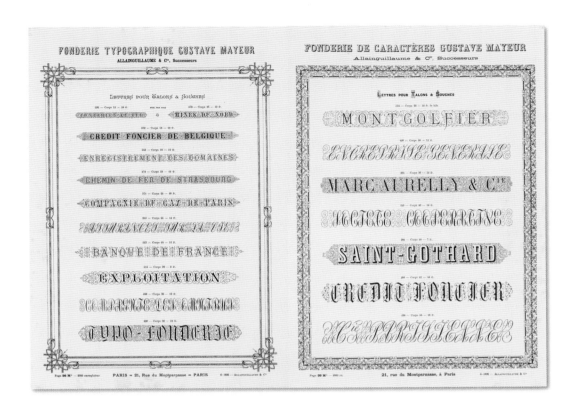

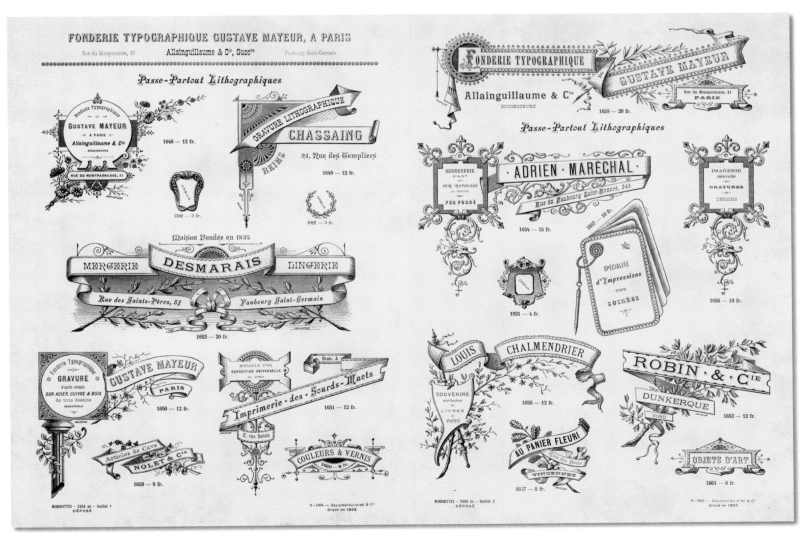

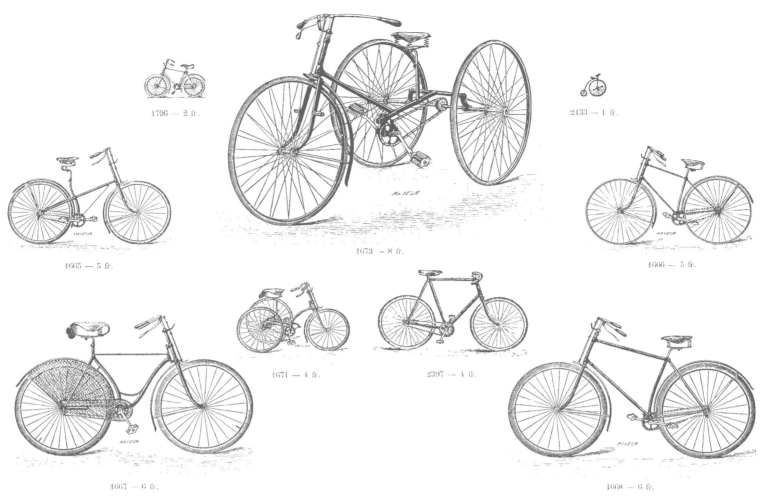

1796 — 2 fr.

2133 — 1 fr.

1673 — 8 fr.

4665 — 5 fr.

4666 — 5 fr.

4671 — 4 fr.

2397 — 4 fr.

4667 — 6 fr.

4668 — 6 fr.

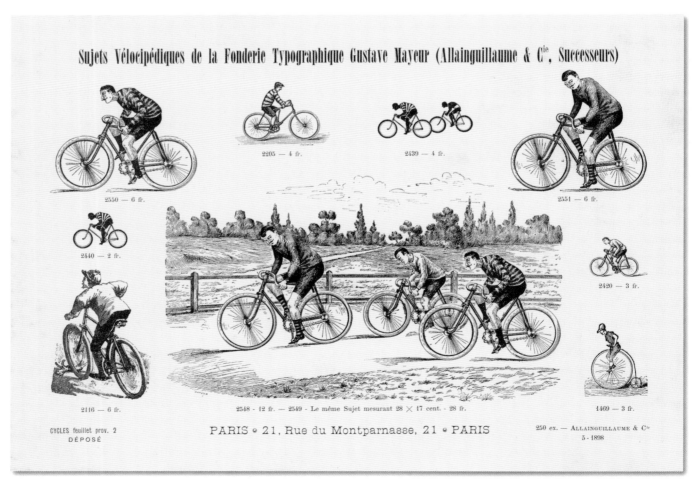

Sujets Vélocipédiques de la Fonderie Typographique Gustave Mayeur (Allainguillaume & Cie, Successeurs)

2205 — 4 fr.

2439 — 4 fr.

2550 — 6 fr.

2551 — 6 fr.

2440 — 2 fr.

2420 — 3 fr.

2116 — 6 fr.

2548 - 12 fr. — 2549 - Le même Sujet mesurant 28 × 17 cent. - 28 fr.

4469 — 3 fr.

CYCLES feuillet prov. 2
DÉPOSÉ

PARIS • 21, Rue du Montparnasse, 21 • PARIS

250 ex. — ALLAINGUILLAUME & Cie
5 - 1898

21. Rue du Montparnasse   21. Rue du Montparnasse

ARMÉNIENNES NOIRES	ARMÉNIENNES NOIRES & BLANCHES	ARMÉNIENNES BLANCHES
Les Mauresques noires	Les Mauresques noires	Les Mauresques noires
TRIPOLITAINE	TRIPOLITAINE	TRIPOLITAINE
Mariage de Figaro	Mariage de Figaro	Mariage de Figaro
·CLERMONT·	·CLERMONT·	·CLERMONT·
Second Empire	Second Empire	Second Empire
·GÉOMÈTRE·	·GÉOMÈTRE·	·GÉOMÈTRE·
Providence	Providence	Providence
HOMÈRE	HOMÈRE	HOMÈRE

Les Lettres Noires sont gravées pour retomber exactement dans les Lettres Blanches. Chaque lettre étant complète, ce type peut s'employer isolément pour un seul tirage.

Les Corps 12 & 18 en gravure « ront terminés prochainement

Les Lettres Blanches sont gravées pour retomber exactement dans les Lettres Noires. Chaque lettre étant complète, ce type peut s'employer isolément pour un seul tirage.

1900, Spécimen Album, *Fonderie Gustave Mayeur,* Paris

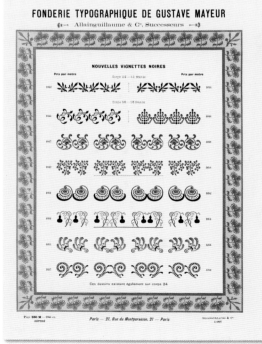

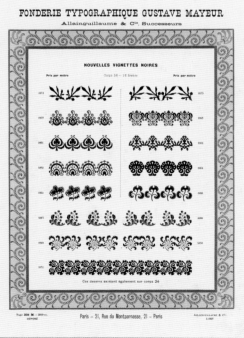

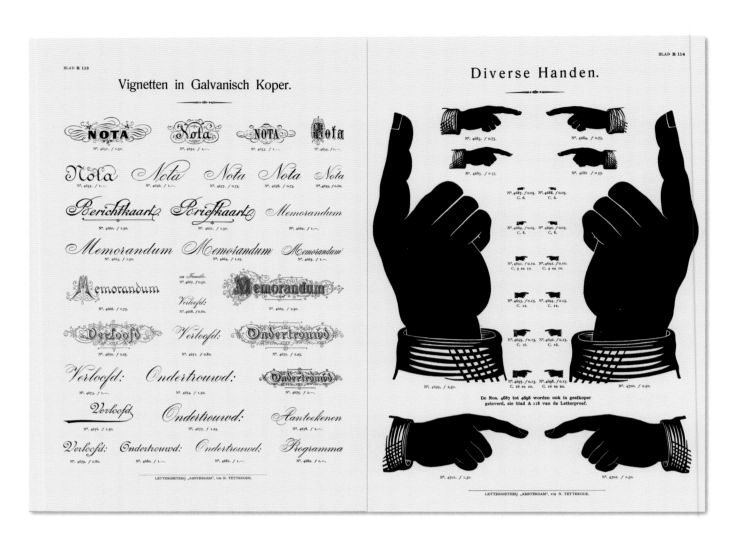

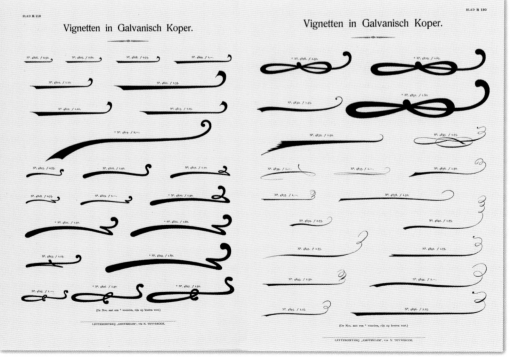

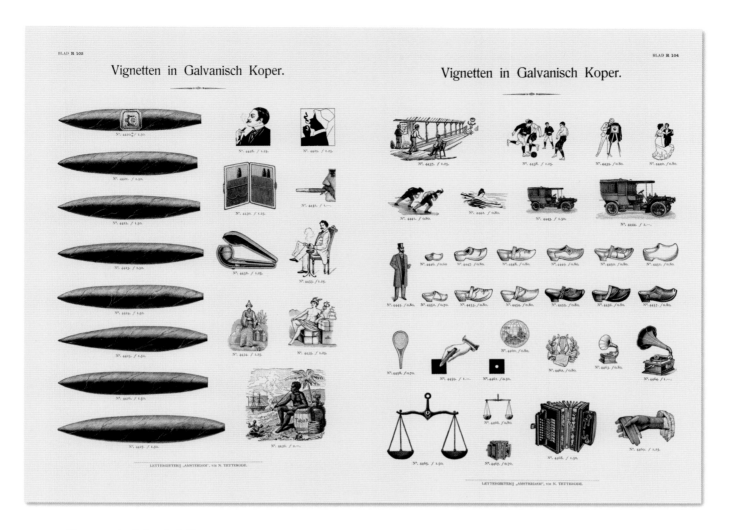

1900, **Vignetten in Galvanisch Koper,**
Lettergieterij Amsterdam, Amsterdam

An ample selection of hands—
and cigars and clogs, too!

Eine üppige Auswahl an Händen,
aber auch an Zigarren und Pantinen!

Une vaste sélection de mains –
mais aussi de cigares et de sabots !

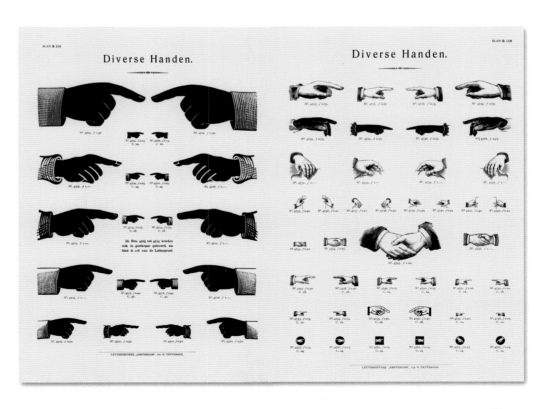

Vignetten in Galvanisch Koper.

N°. 4408. ƒ 0.80.   N°. 4409. ƒ 1.—.   N°. 4410. ƒ 1.50.   N°. 4411. ƒ 1.25.   N°. 4412. ƒ 1.—.

N°. 4413. ƒ 1.75.   N°. 4414. ƒ 2.—.   N°. 4415. ƒ 2.—.

N°. 4416. ƒ 2.50.   N°. 4417. ƒ 2.50.

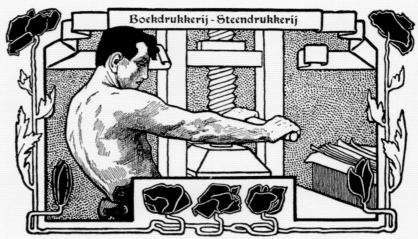

N°. 4418. ƒ 2.25.

N°. 4419. ƒ 4.—.   Voor 2 kleuren ƒ 5.50.

LETTERGIETERIJ „AMSTERDAM", v/h N. TETTERODE.

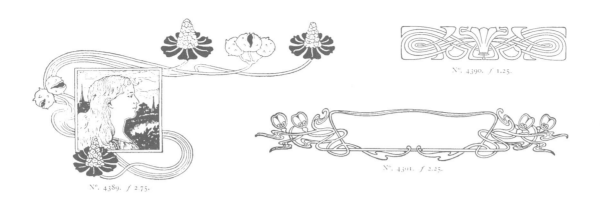

N°. 4389. ƒ 2.75.

N°. 4390. ƒ 1.25.

N°. 4391. ƒ 2.25.

N°. 4395. ƒ 1.25.

N°. 4396. ƒ 1.50.

N°. 4397. ƒ 1.50.

N°. 4404. ƒ 1.—.

N°. 4405. ƒ 1.—.

N°. 4406. ƒ 1.25.

N°. 4400. ƒ 1.25.

N°. 4401. ƒ 1.25.

N°. 4402. ƒ 1.25.

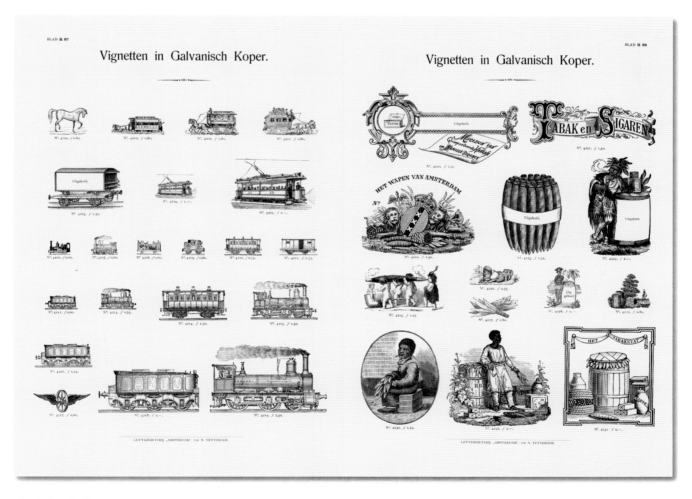

Vignetten in Galvanisch Koper.

Vignetten in Galvanisch Koper.

INDEX

IMPRINT

© 2009 TASCHEN GmbH
Hohenzollernring 53, D–50672 Köln
www.taschen.com

To stay informed about upcoming TASCHEN titles, please request
our magazine at www.taschen.com/magazine or write to TASCHEN,
Hohenzollernring 53, D-50672 Cologne, Germany; contact@taschen.com;
Fax: +49-221-254919. We will be happy to send you a free copy of
our magazine, which is filled with information about all of our books.

All images are taken from the collection of type specimens by
Jan Tholenaar, Reinoud Tholenaar and Saskia Ottenhoff-Tholenaar
and are reproduced with kind permission by the owners.

Design: Sense/Net, Andy Disl and Birgit Eichwede, Cologne
Concept: VK Projects/Cees W. de Jong
Editorial coordination: Florian Kobler, Kathrin Murr, Cologne
Production: Ute Wachendorf, Cologne
German translation: Holger Wölfle, Berlin
French translation: Blandine Pélissier, Paris

Printed in China
ISBN: 978-3-8365-1101-8